Lifespan Acquisition and Language Change

Advances in Historical Sociolinguistics (AHS)
ISSN 2214-1057

Over the last three decades, historical sociolinguistics has developed into a mature and challenging field of study that focuses on language users and language use in the past. The social motivation of linguistic variation and change continues at the forefront of the historical sociolinguistic enquiry, but current research does not stop there. It extends from social and regional variation in language use to its various communicative contexts, registers and genres, and includes issues in language attitudes, policies and ideologies. One of the main stimuli for the field comes from new digitized resources and large text corpora, which enable the study of a much wider social coverage than before. Historical sociolinguists use variationist and dialectological research tools and techniques, perform pragmatic and social network analyses, and adopt innovative approaches from other disciplines. The series publishes monographs and thematic volumes, in English, on different languages and topics that contribute to our understanding of the relations between the individual, language and society in the past.

For an overview of all books published in this series, please see
benjamins.com/catalog/ahs

Editors

Marijke J. van der Wal
Leiden University

Terttu Nevalainen
University of Helsinki

Editorial Board

Wendy Ayres-Bennett
University of Cambridge

Martin Durrell
University of Manchester

Agnieszka Kiełkiewicz-Janowiak
Adam Mickiewicz University, Poznań

William A. Kretzschmar Jr.
University of Georgia, Athens GA

Mieko Ogura
Tsurumi University, Yokohama

Suzanne Romaine
University of Oxford

Daniel Schreier
University of Zurich

Merja Stenroos
University of Stavanger

Sali A. Tagliamonte
University of Toronto

Ingrid Tieken-Boon van Ostade
Leiden University

Donald N. Tuten
Emory University, Atlanta GA

Wim Vandenbussche
Vrije Universiteit Brussel

Anna Verschik
Tallinn University

Volume 14

Lifespan Acquisition and Language Change
Historical sociolinguistic perspectives
Edited by Israel Sanz-Sánchez

Lifespan Acquisition and Language Change

Historical sociolinguistic perspectives

Edited by

Israel Sanz-Sánchez
West Chester University

John Benjamins Publishing Company
Amsterdam / Philadelphia

The paper used in this publication meets the minimum requirements of the American National Standard for Information Sciences – Permanence of Paper for Printed Library Materials, ANSI Z39.48-1984.

DOI 10.1075/ahs.14

Cataloging-in-Publication Data available from Library of Congress:
LCCN 2024000097 (PRINT) / 2024000098 (E-BOOK)

ISBN 978 90 272 1459 1 (HB)
ISBN 978 90 272 4707 0 (E-BOOK)

© 2024 – John Benjamins B.V.
No part of this book may be reproduced in any form, by print, photoprint, microfilm, or any other means, without written permission from the publisher.

John Benjamins Publishing Company · https://benjamins.com

To Kim Geeslin, a dear mentor, colleague, friend, and inspiration to the authors in this volume, gone too soon.

Table of contents

Acknowledgements	IX

PART I. Introduction
CHAPTER 1. Language acquisition across the lifespan in historical sociolinguistics — 2
Israel Sanz-Sánchez

PART II. Perspectives on acquisition and change
CHAPTER 2. Monolingual and bilingual child language acquisition and language change — 44
Naomi Shin

CHAPTER 3. The second language acquisition of variation in adulthood and language change — 64
Kimberly Geeslin, Travis Evans-Sago, Stephen A. Fafulas & Thomas Goebel-Mahrle

CHAPTER 4. The dynamics of lifelong acquisition in dialect contact and change — 84
Jennifer Hendriks

CHAPTER 5. Multilingual acquisition across the lifespan as a sociohistorical trigger for language change — 104
Suzanne Aalberse

CHAPTER 6. Language acquisition across the lifespan and the emergence of new varieties — 127
Devyani Sharma

PART III. Case studies
CHAPTER 7. Tracing the emergence of the *voseo/tuteo* semantic split in Río de la Plata second person subjunctives: The role of child language acquisition — 150
María Irene Moyna & Pablo E. Requena

CHAPTER 8. The influences of adult and child speakers in the emergence of Light Warlpiri, an Australian mixed language   179
   Carmel O'Shannessy

CHAPTER 9. Child and adolescent transmission and incrementation in acquisition in historical sociophonetic data from English in Missouri, 1880–2000   203
   Christopher Strelluf

CHAPTER 10. Language dominance across the lifespan in Wisconsin German and English varieties: Voice onset time and final obstruent neutralization, 1863–2013   234
   Samantha M. Litty

CHAPTER 11. The contact origin(s) of 'hand' and 'foot' > 'limb' in Antioquian Spanish: Tracing historical adult L1 transfer   264
   Eliot Raynor

CHAPTER 12. Adult L2 acquisition of *for*-complementation in Chinese Pidgin English and Hong Kong English: A sociohistorical perspective   294
   Michelle Li

PART IV. Future directions

CHAPTER 13. Towards an acquisitionally informed historical sociolinguistics   318
   Israel Sanz-Sánchez

Language index   327

Subject index   331

Acknowledgements

The present volume is a collaboration by an international team of dedicated scholars at various points of their respective careers, who have been working together since April 2021. As its editor, I am happy to share the results of this collaboration with our global academic community, and I would like to thank the people who have made this project possible.

I would first like to thank the authors for sharing their research and contributing to this volume. From the very beginning, they graciously accepted my invitation to be a part of this project, and have since remained committed to it by promptly responding to my requests for drafts and revisions, by being open to the peer reviewers', the series editors' and my feedback, and (most importantly) by respecting and embracing the overall goal of the volume to showcase research on the acquisition of linguistic variation and language change from a sociohistorical perspective. It has been my privilege as volume editor to be able to work with and learn from such a brilliant and collegial group of scholars.

I am also grateful to our expert reviewers, who have selflessly carved time out of their busy schedules to provide insightful comments on the chapters in this volume. They are, in last name alphabetical order, the following: Suzanne Aalberse (Universiteit van Amsterdam), Albert Backus (Tilburg University), Josh Brown (University of Wisconsin-Eau Claire), Joseph Clancy Clements (University of Indiana, Bloomington), Ailís Cournane (New York University), Melisa Dracos (Baylor University), Alexandra D'Arcy (University of Victoria), David Durian (The Pennsylvania State University), Kimberly Geeslin (University of Indiana, Bloomington), Jennifer Hendriks (The Australian National University), Samantha Litty (Europa-Universität Flensburg), Stephen Matthews (University of Hong Kong), María Irene Moyna (Texas A&M University), Randi Neteland (Høgskulen på Vestlandet), Carmel O'Shannessy (The Australian National University), Eliot Raynor (Princeton University), Pablo E. Requena (University of Texas at San Antonio), Yael Reshef (Hebrew University of Jerusalem), Devyani Sharma (Queen Mary University of London), Naomi Shin (University of New Mexico), Eivind Torgersen (Norges teknisk-naturvitenskapelige universitet), and Sarah Zahler (State University of New York at Albany). Their priceless feedback has greatly improved the overall quality of the volume.

I would also like to express my sincerest gratitude to the coeditors of the series *Advances in Historical Sociolinguistics* at John Benjamins, Terttu Nevalainen

(Helsingin yliopisto) and Marijke van der Wal (Universiteit Leiden). Their expert guidance, attention to detail, responsiveness, suggestions, and patience throughout this project have been extremely helpful and have greatly enhanced the overall scholarly quality of the volume. I am also thankful to the editing team at John Benjamins, whose professional assistance has been critical as the volume neared the publishing stage.

Lastly, a particularly heartfelt 'thank you' goes to our dear colleague Kimberly (Kim) Geeslin (University of Indiana, Bloomington), who sadly passed away in January 2023. Kim was an internationally renowned scholar in the study of the second-language acquisition of variation, who inspired whole cohorts of students and colleagues and left an indelible impression in our field. Throughout my communication with her as the first author of one of the chapters in this volume, she was an example of expertise, dedication, professionalism, and passion for one's scholarship. May she rest in peace.

PART I

Introduction

CHAPTER 1

Language acquisition across the lifespan in historical sociolinguistics

Israel Sanz-Sánchez
West Chester University

The study of language variation and change has long been rooted in the effects of acquisition at different points of the lifespan, but the potential for language acquisition theory and data to inform sociohistorical approaches to language diachrony has not always been recognized. In this introductory chapter, the application of an acquisitionally informed lens to the research on language variation and change is justified on theoretical, methodological, and heuristic grounds. Following an overview of the existing research on the role of age in the acquisition of variation and the emergence of sociolinguistic norms, the chapter summarizes previous applications of acquisition theory in historical sociolinguistics. This panoramic review is then used to articulate the potential for a lifelong view of language acquisition to serve as a powerful instrument in the historical sociolinguist's toolkit. Ultimately, the goal is to supplement other methodologies to produce more thorough explanations of language change by centering a language developmental perspective in the praxis of historical sociolinguistics.

Keywords: age, children, adolescents, adults, language acquisition, language variation, language change, historical sociolinguistics, language contact, dialect contact

1. Introduction

The present volume connects the latest research on language acquisition across the lifespan with the explanation of language change in specific sociohistorical settings. This dialogue benefits from recent advances in two research areas: on the one hand, the study of how learners of various ages and in various sociolinguistic contexts acquire language variation; on the other, historical sociolinguistics as the field that seeks to understand historical patterns of language variation and change. The overarching rationale for this interdisciplinary conversation is that all language changes start and spread as the result of individual acts of acquisition throughout the speakers' lives.

By now, much research on language variation and change relies on the age-specific effects of language learning at various points across the human lifespan (Diskin Ravid 1995; Gregersen et al. 2009; Kerswill 1996; Labov 2001, 2007; Nevalainen 2015; Sankoff 2019; Tagliamonte & D'Arcy 2009), which are assumed to be rooted in universal processes of neurocognitive maturation. Further proof of the importance of age in the acquisition of variation and of its potential role in language change can be found in a growing body of research on various forms of monolingual and bilingual acquisition (Cournane 2019; Geeslin et al. 2013; Hudson Kam & Newport 2005, 2009; Shin and Miller 2022; Regan 2021). The picture emerging from this literature is that language acquisition is a lifelong process, with different manifestations at various ages (Anthonissen & Petré 2019; Fløgstad & Lanza 2019; Røyneland & Blackwood 2022). This lifespan perspective on language acquisition is enriched (and complexified) by incorporating the many socioculturally contingent aspects of age (Cameron 2011; Wagner 2012).

Historical sociolinguistics has also contributed to this conversation, going beyond its initial focus on textual variation (Nevalainen & Raumolin-Brunberg 1996; Romaine 1982) to embrace a much broader range of research questions, theoretical frameworks, and interpretive protocols. Given the growing evidence that age-dependent acquisitional behavior is a key factor in sociolinguistic variation, we would expect historical sociolinguistics to have embraced acquisition theory and data as core components of the field. While individual historical sociolinguistic studies have incorporated this perspective (e.g., Clements 2009; Schwegler et al. 2016; Sanz-Sánchez & Moyna 2023; Trudgill 2004) current definitions of theory and methods in historical sociolinguistics do not always do justice to the capital role that an acquisitionally informed view of language variation can play in informing historical sociolinguistic approaches to language change. By bringing together researchers working on the acquisition of language variation across the lifespan and historical sociolinguists that incorporate language acquisition in the study of language variation and change, this volume contributes to this theoretical and methodological conversation in the historical sociolinguistic literature.

This introduction starts with an overview of the existing research on the role of age in acquisition and articulates the lifespan perspective adopted in this volume (Section 2), followed by a summary of several important interactions between age and the acquisition of variation (Section 3). These age-dependent effects are then linked to the emergence of norms in various sociolinguistic contexts (Section 4). Then, previous applications of acquisition theory and data in historical sociolinguistics are surveyed (Section 5) and the potential for a lifelong view of language acquisition to inform future research agendas in historical sociolinguists is articulated (Section 6). The introduction ends with an overview of the sections and chapters in the volume (Section 7).

2. What is language acquisition? The lifelong development of variation

Understanding language acquisition has been a central concern in linguistics since at least the 1950s. Much of this research has investigated the role of age in the acquisition process: do individuals of different ages process linguistic input differently, and if so, how do these differences correlate with language use? How does age interact with other personal and social variables to determine the outcome of language learning throughout the lifespan? Two related complications have impacted research agendas on the interaction between age and language acquisition. First, *age* is not only a chronological dimension. Second, language acquisition is a multifaceted process mediated by multiple biological and non-biological factors.

In relation to the first question, there is by now widespread consensus that age is a complex construct mediated by multiple biological and environmental determinants, all of which play a role in the outcome of learning processes throughout our lives. Indeed, "aging may best be researched at the intersection of aging and categories of experience such as gender, ethnicity, class, social network, religion, or other community-specific categories and micro-sociological contexts" (Cameron 2011: 207). Research strongly suggests that changes in brain maturation throughout the lifespan can be assumed to follow at least some biologically determined basis (for instance, the decrease in grey matter density and its effects on brain plasticity, Isel & Kail 2019; see also Birdsong 2018). Inasmuch as these changes are a function of the architecture of the human brain, they offer a basis for an age-based uniformitarian approach to at least some psycholinguistic mechanisms (Labov 1994; Walkden 2019; see Section 3). However, these biologically determined neural changes interact with other environmental factors to yield specific patterns of learning and behavior that are anything but universal (Section 4). For instance, literacy (clearly a sociocultural factor) has been shown to shape phonological awareness and related processes of lexical acquisition among bilingual adults (Smalle et al. 2019; Tarone & Bigelow 2005).

If aging is a multidimensional process shaped by universal and local determinants, it follows that definitions of human life stages such as 'childhood' or 'adulthood' also rest on local cultural expectations at the social, legal, economic, educational, and even sexual or moral level. As Fløgstad and Lanza point out, "[d]ifferent approaches to age thus have sociolinguistic consequences. [For instance, i]n societies in which adolescents are expected to work [...], they do not form age homogeneous groups similar to those found in current Western societies' systems of secondary education, where linguistic innovation flourishes" (176). Consequently, many fine-grained life stage constructs that have been instrumental in studies of the acquisition of linguistic variation are not necessarily generalizable beyond the social contexts for which they have been operationalized. This includes, for instance, who qualifies as a 'caregiver' in child language acquisition (Smith & Durham 2019; Stanford 2008), the distinction between early childhood, later childhood, and adolescence that has guided much research into the acquisition of variation in western societies (Kerswill 1996; Kerswill & Williams 2000; Tagliamonte & D'Arcy 2007, 2009), or the expectation that adolescence and early adulthood will be a time of sociolinguistic negotiation of linguistic features as individuals enter the labor market in industrialized societies (Eckert & McConnell-Ginet 2013). Similarly, as average life expectancies continue to grow in many parts of the world, definitions of 'old age' also change.

Many of the same questions about the interconnected role of biological and environmental factors that are relevant to definitions of age also complicate the study of the interaction between aging and language acquisition. Historically, research in this area has focused on different aspects of this interaction. For instance, much of the initial thrust in the study of language acquisition came from innatist researchers that saw child L1 acquisition as a window into the properties of the human *Language Acquisition Device* (LAD) or the *Universal Grammar* (UG) or other types of inborn cognitive representation mechanisms. In this tradition, complete language acquisition was seen primarily as a childhood phenomenon that relied on innate cognitive processes that are inactive or severely limited in adulthood (i.e., a *critical period* for language learning, Lenneberg 1967). Consequently, language learning in adulthood was seen as an imperfect or incomplete phenomenon (Klein 1997). By emphasizing the role of *errors* as indicative of an individual's degree of proficiency development (see *interlanguage*, Selinker 1972), these early approaches to L2 acquisition assumed a monolingual native target and rested on a clear-cut contrast between childhood and adulthood as distinct developmental periods – although some earlier approaches did question several of these assumptions (e.g., connectionist approaches, see Gasser 1990).

In many of these early articulations, acquisition was seen as consisting primarily of the learning of categorical grammatical options in the input, such as the basic parametric settings of the language. As early sociolinguistic work (Labov 1972; Weinreich et al. 1968) centered the study of language variation as part of the broader study of human language, the acquisition of variation increasingly became critical to an understanding of how individuals of various ages learn language (e.g., Payne 1980; Roberts 1997). L2 acquisition studies also started to pay attention to the acquisition of variation. In this area, attention progressively shifted from an early focus on the alternation between target (i.e., 'native') forms and non-target errors (Tarone 1988) to investigations on the acquisition of variable conditioning by adult learners (Adamson & Regan 1991). Initially, acquisition-minded sociolinguists did not challenge the assumption that humans do most of their acquisitional work in their L1 before early adolescence. It is precisely the malleability of young learners' systems and the assumed stability of adult systems that has been invoked to justify the *apparent time* approach to language change, i.e., the study of language variation and change in a community via a cross-section of generational differences in language use (see Section 4.3). Recent research has supported the view that at least some forms of variation are acquired quite early (e.g., between ages 2 and 4, Chevrot & Foulkes 2013; Smith & Durham 2019), confirming that, for children, the acquisition of variation is an "integral part of acquisition itself" (Roberts 2005: 154; see also Chapter 2 in this volume).

While some forms of variation do seem to emerge in early childhood, others develop well past the assumed end of the critical period. For instance, late childhood and adolescence are often a time of adjustment to the sociolinguistic landscape of the community (Chevrot et al. 2000; Guy & Boyd 1990; Labov 1989, 2001; Renn & Terry 2009; Tagliamonte & D'Arcy 2007, 2009). Similarly, work on variable linguistic behavior in adulthood has shown that individuals may modify the frequency of certain variants or incorporate new forms of variation long past adolescence (Sankoff 2018, 2019; Sankoff & Blondeau 2007), which suggests that at least some components of linguistic competence are open to change throughout life. By now, there is strong consensus that the age of L1 acquisition of a variable depends on both its linguistic profile (Chambers 1992; Kerswill 1996) as well as the kind of input that individual learners are exposed to as their social world changes (e.g., going from caregiver influence to participating in peer networks in many societies). In addition, adult L2 learners can also build systematic variable grammars (Geeslin et al. 2013). Over the past 20 years, a burgeoning body of sociolinguistic and experimental research has studied the acquisition of L1 variation (Hall & Maddeaux 2020; Miller & Schmitt 2012; Nardy et al. 2014; Shin 2016; Shin & Erker 2015; Shin & Miller 2022; Smith 2021; Smith & Durham 2019; Smith et al. 2007; see also Chapter 2 in this volume), L2 variation (Geeslin & Long 2014; Gudmestad 2014; Regan 2013, 2021; see also Chapter 3 in this volume) or both (Ghimenton et al. 2021). This literature underscores the importance of the interface between the biological timing of general learning processes and the social environment of language use to understand the outcome of acquisition for learners of various ages.

As findings on the effects of age on language acquisition continue to accumulate, recent studies have emphasized the operation of acquisitional processes throughout the life of the individual, i.e., *language acquisition across the lifespan* (e.g., Anthonissen & Petré 2019; Baxter & Croft 2016; de Bot & Schrauf 2009; Fløgstad & Lanza 2019; Gaskell & Ellis 2009; Ghimenton et al. 2021; Nicoladis & Montanari 2016; Petré & Van de Velde 2018; Røyneland & Blackwood 2022). A basic tenet in this literature is that linguistic competence does not emerge via the fixing of categorical information during early childhood. Instead, various forms of linguistic knowledge can be shown to evolve at various points of our lives, as our cognitive affordances (and their underlying biological mechanisms) continue to interact dynamically with our social environment and our individual identities to produce changes in linguistic knowledge and in how this knowledge is deployed socially (Brown & Gaskins 2014; Smalle et al. 2019). While this research does not deny that biological age is an important mediator in how we learn language, it shifts the focus from *what can/cannot happen* to *what tends to happen when*, and how these observed effects may come to shape individual patterns of use dynamically throughout the lifespan.

Lifespan approaches ultimately advocate for a *developmental* view of language acquisition, where individual linguistic knowledge adapts to lifelong neural and social changes (Cournane 2015; Filippi et al. 2018; Gerstenberg & Voeste 2015; Leather & Van Dam 2003). A lifespan approach to language acquisition allows for the integration of previously marginalized acquisitional experiences that go beyond the clear-cut typologies of earlier research. For instance, heritage language acquisition shows characteristics that cannot be easily ascribed to either monolingual L1 or bilingual L2 acquisition (Montrul 2008; Montrul & Silva-Corvalán 2019; see also Chapters 5 and 6 in this volume). Heritage grammars also call into question the validity of L1 systems as the universal benchmark of 'complete' or 'successful' learning, as well as the very notion of 'nativeness' or 'target' that has been central to much research on language acquisition historically (García & Wei 2014; Slavkov et al. 2022). In a similar vein, studies of language attrition in adult bilingual individuals have evolved from a perspective of loss to approaches that see attrition as a form of adaptation of the speaker's linguistic representations to their personal changing environment (De Leeuw et al. 2013; Ng & Cavallaro 2022).

Our approach to language acquisition in this volume is in full agreement with this lifelong developmental view. We understand acquisition broadly as any form of learning resulting in changes to the linguistic repertoire of an individual throughout the lifespan, rather than the fixation of stable grammatical systems in imitation of adult input in childhood (as typically assumed in the generative tradition as well as in some recent approaches to the relationship between language acquisition and language change, e.g., Ozón & Eppler 2019). Via communication, individuals are exposed to input from multiple agents throughout their lives, and they treat this input by means of universal cognitive constraints that interact with the local social environment. This lifelong process is the basis for linguistic perpetuation in every population, which we consider as an aggregate of individuals whose linguistic behavior ultimately determines the course of linguistic variation and change for the whole community (Baxter & Croft 2016; Blythe & Croft 2021; Croft 2000; Gleitman & Newport 1995; Mufwene 2008). Besides the reproduction of features available in the input, acquisition could result in the addition or elimination of forms, the formulation of new form-meaning mappings, or shifts in the frequency of use of specific variants or in the ranking of constraints of specific variables. Due to environmental differences, the linguistic experiences that each learner is presented with throughout their life are unlikely to be identical to those of other learners. Consequently, not every learner in the same community will make the same acquisitional choices (Cournane 2019; Tomasello 2003).

The studies in this volume are rooted in this lifelong developmental approach to language acquisition, where age is an important (though by no means the only) predictor in the acquisition process. Insofar as these acquisitional tendencies have consequences for the broader patterns of language variation across the whole community, they are highly relevant to sociolinguistically inspired approaches to language change. The following section offers a summary of the most salient effects of age on the acquisition of variation as described in the literature.

3. The effects of age on the acquisition of language variation: A summary

A primary concern in the literature on the acquisition of variation from a lifelong perspective is whether different acquisitional behaviors can be expected from specific age cohorts. In turn, exploring the effects of age on the acquisition of variation necessarily directs us to questions about language acquisition and the human brain: do learners of different ages acquire language (and language variation) differently? If not, what are the reasons for these differences? Research on the relationship between age and acquisition has yielded different answers to these questions.

Broadly speaking, authors tend to be divided between those who defend that language acquisition responds to age-specific maturational stages in the human brain, with only children attaining full command of the target grammars (Clahsen & Muysken 1996; Crain et al. 2006; Hartshorne et al. 2018; Li 1996; Meisel 2011; Meisel et al. 2013; Newport 2020; Weerman 1993) and those who argue that observable age-based differences are not due to fundamental cognitive differences between younger and older learners but are the function of other factors, such as the amount and types of input various age cohorts have access to or their respective degrees of sociocultural motivation to conform to other speakers (Dąbrowska et al.

2020; Flege 1987; Montrul 2008; Unsworth 2016). In usage-based approaches, language structure emerges in everyday communication from the activity of domain-general cognitive processing mechanisms (e.g., priming, analogy) that are present in learners of all ages (Bybee 2010; Larsen-Freeman 2007; Ortega & Tyler 2016; Tomasello 2003). Ultimately, this is not just a conversation about language acquisition: neurological, cognitive, and social factors are deeply intertwined with language development. For instance, brain maturation affects language acquisition, but exposure to linguistic input also affects brain development at various ages (Cheng et al. 2023; Li et al. 2014).

Without denying the important theoretical ramifications of some of these conversations, from a historical sociolinguistic perspective we are ultimately interested in how age determinants on acquisition interact with social factors to shape individual learning trajectories and how these translate into language change in the community. If, as research from various theoretical angles has demonstrated, age matters in the acquisition of variation, how does age shape acquisition in the presence of various kinds of input (monolingual vs bilingual, bidialectal, etc.) and varying motivations to conform to specific norms? Relevant evidence can be obtained from experimental studies of learners of various ages, studies of naturalistic sociolinguistic or acquisitional data, and sociolinguistic longitudinal panel or trend studies.

Studies comparing children and adults have identified significant differences between both groups. Children and adults alike pay close attention to frequency, but they rely on it in different ways. Children tend to acquire highly productive patterns (e.g., *-s* for plural or *-ed* for past tense in English) very early. If the target, however, is variable, young children tend to acquire it only if it is predictable, namely, when they receive robust evidence of linguistic and/or sociolinguistic conditioning. By contrast, if variation is not predictable, children show a strong tendency to overregularize, typically based on the most frequent pattern (Hudson Kam & Newport 2005, 2009; Newport 2020; Shin & Miller 2022). Children's tendency to regularize surfaces even in the face of predictable variation (Cournane 2019; Hall & Maddeaux 2020), although with abundant evidence of this variation, the relevant constraints are eventually acquired. These are the conditions we can expect in communities where social stratification and sociolinguistic norms are clear (e.g., many industrialized Western communities). In bilingual or multilingual communities, however, the target norm might be more equivocal. In these cases, the nature of the input and the social context in which children acquire it determine the outcome, whether bilingual first language acquisition (De Houwer 2009), code-switching patterns (Phillips & Deuchar 2022), or options that reflect the changing levels of input in the child's immediate environment (e.g., attrition in child heritage language learning, Montrul 2008) or the effects of regularization in the face of highly irregular and unstructured input (Singleton & Newport 2004).

Adults, on the other hand, seem to show a positive bias towards acquiring variation. They do this by probability-matching, acquiring the overall frequency rates of variation without the associated conditioning and only beginning to over-regularize when the input is too irregular and/or unpredictable (Hudson Kam & Newport 2005, 2009; Newport 2020; Shin & Miller 2022). While adults have historically been regarded as imperfect or deficient learners, more recent research has shown that, with sufficient input, adults can acquire many of the same linguistic and sociolinguistic constraints as L1 speakers – even if the overall frequencies of use of each variant may still tell them apart from younger learners (Geeslin 2018; Gudmestad 2014; see also Chapter 3 in this volume). Recent psycholinguistic approaches also confirm that post-childhood bilingual learning makes individuals more tolerant to innovative structures in their L1 than monolinguals, and this higher tolerance may explain the spread of these structures in sociolinguistic settings where bilinguals constitute a higher share of the population (Fernández et al. 2017).

While research shows that children and adults apply different acquisitional strategies, a categorical distinction between both age groups is unsatisfactory, and not only because of local social understandings of age (Section 2). One reason is that the effects of age on acquisition seem to be modular: while individuals may modify their systems throughout life, not all elements are as impervious to change to the same degree. For instance, Werker & Tees (2005) propose that *optimal periods* apply to specific components of grammar. Some of these age effects fall within the traditional definition of the critical period for child language acquisition. For instance, certain components might have to be mastered by age 3 to exhibit native competence, like phonological contrasts (Meisel 2009), or by age 6–7 for syntax (Meisel 2011; Schwartz 2004). Therefore, older children have been shown to already be 'imperfect' (i.e., not matching L1 speakers) in the acquisition of specific dialectal features, as demonstrated by individual studies of second dialect acquisition (e.g., the Canadian children studied by Tagliamonte and Molfenter (2007) had arrived in Britain before age 5 and still had not matched their local peers six years after arrival) or in cases of new dialect formation (Kerswill 1996; Kerswill & Williams 2000; see also Section 4.4 in this chapter, and Chapters 4 and 6 in this volume). In other ways, however, personal grammars must be malleable well into adolescence, as shown by the fact that L2 acquirers show native or near-native attainment for certain structural components well past the traditional end of the critical period (possibly as late age 17, Hartshorne et al. 2018). In turn, this flexibility appears to be connected to adolescents' participation in the incrementation of sociolinguistic norms (Fløgstad

& Lanza 2019: 175–177; Kirkham & Moore 2013).[1] At the opposite end of the age spectrum, elderly speakers have been observed to exhibit declines in form-function components of language, such as lexical retrieval or discourse comprehension, to a larger degree than more structural components like phonology or syntax, but other elements (like the addition of new vocabulary) can continue to evolve well into old age (Neumann et al. 2010).

While these studies allow us to chart important age-based acquisition differences between children and adults, or between younger adults and the elderly, there are still important gaps in our knowledge of the evolution of language acquisition throughout life. As commonly decried in studies of lifelong language development (Fløgstad & Lanza 2019; Gerstenberg & Voeste 2015: 4; Wagner 2012: 376), the span between early adulthood and the onset of cognitive decline associated with healthy aging in elderly individuals is still the least researched. This gap is particularly glaring in linguistically diverse environments, where speakers are expected to interact with heterogenous ways of saying things throughout their lives.

But even with these limitations, some conclusions can be extracted from this brief review of the literature on the acquisition of variation throughout the lifespan: (a) learners of various ages typically exhibit different outcomes in the acquisition of variation; (b) these differences cannot be reduced to a simple dichotomy between 'complete' learning in children vs. 'incomplete' learning in adults; (c) age effects on language acquisition are shaped by many factors, including not just biological age but also the structural characteristics of the linguistic variable, the type of input that learners have access to, and the degree of sociocultural motivation for learners to acquire it; and (d) the social embedding of language acquisition is key to whether and how speakers of various ages will acquire and use a certain element or pattern.

From a historical sociolinguistic perspective, the question about age-specific acquisitional behaviors is closely connected to the kinds of contribution to community-wide patterns of variation and change that we may expect from each of these age groups. How do these universal age-specific tendencies in language learning constrain the kinds of innovations that speakers may generate or learn throughout their lives? And how have specific historical social environments shaped these acquisitional effects and their consequences for local patterns of language change? We survey some of the responses to these questions in the next section.

---

1. See Chapter 9 in this volume for an example.

4. Language acquisition across the lifespan and language change: Previous approaches

4.1 Early approaches

Diachronic linguists have long posited a causal connection between language acquisition and language change. For instance, as early as 1880, Paul attributed language change to the agency of children: "[i]t is obvious that the processes of language acquisition are of prime importance for the explanation of changes in language use [and] they represent the primary cause of these changes" (quoted and translated in Meisel 2011: 124). Some of these early approaches also underscored the importance of language learning at various points across the lifespan in the actuation of specific changes. For instance, comparing the English and Gothic inflectional systems, Jespersen invoked the acquisitional biases of both children and adults as a causative factor: "[i]t is clear […] that the English form[s] sav[e] a considerable amount of brainwork to all English-speaking people – not only to children, who have fewer forms to learn, but also to adults, who have fewer forms to choose between and to keep distinct whenever they open their mouths to speak" (1964 [1922]: 332).

Some early approaches also paid attention to the demographic or social characteristics of the acquisition environment as a factor in the diachronic emergence of communal norms. For instance, Haugen (1953) incorporated the differences between adult and child language acquisition, as well as the place of each age group in the demographic structure of the community, among the factors predicting the outcome of contact.

4.2 Generative and usage-based approaches

Unlike some of these early formulations, generative approaches to language change largely ignored social factors in their discussion of the roots of language change. According to the prevalent generativist line of thinking, child acquisition plays a central role in the instantiation of language change. From this perspective, children can introduce changes in the grammar shared by a community by reanalyzing the input offered by adults and developing an alternative abstract representation of the underlying grammar. In this view, *reanalysis* offers us a way out of the so-called *logical problem of language change*: "if [child] learners have both the capacity and the motivation to acquire an exact replica of the language around them, how is change even possible?" (Kiparsky 2014: 16). For most generativists, the answer to this conundrum must be sought in diachronic differences in the primary linguistic data presented to different cohorts of young learners:

if generation b has access to a different distribution of features in their input from generation a (e.g., different frequencies in each of the alternatives for the same syntactic context), they may postulate an innovative underlying grammar (Lightfoot 2006; Lightfoot & Westergaard 2007; Meisel 2011; Yang 2002). In some generative approaches, child acquisition naturally results in at least some errors, especially if primary data offer evidence for alternatives, which in turn may lead to a new grammar (Hróarsdóttir 2003; Kroch 2005). For at least some generativists, true parametric change can only be observed in situations where adults have introduced enough deviations from the original grammar in the community input, so that L2 learners (and not children) must be considered the true innovators (Kroch et al. 2000; Meisel et al. 2013).

While generativists are concerned with internal (i.e., underlying) grammar change, their focus on reanalysis necessarily implies an appeal to external factors in language change: *something* must have triggered a shift in the distribution of data that the innovating learners were presented with. The possible culprits include shifts in stylistic preferences or other patterns of use in the community, or a demographically high proportion of bilingual or non-native adult speakers bringing new options into the community. While many generative authors do not see these social mechanisms as part of a theory of language change (they are "interesting and important topics of research, but not relevant for a formal model of language change," Yang 2002:130), other generative approaches do recognize the importance of these social factors in the explanation of specifics language changes – if only because they necessarily determine the conditions of acquisition at the individual level (Meisel 2011:139–140; Meisel et al. 2013). To sum up, for most generative-inspired authors, language change is the result of a failure to acquire the adult grammar, which differs from assumedly 'typical' acquisition settings where we should expect learners to be presented with monolingual or otherwise linguistically unequivocal input.

Usage-based approaches reject this form of the abrupt-acquisition-to-change scenario (Aitchison 2003; Bybee 2010; Bybee & Slobin 1982; Diessel 2012). In these approaches, learners are always faced with variable input, where options are used with different degrees of frequency. In this view, true acquisition errors in child language can only be of the developmental kind (e.g., phonological substitutions, morphological overgeneralizations, etc.), and these errors do not usually match the innovations typical of language change. While usage-based approaches differ from generative ones in acknowledging that input is always variable, like generativists, they assume that learners are presented with some type of unequivocal target: "As children grow older, they eliminate their linguistic errors and *conform to the rules*" (Diessel 2012:1609, my emphasis). In this scenario, innovations spread from speaker to speaker as they progressively adjust their individual frequencies in everyday communication with each other. This process could in principle occur at any stage of life, but notably not in early childhood, as small children "simply do not have the social clout" that they would need to act as influential language models (Bybee 2010: 119).

4.3 Variationist sociolinguistic approaches

Starting in the 1960s, variationist sociolinguistics and contact studies have fostered a social turn in the understanding of the contribution of acquisitional trajectories to language change (see Section 2). From this perspective, the interface between language acquisition and language change emerges as a critical area to address several of the problems articulated by Weinreich et al. (1968) as central to a social theory of language change. These include most notably the *transmission* question (the factors that explain the spread of an innovation in a community), the *embedding* question (the social and linguistic environment in which a change takes place), and the *actuation* question (the linguistic and social triggers that set off a change).

Variationist sociolinguists have thoroughly researched this interaction between lifelong changes in individual variable repertoires and community-wide patterns of change. In many variationist studies, the progression of language change is commonly credited to the ability of old children and adolescents to modify parts of their variable grammars for years after the critical period. In this process of *vernacular reorganization*, they often boost the vectors of ongoing change as they shift from their early uses (modeled after their caregivers) to align with the community norm (Labov 2001, 2007; Sankoff 2018, 2019; Tagliamonte & D'Arcy 2007, 2009; Wagner 2012). This process of *incrementation* takes place as older children come to participate in peer networks outside of the home and presumably gravitate towards a more advanced version of whatever variables they can identify as indexical of sociocultural innovation. As individuals in these social contexts enter adult institutions that value conservatism (e.g., family, labor market), they settle on a given norm or even retreat into slightly more conservative uses, but still at a level of change that is more advanced than that of older peers (Chambers 2003: 135). The repetition of this *adolescent peak* across successive generations of learners can then bring a change to completion (see Chapter 9 in this volume for an example).

Unlike age-graded patterns, changes that proceed according to this prototypical route may be tracked in apparent time through the lens of generational differences (Bailey 1991; Baxter & Croft 2016; Wagner 2012). Many of the intuitions afforded by the apparent time approach have been confirmed based on *trend studies* (collecting data from the same community at different time intervals, e.g., Sankoff & Blondeau 2007) and *panel studies* (collecting information from the same individuals at various ages, e.g., Gregersen & al. 2009). The latter kind of studies is particularly revealing from a lifelong sociolinguistic acquisitional perspective, insofar as they allow us to trace whether individuals modify their sociolinguistic repertoires after adolescence, and whether these personal changes contribute to communal trends of change. Table 1 summarizes some of the most prominent connections between individual and communal language change postulated in the literature. Note that a 'stable' individual pattern here implies post-adolescent stability:

Table 1. Patterns of post-adolescent change in the individual and the community (adapted from Sankoff 2019: 199 and Wagner 2012: 373)

Overall sociolinguistic pattern	Individual	Community	Apparent time synchronic patterns
Stability	Stable	Stable	Flat
Age-grading	Unstable	Stable	Increasing/decreasing slope with age
Generational change	Stable	Unstable	Increasing/decreasing slope with age
Communal change	Unstable	Unstable	Flat
Lifespan change	Unstable	Unstable	Increasing/decreasing slope with age

Table 1 reveals several nuanced relationships between the individual and the community. While post-adolescence individual changes typically follow the same vector as adolescent-led changes in progress at the community level, age-graded individual changes may have the opposite function (e.g., maintaining the correlation between the linguistic variable and age already expected by the members of the community). Individual change may even be opposite to the direction of change in the community, as when some speakers become more conservative as they age (see *retrograde change*, Sankoff 2019; Sankoff & Blondeau 2007).

While these correlations between individual lifelong changes and community changes are supported by a robust body of variationist literature from many communities, the local sociodemographic profile of a change may result in alternative patterns. For instance, Labov (2007) has proposed an influential variationist model that relies on the difference between childhood and adult acquisition as the key to understanding the specific sociolinguistic profile of a language change. This model establishes a fundamental difference between two processes: *transmission*, where young learners acquire (and potentially increment) the sociolinguistic model of their community, and *diffusion*, where parts of the conditioning of a sociolinguistic norm are lost via post-childhood acquisition. The latter can be expected whenever demographic changes (e.g., immigration from other dialectal areas) result in young learners being presented with a diffuse sociolinguistic model.

Overall, variationist studies confirm the possibility of post-adolescent changes, but such changes are typically seen as less pervasive and more idiosyncratically variable than childhood and adolescent changes (Cameron 2011; Sankoff 2018). These findings match those provided by psycholinguistic approaches to L2 acquisition (Birdsong 2018), suggesting a common rooting in biologically determined cognition changes. Many of these studies have been conducted in socially stratified monolingual Western communities sharing many common values about the symbolic value of standard vs. non-standard variants and institutions (media, education systems, etc.), and the role of linguistic innovations at each stage of life. In the next section, we survey some of the interactions between acquisition and change observed in more diverse social settings.

4.4 Contact-based approaches: Dialect contact, language contact, pidginization and creolization

Compared to the patterns of variation and change expounded in variationist literature, the relationship between these communal patterns and individual acquisition trajectories is much more equivocal in settings featuring pervasive contact among multilingual or multidialectal users. Broadly speaking, three strands of literature have explored the role of acquisition in such settings from a socially situated perspective: dialect contact studies, language contact literature, and research on the emergence of pidgins and creoles. Each of these strands can be understood as focusing on different portions of the sociohistorical contact spectrum, rather than as discrete research areas. The challenge for these studies is double: to relate the specific linguistic features in the resulting contact codes to a specific acquisitional trigger (features from the learners' L1s, the application of innate linguistic processes, or domain-general learning strategies, see Winford 2020:26); and to explain how these acquisitional strategies may have led to language change in their sociolinguistic contact environment (van Gijn et al. 2023). The following paragraphs review the most prominent incorporations of age-based acquisitional perspectives in each of these lines of inquiry.

Dialect contact studies have often been concerned with the role of age-based acquisition differences in the emergence of new norms. Age of exposure to certain linguistic categories appears to be critical for their 'successful' (i.e., native) acquisition, as observed in second dialect acquisition in situations of migration (Chambers 1992; Kerswill 1996; Siegel 2010; Tagliamonte & Molfenter 2007). Overall grammatical complexity is sometimes analyzed as a predictor for variation, and this relationship is in turn predicated on age-based learning affordances (Diskin Ravid 1995). For instance, features that are underdetermined or underspecified in the grammar (i.e., less salient for learners) have been hypothesized to require continued exposure to input to develop. In turn, this difference would explain why late acquired phenomena are more diachronically unstable, and more prone to not be acquired in situations of contact (e.g., Cornips et al. 2016). The contribution of individual learning trajectories to the historical outcome of contact is particularly clear in situations of *new dialect formation* via colonization settlement or the founding of new towns. In this model, adults contributing vernacular forms from various dialects reduce some of the initial variation by accommodating to each other's vernaculars. Children are then in charge of the emergence of a new vernacular, by leveling out the variation provided by adults and favoring frequent or structurally transparent forms (Kerswill 1996; Kerswill & Williams 2000; see also Chapters 4 and 6 in this volume).

The combined action of speakers of various ages is also apparent in language contact settings. The study of bilingual individuals as agents of language change was adumbrated by language contact pioneers like Haugen (1953) and Weinreich (1953). Building on these early studies, Thomason and Kaufman (1988) proposed an influential typology of diachronic contact processes that relies on the action of bilingual learners: settings of stable bilingualism favor *borrowing* (i.e., elements from language a are incorporated into language b), whereas community-level language shift favors *linguistic interference* (when a grammatical pattern in language a is mapped onto the lexicon of language b). In this framework, social factors (e.g., intensity of contact, prestige) interact with linguistic factors (such as the markedness of a given form or the typological distance between the grammatical options of each language) to determine the outcome of contact. Adult learners are seen as the main innovators in this process: children perpetuate adult innovations via learning, but they do not typically introduce new changes.

Adult learners have also taken the centerstage in later contact models, several of which have advocated strongly for a psycholinguistic perspective. For instance, van Coetsem's speaker agency model (2000) uses relative language dominance as the central predictor of the types and direction of change. He distinguishes between the *recipient language* (RL) and the *source language* (SL) and classifies changes into two main processes. In *borrowing*, the RL is the speaker's dominant language, and it operates as the morphosyntactic basis into which elements from the SL are integrated. By contrast, in *imposition*, competence in the RL is lower than in the SL and as a result the bilingual speaker relies on the grammatical or semantic patterns of their stronger language. In this model, adult L2 acquisition plays a key role: as speakers build their interlanguage, they resort to general psycholinguistic processing strategies to achieve communication. Besides borrowing and imposition, these L2 learning strategies include the generalization of analogical options or the reduction of grammatical categories.

While Thomason and Kaufman's and van Coetsem's models are rooted in the relationship between individual acquisition and its linguistic outcomes, they also incorporate social factors as key to whether and how specific contact features become part of community repertoires. Subsequent reflections on the diachronic role of bilingual acquisition strategies have also reflected on the social rooting of contact-based changes beyond their initial psycholinguistic motivation (Eckman & Iverson 2015; Kupisch & Polinsky 2022; Muysken 2013; Siegel 2012; Winford 2013, 2020; see also Chapter 5 in this volume). Consequently, many of the acquisitional questions raised by language contact studies have been embraced by studies on the effects of language contact in specific social settings. For instance, in heritage language communities, language change can be connected to individual patterns of language acquisition, but also to lifelong shifts in individual language dominance and language attrition which are ultimately governed by social pressures towards linguistic assimilation or the maintenance of linguistic practices in the minority language (Aalberse et al. 2019; Bondi Johannessen & Salmons 2015). Another sociolinguistic development commonly tied to the agency of specific cohorts of learners is the emergence of urban *multiethnolects* (e.g., Cheshire et al. 2013 and Sharma & Sankaran 2011 for London; Gardner-Chloros & Secova 2018 for Paris; Nortier & Dorleijn 2013 for various multiethnolects across western Europe), typically in immigration settings where younger speakers grow up in contact with multiple native and non-native forms of speaking the majority language. In these contexts, specific innovations appear to generalize via communication among older children and adolescents in peer networks, where deviance from the standard rules of the majority language symbolizes new multiethnic urban identities.[2]

Not all approaches to language contact treat the age of acquisition as a meaningful variable in the social actuation of specific changes. In some proposals, the focus is instead on age-independent, universal psycholinguistic processes that determine the degree of learnability of a given form in any sociolinguistic context (e.g., *vernacular universal*, Chambers 2004). Similarly, in evolutionary-ecological approaches (Aboh 2015; Clements 2009; Croft 2000; Mufwene 2008) language change is seen as the result of a process whereby learners of any age select alternatives in a piece-meal fashion from a set of options (*feature pool*) originating in the same or different linguistic systems (dialects or languages). The process operates according to an equation applied by the individual language learner. In this calculation, both internal and external ecological factors conspire to increase or

---

2. See Chapter 6 in this volume for a more detailed review of the literature on multiethnolects.

decrease the chances that a given alternative may be selected, in a manner analogous to the recombination of genes in biological replication. Some recent adaptations of the ecological framework do emphasize the operation of age-specific acquisition processes in the history of contact varieties (Winford 2017, 2020).

While language learning processes are central to many approaches to dialect and language contact, nowhere in the contact literature has the role of age-specific forms of acquisition been as contentious as in the study of the emergence of pidgins and creoles. This area has stood as a testing ground for the application of acquisition-based arguments to historical language data, ever since Bickerton's (1981) groundbreaking but polemical *Language Bioprogram Hypothesis*. According to Bickerton, many creoles were created abruptly in colonial plantation settings by the first generation of children born to non-native speakers. These children turned their parents unstructured approximation to the colonizers' language (i.e., a pidgin) into a regular code by relying on a set of universal innate mechanisms. The universality of these learning strategies explains the similarities among many creoles (SVO word order, TMA systems, etc.). Although Bickerton's abrupt genesis proposal was subsequently refuted by other authors (e.g., Roberts 2000; Veenstra 2009), it did shape the subsequent debate on the role of speakers of various ages in the emergence of creoles. For some authors, creoles emerged gradually as several cohorts of adult L2 learners progressively expanded upon the functions of their non-native approximations to the lexifier via various strategies (relexification of the L1, Lefebvre 1998; interlanguage conventionalization, Plag 2008; approximation to the L2 lexifier language, Chaudenson 2003; general L2 learning strategies, Mather 2006; Sessarego 2020). For other authors, children did play a role as stabilizers of the input offered by adults (Aboh 2015; DeGraff 1999, 2009).

As this brief review shows, various strands of research have long paid attention to the contribution by individual learners as historical language variation and change actors via their age-specific acquisitional behaviors. From a historical sociolinguist perspective, the question becomes how to incorporate what we have learned from this robust body of research on language acquisition throughout the lifespan to the sociohistorical study of language variation and change. As shown in the next section, historical sociolinguists have already started to answer this question.

5. Language acquisition across the lifespan and historical sociolinguistics: Previous approaches

As the discipline that focuses on the historical progression of language change as a function of the social context in which speakers communicate and acquire language, historical sociolinguistics is particularly well poised to theorize and explore the application of acquisition theory and data to the sociohistorical archive. The interpretation of historical language data through the lens afforded by the more synchronic work on the acquisition of variation by individuals of various ages (Section 3) has opened new avenues for the application of acquisition-based perspectives to the study of language variation and change in sociohistorical contexts.

By now, a robust body of explicitly sociohistorical work is rooted in language acquisition at various points of the lifespan as a component of language change, or even tests the applicability of specific theories of acquisition against the extant historical evidence. Focusing on the last two decades only, these studies include Palander-Collin (2018) and Petré & Van de Velde (2018) on British English; Bekker (2014), Deumert (2004); Sharma & Shankaran (2011); Sharma (2017), Schreier (2009, 2016) and Winford (2017) on post-colonial Englishes; Tuten (2003) and Sanz-Sánchez & Tejedo-Herrero (2021) on medieval and colonial Spanish; Lipski (2005); Moyna (2009); Moyna & Sanz-Sánchez (2023), Sanz-Sánchez (2013, 2019), Sanz-Sánchez & Moyna (2023) and Winford (2020) on Latin American Spanish; Schwegler et al. (2016) on Iberian (Spanish and Portuguese-lexified) creoles; Aboh (2015) on Atlantic Creoles; Muysken (2019) on Papiamentu; Howell (2006) on early modern Dutch; and Lucas & Lash (2014) on Arabic and Coptic, to name but a few. While all these studies rely on an understanding of individual acquisitional histories as central to the linguistic evolution of their communities, the exact methodological protocol to enlist acquisition theory in the interpretation of historical evidence depends on the particular questions posed by of each study as well as on the availability of data to address these questions.

For instance, in line with many variationist studies (Section 4.3), analyses of the linguistic production of specific individuals over part of their lives by means of historical written and audiovisual corpora have confirmed that language use across an individual's lifespan is not always stable after childhood. Examples of this approach include Harrington (2006) on Queen Elizabeth II; Kwon (2014) on American linguist Noam Chomsky; or Shapp et al. (2014) on US Supreme Court Justice Ruth Ginsburg. Other studies have analyzed corpora of writings by several individuals over a period of their lives (i.e., a historical sociolinguistic take on panel studies), including Anthonissen & Petré (2019); Nevalainen (2015); Palander-Collin (2018); Petré & Van de Velde (2018) and Raumolin-Brunberg (2005, 2009). Besides confirming that personal grammars can continue to change after childhood, these studies have assessed the degree to which lifelong individual changes may have contributed (or resisted) specific changes in progress (i.e., more progressive vs. more conservative individuals).

Attention to conditions of acquisition across the lifespan is particularly common among studies focusing on the sociohistorical dynamics of contact and change (see Section 4.4). For instance, Clements (2009) analyzes several situations of historical contact in the colonial expansion of Spanish and Portuguese (including Andean Spanish, Portuguese- and Spanish-lexified creoles, and Barranquenho Portuguese) as the result of the conventionalization of forms emerging from L1/L2 bootstrapping acquisition strategies that rely on domain-general principles like frequency-based analogy or perceptual salience. His account incorporates demographic, sociolinguistic and acquisitional evidence. To illustrate how non-native acquisition could have given rise to the attested patterns, Clements incorporates comparisons between recent corpora and historical materials that show the application of the same learning strategies (e.g., some of the features typical of current Spanish-Quechua contact varieties are already present in a 16th-century corpus of letters in Spanish by an L1-Quechua artist, and observation of Chinese immigrants in 21st-century Madrid reveals commonalities with the historical corpus of L2 approximations to Spanish by Chinese laborers in 19th-century Cuba).[3]

Other studies focus on the distribution of features in a sociohistorical corpus, and then interpret the data based on how individuals of various ages have been observed to acquire language variation in comparable settings. For instance, Schreier (2016) studies *be* leveling in Tristan da Cunha English as attested in a corpus of interviews with speakers born 1895–1988. Older speakers show very high or nearly categorical use of leveled *is* in singular forms of *to be*, but younger speakers exhibit variation between leveled *is* and standard forms. Based on the available demographic and sociolinguistic information, the author concludes that adult speakers must have presented the first generations of Tristanians with a diffuse acquisition target that included L2 forms and dialectal variation imported from the British Isles. In a process parallel to other situations of new dialect formation (see Section 4.4 in this chapter, and Chapters 4 and 6 in this volume), younger learners ("children and adolescents") subsequently nativized this sociolinguistically diffuse input into a more systematic dialectal norm. Over the course of the 20th century, increased exposure to British varieties and universal schooling have led to the introduction of standard forms, which now alternate with the vernacular pattern. In this account, age-specific acquisitional behaviors are invoked to explain the evolution from a situation of initial unstructured variation to a regular dialectal norm.

Other studies test whether specific processes of acquisition can explain attested typological trends. In this line of inquiry, the goal is to establish connections between historical conditions of acquisition and crosslinguistic grammatical patterns, according to the rationale that certain types of structures may be more easily

---

3. See Chapters 11 and 12 in this volume for examples of a similar approach.

learned by individuals in certain demographic or social environments (Operstein 2015; Trudgill 2011; Weerman 2011). Several of these generalizations have been tested. For instance, Kortmann and Szmrecsanyi (2009) classify a number of morphosyntactic features in post-colonial varieties of English according to their level of structural complexity, which they operationalize in terms of quantitative complexity (e.g., more phonemes > fewer phonemes), L2 acquisition complexity (i.e., features common in adult interlanguages are simpler) and transparency and irregularity (e.g., irregular elements that are infrequent are harder to acquire). They then survey these features across a range of non-standard varieties of English, including low-contact varieties, L2 varieties, and creoles. Their analysis reveals clear trends according to the historical contact profile of these varieties: low-contact varieties show more opacity and irregularity than L2 varieties and creoles. The overall verdict from this crosslinguistic quantification is that a history of language contact is systematically correlated with a lower degree of complexity, which the authors attribute to the acquisitional action of adult L2 learners (for a similar argument, see Operstein 2015; Sinnemäki 2020; Walkden & Breitbarth 2019).

A common type of acquisition-based argumentation in historical sociolinguistics involves the identification of specific age cohorts as prominent agents of language change in a particular historical ecology. Adults are commonly credited as innovators due to their reduced ability to acquire some forms of grammatical conditioning (Section 3). Sharma (2017) tests some of these assumptions in relation to various features in post-colonial varieties of English, including Indian English and Singapore English. She considers several factors commonly attributed to adult non-native learning, including the influence of universal processes of learning; transfer from L1 substrates; and processes specific to adult acquisition (e.g., *interface effects*, see Sorace 2006, and *input demand*, Davydova 2011). She concludes that, while putative universal processes do not adequately explain the grammatical features attested in these varieties, these characteristics do appear to reflect the interplay between substrate influences and the learnability of each feature (for instance, features that require high levels of input to develop, like the use of definite vs. indefinite articles, are less learnable and thus more diachronically unstable). This study invites us to think of the emergence of these post-colonial varieties as both a sociohistorical and as a psycholinguistic process.

The imprint from even younger learners, such as older children and adolescents, can be felt in the emergence of other community repertoires. While the studies showing that this age group can be instrumental in the incrementation of new norms typically only cover a few decades (Sections 3 and 4.3), occasionally historical corpora with a deeper chronological reach and offering sufficient linguistic detail are available. This possibility is illustrated by historical sociophonetic research (see Hickey 2017 and Chapter 10 in this volume). For instance, a

Montreal corpus includes data from speakers born as early as 1886 (Sankoff & Blondeau 2007; Sankoff 2018, 2019). Audio records from New Zealand English go back to at least 1850 (Trudgill 2004). When available, this type of evidence can be used to gauge how several cohorts of speakers participated in the spread of a chance. As an example, Gordon and Strelluf (2017) trace some changes in the vowel system of Missouri English back to speakers born as early as the 1880s, with older children and adolescents playing a critical role in the incrementation of these changes (see also Chapter 9 in this volume), as observed in more recent cases of language change.

Attention to various sociohistorical contexts of acquisition has also shed light on classical controversies, such as whether young children can contribute to language change via acquisition (Section 3). In this area, the observation of recently emerged sign languages and mixed codes has been particularly informative. These situations share certain environmental components, including high variability in the input; opportunities for young children to communicate in peer networks; and few normative pressures. Examples include Nicaraguan Sign Language (Kocab et al. 2016; Senghas & Coppola 2001), Israeli Sign Language (Meir et al. 2012), and Light Warlpiri (O'Shannessy 2013, 2015; O'Shannessy & Davidson 2020; and Chapter 8 in this volume). In these settings, young children well within the period traditionally considered as critical for native acquisition (i.e., before age 8) have been observed to regularize and systematize the more irregular input provided by older speakers, reproducing the bias towards linguistically predictable grammars revealed by the experimental literature on L1 acquisition (Section 3). These cases confirm that, given certain sociolinguistic triggers, young children can actively contribute to the emergence of new varieties.

Not only have historical sociolinguists applied language acquisition theory to their diachronic materials. A growing body of sociohistorical research also utilizes recently collected acquisition corpora and other acquisition data sources to shed light on how the learners of the past may have processed their linguistic input. The operating principle in these studies is that interactions between the age of acquisition and their observed linguistic outcomes can be projected backwards in time if the available sociohistorical information allows us to hypothesize that learners were presented with similar forms of variation in their input (Aboh 2015; DeGraff 1999, 2009; Winford 2017, 2020). From this perspective, recent acquisitional data offer an analogue to how these learners from yesteryear may have dealt with their respective input, provided that the potential confounding effect of local social conditions be accounted for to avoid anachronic reconstructions (Bergs 2012).

A study that applies this reasoning is Sanz-Sánchez & Moyna (2023). Using a combination of archival, metalinguistic, and acquisitional evidence, they revisit the history of several phonological sibilant mergers in Latin American Spanish that have traditionally been interpreted as the function of adult accommodation in the colonial period. The authors argue that the attested archival data can be better accounted for by invoking a more complex mixture of environmental triggers. These include the same acquisitional tendencies towards perceptually and articulatorily simple sibilant systems that has been recorded for young learners in recent contact situations. To support their analysis, several types of data are enlisted, including experimental studies of L1 and L2 acquisition, heritage language data, and crosslinguistic distributions. All these sources allow us to tentatively reconstruct how children in the early (16th–17th century) Spanish colonies would have processed the phonological distributions in the unfocused input they received from older speakers. A similar methodological protocol is applied by Moyna and Sanz-Sánchez (2023) to explain the attested changes in the 2nd-person singular forms of address in 19th-century Río de la Plata Spanish (see also Chapter 7 in this volume).

An important corollary to the sociolinguistic literature on lifespan change (Sections 3 and 4) is that learners of various ages contribute to the emerging collective repertoires in different ways. From this perspective, the issue of which age group actuated a given change is a moot point: "all individuals present in a communicative ecology participate in the negotiation and selection of language features that constitute the basis of language change at the population level as allowed by their respective age-based cognitive affordances – even though [...] some of these features may be more competitive for demographic, sociolinguistic, and acquisitional reasons" (Sanz-Sánchez & Tejedo-Herrero 2021: 129). Consequently, an awareness of both the age-mediated manifestations of human cognitive affordances operative in language learning as well as the sociohistorical and cultural embedding of acquisition can assist historical sociolinguists in calibrating how language users of various ages may have collaborated in the emergence of historical sociolinguistic repertoires. The following section outlines some ideas on how to incorporate this acquisitionally based perspective as a core theoretical and methodological component in historical sociolinguistics.

6. Towards an acquisitionally informed historical sociolinguistics

Despite the proven potential for acquisition theory and data to inform historical sociolinguistic research, recent articulations of the field (e.g., Auer et al. 2015; Hernández-Campoy & Conde Silvestre 2012; Russi 2016; Tuten & Tejedo-Herrero 2011) do not typically acknowledge the possibility of this interface. In these definitions, references to acquisition theory are often absent or are included only tangentially in the context of dialect or language contact studies. This absence is surprising considering the robust body of historical sociolinguistic work that incorporates acquisition-based perspectives (Section 5) and the markedly interdisciplinary nature of our field. As an illustration, Figure 1 provides an overview of some of these interdisciplinary interactions – language acquisition theory is conspicuously missing from this selection:

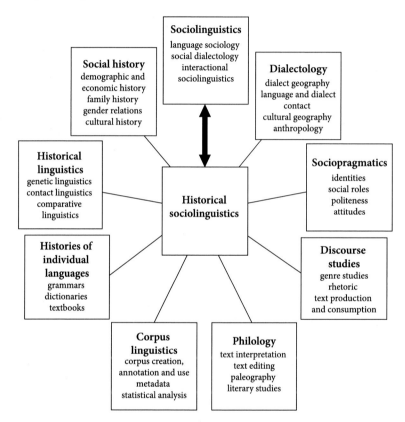

Figure 1. Historical sociolinguistics from a cross-disciplinary perspective (from Nevalainen & Raumolin-Brunberg 2012: 27)

The marginality of acquisition theory in current conceptualizations of historical sociolinguistics as a field is clearly at odds with the recent research on the learning of sociolinguistic variation (see Sections 3 and 4 in this chapters), as well as with the sociohistorical work on language variation and change reviewed in the preceding section. In this sense, there is a mismatch between how the field is conceptualized to this day and what many practitioners in our field are already doing. This mismatch also obscures the potential for new research agendas in historical sociolinguistics.

In all fairness, there are important heuristic limitations to the use of acquisition theory and data in historical sociolinguistics. Even if we accept that lifelong language acquisition trajectories must have played a critical role in many of the attested changes, this role is unlikely to be directly confirmed by the archival data that historical sociolinguists typically work with. Most acquisitional corpora and the theories that are based on them are but a few decades old: Louis XIII of France's physician's development notes (collected between 1601–1628) or several child development studies from Western Europe from the late 1800s (Behrens 2008) are exceptional. Data collection has also privileged a small number of commonly spoken languages. For most sociohistorical contexts, direct acquisition evidence is simply lacking. Therefore, if we seek to gauge the role of specific cohorts of learners in a specific change, we must be open minded and embrace forms of evidence beyond those that historical sociolinguists typically rely on.

This methodological broadening, however, does not require us to step into mere speculation. Reflecting on the uniformitarian nature of the biological basis of language change, DeGraff argues in favor of the incorporation of acquisitional analogues in the study of language history, since, after all, "much more is known and knowable about contemporary, thus observable and measurable, instances of [language acquisition], than about their counterparts in the early stages" (2009: 933). In a similar vein, Meisel et al. (2013) defend acquisitional uniformitarianism as an interpretive tool in the study of language change:

> Although the relevance of acquisition research for explanations of diachronic change has long been acknowledged, it happens only very rarely that studies in historical linguistics actually take such insights into account. This is truly surprising, given that speech communities and consequently also the grammar of the language shared by the members of such a community are idealized abstract objects represented in the mental grammars of the individuals who constitute the speech community. [Therefore,] every hypothesis about principles determining the properties of grammars or the processes leading to their restructuring must necessarily conform to the principles and mechanisms which shape acquisition, representation, and processing of linguistic knowledge in the mind. (53)

While sociohistorical settings of language change may differ greatly from each other, it seems safe to assume that the biological makeup of our human language learning affordances is much more stable, at least within the time scales that historical sociolinguistic research can feasibly hope to encompass. From this perspective, the incorporation of acquisition theory and data is a logical step to address the classical questions of embedding, transmission and actuation in the explanation of language change in Weinreich et al. (1968), as articulated in Section 4.3. While traditionally these questions have been interpreted exclusively from a linguistic or sociolinguistic angle, an acquisitionally informed approach can shed light on how the specific local conditions of socialization and communication yielded the structural or social profile of the innovations present in the historical sociolinguistic record.

Building on the growing body of evidence on the centrality of variation to the overall task of language acquisition across the lifespan (Section 3), the papers in this collection make a strong case that this perspective can be applied fruitfully to historical sociolinguistic approaches to language change. This rationale is also in line with recent proposals that have called for the integration of a psycholinguistic lens in the study of language change. For instance, commenting on the applicability of ecological theories to the sociohistorical study of the colonial expansion of European languages, Winford (2017, 2020) decries the fragmentation of the field into subareas that focus on separate portions in the contact continuum, from so-called L1 varieties to pidgins and creoles. To overcome this division, he calls for an integrated historical sociolinguistic model that incorporates acquisition theory and data:

> Linguistic approaches to these varieties have devoted a great deal of attention to the structural properties of contact phenomena and their sources in the input languages, but by and large pay little attention to the role of social factors. Sociolinguistic or socio-ecological approaches focus more on social contexts at the expense of structural factors. And both types of approach generally have little to say about the role of psycholinguistic factors, hence they fall short of providing a comprehensive picture of the evolution of post-colonial [varieties]. A truly integrative model of language contact must establish links between linguistic, sociolinguistic and psycholinguistic approaches to language evolution. (2017: 26)

If valid to understand the expansion of European languages into new sociolinguistic settings and their eventual diversification, Winford's call for an integration of various strands of research should be equally applicable to any other linguistic setting.

A major take-away from the body of research reviewed in the preceding sections is that language change can be conceptualized as the summation of multiple acts of acquisition throughout the speakers' lifespan, and that these individual acquisitional trajectories are mediated by their respective sociolinguistic context. If linguistic innovations as well as their spread are taken as individual phenomena with community-level consequences, accounting for the actuation of language changes must involve at minimum the following four ingredients (after Petré & Van de Velde 2018: 869):

1. The cognitive mechanisms and motivations underlying the creation of new patterns by the individual;

2. The social-psychological mechanisms and motivations underlying the creation or adoption of new patterns by the individual;
3. The mechanisms underlying propagation at the communal level; and
4. The way (1), (2), and (3) interact

As we consider these factors, we must be careful not to equate acquisition only with (1): on the contrary, the adoption of new patters in (2), and their propagation across the community as speakers interact with each other in specific social networks expressed in (3) are also incumbent upon individual acts of acquisition (see Section 2 in this chapter).

A lifespan acquisitional perspective can be seen as contributing to the development of historical sociolinguistics in several ways: (a) theoretically, the incorporation of individual language acquisition as a trigger for language change at the community level allows researchers to address some of the basic problems in historical sociolinguists, such as the relationship between individual innovations and community-wide changes (Raumolin-Brunberg 1996: 16–17; Tuten & Tejedo-Herrero 2011: 284–285); (b) methodologically, the use of acquisition data allows historical sociolinguists to alleviate the dependence on written data, which are often scarce or frustratingly unrepresentative (Auer et al. 2015: 5; Nevalainen 1999); and (c) heuristically, acquisition theory and data can make it possible to supplement previous accounts of language change by allowing us to sketch richer, more plausible sociohistorical scenarios despite a paucity of direct linguistic evidence. By bringing together the research on language acquisition at various points across the lifespan and several sample applications of this research to the study of language change in specific historical environments, this volume seeks to contribute to move our field in this direction.

7. Structure of the volume

To illustrate the opportunities afforded by the integration of a lifelong developmental language acquisition lens in historical sociolinguistics, the remaining chapters in this volume are organized in two main parts: Part II (*Perspectives on acquisition and change*), which summarizes the literature on language acquisition at various points of our life and in various sociolinguistic settings as a factor in language change, and Part III (*Case studies*), where the theory and data on lifespan acquisition are applied to specific historical cases of language variation and change. Closing the volume, Part IV (*Future directions*) consists of a chapter that outlines some of the possible applications of acquisition literature and data to create new avenues of research in historical sociolinguistics.

Part II of the volume surveys the existing literature on age and acquisition to provide an understanding of how individual acquisitional trajectories contribute to language variation and change. The chapters in this section do not attempt to offer a comprehensive summary of the conversation about the multifaceted relationship between age of acquisition and language change. Instead, these papers zero in on areas of burgeoning research that show potential for fruitful cross-fertilization between acquisition theory and historical sociolinguistic studies, as suggested by recent trends in our field (Section 5). These include monolingual and bilingual child language acquisition (Chapter 2, by Naomi Shin), the adult L2 acquisition of variation (Chapter 3, by Kimberly Geeslin, Travis Evans-Sago, Stephen Fafulas, and Thomas Goebel-Mahrle), the role of age in lifelong acquisition patterns as a factor in dialect contact and change (Chapter 4, by Jennifer Hendriks), bilingual acquisition strategies in language contact and heritage language settings (Chapter 5, by Suzanne Aalberse), and the emergence of new language varieties in post-colonial and multiethnic immigration settings via both dialect contact and language contact (Chapter 6, by Devyani Sharma). In addition to providing a panoramic review of literature in their respective areas of concentration, all chapters in this part of the volume end with a section that explicitly outlines challenges and opportunities for the application of the theory surveyed in each chapter to the study of language variation and change from a historical sociolinguistic perspective.

In Part III of the volume, our attention shifts to how historical sociolinguists may apply what we have learned from the acquisition literature reviewed in Part II to the available historical sociolinguistic record. This application is illustrated by six case studies targeting sociohistorical contexts in the Americas, Oceania, and Asia, thus moving beyond the Western European contexts where much historical sociolinguistic research has been carried out. While this section is organized along a lifespan sequence (from cases where young learners appear to have played a critical role to situations where adult speakers seem to have operated as the most decisive innovators), the case studies do not seek to identify one given age group as the only agents of change (see Section 5). Instead, their purpose is to underscore how the interaction among learners of various ages has shaped community repertoires historically, in ways that reflect the local demographic and sociocultural environment of language learning. To this end, these studies integrate various theoretical, methodological, and analytical protocols to explore the role of age-based acquisitional trajectories in their respective sociohistorical situations, resulting in more comprehensive accounts than approaches that do not incorporate acquisitional analogues.

The first two case studies illustrate the action of young children in the emergence of new norms. Chapter 7 (by María Irene Moyna and Pablo Requena) studies the creation of a mixed paradigm in the expression of the 2nd person singular in Río de la Plata Spanish between the 19th and the 20th century, and Chapter 8 (by Carmel O'Shannessy) analyzes the conventionalization of Light Warlpiri as a new mixed language out of adult code-switching practices in an Australian Northern Territories Aboriginal community starting in the 1980s. The role of slightly older learners is illustrated in Chapter 9 (by Christopher Strelluf), which offers sociophonetic evidence for the actuation of a new pattern of allophonic variation in /æ/ in Missouri English since the late 1800s via incrementation by older children and adolescents. The remaining chapters exemplify how innovations emerging from adult L2 acquisition can become entrenched as part of new norms. In Chapter 10 (by Samantha Litty), a bilingual corpus combining written and audio materials from a heritage North American German community is used to track the historical presence of non-standard phonological simplification patterns in the local English and German varieties, and the interaction among speakers of various ages and levels of language dominance is invoked to explain the attested features. Chapter 11 (by Eliot Raynor) surveys the action of ethnolinguistically diverse non-native Spanish learners in the 16th and 17th centuries via imposition from their L1s as creators of a dialectally idiosyncratic semantic pattern to designate body limbs in a variety of Colombian Spanish. Chapter 12 (by Michelle Li) examines the selection of *for* + infinitive as a purpose complementizer construction in Chinese Pidgin English (18th–19th centuries) and compares this process to the more recently attested use of the same feature in Hong Kong English under partially similar sociolinguistic conditions.

Besides the broad range of geographical environments, sociohistorical scenarios and linguistic features covered by the chapters in Part III, these case studies are valuable in that they illustrate many of the applications of acquisition theory and data to historical sociolinguistic research adumbrated by the literature surveyed in Parts I and II. All these case studies apply analytical protocols that rely on the combination of various forms of data as a tool in reconstructing the historical acquisitional evolution of their communities of focus, thus helping to fill the gaps in the historical record. The precise combination of data sources featured in these chapters includes sociolinguistic interviews and experimental acquisition tasks (Chapter 7), fieldwork naturalistic interactions and elicited production recordings (Chapter 8), archival recordings and sociolinguistic interviews (Chapter 9), written documents and audio recordings (Chapter 10), demographic data and crosslinguistic surveys (Chapter 11), and pedagogical materials and written L2 production corpora (Chapter 12). Working with vastly different forms of evidence, the authors of these studies pose sociohistorical research questions that go beyond those that would be feasible if relying exclusively on more traditional data, such as demographic records or written archival evidence. By providing contextualized examples of the application of acquisition theory and data to a variety of archival materials and sociohistorical contexts, these studies contribute to the broader goal of this volume: to articulate a rationale for the incorporation of language acquisition theory and data as central ingredients in the field of historical sociolinguistics, and to exemplify this approach with the study of specific cases of language change.

References

Aalberse, Suzanne, Ad Backus & Pieter Muysken. 2019. *Heritage languages: A language contact approach.* Amsterdam: John Benjamins.

Aboh, Enoch Oladé. 2015. *The emergence of hybrid grammars: Language contact and change.* Cambridge: Cambridge University Press.

Adamson, Hugh Douglas & Vera Regan. 1991. The acquisition of community norms by Asian immigrants learning English as a second language: A preliminary study. *Studies in Second Language Acquisition* 13. 1–22.

Aitchison, Jean. 2003. Psycholinguistic perspectives on language change. In Joseph Brian & Richard Janda (eds.), *The handbook of historical linguistics*, 736–743. Malden, MA: Wiley-Blackwell.

Anthonissen, Lynn & Peter Petré. 2019. Grammaticalization and the linguistic individual: New avenues in lifespan research. *Linguistics Vanguard* 5(2). 20180037.

Auer, Anita, Catharina Peersman, Simon Pickl, Gijsbert Rutten & Rik Vosters. 2015. Historical sociolinguistics: The field and its future. *Journal of Historical Sociolinguistics* 1(1). 1–12.

Bailey, Guy. 1991. Directions of change in Texas English. *The Journal of American Culture* 14(2). 125–134.

Baxter, Gareth & William Croft. 2016. Modeling language change across the lifespan: Individual trajectories in community change. *Language Variation and Change* 28. 129–173.

Behrens, Heike. 2008. Corpora in language acquisition research: History, methods, perspectives. In Heike Behrens (ed.), *Corpora in language acquisition research: History, methods, perspectives*, xi–xxx. Amsterdam: John Benjamins.

Bekker, Ian. 2014. South-African English as a late 19th-century extraterritorial variety. *English World-Wide* 33. 127–146.

Bergs, Alexander. 2012. The uniformitarian principle and the risk of anachronisms. In Juan Manuel Hernández-Campoy & Juan Camilo Conde-Silvestre (eds.), *The handbook of historical sociolinguistics*, 83–101. Malden, MA: Wiley-Blackwell.

Bickerton, Derek. 1981. *Roots of language.* Ann Arbor, MI: Karoma Publishers.

Birdsong, David. 2018. Plasticity, variability and age in second language acquisition and bilingualism. *Frontiers in Psychology* 9. 1–17.

Blythe, Richard & William Croft. 2021. How individuals change language. *PLoS ONE* 16(6). e0252582.

Bondi Johannessen, Janne & Joseph Salmons (eds.). 2015. *The study of Germanic heritage languages in the Americas.* Amsterdam: John Benjamins.

Brown, Penelope & Suzanne Gaskins. 2014. Language acquisition and language socialization. In N. J. Enfield, Paul Kockelman & Jack Sidnell (eds.), *The Cambridge handbook of linguistic anthropology*, 187–226. Cambridge: Cambridge University Press.

Bybee, Joan. 2010. *Language, usage and cognition.* Cambridge: Cambridge University Press.

Bybee, Joan & Dan Slobin. 1982. Rules and schemas in the development and use of the English past tense. *Language* 58(2). 265–289.

Cameron, Richard. 2011. Aging, age, and sociolinguistics. In Manuel Díaz-Campos (ed.), *The handbook of Hispanic sociolinguistics*, 207–229. Malden, MA: Wiley-Blackwell.

Chambers, Jack K. 1992. Dialect acquisition. *Language* 68(4). 673–705.

Chambers, Jack K. 2003. *Sociolinguistic theory.* 2nd ed. Malden, MA: Wiley-Blackwell.

Chambers, Jack K. 2004. Dynamic typology and vernacular universals. In Bernd Kortmann (ed.), *Dialectology meets typology: Dialect grammar from a cross-linguistic perspective*, 127–145. Berlin: De Gruyter Mouton.

Chaudenson, Robert. 2003. *La créolisation: Théorie, applications, implications.* Paris: L'Harmattan.

Cheng, Qi, Austin Roth, Eric Halgren & Rachel Mayberry. 2023. Restricted language access during childhood affects adult brain structure in selective language regions. *PNAS* 120(7). e2215423120.

Cheshire, Jenny, Susan Fox, Paul Kerswill & Eivind Torgersen. 2013. Language contact and language change in the multicultural metropolis. *Revue Française de Linguistique Appliquée* 18(2). 63–76.

Chevrot, Jean-Pierre, Laurence Beaud & Renata Varga. 2000. Developmental data on a French sociolinguistic variable: Post-consonantal word-final /R/. *Language Variation and Change* 12. 295–319.

Chevrot, Jean-Pierre & Paul Foulkes. 2013. Introduction: Language acquisition and sociolinguistic variation. *Linguistics* 51(2). 251–254.

Clahsen, Harald & Pieter Muysken. 1996. How adult second language learning differs from child first language development. *Behavioral and Brain Sciences* 19(4). 721–723.

Clements, J. Clancy. 2009. *The linguistic legacy of Spanish and Portuguese: Colonial expansion and language change.* Cambridge: Cambridge University Press.

Cornips, Leonie, Jos Swanenberg, Wilbert Heeringa & Folkert de Vriend. 2016. The relationship between first language acquisition and dialect variation: Linking resources from distinct disciplines in a CLARIN-NL project. *Lingua* 178. 32–45.

Cournane, Ailís. 2015. In defence of the child innovator. In Eric Mathieu & Robert Truswell (eds.), *Micro-change and macro-change in diachronic syntax*, 10–24. Oxford: Oxford University Press.

Cournane, Ailís. 2019. A developmental view on incrementation in language change. *Theoretical Linguistics* 45. 127–150.

Crain, Stephen, Takuya Goro & Rosalind Thornton. 2006. Language acquisition is language change. *Journal of Psycholinguistic Research* 35(1). 31–49.

Croft, William. 2000. *Explaining language change: An evolutionary approach.* London: Longman.

Dąbrowska, Ewa, Laura Becker & Luca Miorelli. 2020. Is adult second language acquisition defective? *Frontiers in Psychology* 11.1839. ⟨https://www.frontiersin.org/articles/10.3389/fpsyg.2020.01839/full#ref90⟩

Davydova, Julia. 2011. *The present perfect in non-native Englishes: A corpus-based study of variation.* Berlin: De Gruyter Mouton.

de Bot, Kees & Robert W. Schrauf (eds.). 2009. *Language development over the lifespan.* New York: Routledge.

DeGraff, Michel. 1999. Creolization, language change, and language acquisition: An epilogue. In DeGraff, Michel (ed.), *Language creation and language change. Creolization, diachrony, and development,* 473–544. Cambridge, MA: MIT Press.

DeGraff, Michel (ed.). 1999. *Language creation and language change. Creolization, diachrony, and development.* Cambridge, MA: MIT Press.

DeGraff, Michel. 2009. Language acquisition in creolization and, thus, language change: Some cartesian-uniformitarian boundary conditions. *Language and Linguistics Compass* 3/4. 888–971.

De Houwer, Annick. 2009. *Bilingual first language acquisition.* Bristol: Multilingual Matters.

De Leeuw, Esther, Conny Opitz & Dorota Lubińska. 2013. Dynamics of first language attrition across the lifespan. *International Journal of Bilingualism* 17(6). 667–674.

Deumert, Ana. 2004. *Language standardization and language change: The dynamics of Cape Dutch.* Amsterdam: John Benjamins.

Diessel, Holger. 2012. New perspectives, theories and methods: Diachronic change and language acquisition. In Alex Bergs & Laurel Brinton (eds.), *Historical linguistics of English,* 1599–1613. Berlin: De Gruyter Mouton.

Diskin Ravid, Dorit. 1995. *Language change in child and adult Hebrew: A psycholinguistic perspective.* Oxford: Oxford University Press.

Eckert, Penelope & Sally McConnell-Ginet. 2013. *Language and gender.* Cambridge: Cambridge University Press.

Eckman, Fred & Gregory Iverson. 2015. Second language acquisition and phonological change. In Patrick Honeybone & Joseph Salmons (eds.), *The Oxford handbook of historical phonology,* 637–643. Oxford: Oxford University Press.

Fernández, Eva, Ricardo Augusto de Souza & Agustina Carando. 2017. Bilingual innovations: Experimental evidence offers clues regarding the psycholinguistics of language change. *Bilingualism: Language and Cognition* 20(2). 251–268.

Filippi, Roberto, Dean D'Souza & Peter Bright. 2018. A developmental approach to bilingual research: The effects of multi-language experience from early infancy to old age. *International Journal of Bilingualism* 23(5). 1195–1207.

Flege, James. 1987. The production of "new" and "similar" phones in a foreign language: Evidence for the effect of equivalence classification. *Journal of Phonetics* 15(1). 47–65.

Fløgstad, Guro Nore & Elizabeth Lanza. 2019. Language contact across the lifespan. In Jeroen Darquennes, Joseph Salmons & Wim Vandenbussche (eds.), *Language contact: An international handbook,* 172–184. Berlin: De Gruyter Mouton.

García, Ofelia & Li Wei. 2014. *Translanguaging: Language, bilingualism, and education.* London: Palgrave Macmillan.

Gardner-Chloros, Penelope & Maria Secova. 2018. Grammatical change in Paris French: In-situ question words in embedded contexts. *Journal of French Language Studies* 28(2). 181–207.

Gaskell, Gareth & Andrew Ellis. 2009. Word learning and lexical development across the lifespan. *Philosophical Transaction of the Royal Society* 364. 3607–3615.

Gasser, Michael. 1990. Connectionism and universals of second language acquisition. *Studies in Second Language Acquisition*, 12. 179–199.

Geeslin, Kimberly L. 2018. Variable structures and sociolinguistic variation. In Paul Malovrh & Alessandro Benati (eds.), *The handbook of advanced proficiency in second language acquisition*, 547–565. Oxford: Wiley-Blackwell.

Geeslin, Kimberly, Stephen Fafulas & Matthew Kanwit. 2013. Acquiring geographically-variable norms of use: The case of the present perfect in Mexico and Spain. In Chad Howe, Sarah Blackwell & Margaret Quesada (eds.), *Selected proceedings of the 15th Hispanic Linguistics Symposium*, 205–220. Somerville, MA: Cascadilla Press.

Geeslin, Kimberly & Avizia Long. 2014. *Sociolinguistics and second language acquisition: Learning to use language in context*. London: Routledge.

Gerstenberg, Annette & Anja Voeste (eds.). 2015. *Language development: The lifespan perspective*. Amsterdam: John Benjamins.

Ghimenton, Anna, Aurélie Nardy & Jean-Pierre Chevrot (eds.), 2021. *Sociolinguistic variation and language acquisition across the lifespan*. Amsterdam: John Benjamins.

Gleitman, Lila & Elissa Newport. 1995. The invention of language by children: Environmental and biological influences on the acquisition of language. In Lila Gleitman & Mark Liberman (eds.), *Language: An invitation to cognitive science*. 2nd edition, 1–24. Cambridge, MA: MIT Press.

Gordon, Matthew J. & Christopher Strelluf. 2017. Evidence of American regional dialects in early recordings. In Raymond Hickey (ed.), *Listening to the past: Audio records of accents of English*. Cambridge: Cambridge University Press: 232–256.

Gregersen, Frans, Marie Maegaard & Nicolai Pharao. 2009. The long and short of (æ)-variation in Danish: A panel study of short (æ)-variants in Danish in real time. *Acta Linguistica Hafniensia* 41. 64–82.

Gudmestad, Aarnes. 2014. Variationist approaches to second language Spanish. In Kimberly Geeslin (ed.), *The handbook of Spanish second language acquisition*, 80–95. Malden, MA: Wiley-Blackwell.

Guy, Gregory & Sally Boyd. 1990. The development of a morphological class. *Language Variation and Change* 2. 1–18.

Hall, Erin & Ruth Maddeaux. 2020. /u/-fronting and /æ/-raising in Toronto families. *University of Pennsylvania Working Papers in Linguistics* 25(2). Article 7. (https://repository.upenn.edu/pwpl/vol25/iss2/7)

Harrington, Jonathan. 2006. An acoustic analysis of 'happy-tensing' in the Queen's Christmas broadcasts. *Journal of Phonetics* 34(4). 439–457.

Hartshorne, Joshua, Joshua Tenenbaum & Steven Pinker. 2018. A critical period for second language acquisition: Evidence from 2/3 million English speakers. *Cognition* 177. 263–277.

Haugen, Einar. 1953. *The Norwegian language in America: A study in bilingual behavior*. Philadelphia: University of Pennsylvania Press.

Hernández-Campoy, Juan Manuel & Juan Camilo Conde-Silvestre. 2012. *The handbook of historical sociolinguistics*. Malden, MA: Wiley-Blackwell.

Hickey, Raymond (ed.), 2017. *Listening to the past: Audio records of accents of English*. Cambridge: Cambridge University Press.

Howell, Robert. 2006. Immigration and koineisation: The formation of early modern Dutch urban vernaculars. *Transactions of the Philological Society* 104(2). 207–227.

Hróarsdóttir, Thorbjörg. 2003. Language change and language acquisition. *Nordlyd* 31(1). 116–131.

Hudson Kam, Carla & Elissa Newport. 2005. Regularizing unpredictable variation: The roles of adult and child learners in language formation and change. *Language Learning and Development* 1(2). 151–195.

Hudson Kam, Carla & Elissa Newport. 2009. Getting it right by getting it wrong: When learners change languages. *Cognitive Psychology* 59(1). 30–66.

Isel, Frédéric & Michèle Kail. 2019. Neuroplasticity, network connectivity and language processing across the lifespan. *Brain and Cognition* 134. 67–70.

Jespersen, Otto. 1964. *Language: Its nature, development, and origin*. New York: Norton & Company. Originally published in 1922.

Kerswill, Paul. 1996. Children, adolescents, and language change. *Language Variation and Change* 8. 177–202.

Kerswill, Paul & Ann Williams. 2000. Creating a new town koine: Children and language change in Milton Keynes. *Language in Society* 29. 65–115.

Kiparsky, Paul. 2014. New perspectives in historical linguistics. In Claire Bowern (ed.), *The Routledge handbook of historical linguistics*, 64–102. London: Routledge.

Kirkham, Sam & Emma Moore. 2013. Adolescence. In Jack K. Chambers & Natalie Schilling (eds.), *The handbook of language variation and change*, 277–296. Oxford: Wiley-Blackwell.

Klein, Wolfgang. 1997. Language acquisition at different ages. In David Magnusson (ed.), *The lifespan development of individuals: Behavioral, neurobiological, and psychosocial perspectives: A synthesis*, 244–264. Cambridge: Cambridge University Press.

Kocab, Annemarie, Ann Senghas & Jesse Snedeker. 2016. The emergence of temporal language in Nicaraguan Sign Language. *Cognition* 156. 147–163.

Kortmann, Bernd & Benedikt Szmrecsanyi. 2009. World Englishes between simplification and complexification. In Lucia Siebers & Thomas Hoffmann (eds.), *World Englishes: Problems, properties and prospects. Selected papers from the 13TH IAWE Conference*, 265–285. Amsterdam: John Benjamins.

Kroch, Anthony. 2005. Modeling language change and language acquisition. Expansion of an LSA Institute forum lecture. Online publication. (https://www.ling.upenn.edu/~kroch/papers/lsa-forum.pdf).

Kroch, Anthony, Ann Taylor & Donald Ringe. 2000. The Middle English verb-second constraint: A case study in language contact and language change. In Susan Herring, Pieter van Reenen & Lene Schøsler (eds.), *Textual parameters in older languages*, 353–391. Amsterdam: John Benjamins.

Kupisch, Tanja & Maria Polinsky. 2022. Language history on fast forward: Innovations in heritage languages and diachronic change. *Bilingualism* 25(1). 1–12.

Kwon, Soohyun. 2014. Vowel change across Noam Chomsky's lifespan. *University of Pennsylvania Working Papers in Linguistics* 20(2). Article 11. ⟨https://repository.upenn.edu/pwpl/vol20/iss2/11⟩

Labov, William. 1972. *Sociolinguistic patterns*. Philadelphia: University of Pennsylvania Press.

Labov, William. 1989. The child as linguistic historian. *Language Variation and Change* 1. 85–97.

Labov, William. 1994. *Principles of linguistic change. Volume 1: Internal factors*. Oxford: Blackwell.

Labov, William. 2001. *Principles of linguistic change. Volume 2: Social factors*. Oxford: Blackwell.

Labov, William. 2007. Transmission and diffusion. *Language* 83(2). 344–387.

Larsen-Freeman, Diane. 2007. Reflecting on the cognitive-social debate in second language acquisition. *The Modern Language Journal* 91. 773–787.

Leather, Jonathan & Jet van Dam. 2003. Towards an ecology of language acquisition. In Jonathan Leather & Jet van Dam (eds.), *Ecology of language acquisition*, 1–29. Dordrecht: Springer.

Lefebvre, Claire. 1998. *Creole genesis and the acquisition of grammar: The case of Haitian Creole*. Cambridge: Cambridge University Press.

Lenneberg, Eric. 1967. *Biological foundations of language*. New York: John Wiley and Sons.

Li, Ping. 1996. Why don't L2 learners end up with uniform and perfect linguistic competence? *Behavioral and Brain Sciences* 19(4). 733–734.

Li, Ping, Jennifer Legault & Kaitlyn Litcofsky. 2014. Neuroplasticity as a function of second language learning: Anatomical changes in the human brain. *Cortex* 58. 301–324.

Lightfoot, David. 2006. *How new languages emerge*. Cambridge: Cambridge University Press.

Lightfoot, David & Marit Westergaard. 2007. Language acquisition and language change: Inter-relationships. *Language and Linguistics Compass* 1(5). 396–415.

Lipski, John. 2005. *A history of Afro-Hispanic language: Five centuries, five continents*. Cambridge: Cambridge University Press.

Lucas, Christopher & Elliott Lash. 2014. Contact as catalyst: The case for Coptic influence in the development of Arabic negation. *Journal of Linguistics* 46(2). 379–413.

Mather, Patrick-André. 2006. Second language acquisition and creolization: Same (i-)processes, different (e-)results. *Journal of Pidgin and Creole Languages* 21. 231–274.

Meir, Irit, Assaf Israel, Wendy Sandler, Carol Padden & Mark Aronoff. 2012. The influence of community on language structure: Evidence from two young sign languages. *Linguistic Variation* 12(2). 247–291.

Meisel, Jürgen. 2009. Second language acquisition in early childhood. *Zeitschrift für Sprachwissenschaft* 28. 5–34.

Meisel, Jürgen. 2011. Bilingual language acquisition and theories of diachronic change: Bilingualism as cause and effect of grammatical change. *Bilingualism: Language and Cognition* 14. 121–145.

Meisel, Jürgen, Elsig Martin & Rinke Esther. 2013. *Language acquisition and change: A morphosyntactic perspective*. Edinburgh: Edinburgh University Press.

Miller, Karen & Cristina Schmitt. 2012. Variable input and the acquisition of plural morphology. *Language Acquisition* 19. 223–261.

Montrul, Silvina. 2008. *Incomplete acquisition in bilingualism: Re-examining the age factor.* Amsterdam: John Benjamins.

Montrul, Silvina & Carmen Silva-Corvalán. 2019. The social context contributes to the incomplete acquisition of aspects of heritage languages. *Studies in Second Language Acquisition* 41(2). 269-273.

Moyna, María Irene. 2009. Child acquisition and language change: Voseo evolution in Río de la Plata Spanish. In Joe Collentine, Barbara Lafford, MaryEllen García & Francisco Marcos Marín (eds.), *Proceedings of the 2007 Hispanic Linguistics Symposium*, 131-142. Somerville, MA: Cascadilla.

Moyna, María Irene & Israel Sanz-Sánchez. 2023. Out of the mouths of babes: The role of children in the formation of the Río de la Plata address system. *Journal of Historical Sociolinguistics* 9(2). 189-210.

Mufwene, Salikoko. 2008. *Language evolution: Contact, competition, and change.* London: Continuum.

Muysken, Pieter. 2013. Language contact outcomes as the result of bilingual optimization strategies. *Bilingualism: Language and Cognition* 16(4). 709-730.

Muysken, Pieter. 2019. Heritage languages in post-colonial settings: Focus on Papiamentu. In Suzanne Aalberse, Ad Backus & Pieter Muysken (eds.), *Heritage languages: A language contact approach*, 203-223. Amsterdam: John Benjamins.

Nardy, Aurelie, Jean-Pierre Chevrot & Stéphanie Barbu. 2014. Sociolinguistic convergence and social interactions within a group of preschoolers: A longitudinal study. *Language Variation and Change* 28. 273-301.

Neumann, Yael, Linda Carozza & Anastasia Georgiou. 2010. Neurolinguistics and psycholinguistics: Contributions to understanding healthy aging and dementia. In Susan Behrens & Judith Parker (eds.), *Language in the real world: An introduction to linguistics*, 314-330. London: Routledge.

Nevalainen, Terttu. 1999. Making the best use of 'bad' data: Evidence for sociolinguistic variation in Early Modern English. *Neuphilologische Mitteilungen* 100. 499-533.

Nevalainen, Terttu. 2015. Age-related variation and language change in Early Modern English. In Anette Gerstenberg & Anja Voeste (eds.), *Language development: The lifespan perspective*, 129-146. Amsterdam: John Benjamins.

Nevalainen, Terttu & Helena Raumolin-Brunberg (eds.). 1996. *Sociolinguistics and language history: Studies based on the Corpus of Early English Correspondence.* Amsterdam: Rodopi.

Nevalainen, Terttu & Helena Raumolin-Brunberg. 2012. Historical sociolinguistics: Origins, motivations, and paradigms. In Juan Manuel Hernández-Campoy & Juan Camilo Conde-Silvestre (eds.), *The handbook of historical sociolinguistics*, 22-40. Malden, MA: Wiley-Blackwell.

Nicoladis, Elena & Simona Montanari (eds.). 2016. *Bilingualism across the lifespan: Factors moderating language proficiency.* Berlin: De Gruyter.

Newport, Elissa. 2020. Children and adults as language learners: Rules, variation and maturational change. *Topics in Cognitive Science* 12. 153-169.

Ng, Bee Chin & Francesco Cavallaro. 2022. Where have all my languages gone? Aging and the changing multilingual linguistic ecology. In Unn Røyneland & Robert Blackwood (eds.), *Multilingualism across the lifespan*, 147-168. London: Routledge.

Nortier, Jacomine & Margreet Dorleijn. 2013. Multi-ethnolects: Kebabnorsk, Perkerdansk, Verlan, Kanakensprache, Straattaal, etc. In Peter Bakker & Yaron Matras (eds.), *Contact languages: A comprehensive guide*, 229–272. Berlin: De Gruyter Mouton.

Operstein, Natalie. 2015. Contact-genetic linguistics: Toward a contact-based theory of language change. *Language Sciences* 48. 1–15.

Ortega, Lourdes & Andrea Tyler. 2016. Introduction: The vibrant and expanded study of usage-based language learning and multilingualism. In Lourdes Ortega, Andrea Tyler, Hae In Park & Mariko Uno (eds.), *The usage-based study of language learning and multilingualism*, 1–12. Georgetown: Georgetown University Press.

O'Shannessy, Carmel. 2013. The role of multiple sources in the formation of an innovative auxiliary category in Light Warlpiri, a new Australian mixed language. *Language* 89. 328–353.

O'Shannessy, Carmel. 2015. Multilingual children increase language differentiation by indexing communities of practice. *First Language* 35. 305–326.

O'Shannessy, Carmel & Lucinda Davidson. 2020. Language contact and change through child first language acquisition. In Raymond Hickey (ed.), *The handbook of language contact*, 2nd edition, 67–91. Malden, MA: Wiley-Blackwell.

Ozón, Gabriel & Eva Duran Eppler. 2019. First- and second-language acquisition and CILC. In Anthony Grant (ed.), *The Oxford handbook of language contact* (online edition), 215–240. Oxford: Oxford University Press.

Palander-Collin, Minna. 2018. Ongoing change: The diffusion of the third-person neuter possessive *its*. In Terttu Nevalainen, Minna Palander-Collin & Tanja Säily (eds.), *Patterns of change in 18th-century English: A sociolinguistic approach*, 159–178. Amsterdam: John Benjamins.

Payne, Arvilla. 1980. Factors controlling the acquisition of the Philadelphia dialect by out-of-state children. In William Labov (ed.), *Locating language in time and space*, 143–178. New York: Academic Press.

Petré, Peter & Freek Van de Velde. 2018. The real-time dynamics of the individual and the community in grammaticalization. *Language* 94(4). 867–901.

Phillips, Shannon & Margaret Deuchar. 2022. The role of the input in the acquisition of code-switching. In Unn Røyneland & Robert Blackwood (eds.), *Multilingualism across the lifespan*, 56–79. London: Routledge.

Plag, Ingo. 2008. Creoles as interlanguages: Inflectional morphology. *Journal of Pidgin and Creole Languages* 23. 109–130.

Raumolin-Brunberg, Helena. 1996. Historical sociolinguistics. In Terttu Nevalainen & Helena Raumolin-Brunberg (eds.), *Sociolinguistics and language history: Studies based on the Corpus of Early English Correspondence*, 11–37. Amsterdam: Rodopi.

Raumolin-Brunberg, Helena. 2005. Language change in adulthood: Historical letters as evidence. *European Journal of English Studies* 9. 37–51.

Raumolin-Brunberg, Helena. 2009. Lifespan changes in the language of three early modern gentlemen. In Arja Nurmi, Minna Nevala & Minna Palander-Collin (eds.), *The language of daily life in England (1400–1800)*, 165–196. Amsterdam: John Benjamins.

Regan, Vera. 2013. Variation. In Julia Herschenson & Martha Young-Scholten (eds.), *The Cambridge handbook of second language acquisition*, 272–291. Cambridge: Cambridge University Press.

Regan, Vera. 2021. Second language acquisition and dialectal variation in adults. In Anna Ghimenton, Aurélie Nardy & Jean-Pierre Chevrot (eds.), *Sociolinguistic variation and language acquisition across the lifespan*, 185–198. Amsterdam: John Benjamins.

Renn, Jennifer & Michael Terry. 2009. Operationalizing style: Quantifying the use of style shift in the speech of African American adolescents. *American Speech* 84(4). 367–390.

Roberts, Julie. 1997. Hitting a moving target: Acquisition of sound change in progress by Philadelphia children. *Language Variation and Change* 9. 249–266.

Roberts, Julie. 2005. Acquisition of sociolinguistic variation. In Martin Ball (ed.), *Clinical sociolinguistics*, 151–164. Malden, MA: Wiley-Blackwell.

Roberts, Sarah. 2000. Nativization and the genesis of Hawaiian Creole. In John McWhorter (ed.), *Language change and language contact in pidgins and creoles*, 257–300. Amsterdam: John Benjamins.

Romaine, Suzanne. 1982. *Socio-historical linguistics*. Cambridge: Cambridge University Press.

Røyneland, Unn & Robert Blackwood (eds.). 2022. *Multilingualism across the lifespan*. London: Routledge.

Russi, Cinzia (ed.). 2016. *Current trends in historical sociolinguistics*. Berlin: De Gruyter.

Sankoff, Gillian. 2018. Language change across the lifespan. *Annual Review of Linguistics* 4. 297–316.

Sankoff, Gillian. 2019. Language change across the lifespan: Three trajectory types. *Language* 95. 197–229.

Sankoff, Gillian & Hélène Blondeau. 2007. Language change across the lifespan: /r/ in Montreal French. *Language* 83(3). 560–588.

Sanz-Sánchez, Israel. 2013. Diagnosing dialect contact as the cause for dialect change: Evidence from a palatal merger in colonial New Mexican Spanish. *Diachronica* 30. 61–94.

Sanz-Sánchez, Israel. 2019. Documenting feature pools in language expansion situations: Sibilants in early colonial Latin American Spanish. *Transactions of the Philological Society* 117(2). 199–233.

Sanz-Sánchez, Israel & Fernando Tejedo-Herrero. 2021. Adult language and dialect learning as simultaneous environmental triggers for language change. In Whitney Chappell and Bridget Drinka (eds.), *Spanish socio-historical linguistics: Isolation and contact*, 104–137. Amsterdam: John Benjamins.

Sanz-Sánchez, Israel & María Irene Moyna. 2023. Children as agents of language change: Diachronic evidence from Latin American Spanish phonology. *Journal of Historical Linguistics* 13(3). 327–374.

Schreier, Daniel. 2009. Language in isolation, and its implications for variation and change. *Language and Linguistics Compass* 3. 682–699.

Schreier, Daniel. 2016. Super-leveling, fraying-out, internal restructuring: A century of present *be* concord in Tristan da Cunha English. *Language Variation and Change*, 28. 203–224.

Schwartz, Bonnie. 2004. On child L2 development of syntax and morphology. *Lingue e Linguaggio* 3. 97–132.

Schwegler, Armin, John McWhorter & Liane Ströbel (eds.). 2016. *The Iberian challenge: Creole languages beyond the plantation setting*. Madrid: Iberoamericana/Vervuert.

Selinker, Larry. 1972. Interlanguage. *International Review of Applied Linguistics in Language Teaching* 10. 209–241.

Senghas, Ann & Marie Copola. 2001. Children creating language: How Nicaraguan Sign Language acquired a spatial grammar. *Psychological Science* 12. 323–328.

Sessarego, Sandro. 2020. Not all grammatical features are robustly transmitted during the emergence of creoles. *Humanities and Social Sciences Communications* 7(1). 130.

Shapp, Allison, Nathan LaFave & Singler John Victor. 2014. Ginsburg v. Ginsburg: A longitudinal study of regional features in a Supreme Court Justice's speech. *University of Pennsylvania Working Papers in Linguistics* 20(2). Article 17. ⟨https://repository.upenn.edu/pwpl/vol20/iss2/17⟩

Sharma, Devyani. 2017. A dynamic typology of syntactic change in Postcolonial Englishes. Presentation at the Societas Linguistica Europea. September 12, 2017.

Sharma, Devyani & Lavanya Sankaran. 2011. Cognitive and social forces in dialect shift: Gradual change in London Asian speech. *Language Variation and Change* 23. 399–428.

Shin, Naomi. 2016. Acquiring constraints on morphosyntactic variation: Children's Spanish subject pronoun expression. *Journal of Child Language* 43. 914–947.

Shin, Naomi & Daniel Erker. 2015. The emergence of structured variability in morphosyntax: Childhood acquisition of Spanish subject pronouns. In Ana Carvalho, Rafael Orozco, and Naomi Shin (eds.), *Subject pronoun expression in Spanish: A cross-dialectal perspective*, 171–191. Georgetown, DC: Georgetown University Press.

Shin, Naomi & Karen Miller. 2022. Children's acquisition of morphosyntactic variation. *Language Learning and Development* 18(2). 125–150.

Siegel, Jeff. 2010. *Second dialect acquisition*. Cambridge: Cambridge University Press.

Siegel, Jeff. 2012. Two types of functional transfer in language contact. *Journal of Language Contact* 5. 187–215.

Singleton, Jenny & Elissa Newport. 2004. When learners surpass their models: The acquisition of American Sign Language from inconsistent input. *Cognitive Psychology* 49(2). 370–407.

Sinnemäki, Kaius. 2020. Linguistic system and sociolinguistic environment as competing factors in linguistic variation: A typological approach. *Journal of Historical Sociolinguistics* 6. 1–39.

Slavkov, Nikolay, Sílvia Melo-Pfeifer & Nadja Kerschhofer-Puhalo. 2022. *The changing face of the "native speaker": Perspectives from multilingualism and globalization*. Berlin: De Gruyter.

Smalle, Eleonore, Arnaud Szmalec, Louisa Bogaerts, Mike Page, Vaishna Narang, Deepshikha Misra, Susana Araújo, Nishant Lohagun, Ouroz Khan, Anuradha Singh, Ramesh Mishra & Falk Huettig. 2019. Literacy improves short-term serial recall of spoken verbal but not visuospatial items: Evidence from illiterate and literate adults. *Cognition* 185. 144–150.

Smith, Jennifer. 2021. Child language acquisition and sociolinguistic variation. In Anne Ghimenton, Aurélie Nardy & Jean-Pierre Chevrot (eds.), *Sociolinguistic variation and language acquisition across the lifespan*, 12–19. Amsterdam: John Benjamins.

Smith, Jennifer, Mercedes Durham & Liane Fortune. 2007. "Mam, my trousers is fa'in doon!": Community, caregiver, and child in the acquisition of variation in a Scottish dialect. *Language Variation and Change* 19. 63–99.

Smith, Jennifer & Mercedes Durham. 2019. *Sociolinguistic variation in children's language: Acquiring community norms*. Cambridge: Cambridge University Press.

Sorace, Antonella. 2006. Pinning down the concept of "interface" In bilingualism. *Linguistic Approaches to Bilingualism*, 1(1). 1–33.

Stanford, James. 2008. Child dialect acquisition: New perspectives on parent/peer influence. *Journal of Sociolinguistics* 12(5). 567–596.

Tagliamonte, Sali & Alexandra D'Arcy. 2007. Frequency and variation in the community grammar: Tracking a new change through the generations. *Language Variation and Change* 19. 1–19.

Tagliamonte, Sali & Alexandra D'Arcy. 2009. Peaks beyond phonology: Adolescence, incrementation, and language change. *Language* 85(1). 58–108.

Tagliamonte, Sali & Sonja Molfenter. 2007. How'd you get that accent? Acquiring a second dialect of the same language. *Language in Society*, 36(5). 649–675.

Tarone, Elaine. 1988. *Variation in interlanguage.* London: Edward Arnold.

Tarone, Elaine & Martha Bigelow. 2005. Impact of literacy on oral language processing: Implications for second language acquisition research. *Annual Review of Applied Linguistics* 25. 77–97.

Thomason, Sarah & Terrence Kaufman. 1988. *Language contact, creolization, and genetic linguistics.* Berkeley: University of California Press.

Tomasello, Michael. 2003. *Constructing a language: A usage-based theory of language acquisition.* Cambridge, MA: Harvard University Press.

Trudgill, Peter. 2004. *New-dialect formation: The inevitability of colonial Englishes.* Edinburgh: Edinburgh University Press.

Trudgill, Peter. 2011. *Sociolinguistic typology: Social determinants of linguistic complexity.* Oxford: Oxford University Press.

Tuten, Donald. 2003. *Koinéization in Medieval Spanish.* Berlin: De Gruyter.

Tuten, Donald & Fernando Tejedo-Herrero. 2011. The relationship between historical linguistics and sociolinguistics. In Manuel Díaz-Campos (ed.), *The handbook of Hispanic sociolinguistics*, 283–302. Malden, MA: Wiley-Blackwell.

Unsworth, Sharon. 2016. Early child L2 acquisition: Age or input effects? Neither, or both? *Journal of Child Language* 43(3). 608–634.

van Coetsem, Frans. 2000. *A general and unified theory of the transmission process in language contact.* Heidelberg: Winter.

van Gijn, Rik, Hanna Ruch, Max Wahlstrom & Anja Hasse (eds.). 2023. *Language contact: Bridging the gap between individual interactions and areal patterns.* Berlin: Language Science Press.

Veenstra, Tonjes. 2009. Creole genesis: The impact of the Language Bioprogram Hypothesis. In Silvia Kouwenberg & John Victor Singler (eds.), *The handbook of pidgin and creole studies*, 219–241. Malden, MA: Wiley-Blackwell.

Wagner, Suzanne. 2012. Age grading in sociolinguistic theory. *Language and Linguistics Compass* 6(6). 371–382.

Walkden, George. 2019. The many faces of uniformitarianism in linguistics. *Glossa* 4(1). 52.

Walkden, George & Anne Breitbarth. 2019. Complexity as L2-difficulty: Implications for syntactic change. *Theoretical Linguistics* 45(3–4). 183–209.

Weerman, Fred. 1993. The diachronic consequences of first and second language acquisition: The change from OV to VO. *Linguistics* 31(5). 903–931.

Weerman, Fred. 2011. Diachronic change: Early versus late acquisition. *Bilingualism: Language and Cognition* 14(2). 149–151.

Weinreich, Uriel. 1953. *Languages in contact: Findings and problems*. The Hague: Mouton.

Weinreich, Uriel, William Labov & Marvin Herzog. 1968. Empirical foundations for a theory of language change. In Winfred Lehmann & Yakov Malkiel (eds.), *Directions for historical linguistics*, 95–195. Austin: University of Texas Press.

Werker, Janet & Richard Tees. 2005. Speech perception as a window for understanding plasticity and commitment in language systems of the brain. *Developmental Psychobiology* 46. 233–251.

Winford, Donald. 2013. Social factors in contact languages. In Yaron Matras & Peter Bakker (eds.), *Contact languages: A comprehensive guide*, 363–416. Berlin: De Gruyter Mouton.

Winford, Donald. 2017. The ecology of language and the New Englishes: toward an integrative framework. In Markku Filppula, Juhani Klemola, Anna Mauranen & Sveltana Vetchinnikova (eds.), *Changing English: Global and local perspectives*, 25–55. Berlin: De Gruyter Mouton.

Winford, Donald. 2020. The New Spanishes in the context of contact linguistics: Toward a unified approach. In Luis A. Ortiz-López, Rosa E. Guzzardo Tamargo & Melvin González-Rivera (eds.), *Hispanic contact linguistics: Theoretical, methodological, and empirical perspectives*, 11–41. Amsterdam: John Benjamins.

Yang, Charles. 2002. *Knowledge and learning in natural language*. Oxford: Oxford University Press.

PART II

Perspectives on acquisition and change

CHAPTER 2

Monolingual and bilingual child language acquisition and language change

Naomi Shin
University of New Mexico

This chapter reviews research on children's monolingual and bilingual acquisition of linguistic variation to consider children's role in language change. Many patterns of variation are learned early and veridically, but some are acquired late and may be more susceptible to change. Further, children sometimes regularize variable input and may create novel patterns when exposed to different dialects or languages, which suggests that contact settings can serve as breeding grounds for language change. The chapter thus turns to the topic of childhood bilingualism and reviews research on child heritage speakers, whose divergences from their input sometimes persist into adulthood. The chapter culminates by considering the implications of the research reviewed for socially informed models of language change and historical sociolinguistics.

Keywords: child language, bilingual language development, child heritage speakers, heritage grammars, acquisition of linguistic variation, sociolinguistic variation, language change

1. Introduction

This chapter brings together two lines of inquiry – children's acquisition of (socio)linguistic variation and bilingual language acquisition – in order to better understand children's role in initiating and advancing language change. Much of the growing body of research on children's acquisition of sociolinguistic variation rests on the assumption that the primary language data presented to children during the first few years of their lives tends to be consistent, and that children replicate input patterns veridically and quite early (Labov 1989; Roberts 1997; Smith & Durham 2019). According to this view, young children are not the primary drivers of language change. Instead, children first learn the patterns of their primary caregivers, and later they diverge from their caregivers as they emulate community norms (Baxter & Croft 2016; Holmes-Elliot 2021; Labov 2007, 2012; Smith & Holmes-Elliot 2022; see also Chapter 9 in this volume). Children appear to adjust their language usage to mirror patterns of speakers who are just a little older than they are, and they advance language change at the community level by situating themselves at the vanguard of changes in progress (Bermúdez-Otero 2020; Holmes-Elliot 2021).

In contrast to the view that young children do not initiate change, some scholars argue that children create innovations that can become the source of community-level changes. Yang (2002:125) argues that "[u]ltimately, language changes because learners acquire grammars that are different from their parents." Evidence for this position includes the observation that children's innovations parallel diachronic changes (e.g., Cournane 2017, 2019; Cournane & Pérez-Leroux 2020; Hall & Pérez-Leroux 2020; Lightfoot 2006), and that the patterns to which children are exposed provide the basis for children's misanalyses, which in turn result in innovations (Kodner 2020; Lightfoot 2006; O'Shannessy 2021; see also Chapter 8). In addition, children have been shown to regularize when faced with variation in the input (Hudson Kam & Newport 2005; see also Chapter 7). Learning biases like the tendency to regularize can be amplified across generations of learners and thus can shape language change (Smith & Wonnacott 2010). Finally, complexity of variation can prolong acquisition of variable patterns (Holmes-Elliot 2021; Shin 2016), calling into question the generalization that young children veridically replicate variable patterns in the input.[1]

The question of whether children replicate patterns in the input becomes even more intricate whenever children are learning more than one language. Indeed, children have been shown to create novel grammars in the face of mixed input (Kodner 2020; O'Shannessy 2021; see Chapter 8 in this volume). Further, restricted input and crosslinguistic influence impact bilingual language development (e.g., Mitrofanova et al. 2018; Sánchez 2019). Child heritage speakers in particular offer an excellent opportunity for understanding bilingual children's role in language change, since some of their language patterns persist into adulthood (Montrul 2015; Polinsky 2018). Of course, whether bilingual children's innovations translate into community-wide language change will depend on population structure (Mufwene 2011), including the predominance of bilinguals in a given community and whether they are in frequent contact with speakers of other (including monolingual) varieties (Lipski 2008; Lupyan & Dale 2010; see also Chapter 6 in this volume).

---

1. For additional elaboration on the role of young learners in situations of dialect contact and new dialect formation, see Chapters 4 and 6 in this volume, respectively.

The goal of the current chapter is to consider what circumstances and linguistic structures might lend themselves to child-initiated change. After a review of trends in monolingual (Section 2) and bilingual (Section 3) child acquisition of variation, including research on several illustrative phenomena, the chapter proposes applications of this research to the sociohistorical study of language change (Section 4). Ultimately, the chapter raises more questions than it answers, and culminates with a call for continued research on children's acquisition of linguistic variation and bilingual language development.

2. Children's acquisition of (socio)linguistic variation

Since linguistic variation is a precondition for language change (Bybee 2015), the growing body of research on children's acquisition of variation is highly relevant for assessing children's role in language change. Current models of language change, such as the *incrementation model* (Labov 2007) and the *momentum-based model* (Bermúdez-Otero 2020), assume that children initially replicate patterns of variation in the input provided by primary caregivers and later reject some of these patterns in favor of community norms, especially those of slightly older peers (Holmes-Elliot 2021). The sections that follow review research that assesses how long patterns of variation take to acquire, how closely children mirror variation in the input, and which learning biases shape the course of development.

2.1 Timing of acquisition

With respect to timing of acquisition of variation, children appear to acquire many variable patterns very early. In a study of English in Philadelphia, Roberts & Labov (1995) found that the same lexical and phonetic factors conditioned tense versus lax short *a* among both adults and 3- and 4-year-olds. Both children and adults tensed short *a* in the words *mad* and *bad* and never in the word *sad*. They also tensed short *a* before a nasal and a syllable boundary (e.g., *sandals*), but not in initial position followed by a nasal and vowel (e.g., *animal*). Early acquisition of constraints on variation in Philadelphia has also been demonstrated for variable (ING) (e.g., *fishing ~ fishin'*) (Labov 1989; Roberts 1997). In a study of Chilean Spanish, Miller (2013) found that the same linguistic contexts favored –s deletion among caregivers and their children, ages 2;04–5;09, including word final position (e.g., *más*) and when –s was a plural marker. Moreover, the children's –s deletion rates in the various conditioning contexts closely matched those of their caregivers.

Evidence for children's early acquisition of sociolinguistic variation is also found in research on caregivers' and children's natural conversations in Buckie, a fishing village in Scotland (Smith & Durham 2019; Smith et al. 2007; Smith et al. 2013). These studies, which included 29 children, ages 2;10 to 4;2, and their caregivers, found tight correlations between caregivers' and children's variation between 'local' forms, which are endemic to Buckie, and 'standard' forms more widely used across varieties of English. For example, both children and caregivers varied between third person singular and plural verb forms with third person plural subjects, as in *my trousers is/are falling down*. Moreover, the same linguistic factors constrained the children's and the caregivers' variation. Both produced third person singular forms in plural contexts (1) when the subject was a lexical noun phrase, as in *the grapes is open*, but not when the subject was the personal pronoun *they*; (2) with existentials, as in *there's jelly sweeties*; and (3) more often with interrogatives than with declaratives (Smith et al. 2007: 83–88; Smith et al. 2013: 314). The authors conclude that children acquire the linguistic constraints on morphosyntactic variation very early. Furthermore, given the close correlations between the children's and adults' rates of forms produced in each linguistic context, illustrated in Figure 1, the results suggest that the children replicate the patterns of variation in the input veridically.

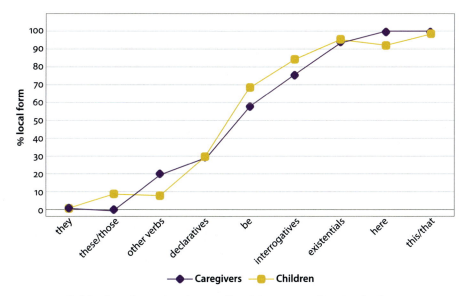

Figure 1. Children's and caregivers' rates of local forms in Buckie, Scotland (from Smith et al. 2013: 314)

While the studies discussed above support the conclusion that children learn the patterns of variation in the input very early and reproduce those patterns veridically, other studies suggest that this is not always the case. Some patterns take a long time to learn, only emerging during school age. Kovac and Adamson (1981) found that children acquiring African American English varied between expressing and deleting finite *be*, as in *she going ~ she is going*, but the patterns of variation were not constrained by the same factors that constrain adult usage until age seven. Research on English word-final -t/-d deletion, as in *mist* or *missed* pronounced as 'mis' indicates that very young children's variable production of -t/-d is constrained by the same articulatory factors that constrain adult usage (Roberts 1997; Smith et al. 2009). However, the morphemic status of the word constrains variation among adults, but not children. Children delete -t/-d just as often with semiweak verbs such as *lost* and *told*, as with monomorphemic words, such as *mist* (Roberts 1997). Guy and Boyd (1990) found that excessive -t/-d deletion with semi-weak verbs persists into adolescence.

Late acquisition of grammatical variation is also evident in Shin's (2016) study of 154 Mexican children's Spanish subject pronoun expression. The children, ages 6 to 16, all alternated between expressing and omitting subject pronouns; however, some of the linguistic contexts that constrain adult variation were not active among children until after age eight. Shin argues that the linguistic constraints that emerge first are the ones that are most frequent in discourse and, as such, children have ample evidence to track pronoun use in these contexts. In addition to frequency, complexity of the structure may also prolong acquisition of variation (Holmes-Elliot 2021; Shin 2016). As such, the window of time during which children acquire variable patterns can extend into school age, when language input diversifies due to contact with people outside the home, which in turn has implications for understanding children's role in language change. Later-acquired parts of their grammars may be even more influenced by community members rather than children's own caregivers (see Chapters 7 and 9 in this volume for examples).

2.2 Children's innovations

Although several of the studies mentioned above indicate that children replicate variation in their input veridically, there is also research showing that children innovate. For example, when faced with variable patterns in the input, children may regularize and thus generate a simpler grammar. Hudson Kam and Newport (2005) presented adults and children with an artificial language called *Silly Speak*, which included 12 made-up nouns like *nerk, melnag, flerbit*, etc, as well as *po*, which functioned like a determiner. To mimic variation, the input included nouns with *po* 60% of the time and without *po* 40% of the time. When asked to produce sentences in Silly Speak, adults matched the variation in the input and produced *po* with nouns about 60% of the time. In contrast, the children developed more regular grammars by always producing *po* or never producing it. Children may also depart from variation in the input by boosting one form over the other without fully regularizing (Cournane 2019; Hall & Maddeaux 2020; Samara et al. 2017; Shin & Miller 2022). For example, Miller (2015) found that a child who was exposed to input in which *isn't* varied with *ain't* passed through stages in which first she relied only on *isn't* and later produced both *isn't* and *ain't* but she partitioned the forms such that *isn't* was relegated to interrogatives and *ain't* to declaratives. The tendency to use *isn't* in tag questions is found among adults who vary between *isn't* and *ain't* (Washington & Craig 2002). Thus, the child boosted the frequency of *isn't* in a context in which it is commonly used in the input, but she overshot the mark, extending the pattern beyond the distribution found among adults (see also Hall & Maddeaux 2020).

Children's quantitative boosts can potentially lead to qualitative changes provided that the boost has a lasting effect. Indeed, for language change to happen, child-initiated innovations must be adopted at the community level. Artificial language learning studies that model transmission of language across generations of learners indicate that even weak biases can result in changes that reduce variation and increase systematicity (Smith et al. 2017; Smith & Wonnacott 2010). Besides experimental evidence, support for this hypothesis also comes from observational historical and present-day data. For instance, Westergaard (2009) supports the idea that frequency boosts in child language acquisition may result in language change. Her analyses of variable word order in Old and Middle English as well as present-day Norwegian suggest that when a given word order becomes less frequent in a specific discourse context, children rely on the more frequent word order in that discourse context. Overtime and across generations, this may result in the loss of a word order and, ultimately, the loss of variation, across discourse contexts, as in the case of verb-second word order in English. Further evidence that children's boosting of one variant over another may play a role in language change comes from Cournane and Pérez-Leroux's (2020) study of modal verb 'must', which is in the process of losing its deontic meaning in favor of the epistemic meaning. Cournane and Pérez-Leroux found that children preferred the epistemic meaning for 'must' more than adults did. Similarly, Hall and Maddeaux (2020) found that young children in Toronto produced more /ae/-raising and /u/-fronting as compared to the adults in their study. Further, /u/-fronting is a change in progress and the youngest children in the study were the most advanced in this change. Thus, these studies suggest that children may play an important role in the incrementation of changes in progress.

In addition to regularizing or boosting one form over another, children may also create novel patterns in the face of variation. Lightfoot (2006) argues that sweeping changes in Middle English morphology resulted in a set of verbs becoming distinctive in form from other verbs, which children then reanalyzed as the class of verbs that now constitute the English modals.

Another interesting, more recent example of an emerging novel pattern in the face of variation is related to /ai/ raising in North American English. In some dialects, including Canadian dialects, /ai/ is raised before voiceless consonants, yielding /ʌi/ in words like 'right' and 'knife'. In addition, /ai/ is raised before underlying voiceless segments yielding /ʌi/ in 'writer' but not in 'rider', even though both are pronounced with an intervocalic flap. This is the more 'traditional' or 'canonical' raising pattern. Some speakers, however, produce what is called *transparent raising* or *phonetic raising*, where /ai/ is raised only before surface voiceless segments. For these speakers, /ai/ is raised in 'right' and 'write', but not in 'writer'. Kodner (2020) and Kodner and Richter (2020) argue that transparent raising is an innovation that emerges when children are exposed to mixed input, i.e., input that includes traditional raising as well as no raising. They find that this mixed input includes the necessary conditions that yield children's creation of the innovative grammar in which /ai/ is raised before voiceless surface segments only. Kodner (2020) makes similar arguments for children's role in changes that are already complete, such as the emergence of the to-dative in Middle English, analogical change in Proto-Germanic strong verbs, and the past participles and t-deverbals in Classical and Late Latin.

Artificial language learning studies also reveal children's sensitivity to distributions in the input that potentially yield novel patterns. In Hudson Kam's (2015) artificial language learning study, novel determiners occurred with nouns either 40% or 60% of the time. In addition, the determiners were distributed syntactically, occurring more often with subject nouns in one condition and more often with direct object nouns in another condition. Results showed that adult learners were sensitive to the syntactic distribution of the determiners, but 5-7-year-olds were not. Interestingly, six children evinced a different, but systematic pattern: they produced the determiner most often with intransitive subjects, less often with objects in transitive sentences, and least often with transitive subjects. Hudson Kam notes that these children seem to have innovated by imposing an ergative-absolutive pattern. An important take-away from this research is that the input contains distributions that lead children to an unexpected analysis of the data, which in turn results in an innovative grammar.

The observation that children may regularize, boost the frequency of a particular form or meaning, or create novel patterns in the face of variation is particularly relevant to the study of language change in high-contact social environments, where children are likely to have access to multiple variable grammars in their input (Sanz-Sánchez & Moyna 2023). As Yang (2002: 133–134) writes, "heterogeneity in the linguistic evidence, however introduced, is a prerequisite for language change." Mixed input from speakers of different dialects or languages increases heterogeneity in the input and thus may present the type of linguistic evidence that yields innovations among children.

3. Child heritage speakers

Explorations of children's role in language change must consider bilingual settings, which are more common than monolingual settings worldwide (Grosjean 2021) and which may precipitate major changes in languages (e.g., Heine & Kuteva 2006; Trudgill 2011; Walkden et al. 2023). Although some scholars have argued that only second language learners introduce contact-induced change (Meisel 2010; Weerman 2011), several studies have found evidence of bilingual child-initiated language change (e.g., O'Shannessy 2021; Queen 2001; Szeto et al. 2019; Thomason 2011). O'Shannessy (2021) demonstrates how children create the mixed language Light Walpiri through exposure to mixed utterances in Walpiri, Kriol, and English. For example, children reanalyze the Walpiri pronoun *im* as consisting of two separate morphemes *i-m*, and out of this reanalysis emerges a new non-future verbal marker *-m*. Thus, processes involved in child language acquisition in general, such as reanalysis, can lead to the creation of innovative grammars (see also Kodner 2020, discussed in Section 2.2, and Chapter 8). Of course, not all bilingual children's innovations will be adopted at the community level, but with enough bilingual speakers, it seems that bilingual innovations can spread throughout a community.

Studying heritage speakers provides an especially promising avenue for investigating the effects of bilingualism on community language norms, since some of the phenomena found among child heritage speakers persist into adulthood (Dracos & Requena 2022; Montrul 2023; Montrul et al. 2014; Shin 2018; Silva-Corvalán 2014, 2018). The growing body of research on child heritage acquisition suggests that restricted input in a minority language (Dracos & Requena 2022; Pérez-Leroux et al. 2018; Pirvulescu et al. 2014; Silva-Corvalán 2014) and crosslinguistic influence (Sánchez 2019; Shin 2018; Shin et al. 2023) can affect linguistic development in terms of both pace (Gathercole 2007) and developmental pathway (Shin et al. 2021). As such, this section reviews various phenomena that have been argued to illustrate such child heritage 'bilingual effects' and asks, for each phenomenon, whether child heritage speakers may play a role in initiating and spreading language change at the community level.

3.1 Null objects

Bilingual children, including child heritage speakers, experience an extended *null object stage*, that is, they omit more direct objects and do so for a longer period of time than their monolingual counterparts (Castilla-Earls et al. 2016; Castilla-Earls et al. 2020; Pirvulescu et al. 2014; Shin et al. 2019, Shin et al. 2023). Some scholars have suggested that this 'bilingual effect' is the result of crosslinguistic influence (Larrañaga & Guijarro-Fuentes 2012). Indeed, extensive direct object omission in one language, such as Basque or Quechua, appears to beget more direct object omission in another language (e.g., Spanish) among child bilinguals (Larrañaga & Guijarro-Fuentes 2012; Sánchez 2003). Nevertheless, more direct object expression in one language does not appear to result in increased direct object expression in the other language. For example, direct object expression is more frequent in child-directed English than in child-directed French, but French-English bilingual children omit direct objects more often than French-speaking monolingual children (Pirvulescu et al. 2014). Similarly, Spanish-English bilingual children in the U.S. omit more direct objects in Spanish than monolingual children in Mexico (Shin et al. 2023). The bilingual children's elevated object omission rates in Spanish are not due to English influence; in fact, the same children produce higher rates of direct objects in English than in Spanish. Restricted input, which can slow vocabulary development, offers a better explanation for the higher rates of null objects among these bilingual children (Pérez-Leroux et al. 2018; Pirvulescu et al. 2014; Shin 2023).

Regardless of the source of the increase in null objects among bilingual children, the phenomenon is widespread and thus relevant to the question of whether bilingual children play a role in language change. Null objects in one language appear to beget increased amounts of null objects in another language at the community level. For example, null objects have permeated the Spanish spoken in contact with Basque, Quechua, and Guaraní (Gómez-Seibane 2013; Paredes 1996; Sainzmaza-Lecanda & Schwenter 2017) and have extended to linguistic contexts where they are not generally found outside these regions (Schwenter 2006). Scholars generally agree that the abundance of null objects in these communities is contact-induced, but it is unclear whether bilingual children are their source. One possibility is that bilingual children's extended null object stage has a lasting effect. Another possibility is that adult L2 Spanish learners transfer this feature from their first language to their second language. Indeed, studies have shown that Spanish object omission is more prevalent among adults with high proficiency in Basque (Sainzmaza-Lecanda & Schwenter 2017) or Quechua (Paredes 1996). If these adult learners are the source of elevated direct object omission rates at the community level, then bilingual Basque and Andean children's high omission rates are the result of learning a variety of Spanish in which there is already an elevated rate of direct object omission. At the same time, given the evidence that children can boost the frequency of structures in their input (Samara et al. 2017; Shin & Miller 2022), it is possible that adult second language learners and bilingual children are both a source of increased null objects in bilingual settings. If adult heritage speakers of Spanish whose other language is not a null-object language (e.g., Spanish-English bilinguals) show elevated rates of null objects in Spanish, that would suggest that childhood bilingualism may play a role in the proliferation of null objects in contact settings.

3.2 Gender agreement

Research consistently shows notable differences between heritage and monolingual speakers' acquisition of gender agreement across languages (Polinsky 2018: 206). An interesting question is whether the gender system of adult heritage speakers finds its origin in childhood bilingualism. Indeed, child heritage speakers produce more gender mismatches as compared to monolingual children in Spanish (Cuza & Pérez-Tattam 2016; Goebel-Mahrle & Shin 2020) and in Russian (Mitrofanova et al. 2018; Rodina & Westergaard 2017; Schwartz et al. 2015). Both quantity of input in the heritage language as well as complexity of the structure involved have been shown to influence children's gender mismatching (Mitrofanova et al. 2018; Rodina & Westergaard 2017). Among heritage speakers of Spanish in the U.S., children's gender mismatches are particularly evident in adjectives referring to nouns with less predictable gender (Cuza & Pérez-Tattam 2016; Goebel-Mahrle & Shin 2020), as well as in their production of direct clitics *lo* and *la* (Goebel-Mahrle & Shin 2020; Shin et al. 2019; Shin et al. 2023). With respect to noun-adjective agreement, Cuza & Pérez-Tattam (2016) found no age effects in their study of 32 Spanish–English bilingual children, ages 5;0–10;8. However, age effects have been found for direct object clitic gender. As children age and, in many cases, undergo language dominance shift (see Castilla-Earls et al. 2019), they rely more heavily on masculine direct object clitic *lo* to refer to masculine and feminine inanimate objects alike (Goebel-Mahrle & Shin 2020; Shin et al. 2019; Shin et al. 2023). This body of research suggests that even if child heritage speakers replicate their input in the early stages of language acquisition, their grammars may become more innovative as they age. At the same time, age effects differ depending on the structure; when the grammatical feature relies heavily on lexical learning, as is the case for noun-adjective agreement with noncanonical nouns, children may plateau (Cuza & Pérez-Tattam 2016) or may gender match more as their lexicon grows (Shin 2018). In contrast, other features such as clitic gender may show increasing innovation with age, perhaps due to language dominance shift and increased influence from the dominant language.

3.3 Differential object marking

Another widely studied phenomenon in heritage language research is differential object marking (DOM). The research tends to show higher rates of DOM omission among child and adult heritage speakers of various languages (e.g., Montrul 2023). For example, in Spanish, animate and specific direct objects are generally preceded by *a*, as in *veo **a** la mujer* 'I see the woman'. In contrast, inanimate as well as nonspecific direct objects are not preceded by DOM marker *a* (e.g., *veo la mesa*, 'I see the table). Ticio (2015) investigated DOM in Spanish produced by seven Spanish-English bilingual children, ages 1;1 to 3;6. She found much lower rates of DOM marking before animate, specific nouns as compared to a prior study of monolingual children. In a subsequent analysis of these children's data, Requena (2023) found that when contexts that permit variation are considered (e.g., non-human animates), both monolingual and bilingual children alike perform similarly to their caregivers. Requena's research underscores the importance of understanding the nature of structured variation in the input to investigate whether children's own variation replicates the input or departs from it (see also Flores & Rinke 2020; Shin 2022).

While pre-school bilingual children may replicate patterns in their input, research on school-age bilingual children suggests protracted development of DOM. Montrul and Sánchez-Walker (2013) compared Spanish-English speaking children in Chicago to monolingual children in Mexico, all between ages 6–17 years old. The monolingual children produced *a* before animate, specific DOs significantly more often than the bilingual children did. Thus, like direct object clitic gender, DOM may be susceptible to age effects: as children age and undergo language dominance shift, they may depart more from their caregivers' grammar. It remains an open question whether adult heritage speakers' differential object omission finds its source in early childhood bilingualism. Indeed, Montrul and Bateman (2020) find that adults who experienced early simultaneous bilingualism omitted DOM in heritage Romanian more often than adults who first learned Romanian and then started learning English as a second language during childhood. Another possibility is that speakers' production of DOM ebbs and flows over the lifespan concomitant with the ebb and flow of linguistic experience with the heritage language. In either case, the preponderance of DOM omission among adult heritage speakers suggests that this bilingual effect may leave an imprint at the community level.

3.4 Child heritage speakers and linguistic variation

The bilingual phenomena discussed above – null objects, gender mismatching, and DOM omission – are generally analyzed as bilingual effects that represent departures from monolingual norms and from bilingual children's own input. A related question with sociohistorical import is whether bilingual children initiate change in the face of variation in the input. Research on bilingual children's acquisition of linguistic variation has yielded divergent outcomes. Some studies show veridical replication of variation in the input, while others suggest bilingual children may promote quantitative shifts towards one variant. For example, U.S. Spanish-English bilingual children's alternation between pre- and post-verbal Spanish clitics is remarkably similar to that of monolingual Spanish speakers (Requena & Dracos 2018; Shin et al. 2017; Silva-Corvalán 2018). In contrast, there is evidence that child heritage speakers of Spanish differ quantitatively from monolinguals in that the former produce higher rates of expressed subject pronouns and pre-verbal subjects (Silva-Corvalán 2014, 2018).

While different variable structures may reveal divergent outcomes, linguistic variability may be particularly important for understanding the relationship between bilingualism during childhood and lasting contact-induced language change. In a review of research on child heritage Spanish, Shin (2018) compares more versus less variable morphosyntactic structures to determine the extent to which crosslinguistic influence from English is evident in the children's Spanish. English appears to affect even invariant structures in Spanish among child heritage speakers under five years of age. For example, children under this age produce structures that never appear in monolingual Spanish, such as preposition stranding (e.g., Silva-Corvalán 2014), but such structures are rare in older bilingual speech. By contrast, contact effects persist into adulthood for some structures that show ample variation such as the variable expression of subject pronouns and pre- versus post-verbal subject placement in Spanish (Erker et al. 2017; Otheguy & Zentella 2012; Shin 2018). The nature of the structured variation, however, also plays a role, as variable clitic placement seems less susceptible to contact effects, perhaps due to the strong lexical conditioning of this variation.

To summarize, several trends emerge from the growing body of research on child heritage speakers. First, some bilingual effects emerge early and some emerge during school age as a result of increasing contact with the majority language. Second, contact effects that represent bilingual innovations appear to persist into adulthood when the structure in question is variable; however, not all variable structures are equally susceptible to contact effects. These factors related to age and the nature of the linguistic structure in question must be taken into account when considering whether bilingual children play a role in community-level language change.

4. Child language acquisition and the historical sociolinguistics of language change: Challenges and opportunities

The review of the research in this chapter indicates that the field has moved beyond the question of whether children initiate language change or not. Instead, the questions have become more complex, which in turn presents new challenges and opportunities for continued investigations of children's role in language change. For instance, what type of input results in child-initiated language change? The literature suggests that mixed input may provide exactly the right conditions for children to create innovations (Kodner 2020; Lightfoot 2006; O'Shannessey 2021; Sanz-Sánchez & Moyna 2023; Westergaard 2009). In addition, children may regularize in the face of variation in the input (e.g., Hudson Kam & Newport 2005) but not all variable input results in language change. In fact, children are highly adept at replicating complex patterns of variation (Smith & Durham 2019). At the same time, some patterns of variation may take longer to acquire and thus children may be likelier to introduce innovations into these patterns (Cournane 2017; Holmes-Elliot 2021; Shin 2016; Shin & Miller 2022). From a historical sociolinguistic point of view, this research is highly relevant to proposals that identify children as the agents (or active contributors) in specific attested changes, such as the emergence of new dialectal norms (e.g., Trudgill 2004; Sanz-Sánchez 2019; Schreier 2016; see Chapter 7 in this volume) or the grammatical systematization of new languages (DeGraff 2009; Senghas & Coppola 2001; see Chapter 8 in this volume).

Another exciting question is the role bilingual children play in initiating and spreading language change. The current chapter highlighted child heritage speakers in particular, as some of the structures these children produce appear to persist into adulthood. However, more longitudinal research is necessary to fully understand what innovations begin in childhood and then remain in individual speakers' grammars. We now know that individual speakers' language usage patterns change over the lifespan (e.g, Sankoff 2018; see also Chapter 9 for an example). While we also know that heritage speakers' grammars change over the lifespan and that child heritage speakers often undergo language dominance shift during school age, research has rarely tracked such changes within the individual (see Silva-Corvalán 2014).

Finally, an important challenge that remains is understanding which innovations introduced by children result in change at the community level. Current models of language change tend to assume that children replicate their input faithfully and only later begin to participate in, and eventually, lead language change (Baxter & Croft 2016; Labov 2007; Holmes-Elliot 2021; Smith & Holmes-Elliot 2022; Tagliamonte & D'Arcy 2009). Where do children's innovations fit into such models, particularly innovations found among bilingual children? And which demographic or sociocultural conditions favor the incorporation of these innovations into community norms? Child and adult heritage speakers offer an exciting opportunity to re-examine the role that children may play in language change since they demonstrate an important departure from the general trend for children to replicate the input early and veridically. Ultimately, the current volume offers scholars the opportunity to move beyond binary questions like whether children initiate change and instead discover the conditions under which children's innovations spread and permeate language at the community level.

5. Conclusion

To summarize, the available research on child language acquisition shows that, in the presence of consistent input, children learn the patterns of variation characteristic of their community, but the specific frequency and linguistic characteristics of each variable affect the timing of acquisition. Insofar as forms of variation that are acquired late may be diachronically more unstable, timing of acquisition in child language emerges as a potential factor in the actuation of some changes. When input is markedly irregular, as in the case when children grow up in multidialectal or multilingual settings, children have sometimes been shown to regularize this input and create new grammatical options. The chapter has also reviewed the evidence of acquisition by bilingual children, especially in heritage settings: in these situations, the options acquired by children may also diverge from those found in the adult input, and some of these differences may persist into adulthood. Although necessarily brief, this review makes it clear that child language acquisition literature offers tools to historical sociolinguists who wish to assess the potential sociohistorical role of young children as innovators and actors in the spread of specific changes. Using this body of knowledge, other chapters in this volume establish connections between the agency of young learners and that of older peers and adults, and offer case study applications of these connections to the emergence of specific linguistic patterns in historical sociolinguistic settings around the world.

References

Baxter, Gareth & William Croft. 2016. Modeling language change across the lifespan: Individual trajectories in community change. *Language Variation and Change* 28. 129–173.

Bermúdez-Otero, Ricardo. 2020. The initiation and incrementation of sound change: Community-oriented momentum-sensitive learning. *Glossa* 5(1). 121.

Bybee, Joan. 2015. *Language change*. Cambridge University Press.

Castilla-Earls, Anny, David Francis, Aquiles Iglesias & Kevin Davidson. 2019. The impact of the Spanish-to-English proficiency shift on the grammaticality of English learners. *Journal of Speech, Language, and Hearing Research* 62(6). 1739–1754.

Castilla-Earls, Anny, Ana Teresa Pérez-Leroux, Lourdes Martinez-Nieto, Maria Adelaida Restrepo & Christopher Barr. 2020. Vulnerability of clitics and articles to bilingual effects in typically developing Spanish-English bilingual children. *Bilingualism: Language and Cognition* 23(4). 825–835.

Castilla-Earls, Anny, Maria Adelaida Restrepo, Ana Teresa Pérez-Leroux, Shelley Gray, Paul Holmes, Daniel Gail & Ziquiang Chen. 2016. Interactions between bilingual effects and language impairment: Exploring grammatical markers in Spanish-speaking bilingual children. *Applied Psycholinguistics* 37(5). 1147–1173.

Cournane, Ailís. 2017. In defense of the child innovator. In Eric Mathieu & Robert Truswell (eds.), *Micro-change and macro-change in diachronic syntax*, 10–24. Oxford: Oxford University Press.

Cournane, Ailís. 2019. A developmental view on incrementation in language change. *Theoretical Linguistics* 45(3–4). 127–150.

Cournane, Ailís & Ana Teresa Pérez-Leroux. 2020. Leaving obligations behind: Epistemic incrementation in preschool English. *Language Learning and Development* 16(3). 270–291.

Cuza, Alejandro & Rocío Pérez-Tattam. 2016. Grammatical gender selection and phrasal word order in child heritage Spanish: A feature re-assembly approach. *Bilingualism: Language and Cognition* 19(1). 50–68.

DeGraff, Michel. 2009. Language acquisition in creolization and, thus, language change: Some cartesian-uniformitarian boundary conditions. *Language and Linguistics Compass* 3/4. 888–971.

Dracos, Melisa & Pablo E. Requena. 2022. Child heritage speakers' acquisition of the Spanish subjunctive in volitional and adverbial clauses. *Language Acquisition* 30(1). 1–28.

Erker, Daniel, Eduardo Ho-Fernández, Ricardo Otheguy & Naomi Shin. 2017. Continuity and Change in Spanish among Cubans in New York: A Study of Subject Placement with Finite Verbs. In Alejandro Cuza (ed.), *Cuban Spanish dialectology: Variation, contact and change*, 63–82. Washington DC: Georgetown University Press.

Flores, Cristina & Esther Rinke. 2020. The relevance of language-internal variation in predicting heritage language grammars. *Bilingualism: Language and Cognition* 23. 25–26.

Gathercole, Virginia Mueller. 2007. Miami and North Wales, so far and yet so near: A constructivist account of morphosyntactic development in bilingual children. *International Journal of Bilingual Education and Bilingualism* 10. 224–247.

Goebel-Mahrle, Thomas & Naomi Shin. 2020. A corpus study of child heritage speakers' Spanish gender agreement. *International Journal of Bilingualism* 24(5–6). 1088–1104.

Gómez Seibane, Sara. 2013. La omisión y duplicación de objetos en el castellano del País Vasco. In Bruno Camus-Bergareche & Sara Gómez Seibane (eds.), *El castellano del País Vasco*, 193–214. Bilbao: Universidad del País Vasco.

Grosjean, François. 2021. *Life as a bilingual*. Cambridge University Press.

Guy, Gregory & Sally Boyd. 1990. The development of a morphological class. *Language Variation and Change* 2. 1–18.

Hall, Erin & Ruth Maddeaux. 2020. /u/-fronting and /æ/-raising in Toronto families. *University of Pennsylvania Working Papers in Linguistics* 25(2). Article 7. https://repository.upenn.edu/pwpl/vol25/iss2/7

Hall, Erin & Ana Teresa Pérez-Leroux. 2020. Children's comprehension of NP embedding. *Glossa* 7. 1–41.

Heine, Bernd & Tania Kuteva. 2006. *Language contact and grammatical change*. Cambridge: Cambridge University Press.

Holmes-Elliot, Sophie. 2021. Calibrate to innovate: Community age vectors and the real time incrementation of language change. *Language in Society* 50(3). 441–474.

Hudson Kam, Carla. 2015. The impact of conditioning variables on the acquisition of variation in adult and child learners. *Language*. 91(4). 906–937.

Hudson Kam, Carla & Elissa Newport. 2005. Regularizing unpredictable variation: The roles of adult and child learners in language formation and change. *Language Learning and Development* 1. 151–195.

Kodner, Jordan. 2020. Language acquisition in the past. Philadelphia, PA: University of Pennsylvania. PhD dissertation.

Kodner, Jordan & Caitlin Richter. 2020. Transparent /ai/-raising as a contact phenomenon. In Ruaridh Purse and Yosiane White (eds.), *Penn Working Papers in Linguistics* 25(2). *Selected Papers from NWAV 47*, 61–70.

Kovac, Ceil & Hugh Douglas Adamson. 1981. Variation theory and first language acquisition. In David Sankoff & Henrietta Cedergren (eds.), *Variation omnibus*, 403–410. Edmonton: Linguistic Research.

Labov, William. 1989. The child as linguistic historian. *Language Variation and Change* 1. 85–98.

Labov, William. 2007. Transmission and diffusion. *Language* 83. 344–387.

Labov, William. 2012. What is to be learned: The community as the focus of social cognition. *Review of Cognitive Linguistics* 10. 265–93.

Larrañaga, Pilar & Pedro Guijarro-Fuentes. 2012. Clitics in L1 bilingual acquisition. *First Language* 32, 151–175.

Lightfoot, David. 2006. *How new languages emerge*. Cambridge University Press.

Lipski, John M. 2008. *Varieties of Spanish in the United States*. Washington DC: Georgetown University Press.

Lupyan, Gary & Rick Dale. 2010. Language structure is partly determined by social structure. *PLoS ONE* 5(1). E8559.

Meisel, Jürgen. 2010. Bilingual language acquisition and theories of diachronic change: Bilingualism as cause and effect of grammatical change. *Bilingualism: Language and Cognition* 14(2). 121–145.

Miller, Karen. 2013. Acquisition of variable rules: /s/-lenition in the speech of Chilean Spanish-speaking children and their caregivers. *Language Variation and Change* 25. 311–340.

Miller, Karen. 2015. Children's production of ain't. In Patricia Donaher & Seth Katz (eds.), *Ain'thology: The history and life of a taboo word*, 96–112. Cambridge Scholars Publishing.

Mitrofanova, Natalia, Yulia Rodina, Olga Urek & Marit Westergaard. 2018. Bilinguals' sensitivity to grammatical gender cues in Russian: The role of cumulative input, proficiency, and dominance. *Frontiers in Psychology* 9. 1894.

Montrul, Silvina. 2015. *The acquisition of heritage languages.* Cambridge University Press.

Montrul, Silvina. 2023. *Native speakers, interrupted: Differential object marking and language change in heritage speakers.* Cambridge: Cambridge University Press.

Montrul, Silvina & Nicoleta Bateman. 2020. Vulnerability and stability of Differential Object Marking in Romanian heritage speakers. *Glossa* 5(1). 119.

Montrul, Silvina, Justin Davidson, Israel De La Fuente & Rebecca Foote. 2014. Early language experience facilitates the processing of gender agreement in Spanish heritage speakers. *Bilingualism: Language and Cognition* 17. 118–38.

Montrul, Silvina & Noelia Sánchez-Walker. 2013. Differential object marking in child and adult Spanish heritage speakers. *Language Acquisition* 20(2). 109–132.

Mufwene, Salikoko. 2011. Transmission, acquisition, parameter-setting, reanalysis, and language change. *Bilingualism Language and Cognition* 14. 152–155.

O'Shannessy, Carmel. 2021. How ordinary child language processes can lead to the unusual outcome of a mixed language. *The International Journal of Bilingualism* 25(2). 458–480.

Otheguy, Ricardo & Ana Celia Zentella. 2012. *Spanish in New York: Language contact, dialectal leveling, and structural continuity.* Oxford: Oxford University Press.

Paredes, Liliana. 1996. The Spanish continuum in Peruvian bilingual speakers: A study of verbal clitics. Los Angeles: University of Southern California PhD dissertation.

Pérez-Leroux, Ana Teresa, Mihaela Pirvulescu & Yves Roberge. 2018. *Direct objects and language acquisition.* Cambridge University Press.

Pirvulescu, Mihaela, Ana-Teresa Pérez-Leroux, Yves Roberge, Nelleke Strik & Danielle Thomas. 2014. Bilingual effects: Exploring object omission in pronominal languages. *Bilingualism: Language and Cognition* 17. 495–510.

Polinsky, Maria. 2018. *Heritage languages and their speakers.* Cambridge University Press.

Queen, Robin. 2001. Bilingual intonation patterns: Evidence of language change from Turkish-German bilingual children. *Language in Society* 30(1). 55–80.

Requena, Pablo E. 2023. Variation versus deviation: Early bilingual acquisition of differential object marking. *Linguistic Approaches to Bilingualism* 13(6). 801–829.

Requena, Pablo E. & Melisa Dracos. 2018. Impermeability of L1 syntax: Spanish variable clitic placement in bilingual children. In Anne Bertolini & Maxwell Kaplan (eds.), *Proceedings of the 42nd annual Boston University Conference of Language Development*, 644–658. Cascadilla Press.

Roberts, Julie. 1997. Acquisition of variable rules: (-t,d) deletion and (ing) production in preschool children. *Journal of Child Language* 24. 351–372.

Roberts, Julie & William Labov. 1995. Learning to talk Philadelphian: Acquisition of short *a* by preschool children. *Language Variation and Change* 7. 101–112.

Rodina, Yulia & Marit Westergaard. 2017. Grammatical gender in bilingual Norwegian–Russian acquisition: The role of input and transparency. *Bilingualism: Language and cognition* 20(1). 197–214.

Sainzmaza-Lecanda, Lorena & Scott Schwenter. 2017. Null objects with and without bilingualism in the Portuguese and Spanish-speaking world. In Kate Bellamy, Michael Child, Paz González, Antje Muntendam & María del Carmen Parafita Couto (eds.), *Multidisciplinary approaches to bilingualism in the Hispanic and Lusophone world*, 95–119. Amsterdam: John Benjamins.

Samara, Anna, Kenny Smith, Helen Brown & Elizabeth Wonnacott. 2017. Acquiring variation in an artificial language: Children and adults are sensitive to socially conditioned linguistic variation. *Cognitive Psychology* 94. 85–114.

Sánchez, Liliana. 2003. *Quechua-Spanish bilingualism: Interference and convergence in functional categories*. Amsterdam: John Benjamins.

Sánchez, Liliana. 2019. Bilingual alignments. *Languages* 4. 82.

Sankoff, Gillian. 2018. Language change across the lifespan. *Annual Review of Linguistics* 4(1). 297–316.

Sanz-Sánchez, Israel. 2019. Documenting feature pools in language expansion situations: Sibilants in early colonial Latin American Spanish. *Transactions of the Philological Society* 117(2). 199–233.

Sanz-Sánchez, Israel & María Irene Moyna. 2023. Children as agents of language change: Diachronic evidence from Latin American Spanish phonology. *Journal of Historical Linguistics* 13(3). 327–374.

Schreier, Daniel. 2016. Super-leveling, fraying-out, internal restructuring: A century of present *be* concord in Tristan da Cunha English. *Language Variation and Change* 28. 203–224.

Schwartz, Miriam, Mila Minkov, Elena Dieser, Ekaterina Protassova, Victor Moin & Maria Polinsky. 2015. Acquisition of Russian gender agreement by monolingual and bilingual children. *International Journal of Bilingualism* 19. 726–752.

Schwenter, Scott. 2006. Null objects across South America. In Timothy Face & Carol Klee (eds.), *Selected Proceedings of the 8th Hispanic Linguistics Symposium*, 23–36. Somerville, MA: Cascadilla.

Senghas, Ann & Marie Coppola. 2001. Children creating language: How Nicaraguan Sign Language acquired a spatial grammar. *Psychological Science* 12(4). 323–328.

Shin, Naomi. 2016. Acquiring patterns of morphosyntactic variation: Children's Spanish subject pronoun expression. *Journal of Child Language* 43. 914–947.

Shin, Naomi. 2018. Child heritage speakers' Spanish morphosyntax: Rate of acquisition and crosslinguistic influence. In Kim Potowski (ed.), *Handbook of Spanish as a heritage language*, 235–253. Routledge.

Shin, Naomi. 2022. Structured variation in child heritage speakers' grammars. *Language and Linguistics Compass* 16(12). e12480.

Shin, Naomi. 2023. *Está abriendo, la abrió*: Lexical knowledge, verb type, and grammatical aspect shape child heritage speakers' direct object omission in Spanish. *International Journal of Bilingualism* 27(5). 842–861.

Shin, Naomi, Alejandro Cuza & Liliana Sánchez. 2023. Structured variation, language experience, and crosslinguistic influence shape child heritage speakers' direct objects. *Bilingualism: Language and Cognition* 26(2). 317–329.

Shin, Naomi, Mariana Marchesi & Jill Morford. 2021. Pathways of development in child heritage speakers' use of Spanish demonstratives. *Spanish as a Heritage Language* 1(2). 222–246.

Shin, Naomi & Karen Miller. 2022. Children's acquisition of morphosyntactic variation. *Language Learning and Development* 18(2). 125–150.

Shin, Naomi, Pablo E. Requena & Anita Kemp. 2017. Bilingual and monolingual children's patterns of syntactic variation: Variable clitic placement in Spanish. In Alejandra Auza and Richard Schwartz (eds.), *Language development and disorders in Spanish-speaking children*, 63–88. New York: Springer.

Shin, Naomi, Barbara Rodríguez, Aja Armijo & Molly Perara-Lunde. 2019. Child heritage speakers' comprehension and production of direct object clitic gender in Spanish. *Linguistic Approaches to Bilingualism* 9(4/5). 659–686.

Silva-Corvalán, Carmen. 2014. *Bilingual language acquisition: Spanish and English in the first six years.* Cambridge University Press.

Silva-Corvalán, Carmen. 2018. Bilingual acquisition: Difference or incompleteness? In Naomi Shin & Daniel Erker (eds.), *Questioning theoretical primitives in linguistic inquiry*, 245–268. Amsterdam: John Benjamins.

Smith, Jennifer, Mercedes Durham & Liane Fortune. 2007. 'Mam, my trousers is fa'in doon!': Community, caregiver, and child in the acquisition of variation in a Scottish Dialect." *Language Variation and Change* 19. 69–95.

Smith, Jennifer, Mercedes Durham & Liane Fortune. 2009. Universal and dialect-specific pathways of acquisition: Caregivers, children, and t/d deletion. *Language Variation and Change* 21. 63–99.

Smith, Jennifer, Mercedes Durham & Hazel Richards. 2013. The social and linguistic in the acquisition of sociolinguistic norms: Caregivers, children, and variation. *Linguistics* 51. 285–324.

Smith, Jennifer & Mercedes Durham. 2019. *Sociolinguistic variation in children's language. Acquiring community norms.* Cambridge: Cambridge University Press.

Smith, Jennifer & Sophie Holmes-Elliot. 2022. Tracking linguistic change in childhood: Transmission, incrementation, and vernacular reorganization. *Language* 98(1). 98–122.

Smith, Kenny, Amy Perfors, Olga Fehér, Anna Samara, Kate Swoboda & Elizabeth Wonnacott. 2017. Language learning, language use and the evolution of linguistic variation. *Philological Transactions of the Royal Society B* 372. 20160051.

Smith, Kenny & Elizabeth Wonnacott. 2010. Eliminating unpredictable variation through iterated learning. *Cognition* 116. 444–449.

Szeto, Pui Yiu, Stephen Matthews, & Virginia Yip. 2019. Bilingual children as "laboratories" for studying contact outcomes: Development of perfective aspect. *Linguistics* 57(3). 693–723.

Tagliamonte, Sali & Alexandra D'Arcy. 2009. Peaks beyond phonology. Adolescence, incrementation, and language change. *Language* 85(1). 58–108.

Thomason, Sarah. 2011. Is morphosyntactic change really rare? *Bilingualism: Language and Cognition* 14(2). 146–148.

Ticio, Emma. 2015. Differential object marking in Spanish-English early bilinguals. *Linguistic Approaches to Bilingualism* 5(1). 62–90.

Trudgill, Peter. 2004. *New dialect formation: The inevitability of colonial Englishes.* Cambridge: Cambridge University Press.

Trudgill, Peter. 2011. *Sociolinguistic typology: Social determinants of linguistic complexity.* Oxford: Oxford University Press.

Walkden, George, Juhani Klemola & Thomas Rainsford. 2023. An overview of contact-induced morphosyntactic changes in Early English. In Sara M. Pons Sanz & Louise Sylvester (eds.), *Medieval English in a multilingual context*, 239–277. London: Palgrave.

Washington, Julie, & Holly Craig. 2002. Morphosyntactic forms of African American English used by young children and their caregivers. *Applied Psycholinguistics* 23. 209–231.

Weerman, Fred. 2011. Diachronic change: Early versus late acquisition. *Bilingualism: Language and Cognition* 14(2). 149–151.

Westergaard, Marit. 2009. Word order in Old and Middle English: The role of information structure and first language acquisition. *Diachronica* 26(1). 65–102.

Yang, Charles. 2002. *Knowledge and learning in natural language.* Oxford University Press.

CHAPTER 3

The second language acquisition of variation in adulthood and language change

Kimberly Geeslin,[1] Travis Evans-Sago,[1] Stephen A. Fafulas[2] & Thomas Goebel-Mahrle[1]

[1] Indiana University | [2] University of Mississippi

Research on the second language acquisition of sociolinguistic variation is grounded in an understanding of sociohistorical linguistics. The patterns attested in language change provide a foundation for understanding the language of second language learners. This chapter provides an overview of research on adult L2 sociolinguistics and shines a light on studies that demonstrate how linguists might bridge the gap between the fields of historical linguistics and second language acquisition (e.g., Giacalone Ramat (1995) for L2 Italian, Donaldson (2017) for L2 French and Geeslin (2002) for L2 Spanish). Moving from studies that explicitly explore this connection, the chapter identifies other findings in L2 research that bridge this gap, and offers suggestions for future inquiry at the intersection of these two fields.

Keywords: adult SLA, language change, L2 development, interdisciplinary linguistics, sociolinguistic variation, sociolinguistic methods, L2 Spanish, L2 French, L2 Italian

1. Introduction: Sociolinguistics in adult second language

Research on the second language acquisition (SLA) of sociolinguistic variation is grounded in the understanding of sociohistorical linguistics and the processes involved in language change. In fact, the patterns attested in language change provide a foundation for understanding development in the language of second language (L2) learners. Research in the fields of historical and synchronic sociolinguistics informs L2 researchers about the frequency of use of a form, the linguistic and social factors that constrain that use, and how patterns change over time. These facts about language change provide a framework within which the acquisition of those same patterns by L2 speakers can be studied and understood.

This chapter begins with an overview of research on adult SLA of variation, highlighting the main themes and generalizations.

While recent research demonstrates that a full picture of adult SLA must include the strategies that adult speakers apply to identify and learn variable patterns in the L2, sociohistorical research demonstrates that this axiom is also valid for historical settings (Auer et al. 2015; Nevalainen & Raumolin-Brunberg 2012). But in contrast to the wealth of empirical research on L2 variation, studies of SLA that make direct reference to historical changes are relatively scarce. Consequently, this chapter will shine a light on those works that demonstrate how linguists might bridge the gap between these two traditions. Featured studies connecting L2 development and historical patterns of change include Giacalone Ramat (1995), Donaldson (2017) and Geeslin (2002). This focused view lends empirical support to earlier work that connected language change and language acquisition (e.g., Greenberg 1991; Preston 1989) as well as to more recent articulations of the key role that L2 acquisition strategies have had in specific historical situations of language contact (e.g., Clements 2009, 2018; Trudgill 2011; Winford 2020; see also Chapters 10, 11 and 12 for case study examples in this volume).

The final section of this chapter explores research on adult L2 variation that contains grounding in historical facts about language change and might serve as additional loci of connection between the two fields of SLA and historical sociolinguistics (e.g., Kanwit & Geeslin 2018). The final section will demonstrate how data and findings from studies of L2 variation might be extended to additional contexts of bilingualism and language contact and can provide insights to those studying historical change over time. The chapter concludes by showing that the collaboration between sociohistorical linguistics and SLA can, and should, be bidirectional. Overall, our focus on the ways in which adult learners handle variation complements approaches to adult language acquisition that emphasize the operation of general cognitive principles and strategies to separate or integrate knowledge in the learners' L1 and L2 (see Chapter 5 in this volume for an overview).

2. Trends in research on adult second language variation

In this section we review standard practices and findings in the field of adult L2 variation. The primary goal is to explain and illustrate the way L2 variationist researchers communicate their findings and contribute to broader conversations about language variation and change. We also discuss shared concepts and assumptions between research on adult SLA and on language change, and this provides the foundation for the rarer work that addresses the connection between the fields of historical change and SLA in Section 3.

The study of adult L2 variation has two objectives. The first is to describe, and ultimately explain, the patterns of language use that occur in L2s. The second is to understand the path along which this variation changes as experience with the language increases. Consequently, this work shares methods and approaches with variationist sociolinguistics more broadly. In thinking about the first goal, classic studies, such as Adamson and Regan (1991), demonstrate how sociolinguistic interviews and multifactorial analyses can shed new light on L2 variation. In that study, immigrants from Vietnam and Cambodia, residing in Philadelphia, participated in a sociolinguistic interview, which provided data for examining the patterns of production of (ing) in L2 English, a well-documented sociolinguistic variable in first language (L1) English varieties (e.g., Labov 1966). Their analysis showed that L2 speakers varied the use of these forms according to the same linguistic and social factors as L1 speakers.[1] Interestingly, however, the study also showed that male L2 speakers not only patterned according to predicted gender differences, but they also produced the informal *–in* variant (versus *–ing*), even more frequently than monolingual English-speaking counterparts. The male speakers appeared to perceive the gender-based social salience of the form (see Levon & Fox 2014) and "overshot" the L1 norms. This early study is now the cornerstone of a long tradition of investigations of L2 variation among adult learners that covers a range of variants, learning contexts and language pairs (e.g., Li 2014, for Mandarin Chinese; Hansen Edwards 2011, for English; Mougeon et al. 2010, for French; Geeslin 2003, for Spanish).

Like variationist sociolinguistics in general, descriptions of adult L2 variation usually identify a functional context, such as the subject form that accompanies third person singular verbs, and then provide an account of the full range of forms, as well as their frequencies and constraints, that occur in that functional context. This approach facilitates documenting changes over time and across geographic space. For example, in a sociolinguistic study on L1 Spanish subject expression, Holmquist (2012) studied the Castañer variety in the western highlands of Puerto Rico and found that while rates of use of overt subject pronouns were markedly lower in this community than in other Puerto Rican varieties, grammatical and functional constraints showed the same direction of effect. Based on previous sociolinguistic and historical research, he proposed that lower rates of use in the highlands may represent a more conservative stage because of earlier migrations of farmers and original settlers from the coast to the interior highlands, as successive waves of Spaniards from innovative regions arrived at

---

1. The terms 'L1 user' and 'L1 speaker' refer to a person whose first language(s) was or were acquired early in childhood (for a discussion on these and related terms, see Dewaele et al. 2022).

the coast. A similar approach is appropriate for documenting paths of development for L2 learners over time who may produce both native-like and non-native forms[2] prior to reaching higher levels of proficiency (see Geeslin 2018). Studies then report the relative frequency of occurrence of these variants. Additionally, most investigations code each token (i.e., any form appearing in a specific functional context) for a host of linguistic and social variables that may condition those patterns of use. In a study on L2 subject expression, Li (2014) found that although intermediate and advanced L2 speakers of Mandarin produced higher rates of overt subject pronouns than their L1 peers, the linguistic and extralinguistic constraints, such as subject person/number, coreference, and speaker gender, patterned similarly across both the L1 and L2 speakers where overt subjects were used more among women, more likely with singular and animate subject referents, and less likely when there was no switch in reference. Rates of subject pronoun use also decreased as L2 proficiency increased. Studies like Li (2014) have helped us to understand the nature of language use for L2 speakers and how it changes over time.[3] To illustrate this common research outcome, Table 1 provides a summary of adult L2 variation research across a range of language pairs, learning contexts and linguistic phenomena, and gives an example of results for frequency of use of a variant, and conditioning factors of that use.

The studies in Table 1 show that variation is an inherent part of *interlanguage*, and that L2 learners become sensitive to the context of interaction in the way they produce and interpret language, provided sufficient exposure to the target language.[4] For example, Caetano and Vieira's (2021) speakers favored pre-verbal clitics in subordinate clauses, and Raish's (2015) participants used the [g] variant in

---

2. Typically, SLA studies have operationalized non-native forms as those referring to "Type 1" variation, or alternation between forms that are grammatical and ungrammatical in the target language, for example the non-native Spanish form *me no gusta vs. the grammatical *no me gusta* 'I don't like it' (see Tarone 2006). By contrast, native-like forms, or "Type 2" variation, include the full range of variants as employed by first-language (L1) users of the target language. Nevertheless, the concepts of (non-)native speaker, monolingual as target, and even the term 'L2' have been questioned (see Dewaele et al. 2022).

3. For a recent volume-length discussion on the intersection of SLA and sociolinguistics, see Geeslin (2022).

4. The term *interlanguage* (Selinker 1972) refers to a separate linguistic system, "different from both the learner's 'native language' (NL) and the 'target language' (TL) being learned but linked to both NL and TL by interlingual identifications in the perception of the learner" (Tarone 2006: 747). For an integrated view of NL, or L1, and TL among bilingual speakers, however, see Creese and Blackledge (2010) and Canagarajah (2011) for discussions of translanguaging or "the deployment of a speaker's full linguistic repertoire without regard for watchful adherence to the socially and politically defined boundaries of named (and usually national and state) languages" (Otheguy et al. 2015: 281).

Table 1. Sample frequency and constraint results in studies of adult L2 variation

Study	Functional context	Frequency of use	Use constraints
Adamson and Regan (1991)	Occurrence of (ing) in US English	[iŋ] versus [ɪn] in 80% of contexts	[ɪn] variant more likely in progressive and periphrastic future verb forms; among male speakers
Caetano and Vieira (2021)	Clitic placement in Mozambican Portuguese	Pre-verbal versus post-verbal placement in 63% of contexts	Pre-verbal clitics more likely in subordinate clauses; among the youngest and oldest age groups of L1 and L2 speakers
Kanwit et al. (2018)	Use of intensifiers in Mexican and Peninsular Spanish	*Muy* 'very' versus *bien* 'well' selected at rate of 83.6% at Time 2 in Spain and 67.8% in Mexico	Intensifier *bien* more likely with positive adjectives and following *estar* 'to be' among study abroad participants in Mexico versus Spain
Li (2010)	Morphosyntactic particle *de* (genitive, attributive, or nominalization marker) in Mandarin Chinese	Retention versus deletion in 84% of optional contexts	Deletion more likely in [Adj + N] contexts; among male speakers and residents who have four+ years living in China
Raish (2015)	Allophones of *jīm* in Egyptian Arabic	[g] versus [ʒ, dʒ] occurred in 38.9% of contexts at pretest and 61.5% at posttest	[g] variant more likely in word-initial position; among female speakers, Egyptian heritage speakers, and learners with moderate proficiency gains during study abroad
Rehner et al. (2003)	First-person plural pronouns in Canadian French	Less formal *on* versus formal *nous* 'we' in 56% of all contexts	Variant *on* more likely in nonspecific and unrestricted referents; among male, upper-working class speakers and immersion learners with greater francophone exposure

word-initial position. Moreover, L2 speakers come to vary language in sociolinguistically meaningful ways, according to social factors like dialect (Kanwit et al. 2018), gender (Li 2010) or socioeconomic class (Rehner et al. 2003).

While the studies summarized demonstrate the value of researching L2 variation using a variationist sociolinguistic approach, a vital goal for L2 inquiry is disentangling L2 development generally, from the acquisition of sociolinguistic variation, more specifically. That is, it is essential for the researcher to determine whether learner variation is representative of a developmental path in interlanguage towards target-like behavior or whether the learner's variation is at a stage where it reflects a response to the social facts of the context of interaction as we would see in L1 communities. Berdan (1996) addressed this issue by analyzing a single learner's variable forms of negation in L2 English. This learner, Alberto, was a 33-year-old Puerto Rican man acquiring English naturalistically in Massachusetts. Cazden et al. (1975) had previously studied Alberto's negation and concluded that his variation between *don't* and *no* (e.g., *don't look my card* versus *no look my card*) showed no linguistic development, but rather the continued use of a non-target-like pattern. Although the *don't* + *V* variant was the non-dominant form in the interlanguage, Berdan questioned whether a variable rule (VARBRUL, Cedergren & Sankoff 1974) analysis would reveal a shift toward L1 English constraints on negation. Through a series of logistic regression analyses, Berdan provided evidence that Alberto's interlanguage had not fossilized, as the constraints governing his use of *don't* had changed over time. This study provides early support for the use of variationist sociolinguistic methods in the analysis of interlanguage, showing that the application of variationist analyses to L2 data allows us to understand patterns of variation for structures that vary along a developmental dimension as well as a social one.

This brief review shows that several of the concepts employed in the field of adult L2 variation share important assumptions with researchers who examine language change over time. Firstly, diachronic change is often described in similar ways. We see that changes in frequency of use of a given form over time, as well as changes in the contexts or constraints that influence use of a form, provide measurable constructs for describing historical change as well as acquisition over time. Secondly, both historical change and SLA are subject to social, political and individual factors, as well as linguistic ones (on this point, see Chapters 4, 5 and 6 in this volume). Given these similarities, it is unsurprising that the tools of variationist sociolinguistics have been applied to both fields. In the section that follows we will see how researchers have applied these tools and identified common paths of change across these fields.

3. Connections between SLA language variation and language change

In this section we take a deeper look at the substantive connections between the study of language change and SLA. We see common assumptions, such as the parallels between studying samples of language from different time periods (i.e., apparent time studies) and from different proficiency levels (i.e., cross-sectional L2 studies), and shared mechanisms of change, such as processes of regularization or the introduction of innovative forms and their path of spread into the (developing) grammar. Here, we review three sample studies that highlight how predictors of language change may describe changes over the time course of L2 development. For each of these studies, we describe in detail the research itself and we underscore the findings that draw a connection between language change over time and the acquisition of second languages.

Giacalone Ramat (1995, 2009) notes the connection between typological research and studies of SLA: "learner languages also belong to the field of typology and are relevant to the validation of language universals" (2009: 254). Evidence for this comes from L1 and L2 acquisition studies showing that learners earlier in their development (children in L1 studies and adults at lower levels of proficiency) prefer more transparent (e.g., analytic constructions, salient morphology, etc.) forms and often regularize paradigms. For example, Giacalone Ramat discusses the development of tense-mood-aspect (TMA) properties in L2 Italian showing that learners acquire less marked and more analytical forms earlier and may only later move to acquire more marked and synthetic forms. More specifically, interlanguages illustrate the organizing principles of language systems as well as markedness relations, with learner morphology emerging "in a manner consistent with predictions made by typological universals" whereby learners work out "the meaning of the various markings provided by the input on the grounds of general cognitive principles and discourse frequency." Similarly, the *Basic Variety* studies (see Klein & Perdue 1997) show that untutored learner languages are constrained by a limited set of structural, semantic and pragmatic principles, such as the *Controller First Principle*: the more agentive referent appears first, usually before the verb, commonly yielding a syntactic ordering of NP1 V NP2 or NP1 Cop NP2. Remarkably, the data for their study included adult learners representing six L1 and five target languages, with distinct typological characteristics. In other words, these results cannot be attributed merely to the languages in contact, but to higher-order universals of language processing. This is similar to the notion of the *First Noun Strategy* proposed by VanPatten (2004) which shows a similar pattern for tutored classroom learners of Spanish. In his studies, L2 learners assign the role of subject to the first noun in the verb phrase, even in cases where that noun is, in fact, a pre-posed verbal object. In essence, the primacy of the first noun exerts a universal influence on interpretation in L2 Spanish (see also Chapter 5 for more on the role of universal principles of acquisition in adult language learning).

To take this discussion further, if we assume that principles like the First Noun Strategy apply across time and space, it might explain certain historical changes whereby languages were created or restructured in situations of language contact. For example, Clements (2018: 415) explicitly connects studies of SLA and the emergence of pidgin and creole languages: "the Principle of Uniformity would allow us to expect that the same laws governing language acquisition in general, (…) also apply in the conventionalization process that yields a new language variety, as in the case of pidgin/creole genesis." Speakers in situations of language contact, such as enslaved Africans in forced colonial migrations, would process input of the superstrate language "as second-language input," such that they would "acquire content words such as nouns, verbs, and adjectives before function words such as prepositions or verb auxiliaries" as well as "more frequently used forms (…) before less frequently used forms" (2018: 415–416). Clements exemplifies this claim with a series of studies related to the formation of Spanish- and Portuguese-based pidgins, creoles, and immigrant varieties. Clements shows that in each case, much of the resulting language can be explained by assuming that the speakers built their initial grammars/basic varieties on the most frequently used (e.g., 3rd person singular and infinitive) and easily detectable (e.g., Consonant-Vowel structure) verb forms, copula forms and potential TMA-marking forms.

A second example of interdisciplinary work connecting sociolinguistics and SLA with sociohistorical import is Geeslin (2002). This investigation was designed to test the *Mirror-Image Hypothesis*, which posits that the loosening of constraints in the processes of language loss is the mirror-image of the addition of constraints in the process of SLA. Geeslin (2002) focuses on the stages of change in the Spanish [copula + adjective] structure described by Silva-Corvalán (1986). In general, the [copula + adjective] structure in Spanish alternates between two copular verbs roughly equivalent to English 'to be', *ser* and *estar*. Diachronically, *ser* is losing ground while *estar* is encroaching on contexts once dominated by *ser* (see Geeslin 2003). The Mirror-Image hypothesis predicts that (a) linguistic constraints on the copula contrast that are lost early among Spanish-English bilingual speakers will be learned late among English-speaking learners of Spanish and (b) constraints lost late among bilinguals will be learned early among learners. Geeslin's (2002) cross-sectional results from four levels of English-speaking high school students support the hypothesis. The pragmatic factor of 'frame of reference,' whereby an individual frame of reference favors *estar* and a class frame of reference favors *ser*, was lost early among Silva-Corvalán's bilingual speakers, and significantly affected learner use of the copula contrast only at later levels of enrollment. Conversely, the semantic factor of 'susceptibility to change,' which favors use of *estar*, was lost last among the Spanish-English bilinguals, and was a significant predictor of copula use at each learner level.[5] Although Geeslin confirmed the Mirror-Image Hypothesis for her

---

5. 'Frame of reference' (Falk 1979) is a distinction between contexts where referents are compared to a group of like objects (class frame) or to itself at another point in time (individual frame). 'Susceptibility to change' (Silva-Corvalán 1986) distinguishes referent + adjective combinations that are changeable from those that are not.

learner data, she cautions that her analysis revealed several other contextual factors involved in the copula contrast (e.g., adjective class) and that the relationship between language change and SLA is more complex than the mirror-image results she identified (440).

All in all, this study represents an explicit application of historical sociolinguistic research to L2 data and, in turn, participates in an extended conversation about language change in monolingual and bilingual varieties alike. In the first place, Geeslin's results confirm an interplay, albeit opposite, between pragmatic and semantic factors with *estar* extension but for a different set of bilingual speakers, English-dominant L2 learners of Spanish. In the second, confirmation of the Mirror-Image Hypothesis echoes Giacalone Ramat's point on the relevance of learner languages to the validation of language universals, namely in this case that semantic factors like 'susceptibility to change' or 'adjective class' act as powerful constraints on use of *estar*. This assertion is supported further by the importance of these same factors among monolingual varieties undergoing copula change. Gutiérrez (1992) revealed an extension of *estar* in progress among monolingual speakers in Morelia, Michoacán, but at a slower rate than in Silva-Corvalán's generational study. His social data pointed to the conclusion that change is from below–that is, from speakers with lower levels of education and lower socioeconomic backgrounds. Ortiz-López (2000) also found that level of education interacted with bilingualism and offers a counterargument to the hypothesis that contact with English drives this change in progress. Monolinguals in Puerto Rico, who were less likely to be highly educated than their bilingual counterparts, favored *estar* extension, especially with adjectives of age, size, physical appearance, and evaluation. Thus, in his study, we see evidence that bilingualism (or contact with English) itself is not associated with extension of *estar*. Both Gutiérrez and Ortiz-López confirm Silva-Corvalán's (1994) claim that absence of exposure to normative pressures may accelerate change, while in the additive case of L2 learning, increased exposure helps to strengthen and increase the number of constraints on copula use.

A third study that draws explicit connections between language change and L2 sociolinguistic competence is Donaldson (2017), an examination of learner convergence on target-like patterns of *ne*-deletion in French negation. According to analysis of data from adult L1/advanced L2 speaker dyads, L2 speakers omitted the preverbal particle *ne* less frequently than L1 counterparts, but the difference in rates of deletion was statistically nonsignificant. Regarding linguistic and sociostylistic factors influencing *ne*-deletion, L2 speakers also patterned largely like the L1 speakers: *ne*-deletion is more likely in sentences with subject pronouns but less likely in quoted as well as emphatic speech and serious topics. The groups differed only with respect to two linguistic factors, clause type and lexicalized expressions. Specifically, L2 speakers were more likely to retain *ne* in lexicalized expressions and subordinate clauses, while L1 speakers were not. Even so, a large majority of L2 speakers patterned like L1 speakers.

Donaldson's (2017) study demonstrates that L2 learners can acquire target-like norms of complex stylistic variation for variables like *ne*-deletion with extended exposure and social ties to the target language community. It is especially important that, as Donaldson (2017:165) suggests, we evaluate learner performance according to the state of ongoing changes in the L1 community–the moving targets of SLA (Geeslin 2011). The discrepancy, for instance, between L1 and L2 speakers in this study regarding clause type was attenuated by previous studies on L1 French groups (e.g., Ashby 1976, 1981), which found higher rates of *ne* retention in subordinate clauses. L2 speakers may have patterned after a larger trend in the L1 French community, or they may have had some typological awareness that subordinate clauses are a more conservative site of change (Givón 1976, as cited in Donaldson 2017:161). The challenge is understanding whether *ne*-deletion for these L2 speakers is still a change in progress, like for L1 speakers. Longitudinal or panel studies could better elucidate the typological, acquisitional or sociolinguistic factors affecting L2 development over time. Likewise, detailed individual background analyses that consider identity and investment (Norton 2011), ecology and context (Clements 2009; Evans-Sago 2018), and individual differences in aptitude, motivation, and personality, among others (Dörnyei 2005), could help to explain individual variation in convergence among L2 speakers for stable and ongoing changes in the L1 community.

As mentioned at the outset of this section, there are additional, implicit parallels between historical change and SLA in current research, and many of these studies take place in contexts of bilingualism and language contact. One example that shows the connection between language change, linguistic typology and SLA involves the development of tense and aspect in L2 Spanish. Spanish allows two forms to reference ongoing action at speech time, the simple present and present progressive, whereas English predominantly employs the present progressive (see Torres Cacoullos 2000). Thus, subsequent research has tested the hypothesis that Spanish-English bilinguals will use the present progressive form significantly more than monolingual Spanish speakers, as a way of aligning the bilinguals' two languages (Klein 1980). However, although both languages have equivalent constructions, their functions and distribution differ. Critically, diachronic studies (e.g., Torres Cacoullos 2000) show that both Spanish and English progressives resulted from grammaticalization whereby locative constructions evolved into constructions for depicting ongoing action at speech time. Historical data show a remarkable rise in progressives over the last two centuries in both languages, although the English progressive is distributed more widely across lexical classes as an obligatory marker of ongoing action, relegating the simple present to habitual action. The Spanish progressive is currently at an earlier stage of development in which it competes with the simple present for marking ongoing action and still retains frequentative uses.

Geeslin and Fafulas (2022) tested how adult learners of Spanish with an L1 of English manage the differences between the functions of the progressive and simple present which have developed diachronically. In their study, they employed a written contextualized task, a type of preference task which creates a context in the form of a narrative integrating each item. Participants were asked to indicate a preference for one of two sentences, which differed only in the form under investigation. The authors examined patterns of selection across the categories of lexical aspect in combination with the influence of adverbial phrases leading to a reading of 'right now' and 'habitual.' They collected data from learners at four proficiency levels as well as from L1 speakers of Spanish and L1 speakers of English (tested in English). Thus, their design allowed for an analysis of cross-linguistic comparisons to establish the baseline patterns and guide predictions about how the English-speaking learners of Spanish would develop. Their study tested two hypotheses foundational in learner development of tense and aspect: the *Prototype Hypothesis*, predicting that learners will "acquire a linguistic category starting with the prototype of the category and later expand its application to less prototypical cases" (Shirai & Andersen 1995: 758), and the *Aspect Hypothesis* (see Bardovi-Harlig 2000), which claims that progressive marking begins with activities, extends next to accomplishments and then achievements, and will not be overextended to statives.

Their results confirmed that learners had more difficulty pairing the progressive in frequentative/habitual contexts, which was partly predicted by the fact that this form-meaning mapping was more restricted among the English baseline group, while more common in the Spanish baseline group. Thus, the researchers were able to use the crosslinguistic differences which developed historically between the baselines to observe specific acquisitional trends among the learners in their study. Overall, their findings confirmed the core assumptions of the Aspect Hypothesis and Prototype Hypothesis, while also pointing out that input is a key predictor in learner development. Their study showed that certain universals do hold in crosslinguistic and learner tense-aspect comparisons. Although contact-induced change might give way to certain lexical-semantic restructuring among bilinguals (see Chapter 11 in this volume for an example), it does not necessarily lead to replacement of one form for the other, as Spanish is already changing diachronically, regardless of contact with English. This supports the notion that a synchronic analysis of learner language can incorporate findings and tendencies of diachronic research on each of the learner's languages to guide predictions and explain trends in the data.

In related work, Fafulas (2021) tested simple present and present progressive use among monolingual Peruvian Spanish speakers from Lima and Iquitos as well as naturalistic learners from the Amazon region. Importantly, the Spanish bilinguals in the study shared the substrate Indigenous language Yagua, which lacks an overt progressive construction, allowing for a better understanding of how contact with languages other than English fits into the larger picture of simple present/present progressive variation and development. Results showed some cross-dialectal variation as well as language contact effects. Importantly, the Yagua-Spanish bilinguals showed similar overall rates for the *estar* progressive as reported for L2 Spanish speakers in the USA via the same method of data collection. Because English contact is not present in this situation, these results can be interpreted as evidence for language restructuring more generally in that bilinguals opt for a more transparent system with one-to-one mappings between simple present and present progressive forms; the progressive is mapped to 'ongoing action at speech time' and the simple present is mapped to 'habitual/generic events/states.' This is similar to what has been found in diachronic crosslinguistic studies of these forms (Bybee et al. 1994) showing that, as a morpheme takes over progressive territory, the simple present becomes the default marker for present habitual meaning. This also supports Silva-Corvalán's (1994) observation that an increase of periphrastic forms (i.e., progressive constructions) at the expense of synthetic ones (i.e., simple present) may be accelerated in situations of language contact.

To summarize,[6] the study of simple present and present progressive variation in bilingual communities adds to studies of typology, language evolution and our understanding of how specific processes shape languages across time and space. As Donaldson (2022: 1) points out, both SLA and diachronic change are "marked by grammatical instability, variation, and change." By documenting synchronic variation through L2 grammars and different contact settings, we can learn more about diachronic change and the common factors that may have given rise to historical changes and present-day variation.

---

6. Our coverage here is not exhaustive. See, for example, research on the *Interface Hypothesis* (Sorace & Serratrice 2009), which Fischer & Vega Vilanova (2018) tested in Judeo-Spanish, as well as the discussion of other SLA theories with potential application to sociohistorical context in Chapters 5 and 6 in this volume.

4. SLA and the historical sociolinguistics of language change: Challenges and opportunities

We have seen throughout this chapter that the shared constructs, application of similar methods of analysis and potentially connected findings have been mutually beneficial to research on historical sociolinguistics and to SLA. In the current section we first identify some challenges when building disciplinary connections between these two fields and then provide an account of L2 research methodology that might be more explicitly connected to the social study of language change over time. Finally, we suggest expansion to new geographic regions where situations of bilingualism and language contact provide opportunities to move each field forward.

A main difference, and thus challenge, when connecting research in SLA and (historical) sociolinguistics lies in the heavier focus in SLA studies on the individual, while sociolinguistics and diachronic development is more focused on whole communities (see Geeslin & Evans-Sago 2020). One area that illustrates this tension well can be seen in how the construct of language change and its connection to social groups plays out in each field. Labov's (1994) conclusions regarding the social motivations for language change rely on concepts such as social mobility, social stratification, group membership, and larger-scale immigration that affects the local community. Labov proposes the *Nonconformity Hypothesis* which rests on two principles of linguistic change: (1) the *Nonconformity Principle*: ongoing linguistic changes are emblematic of nonconformity to established social norms of appropriate behavior and are generated in the social milieu that most consistently defies those norms; and (2) the *Constructive Nonconformity Principle*: linguistic changes are generalized to the wider community by those who display the symbols of nonconformity in a larger pattern of upward social mobility. Ultimately, the challenge for historical sociolinguists is to gain enough information about the sociolinguistic context in a particular setting so that they may formulate hypotheses about speaker motivations, such as whether speakers indeed move away from or toward perceived norms. Nevertheless, these concepts do not always align with studies of SLA which often focus on small groups of individuals, frequently in the classroom setting, making a community-wide analysis of variation and change in the Labovian sense difficult to apply to L2 cohorts. More importantly still, a related contrast is the role of differing motivation for conforming to norms and standards and, more broadly in the L2 context, for the learning of additional languages (e.g., instrumental motivation, Gardner & MacIntyre 1991). Learners are often assumed to want to 'conform' to the target language community and, thus, would seem to go against the nonconformity that Labov posits as part of the motivations for language change. However, it is worth noting that learners do in fact make choices to align with certain variants, speakers, or speech communities.[7] These choices might be in the direction that Labov mentions, against standard norms, such as in cases of adopting local covert variants (see Schmidt et al. 2022). In any case, we see a promising area of future research related to newer approaches to SLA, such as documenting the acquisition of regional forms, and newer waves of sociolinguistic variation.

A second area where we see a concrete distinction between both fields is the tendency for native or L1 speakers to be designated as the appropriate 'target' for L2 learners. Donaldson (2022: 7) makes this point explicit: "[m]ost SLA research measures learner development toward some native speaker norm, whereas most diachronic work describes change away from the norm(s) of previous generations." There is, in this sense, a shared understanding of the path of change despite differences in direction of that change (toward or away from group norms). Nevertheless, it is also the very field of language variation and change that provides SLA researchers with the information necessary to argue against a monolithic target, or standard, against which all learners should be compared (Geeslin 2011). Instead, we know that learners may be moving toward an international or pan-dialectal variety, rather than a single community's norms. These observations are particularly relevant to the sociohistorical study of contact settings, where researchers may have difficulty reconstructing whether a local norm was available and, if so, what it may have looked like (see Chapters 10, 11 and 12 in this volume). Despite these challenges, the analytical tools and concepts across these two fields can be applied to better understand the individual (e.g., cognitive) and social factors (e.g., upward mobility) that may have led to historical changes, whether among L1, L2 or bilingual speakers. While the focus of the preceding paragraphs is on how the study of various forms of acquisition can inform historical sociolinguistic approaches to language change, we would be remiss not to mention that historical studies can also benefit SLA research, e.g., by informing methodological decisions in L2 research that can build directly from what is known about language change in progress. Studies such as Geeslin (2003), Geeslin & Fafulas (2022), or Kanwit & Geeslin (2018, 2020) provide examples of how the careful study of language change in progress is a necessary precursor for both instrument design and for effective analysis in SLA variation research.

We conclude this section with two examples of how synchronic approaches to SLA have potential to inform the study of ongoing and historical linguistic change in its social environment. The first example comes from the study of Spanish in the U.S. South, a region where recent demographic trends have resulted in

---

7. See Chapters 5 and 6 in this volume for additional discussion of the role of identity alignment in individual trajectories of language acquisition.

widespread contact between English and Spanish in the home, a broad range of proficiency levels in each language across individuals, and an emerging bilingual community which includes generational shift and processes of SLA. According to the Pew Research Center, over the past few decades, the U.S. South accounted for the largest growth in Latinx populations (Pew Research Center 2022). This region is an ideal test case to further our understanding of the formation of new language varieties, such as Latinx English (Thomas 2019). Lipski (2015: 672) notes that "as Spanish speakers in southern states grow in numbers and prominence, the nuanced English and Spanish that result from this cross-fertilization will further enrich the linguistic profile of our communities." However, little work in this region of the U.S. South exists, especially in communities that have not traditionally had large Latinx populations. Exceptions of studies that examine the emerging Spanish and English varieties of these regions among bilingual populations are Limerick (2017) and Wolfram et al. (2004). These studies illustrate the advantages of applying a variationist lens to contact settings because it allows us to understand how acquisition-based processes (e.g., interlanguage, transfer, dialect acquisition, etc.) shape the emergence of new varieties in bilingual communities.

The second example is from South America's Amazonian region, where Spanish is slowly spreading and is in contact with multiple Indigenous languages. There has been an extended period of multilingualism which has shaped the present-day diversity of Spanish dialects in this area since the colonial period. In some communities, more than one Indigenous ethnicity and language are found alongside Spanish. The diversity of environmental, social and linguistic triggers in the Amazon region makes this area a perfect testing ground for the application of SLA theory to the analysis of the recorded historical patterns of contact, variation and change. Recent edited volumes and studies (Fafulas 2020; Fafulas & Rodríguez-Mondoñedo forthcoming) highlight the growing interest in documenting the Spanish of the region and emphasize the interplay among acquisitional, typological and social factors giving rise to the various forms of Spanish used historically in the Amazonian region. Other studies (e.g., Geeslin & Evans-Sago 2020) highlight the need to empirically disentangle features of Amazonian Spanish resulting from more general processes of naturalistic SLA versus contact with Indigenous languages. These studies also show that, when documenting contact varieties in Indigenous settings, researchers should keep in mind their ability to valorize the Indigenous language communities by having their needs and rights acknowledged, which may assist in reversing the tide of losing vital cultural legacies (Fitzgerald 2017: 285). The same can be said for the Latinx populations in the U.S. South, which may include minoritized speakers and immigrant communities with barriers to healthcare and education.

5. Conclusion

We began this chapter by identifying trends in the field of L2 sociolinguistics that align with studies of language change over time. We documented a wealth of research conducted with L2 learners that shows that they can acquire and do exhibit sociolinguistic variation and, importantly, that this variation demonstrates important connections to studies of historical change. We highlighted the few core studies that explicitly draw connections between historical change and SLA, such as discussions of the Mirror-Image Hypothesis and the Principle of Uniformity, showing clear connections between the two fields. Our discussion then turned to studies of language acquisition that draw on knowledge of historical change, even when these connections are not explicitly identified by the authors. Finally, we identified existing challenges and key differences between the two fields as well as areas where there is the potential to expand inquiry through more tightly constructed dialogue between what we know about language change in progress and what we see in contexts of SLA, bilingualism and language contact. We conclude this chapter by urging this volume's readers to consider the myriad ways that these two fields can collaborate and conduct research that is mutually beneficial to the study of language acquisition, language variation and language change.

References

Adamson, Douglas & Vera Regan. 1991. The acquisition of community speech norms by Asian immigrants learning English as a second language: A preliminary study. *Studies in Second Language Acquisition* 13. 1–22.

Ashby, William. 1976. The loss of negative morpheme, *ne*, in Parisian French. *Lingua* 39. 119–137.

Ashby, William. 1981. The loss of negative particle *ne* in French: A syntactic change in progress. *Language* 57(3). 674–687.

Auer, Anita, Catharina Peersman, Simon Pickl, Gijsbert Rutten & Rik Vosters. 2015. Historical sociolinguistics: the field and its future. *Journal of Historical Sociolinguistics* 1(1). 1–12.

Bardovi-Harlig, Kathleen. 2000. *Tense and aspect in second language acquisition: Form, meaning, and use*. Oxford: Wiley-Blackwell.

Berdan, Robert. 1996. Disentangling language acquisition from language variation. In Robert Bayley & Dennis R. Preston (eds.), *Second language acquisition and linguistic variation*, 203–244. Amsterdam: John Benjamins.

Bybee, Joan, Revere Perkins & William Pagliuca. 1994. *The evolution of grammar: Tense, aspect, and modality in the languages of the world*. Chicago: University of Chicago Press.

Caetano, Ana Carolina Alves & Silvia Rodrigues Vieira. 2021. Análise variacionista da ordem dos clíticos pronominais no português de Moçambique. *Revista Diadorim* 23. 171–202.

Canagarajah, Suresh. 2011. Translanguaging in the classroom: Emerging issues for research and pedagogy. *Applied Linguistics Review* 2. 1–28.

Cazden, Courtney B., Herlinda Cancino, Ellen Rosansky & John Schumann. 1975. *Second language acquisition sequences in children, adolescents and adults*. Final Report. National Institute of Education.

Cedergren, Henrietta J. & David Sankoff. 1974. Variable rules: Performance as a statistical reflection of competence. *Language* 50(2). 333–355.

Clements, J. Clancy. 2009. *The linguistic legacy of Spanish and Portuguese: Colonial expansion and language change*. Cambridge: Cambridge University Press.

Clements, J. Clancy. 2018. Speech communities, language varieties, and typology: What does acquisition have to do with it? *Journal of Pidgin and Creole Languages* 33(2). 413–414.

Creese, Angela & Adrian Blackledge. 2010. Translanguaging in the bilingual classroom: A pedagogy for learning and teaching? *The Modern Language Journal* 94(1). 103–115.

Dewaele, Jean-Marc, Thomas Bak & Lourdes Ortega. 2022. Why the mythical "native speaker" has mud on its face. In Nikolay Slavkov, Sílvia Melo-Pfeifer & Nadja Kerschhofer-Puhalo (eds.), *The changing face of the "native speaker": Perspectives from multilingualism and globalization*, 23–43. Berlin: De Gruyter Mouton.

Donaldson, Bryan. 2017. Negation in near-native French: Variation and sociolinguistic competence. *Language Learning* 67. 141–170.

Donaldson, Bryan. 2022. Connecting language change with second language acquisition. In Kimberly Geeslin (ed.), *The Routledge handbook of second language acquisition and sociolinguistics*, 174–185. New York: Routledge.

Dörnyei, Zoltán. 2005. *The psychology of the language learner: Individual differences in second language acquisition*. New York: Routledge.

Evans-Sago, Travis. 2018. A case study of three Chinese-Spanish varieties: Tense-aspect morphology in instructed and non-instructed language use. *Journal of Ibero-Romance Creoles* 8. 4–37.

Fafulas, Stephen (ed.). 2020. *Amazonian Spanish: Language contact and evolution*. Amsterdam: John Benjamins.

Fafulas, Stephen. 2021. Variation of the simple present and present progressive: Peruvian Spanish, 'Pear Story,' and language contact, oh my!. In Manuel Díaz-Campos (ed.), *The Routledge handbook of variationist approaches to Spanish*, 328–344. New York: Routledge.

Fafulas, Stephen & Miguel Rodríguez-Mondoñedo. Forthcoming. Spanish in contact with Peruvian Amazonian languages. To appear in Leonardo Cerno, Hans-Jörg Döhla, Miguel Gutiérrez Maté, Robert Hesselbach & Joachim Steffen (eds.), *Handbook of contact varieties of Spanish and Spanish-lexified contact varieties*. Berlin: De Gruyter Mouton.

Falk, Johan. 1979. Ser y estar con atributos adjetivales: Anotaciones sobre el empleo de la cópula en catalán y en castellano. Uppsala: Uppsala University PhD dissertation.

Fischer, Susann & Vega Vilanova, Jorge. 2018. Contact-induced change in Judeo-Spanish. In Harm den Boer, Anna Lena Menny, Carsten Wilke, David M. Bunis, Ivana Vučina Simović & Corinna Deppner (eds.), *Caminos de leche y miel. Jubilee volume in Honor of Michael Studemund-Halévy*. Volume 2, 135–153. Barcelona: Tirocinio.

Fitzgerald, Colleen. 2017. Understanding language vitality and reclamation as resilience: A framework for language endangerment and 'loss' (Commentary on Mufwene). *Language* 93(4). 281–298.

Gardner, Robert & Peter MacIntyre. 1991. An instrumental motivation in language study: Who says it isn't effective? *Studies in Second Language Acquisition* 13. 57–72.

Geeslin, Kimberly. 2002. The acquisition of Spanish copula choice and its relationship to language change. *Studies in Second Language Acquisition* 24(3). 419–450.

Geeslin, Kimberly. 2003. A comparison of copula choice: Native Spanish speakers and advanced learners. *Language Learning* 53(4). 703–764.

Geeslin, Kimberly. 2011. The acquisition of variation in second language Spanish: How to identify and catch a moving target. In Manuel Díaz-Campos (ed.), *The handbook of Hispanic sociolinguistics*, 303–319. Oxford: Wiley-Blackwell.

Geeslin, Kimberly. 2018. Variable structures and sociolinguistic variation. In Paul Malovrh & Alessandro Benati (eds.), *The handbook of advanced proficiency in second language acquisition*, 547–565. Oxford: Wiley-Blackwell.

Geeslin, Kimberly (ed.). 2022. *The Routledge handbook of second language acquisition and sociolinguistics*. New York: Routledge.

Geeslin, Kimberly & Travis Evans-Sago. 2020. Bilingualism, second language acquisition, and language contact. In Stephen Fafulas (ed.), *Amazonian Spanish: Language contact and evolution*, 35–56. Amsterdam: John Benjamins.

Geeslin, Kimberly & Stephen Fafulas. 2022. Linguistic variation and second language Spanish: A study of progressive and habitual marking by English-speaking learners. In Robert Bayley, Dennis Preston & Xiaoshi Li (eds.), *Variation in second and heritage languages: Crosslinguistic perspectives*, 159–198. Amsterdam: John Benjamins.

Giacalone Ramat, Anna. 1995. Iconicity in grammaticalization processes. In Raffaele Simone (ed.), *Iconicity in language*, 119–139. Amsterdam: John Benjamins.

Giacalone Ramat, Anna. 2009. Typological universals and second language acquisition. In Sergio Scalise, Elisabetta Magni & Antonietta Bisetto (eds.), *Universals of language today. Studies in natural language and linguistic theory, vol. 76*, 253–272. Dordrecht: Springer.

Givón, Talmy. 1976. Topic, pronoun, and grammatical agreement. In Charles Li (ed.), *Subject and topic*, 149–188. New York: Academic Press.

Greenberg, Joseph. 1991. Typology/universals and second language acquisition. In Thom Huebner & Charles Ferguson (eds.), *Cross currents in second language acquisition and linguistic theories*, 37–43. Amsterdam: John Benjamins.

Gutiérrez, Manuel. 1992. The extension of *estar*: A linguistic change in progress in the Spanish of Morelia, Mexico. *Hispanic Linguistics* 5(1–2). 109–141.

Hansen Edwards, Jette. 2011. Deletion of /t, d/ and the acquisition of linguistic variation by second language learners of English. *Language Learning* 61(4). 1256–1301.

Holmquist, Jonathan. 2012. Frequency rates and constraints on subject personal pronoun expression: Findings from the Puerto Rican highlands. *Language Variation and Change* 24. 203–220.

Kanwit, Matthew & Kimberly Geeslin. 2018. Exploring lexical effects in second language interpretation: The case of mood in Spanish adverbial clauses. *Studies in Second Language Acquisition* 40(3). 579–603.

Kanwit, Matthew, Vanessa Elias & Rebecca Clay. 2018. Acquiring intensifier variation abroad: Exploring *muy* and *bien* in Spain and Mexico. *Foreign Language Annals* 51(2). 455–471.

Kanwit, Matthew & Kimberly Geeslin. 2020. Sociolinguistic competence and interpreting variable structures in a second language: A study of the copula contrast in native and second-language Spanish. *Studies in Second Language Acquisition* 42(4). 775–799.

Klein, Flora. 1980. A quantitative study of syntactic and pragmatic indications of change in the Spanish of bilinguals in the U.S. In William Labov (ed.), *Locating language in time and space*, 69–82. New York: Academic Press.

Klein, Wolfgang & Clive Perdue. 1997. The basic variety (or: Couldn't natural languages be much simpler?). *Second Language Research* 13(4). 301–347.

Labov, William. 1966. *The social stratification of English in New York City*. Washington, DC: Center for Applied Linguistics.

Labov, William. 1994. *Principles of linguistic change. Volume one: Internal factors*. Oxford: Blackwell.

Levon, Erez & Sue Fox. 2014. Social salience and the sociolinguistic monitor: A case study of ING and TH-fronting in Britain. *Journal of English Linguistics* 42(3). 185–217.

Li, Xiaoshi. 2010. Sociolinguistic variation in the speech of learners of Chinese as a second language. *Language Learning* 60(2). 366–408.

Li, Xiaoshi. 2014. Variation in subject pronominal expression in L2 Chinese. *Studies in Second Language Acquisition* 36(1). 39–68.

Limerick, Philip P. 2017. Language contact in the US Southeast: The case of Spanish subject expression in an emerging bilingual community in Georgia. *Spanish in Context* 14(1). 53–77.

Lipski, John. 2015. Is "Spanglish" the third language of the South? In Michael Picone & Catherine Evans Davies (eds.), *New perspectives on language variety in the South: Historical and contemporary approaches*, 657–677. Tuscaloosa: University of Alabama Press.

Mougeon, Raymond, Terry Nadasdi & Katherine Rehner. 2010. *The sociolinguistic competence of immersion students*. Bristol: Multilingual Matters.

Nevalainen, Terttu & Helena Raumolin-Brunberg. 2012. Historical sociolinguistics: Origins, motivations, and paradigms. In Juan Manuel Hernández-Campoy & José Camilo Conde-Silvestre (eds.), *The handbook of historical sociolinguistics*, 22–40. Malden, MA: Wiley-Blackwell.

Norton, Bonny. 2011. Identity. In James Simpson (ed.), *The Routledge handbook of applied linguistics*, 318–330. New York: Routledge.

Ortiz-López, Luis. 2000. Extensión de *estar* en contextos de *ser* en el español de Puerto Rico: ¿Evolución interna o contacto de lenguas? *Boletín de la Academia Puertorriqueña de la Lengua Española*, 98–118.

Otheguy, Ricardo, Ofelia García & Wallis Reid. 2015. Clarifying translanguaging and deconstructing named languages: A perspective from linguistics. *Applied Linguistics Review* 6(3). 281–307.

Pew Research Center. 2022. U.S. Hispanic population continued its geographic spread in the 2010s. https://www.pewresearch.org/short-reads/2022/02/03/u-s-hispanic-population-continued-its-geographic-spread-in-the-2010s/ (April 15, 2022).

Preston, Dennis. 1989. *Sociolinguistics and second language acquisition*. Cambridge, MA: Basil Blackwell.

Raish, Michael. 2015. The acquisition of an Egyptian phonological variant by US students in Cairo. *Foreign Language Annals* 48(2). 267–283.

Rehner, Katherine, Raymond Mougeon & Terry Nadasdi. 2003. The learning of sociolinguistic variation by advanced FSL learners: The case of *nous* versus *on* in immersion French. *Studies in Second Language Acquisition* 25(1). 127–156.

Schmidt, Lauren, Bret Linford & Stephen Fafulas. 2022. Regional variation. In Kimberly Geeslin (ed.), *The Routledge handbook of second language acquisition and sociolinguistics*. London: Routledge.

Selinker, Larry. 1972. Interlanguage. *International Review of Applied Linguistics* 10. 209–232.

Shirai, Yasuhiro & Roger W. Andersen. 1995. The acquisition of tense-aspect morphology: A prototype account. *Language* 71(4). 743–762.

Silva-Corvalán, Carmen. 1986. Bilingualism and language change: The extension of *estar* in Los Angeles Spanish. *Language* 62(3). 587–608.

Silva-Corvalán, Carmen. 1994. *Language contact and change*. Oxford: Oxford University Press.

Sorace, Antonella & Ludovica Serratrice. 2009. Internal and external interfaces in bilingual language development: beyond structural overlap. *International Journal of Bilingualism* 13(2). 193–210.

Tarone, Elaine. 2006. Interlanguage. In Keith Brown (ed.), *Encyclopedia of language and linguistics*. 2nd edition, 747–751. Boston: Elsevier.

Thomas, Erik. (ed.). 2019. *Mexican American English: Substrate influence and the birth of an ethnolect*. Cambridge: Cambridge University Press.

Torres Cacoullos, Rena. 2000. *Grammaticization, synchronic variation, and language contact: A study of Spanish progressive -ndo constructions*. Amsterdam: John Benjamins.

Trudgill, Peter. 2011. *Sociolinguistic typology: Social determinants of linguistic complexity*. Oxford: Oxford University Press.

VanPatten, Bill. 2004. *Processing instruction: Theory, research, and commentary*. New York: Routledge.

Winford, Donald. 2020. The New Spanishes in the context of contact linguistics: Toward a unified approach. In Luis Ortiz López, Rosa Guzzardo Tamargo & Melvin González-Rivera (eds.), *Hispanic contact linguistics: Theoretical, methodological and empirical perspectives*, 11–41. Amsterdam: John Benjamins.

Wolfram, Walt, Phillip Carter & Becky Moriello. 2004. Emerging Hispanic English: New dialect formation in the American South. *Journal of Sociolinguistics* 8(3). 339–358.

CHAPTER 4

The dynamics of lifelong acquisition in dialect contact and change

Jennifer Hendriks
The Australian National University

Acquisition research involving speakers of mutually intelligible varieties (dialects) or mutually unintelligible varieties (languages) reveals a wide range of possible acquisition outcomes at different life stages and their potential to shape language change across the community. Since contexts of dialect contact often include language contact, attempts to understand the link between dialect acquisition and dialect change must also consider language contact as a potential factor. This chapter surveys the research on dialect contact and lifespan change in contexts of language maintenance in both non-mobile and mobile languages users as a window into the human capacity for lifelong acquisition and change. The chapter adopts a linguistic repertoire focus, recognizing that bidialectalism/bilingualism is a matter of degree, and that language dominance plays a key role in crosslinguistic transfer. This proposal is illustrated with a case study of dialect and language contact in Early Modern Dutch.

Keywords: dialect contact, lifespan change, language dominance, linguistic repertoire, crosslinguistic transfer

1. Introduction

Sociohistorical investigations of dialect contact and change stand much to gain from acquisition research seeking to understand the human potential for linguistic malleability across the lifespan. Contemporary sociolinguistic studies have established the potential for change earlier in life yet offer only qualified support for change across later life stages. One question that recent acquisition theorizing may be well-placed to clarify is whether these findings reveal more about underlying similarities in the contexts of research, including the types of language users studied, than the human capacity for lifelong acquisition. How much of the potential for lifespan change can we observe, for example, in research contexts which are restricted to monolinguals, or which examine dialect variation and change only in the dominant language of bilingual or multilingual speakers? And what can we learn from linguistically diverse research environments where individuals may become influenced by, and engage in, different ways of speaking regardless of life stage?

Using these questions to guide the discussion, Section 2 offers a brief overview of research on lifespan change involving mutually intelligible varieties of the same language. Section 3 shifts focus to the recent acquisition literature which underscores the importance of speakers' entire linguistic repertoires in the analysis of dialect (and language) contact, variation and change. Section 4 applies insights from the previous sections to a case of dialect (and language) contact and change in Early Modern Dutch – the historical backdrop to a present-day sound change in progress. Section 5 concludes the chapter by highlighting the challenges and opportunities that acquisition research has to offer sociohistorical linguists investigating dialect contact and change.

2. Language variation, dialect contact and change across the lifespan: Past findings, future directions

Longitudinal studies tracking the same speakers across decades of their lives (i.e., *panel studies*) remain a rarity in any sub-discipline of linguistics (for a review of sociolinguistic studies, see Sankoff 2018, 2019). Our present understanding of lifelong acquisition in settings of L1 dialect contact, variation and change derives primarily from quantitative, community-level sociolinguistic research and qualitative, individual-level dialect acquisition studies. In general, longitudinal studies of native speakers offer a local community perspective on lifespan change, while qualitative accounts of individuals or small groups track repertoire changes in mobile individuals, often as they become members of a new dialect community. Thus, the research contexts for these two approaches as well as the types of speakers studied are fundamentally different – a point we will return to below.

Starting with the community-level perspective, several quantitative sociolinguistic studies conducted in the second half of the twentieth century used synchronic, age-stratified, *apparent-time* data to infer ongoing community change (see Sankoff 2005 for an overview). The assumption underlying this approach was that an L1, once acquired, remained stable across the adult lifespan. Subsequent re-samplings of those communities – *trend studies* which often included a small number of the original participants – did not always reveal the progression of change as expected but did provide clear evidence of adult vernacular lability (see Yaeger-Dror 1989). Building on this research, more recent studies have investigated whether, or to what degree, change in adulthood is predictable. Can change after childhood be linked, for example, to the categoricity or variability of a feature at the time of acquisition (e.g., Nahkola & Saanilahti 2004)? Or is adult change less predictable with respect to the frequency of use of an innovative variant (Gregersen et al. 2009)?

These and other panel studies offer glimpses into lifespan change. For instance, in a panel study of the sociophonetics of variation in the allophones of /æ/ (i.e., [æ] and [ɛ]) in two Danish communities over 20 years, Gregersen et al. (2009: 69) report that a middle-class woman became a categorical user of [æ], while her sister, a near-categorical user of [æ] at the time of the first interview, displayed a significant increase in the use of [ɛ]. Working across a similar time span, Sankoff and Blondeau (2007: 572–573) captured two adults (one male, one female) who had changed from being near-categorical users of apical /r/ to dominant users of the dorsal variant in their Montreal French study. While it is unclear why the male's language use had changed so dramatically, the female had experienced significant occupational change; a 24-year-old factory worker at the initial interview, she had become a businesswoman by the second interview and a successful realtor by the third. Such life-course changes can clearly impact speakers' linguistic repertoires (Eckert 1997), but often we lack detailed life biographies of study participants to explore the motivations underlying adult vernacular change.

Community-level sociolinguistic studies using longitudinal methods have been instrumental in providing evidence of lifelong acquisition. While acknowledging the need for more research on lifespan change, Sankoff nevertheless concludes "that reduced malleability is characteristic of later life" (2018: 308). Moreover, "three trajectory types [...] exhaust the logical possibilities of what speakers may do" (Sankoff 2019: 223): they may remain stable across the lifespan; they may change in the direction of community change; or they may retreat from ongoing community change and become more conservative. The types of speakers as well as the contexts of research relevant to the three trajectory types are notably quite specific. Regarding speakers the focus is "on developments *in early-acquired languages that are maintained across speakers' lives*, and on how sociocultural pressures in their speech communities shape lifespan trajectories" (Sankoff 2018: 298, emphasis added). The contexts of research are those "speech communities that have not, during the relevant time period, experienced significant population mobility and change due to language contact" (Sankoff 2005: 1003). Given the specificity of this research environment where the aim is to track variation and change as it progresses through a relatively stable, non-mobile speech community, it does indeed seem likely that change across the lifespan would be restricted to the possibilities Sankoff has identified.[1] What, then, can we learn about the human capacity for lifelong

---

1. See Chapter 9 in this volume for a case study of change in a largely non-mobile community via the incrementation of change in progress by older children and adolescents.

acquisition from dialect contact studies of mobile speakers, when "the social and linguistic processes underlying children's (and adults') speech modifications are at their most visible" (Kerswill 1996: 34)?

Before considering this question, if the research objective is to understand the potential for lifelong acquisition, an immediate challenge investigating contact and change in structurally similar, mutually intelligible varieties is that speakers of closely related varieties need not necessarily modify their speech to communicate. It can therefore be difficult to determine whether speakers *cannot* acquire a second dialect (or dialect features), or whether they simply *have not* done so. Further confounding this issue is the wealth of evidence showing that mobile speakers regularly adjust their speech for a variety of reasons as they become members of a new dialect community. Several studies have researched whether and how children and adolescents are able to modify early acquired features after relocating to a new dialectal area (e.g., Chambers 1992; Tagliamonte & Molfenter 2007, and below in this section). This same question has also been posed for adults. In an early study, Shockey (1984) conducted a pilot study of four American faculty members at the University of Essex who had lived in England between 8 and 27 years. Focusing on the suppression of /t/ and /d/ flapping, in environments where most Americans would flap 100% of the time, study participants had reduced /t/-flapping to between 17% and 50% and /d/-flapping to between 58% and 72%. To explain these results, the author appealed to *accommodation theory*, noting that Giles (1980) had identified "communicational efficiency" as one major reason for speakers to adjust their speech, but that "intelligibility" (92) had not been adequately investigated. With flapping, the /t/ environments had the greatest potential to cause interactional confusion and they happened to be the most numerous.

Adjusting one's speech in a desire to be understood could explain why the participants in this study had reduced flapping in /t/ environments significantly more than in /d/ environments. These individuals had adjusted their speech as adults in response to having settled in a new dialect community – a finding documented across decades of dialect contact research (see Nycz 2015 and Siegel 2010 for overviews). The reasons for these non-random patterns of variation and change may also be as mundane as wanting to communicate without having to repeat oneself and therefore learning which features to modify to achieve that interactional goal. Studying idiolectal lability in migrants who are exposed to a greater variety of second dialect features than members of relatively stable, non-mobile speech communities offers more opportunities to observe the capacity for lifelong acquisition; migration, after all, affects individuals across all life stages. It remains difficult, however, to determine the degree to which individuals in these contexts adjust their speech to serve a purpose such as increased intelligibility, or whether it informs us about age-specific acquisition stages.

In the second dialect acquisition (SDA) literature, the question of why learners or accommodators of different ages exhibit varying degrees of success acquiring a new variety remains contentious, and research into this question offers the greatest potential for a more nuanced understanding of the human capacity for lifelong acquisition. Influenced by the hypothesis that there is a sensitive period for language acquisition, many SDA studies have sought to determine how young learners must be to acquire a second dialect to native-like proficiency. Citing Lenneberg's (1967) *Critical Period Hypothesis* (CPH), Siegel (2010: 96) clarifies that it "was framed with regard to first language acquisition", specifically in circumstances where children had not been exposed to language before puberty, to account for their inability to successfully acquire language. Nevertheless, this hypothesis has been used in SDA (and second language acquisition) research to account for the well-documented failure of speakers to acquire native-like proficiency after childhood. Adding nuance to the discussion, Kerswill (1996) proposes a "difficulty hierarchy for the acquisition of second dialect features" (200). This nine-level hierarchy specifies several types of lifespan change, all of which appear at the less difficult, lower levels. The highest level is comprised of three feature types, with corresponding apparent critical periods: lexically unpredictable phonological rules (by age three), new phonological oppositions (by age three to thirteen), and new grammatical parameters (by age eight).

Kerswill's research brings clarity to the range of dialect features that may be transferable in contexts of dialect contact while acknowledging that different features may have different critical periods. For example, based on his findings from early (12–16 years) and late (17 years and older) adolescent migrants to Bergen, Kerswill (1996) suggested that the critical threshold for dialect acquisition – established by Chambers (1995) to be between 7 and 14 years – may need to be extended to 16 years, since this upper limit captures the period in life when there is a "heightened need for peer acceptance" (197).

The recognition that high motivation to acquire a second dialect in adolescence could push the boundaries of what is generally accepted as the sensitive period for second dialect/language acquisition, combined with the relative scarcity of investigations of language development in adulthood (de Bot 2007: 55), suggests that we may yet discover these upward limits could be extended. To do so, however, will not only require "understanding the balance between the biological and the social" as Sankoff (2018: 312) has recently advocated, but also consideration of the degree to which an understanding of 'the biological' is rapidly changing. Just over a decade ago, Siegel (2010) explained how Lenneberg's assumption that brain function localization was complete by puberty had been superseded by a focus on neural networks and the myelination process that begins before birth and extends at least one to two decades beyond: "[b]rain plasticity decreases as a result of myelination, and therefore learning (including language acquisition) becomes progressively more difficult" (98). More recently, research on brain neuroplasticity has taken a 'soft-wired' turn, as shown in a study of late L2 acquisition in young adults. Investigating a feature from the 'most difficult to acquire' level of Kerswill's (1996) hierarchy (namely, a new phonological opposition), which previous SDA research has shown could be successfully acquired between the ages of three and thirteen, Heidlmayr et al. (2021) found that "neuronal plasticity in the human brain allows for the late acquisition of even hard-wired linguistic features such as the discrimination of phonemic contrasts in a second language" (1). This would explain the ability of at least some learners in some contexts to acquire 'difficult' features after childhood.

Advances in neuroplasticity research enable us already to view past findings through new lenses. For example, given that brain plasticity is experience-dependent (de Bot 2019; Hayakawa & Marian 2019; Heidlmayr et al. 2021), and no two participants in any study are likely to have the same linguistic experiences, we should expect learners to exhibit varying degrees of success in acquiring a new variety. Therefore, rather than assume decreasing neuroplasticity as we age accounts for apparent age-specific limitations on acquisition, we can instead focus on which experiences and learning environments are necessary and sufficient for successful acquisition across the lifespan. Yaeger-Dror (1989: 145) summarized the necessary SDA conditions for children to acquire complex lexicon-dependent phonological rules. These include early exposure (before age eight), sufficient social network beyond the immediate family, and possibly even maternal influence. More recently, Nycz (2019) investigated the acquisition of a phoneme distinction by Canadian migrant spouses of local New Yorkers – an informative adult 'learning environment' that may otherwise have been missed using more traditional study recruitment/data collection methods.

Similarly informative research connecting experience and learning environment to dialect acquisition success is found in Stanford's (2008, 2014) work with the indigenous Sui people of Guizhou province in China. A society with clan exogamy, once married a wife moves to her husband's village. While she is expected to use only her 'outsider dialect' (*matrilect*), her children are expected to acquire and use only the local dialect (their *patrilect*). Language acquisition and dialect contact are compressed in both time and space, within the family and amid strict community norms regarding appropriate ways of speaking. The quality and quantity of input, however, is crucial to acquisition success. One young child, unlike the other children, mixes dialects. Stanford attributes this behavior to the child's *mother's* mobility among clans in *her* early childhood; she mixed clan dialects and passed on this way of speaking to her child.

All in all, SDA literature suggests that 'difficult to acquire' can apply to both first and second dialect/language acquisition, if necessary and sufficient acquisition conditions are not available to the learner. Recent research on neuroplasticity also suggests that acquisition is experience-dependent and more life-stage-*independent* than previously assumed. Given this emerging knowledge, there is considerable scope for lifelong acquisition research to continue to inform theories of dialect contact, variation and change into the future. Moreover, approaches that move beyond dialect or language boundaries to consider speakers' entire linguistic repertoires are well situated to benefit from this lifelong perspective, as examined in the next section.

3. The relevance of speakers' linguistic repertoires to dialect contact and change

Dialect contact, narrowly defined, involves speakers using structurally similar, mutually intelligible varieties of the same language in communication (e.g., Siegel 2010; Trudgill 1986). For many individuals, dialect contact takes this more circumscribed form. With multilingualism the norm rather than the exception (Andrews 2019; de Bot 2019), dialect contact settings are commonly also language contact settings at both the individual and group level. It is also well-established that most bilinguals have different levels of proficiency in each language (see Treffers-Daller 2019; Unsworth et al. 2018). Robust patterns of crosslinguistic transfer, often difficult to detect when speakers' linguistic dominance profiles are not considered (see Arnal 2011; Winford 2020), indicate not all linguistic elements are equally susceptible to transfer depending on the types of speakers involved. The discussion in this section adopts a whole-of-linguistic-repertoire focus to contact, variation and change in lifelong acquisition. After a brief overview of a speaker-centred model of contact, findings from recent acquisition research supporting the model's core components are discussed before considering what is gained by 'looking both ways' – that is, at both the weaker *and* the stronger language varieties of bilinguals in the study of dialect contact and change.

Before proceeding further, we must make explicit that the *dialect* versus *language* contact distinction is not straightforward, either theoretically or practically. For instance, while discussing the case of Spanish in the US, a clear setting where language contact (Spanish-English) overlaps with dialect contact (among varieties of Spanish), Schmid and Köpke (2017:652) question this separation: "[c]an we really consider exposure to two different dialects of the same language as something that is qualitatively distinct from exposure to two different languages (and where do two varieties cease to be dialects of each other and begin to be different languages)?" Focusing solely on dialect contact in multilingual contexts – on only part of bilingual or multilingual speakers' repertoires – will render an incomplete picture of the linguistic and social dynamics of these settings. This limitation is also clear in contexts involving contact across lexically and structurally similar repertoires (e.g., in a European context, Dutch and German, Spanish and Catalan, or Russian and Ukrainian) where language borders are often politically determined. Ecological approaches to language change (Clements 2018; Mufwene 2008) have pointed out the limitations inherent to the traditional *language* vs. *dialect* divide, and further support the need for approaches to contact and change that seek to move beyond it (for a similar argument from a historical sociolinguistic perspective, see Sanz-Sánchez & Tejedo-Herrero 2021).

Van Coetsem's (1988, 2000) influential model of language contact is not alone in recognizing the fundamental importance of the interplay between the linguistic and social elements of a given contact situation. It is distinguished, however, by its psycholinguistic understanding of speaker agency and the dynamic nature of linguistic repertoire expansion and contraction as its point of departure (see Winford 2020 for a critical overview of language contact theories). While each contact situation minimally involves a source language (SL) and a recipient language (RL), it is the nature of speakers' linguistic repertoires, shaped by their social experiences, which dictates whether transfer from the SL to the RL will involve more stable domains of linguistic structure (particularly phonological, but also morpho-syntactic and semantic structure) or less stable ones (e.g., the lexicon). In a process known as *source-language agentivity* or *imposition transfer*, speakers dominant in the SL *impose* more stable structural elements onto the RL.[2] By contrast, speakers who are dominant in the RL *borrow* less stable elements from the SL via *recipient-language agentivity* or *borrowing transfer* (see Van Coetsem 1988: 7–23, 2000: 51–62). These processes capture the fact that speakers rely on the variety they know best in communication, which accounts for their contrasting qualities. As Howell (1993) explains, recipient-language agentivity "typically represents a conscious introduction of a non-native element" (190) into a speaker's stronger language and is more "unpredictable" and "idiosyncratic" (198), whereas source-language agentivity "is systematic" (191) and "represents an unconscious application of structural imperatives" (190) of a speaker's stronger language when communicating in the weaker language. Importantly, the model does not assume the first language or dialect acquired will remain the strongest across the lifespan. Instead, it allows for a speaker's dominant variety (L1, L2, D1,

---

[2]. See Chapter 11 in this volume for an example of the imposition of a semantic pattern on the RL via the agency of SL-dominant adult speakers.

D2...) to shift in response to their changing social circumstances and recognizes as well that speakers' language dominance may vary depending on, for example, domains of use (see Chapter 2 in this volume).

A core component of Van Coetsem's model – the role of language dominance in crosslinguistic transfer – has attracted increasing interest in acquisition research. Unsworth et al., for example, refer to the "broad consensus that bilingual children, even if exposed to both languages from birth, are more proficient or dominant in one of their two languages" (2018: 2; see also Hamann et al. 2019). How best to operationalize language dominance in bilingual studies is a source of ongoing discussion. Recent evidence suggests that patterns of language use, as opposed to the amount of language exposure, are more reliable indicators of proficiency and language dominance (Treffers-Daller 2019; Unsworth et al. 2018), and that dominance, not age, is a significant factor accounting for crosslinguistic transfer (Andrews 2019: 35; Bosch & Unsworth 2021: 811).

More frequent language use as a proxy for language dominance also aligns with a growing number of experimental studies of adults and children showing crosslinguistic structural priming effects from the dominant to the non-dominant language (Filopović 2019; Koostra & Doedens 2016; Schmid & Köpke 2017; Treffers-Daller 2019; Van Gompel & Arai 2018). An oft-cited example of structural priming as well as crosslinguistic transfer involves bilinguals who speak English, a non-null subject language, and a null subject language such as Greek, Spanish, or Tamil. Bilinguals dominant in the non-null subject language will overuse overt pronouns in contexts typically requiring the null subject in their non-dominant language (see Otheguy et al. 2007: 795; Treffers-Daller 2019: 377; Van Rijswijk 2016: 35). Crosslinguistic structural priming in these instances may be facilitated by the fact that subject pronoun expression differs only with respect to the rates of occurrence and linguistic constraints.

In an experimental study using a feature (constituent order in noun-adjective combinations) which differs between the two languages, however, Hsin et al. (2013) have also demonstrated that it is possible to prime ungrammatical utterances in young Spanish/English bilinguals. Bosch and Unsworth (2021) similarly report that surface overlap is not essential for crosslinguistic transfer to occur and "[a]s a result, the interaction between two languages may cause bilinguals to produce qualitatively different structures which monolinguals would never produce" (786). One possible explanation for structural priming effects in studies involving dominant (as opposed to balanced) bilinguals may be connected to the process of language acquisition itself as "[b]ilinguals reuse as much of the syntax of their L1 as possible when learning and using an L2" (Filopović 2019: 43). Such intermediate forms can be accounted for by the fact that linguistic systems do not exist in isolation in the bilingual/bidialectal mind (see Hsin et al. 2013; Putnam et al. 2017; Schmid & Köpke 2017; Filopović 2019; Treffers-Daller 2019).[3]

The importance of language dominance in analysing crosslinguistic influences supports many acquisition researchers' plea to consider bilingual (and bidialectal) speakers' entire linguistic repertoire (see historical review in Treffers-Daller 2019: 377). The difference now is an increasing awareness among linguists of the need to provide *"empirically valid proficiency data"* rather than relying on study participants' self-assessments (Andrews 2019: 22, emphasis in the original), and to recognize that speakers' linguistic repertoires remain dynamic across the lifespan (see Section 2). If patterns of language use are reliable indicators of language dominance, as argued by Bosch and Unsworth (2021) among others, the reasons for language dominance shift can be found in shifting patterns of language use, where "[d]epending on changing [social/individual] circumstances […], the L2 may 'replace' the L1 as the dominant language. In some cases, and for similar reasons, the L1 may return to dominance" (Birdsong 2018: 11; see also Verspoor et al. 2009).

A recent, unidirectional experimental study of crosslinguistic structural priming demonstrates the role that shifting patterns of language use plays in crosslinguistic transfer. Using a language pair with strongly different syntactic preferences, Koostra and Şahin (2018) conducted two experiments involving Papiamento/Dutch bilinguals in Aruba and the Netherlands, respectively. Those living in Aruba were considered 'low-contact variety' bilinguals ("Dutch [used] only in formal settings" (907)) while those living in the Netherlands were deemed high-contact bilinguals ("Dutch [used] regularly in their daily lives" (907)). In their baseline experiment, Koostra and Şahin documented clear differences in the two groups' syntactic preferences for dative constructions in Papiamento; high contact speakers used more Dutch-like structures. Since the younger study participants in the Netherlands used Dutch as their language of communication more often than the older participants, in their second experiment – the Dutch to Papiamento priming task – the authors aimed to simulate the effects of increased language use, finding that "exposure to Dutch sentences can indeed influence syntactic choices in Papiamento" (918). Again, this priming effect was greatest for the younger speakers in the Netherlands who *used* Dutch more than the older study participants.[4]

Van Coetsem's agentivity/transfer types are operative within each individual whenever the acquisition of more than one linguistic variety commences. To be

---

3. For an example of how L1 transfer and L2 learning can simultaneously contribute to the emergence of a new form in a contact setting, see Chapter 12 in this volume.

4. See Chapter 5 in this volume for further discussion of the role of crosslinguistic priming and activation in contact situations.

able to observe both agentivity types, however, we must be able to observe bilingual speakers' use of *both* their weaker and stronger languages. It matters to our understanding of dialect contact and change what types of speakers we observe/obtain data from in linguistically diverse research contexts, just as it matters that we allow for the possibility that crosslinguistic transfer may occur in contexts of dialect contact, which are frequently contexts of language contact, if speakers in these contexts experience a shift in linguistic dominance (see Chapter 10 in this volume).

Moving beyond the dialect/language distinction also allows the similarities in contact-induced 'variety change' to become more apparent. As mentioned in the beginning of this section, not all linguistic elements are equally susceptible to crosslinguistic transfer in a contact situation, and in both dialect and language contact research, the same patterns of transfer emerge. For instance, in their study of bidirectional transfer in Russian/English adult bilinguals who had migrated to the United States as teenagers or young adults, Pavlenko and Jarvis (2002) observe that: "adult L2 users are likely to exhibit L1 transfer in essentially all language areas, while L2 influence on L1 is most likely to appear first in the form of lexical borrowings and semantic extension" (199). Kerswill's SDA difficulty hierarchy (see Section 2) likewise captures the fact that certain structural elements are more easily transferred ('acquired') than others: "borrowings are the easiest to acquire, while lexically unpredictable phonological changes are the most difficult" (1996: 177). Viewed from an RL-dominant perspective, the most difficult to acquire features on Kerswill's hierarchy are those from the most stable domains of linguistic structure, whereas the least difficult features lower down involve subtypes of lexical transfer. In a dialect contact study of Japanese adult migrants to Hawai'i, Hiramoto (2010) adopts an RL-dominant perspective, finding additional "support [for] current acquisition studies" that "adult speakers acquire lexically-bound features more easily than phonological features" (229). For instance, speakers dominant in the Tôhoku dialect adopt the lexical forms of the first-person singular pronouns of Standard Japanese or the Chûgoku dialect, but impose their D1 phonological rules on these lexical forms, yielding innovative, intermediate forms, often documented in contexts of dialect contact and koine formation (see Kerswill 2010; Solheim 2009), and SLA (see above in this section). This line of research illustrates the applicability of agentivity-based L2 acquisition models to the study of dialect contact settings.

To summarize, the study of dialect contact situations will benefit from transcending the traditional dialect/language divide, from an increased awareness of the need to collect bidirectional data, and from recognizing the role that linguistic dominance plays in patterns of transfer. New analyses must also acknowledge that linguistic dominance can shift across the lifespan in response to changes in speakers' social environments. For historical sociolinguists, the question becomes how to incorporate this perspective given the generalized lack of acquisitional data in the historical record. In what follows, I apply these insights to a sociohistorical case: the impact of demographic changes on the linguistic repertoires of individuals caught up in the late sixteenth-century mass exodus from Antwerp.

4. Lifelong acquisition, contact and change: The case of /f/ and /v/ in Early Modern Dutch

In 1980, then Princess Beatrix of the Netherlands gave an interview during which she pronounced 95% (151 tokens) of her word-initial labiodental fricatives as voiceless [f] and just 5% (eight tokens) as voiced [v]; her use of word-initial alveolar fricatives, however, had nearly the opposite distribution: approximately 94% (149 tokens) were voiced [z] and 6% (ten tokens) were voiceless [s] (Gussenhoven & Bremmer 1983: 57, 59). Voicing contrasts in fricatives are considered a main feature distinguishing varieties of standard Dutch spoken in Flanders and those spoken in the Netherlands (Gussenhoven & Bremmer 1983; Kissine et al. 2003; Van de Velde et al. 1996). In a study including labiodental fricatives, Pinget et al. (2020) find the least voicing in Groningen (Netherlands) participants and the most in West Flemish participants, with individuals from the regions between these north/south extremes holding an "intermediate position" in this "rapidly advancing change in progress" towards devoicing (665). Described over two decades earlier as "a hot issue in the linguistic history of Dutch" (Van de Velde et al. 1996: 156), dialectologist Weijnen (1966) found only sketchy details in an 1895 language atlas (*Taalatlas van Noord- en Zuid-Nederland*): [f] is documented for the word *vis* 'fish' in Amsterdam and three other places within the greater Amsterdam region (Osdorp, Sloten and Hoofddorp) (177). The spelling <f> for word-initial /v/, however, already appears in 17th-century Amsterdam farces (Gussenhoven & Bremmer 1983: 56).

While the history of this sound change awaits detailed examination, 17th-century Amsterdam is, in fact, a plausible place to begin an investigation. A relatively modest city of 30,000 inhabitants in 1550, by 1600 it had more than doubled in size to 65,000 and by 1650 nearly trebled in size to 175,000 (De Vries 1984). This migration-fueled population explosion included many thousands of newcomers from across the West Germanic dialect continuum and beyond, among whom were Protestant Antwerp residents forced to leave the city after the Fall of Antwerp to Spanish forces in 1585. The Amsterdam marriage registers for the period 1578–1650 reveal that nearly 60% of migrants who married in Amsterdam hailed from German territories (Knotter 1995). This is noteworthy since "[a]ll of the GMC [Germanic] languages have /f/, but they do not all have a lenis labial fricative, /β/ or /v/" (Harbert 2007: 45). In the oldest sources of Dutch from southern Flanders, West Germanic reflexes of /f/ became voiced in non-final positions e.g., Middle Dutch *velt* 'field', *vloec* 'curse' (Gussenhoven & Bremmer 1983: 56). Thus, present-day descriptions of this sound change refer either to a *devoicing* of /v/ to account for the northern (i.e., Netherlands Dutch) usage (see Van de Velde et al. 1996), while others characterize the northern usage as a *failure* of a voicing rule to apply where it had in the south (i.e., Flanders) (Gussenhoven & Bremmer 1983). As for German, a change was also underway but in the opposite direction: Middle High German /v/ had merged with /f/ (Salmons 2012: 189), and except for a dozen or so words (e.g., *von* 'from' or *Vater* 'father'), the use of <f> reflecting the loss of the voicing distinction displaces <v> from this point onward.

At the risk of oversimplifying this complex contact situation, the sociodemographic changes taking place in early 17th-century Amsterdam *minimally* would have brought thousands of speakers with /f/ (those who spoke varieties of German) into contact with thousands of speakers with /v/ (e.g., those fleeing northward from Antwerp, among other Dutch speakers). One way to account for the presence of /f/ in 17th-century Amsterdam is to focus on the types of language users relevant to that context of contact. German-dominant speakers, for example, likely imposed their voiceless labiodental fricative onto Dutch in the process of acquiring the language of wider communication in their adopted community. Textual evidence to support this hypothesis would be difficult to come by, not only because it would involve the preservation of documents from German-dominant speakers writing in Dutch, but also because it would require these individuals to ignore the Dutch orthographic tradition of using <v> to represent /v/ except in loanwords (e.g., the French loan <fraai> 'beautiful' or the German loan <fris> 'fresh') (see Van Loey 1970: 57). But this type of phonemic substitution is so well-attested in both the language and dialect acquisition literature that the absence of textual documentation does not undermine its plausibility. Incorporating the speakers' entire linguistic repertoires (see Section 3) to understanding the presence of /f/ in Amsterdam in this period, however, offers another potential source of transfer: speakers of Dutch who spent years, if not decades, as Protestant exiles living in German-speaking territories may have experienced a shift in linguistic dominance, in turn facilitating the transfer of structural elements from their L2 German into their L1 Dutch.

Fortunately, sociohistorical evidence from such speakers is extant. Drawing on a 120,000-word corpus of 253 private letters spanning three and a half decades (1583–1618), Hendriks (2018) documents the language use of the members of two Antwerp merchant families who had lived for years in German-speaking territories prior to resettling in the northern Netherlands. While the Van Der Meulen family correspondence shows no discernible effects of these years in exile, structural transfer from German is evident in the De Baccher/Thijs family correspondence. Specifically, variation in <f> and <v> (139) lends additional support to the claim that regular use of their non-native language German could lead to structural transfer into their L1 Dutch. Moreover, given the age of many of the family members, changes in their linguistic repertoires must have occurred well into adulthood. In their correspondence with one another, family members Magdalena Thijs, the second wife of Andreas de Baccher and stepmother to Hedewig, Philip and Anna Doretea, and Magdalena's brother, Francoys Thijs, who was also married to Hedewig, all use <f> in variation with <v> in Dutch words beginning with labiodental fricatives. Certain examples from their correspondence, such as <fader> 'father' and <fan> 'from', are particularly informative. As mentioned above, these are among the few words in German that continued to be spelled with <v> after the merger of /f/ and /v/ in the Middle High German period. Therefore, the De Baccher/Thijs family members' use of <f> in these instances overrides both German *and* Dutch orthographic traditions. Equally significant is Magdalena's abrupt switch in 1599 from categorical use of <v> to categorical use of <f> in her letters – the textual equivalent of a German-dominant speaker's systematic substitution of a native phoneme, /f/, for non-native /v/ while communicating in the non-dominant language Dutch.

The use of <f> in the De Baccher/Thijs family correspondence emerges while they are living in German territories and continues long after they had migrated on to Amsterdam and other Dutch cities (Leiden, Utrecht). Again, Magdalena's writings spanning three decades of her adult life prove highly informative. In her letters from 1599 to 1610, Magdalena uses only <f>. However, in a memorandum book covering the years 1614–1622 (Bibliotheca Thysiana 655), her categorical use of <f> ceases at an inflection point in her life: her husband, Andreas, had passed away in 1616. Estranged from her stepsons Samuel and Philip, Magdalena had remarried and become reintegrated into the 'southern Dutch/Antwerp' migrant community in Leiden in 1617. At this point in her memorandum book, we observe her *variable* use of <f> and <v>.

Reconstructing a plausible historical account for the emergence of /f/ in 17th-century Amsterdam requires a nuanced understanding of the dynamic sociodemographic context. The complex language/dialect contact situation that obtained in the first half of the 1600s involved tens of thousands of speakers of varieties with /f/ – both those who remained L1-dominant in their '/f/ varieties' and those, like the multilingual De Baccher/Thijs family members, whose L1 had become influenced by their regular use of an '/f/ variety' (in their case, German). The sociodemographic details in combination with robust acquisition research findings support a scenario whereby the voiceless labiodental fricative would have been a common 'accent' feature heard over the course of decades in this highly heterogenous, rapidly expanding city. Its frequency of use and persistence to the present day can be attributed to koinéization processes set in motion by extensive dialect (and language) contact (see Howell 2006 and references cited therein). Linguistic evidence for the presence of /f/ in 17th-century Amsterdam manuscript sources may, however, be difficult to find, not because the change did not happen (it did), and not *only* due to the fragmented historical record. A language acquisition-informed approach makes clear that the types of speakers responsible for introducing the change would need to be speaking and writing in their non-dominant language – in this case Dutch, as opposed to, say, German or Frisian – and while this context of contact predates the emergence of a standard orthography, they would nevertheless need to ignore common Dutch orthographic conventions as well. The fact that several members of a prominent Antwerp family, exiled for years in German-speaking territories, continued to write in their (possibly non-dominant) L1 Dutch, while ignoring both Dutch as well as German orthographic traditions in their use of <f> for <v>, provides solid linguistic evidence supporting the account proposed here, and for the fundamental role that lifelong acquisition in dialect contact and change may play.

5. Acquisition across the lifespan and the historical sociolinguistics of dialect contact and change: Challenges and opportunities

A primary challenge for those seeking to understand historical instances of contact, variation and change is that the fragmented, randomly preserved record often offers little or no metalinguistic information about those who have left meager clues to the linguistic past. In our efforts to compile linguistic corpora – our 'data grabs' – we dip into the lives of language users, but rarely know how linguistically (in)significant those moments may have been for them, let alone which aspects of individual life narratives we have captured in the data collection process. Adopting an acquisition across the lifespan perspective in the sociohistorical study of dialect contact, variation and change might therefore appear *too* challenging, as if contending with 'bad data' were not difficult enough. And yet we could approach this challenge differently by acknowledging that bad data, in the sense of not knowing enough about the 'study participants', is a challenge felt by many linguists regardless of subdiscipline.

Andrews (2019), for example, criticizes research on language and the multilingual brain for the failure to assess study participants' linguistic proficiency. Likewise, research into the fundamental role that language dominance plays in understanding crosslinguistic influences (Section 3) also shows that we cannot make assumptions about bilingual (and bidialectal) speakers' linguistic dominance profiles based on, say, the order or age of acquisition, or research contexts that seem to represent long-term language maintenance. Linguistic dominance shift occurs both in contexts of language maintenance and language shift. Again, empirically valid measures of linguistic proficiency, not to mention a whole-of-linguistic repertoire approach, are needed to assess study participants, yet often these fundamental metalinguistic details are missing.

6. Conclusion

Understanding what the linguistic data can or cannot tell us because we cannot be certain what types of speakers have produced it remains a discipline-wide challenge, experienced most keenly perhaps by (socio)historical linguists. As argued for throughout this chapter, adopting an acquisition across the lifespan perspective in sociohistorical investigations of dialect contact and change, however, can offer new opportunities to address this seemingly intractable problem. While sociohistorical linguists have no control over what has been preserved from the past, we can apply insights from acquisition research to help us understand how the historical data may be biased towards a certain type of language user, for example, and how other types of language user might be absent from the historical record altogether.

The recognition, too, that we are experiential learners and that our life experiences shape our linguistic repertoires across the lifespan, throws the research context and types of speakers studied (i.e., monolingual, bilingual, L1 dominant, L2 dominant, etc.) into sharp relief, also for historical situations. As the call for more longitudinal research at both the individual and group level is heeded, our understanding of how speakers' life experiences shape their linguistic repertoires across the lifespan will provide ongoing opportunities for sociohistorical linguists to deepen our understanding of the linguistic past. The case study chapters in this volume propose strategies to utilize our knowledge of these dynamic acquisitional trajectories at the individual level to understand the sociolinguistic history of specific language varieties.

References

Manuscript sources

Bibliotheca Thysiana 655. *Memoriaal van Magdalena Thijs, 1614–1622*. Bijzondere Collecties, Universiteitsbibliotheek Leiden.

Secondary sources

Andrews, Edna. 2019. Cognitive neuroscience and multilingualism. In John Schwieter (ed.), *The handbook of the neuroscience of multilingualism*, 21–47. Hoboken, NJ: John Wiley & Sons.

Arnal, Antoni. 2011. Linguistic changes in the Catalan spoken in Catalonia under new contact conditions. *Journal of Language Contact* 4(1). 5–25.

Birdsong, David. 2018. Plasticity, variability and age in second language acquisition and bilingualism. *Frontiers in Psychology* 9. 1–17.

Bosch, Jasmijn & Sharon Unsworth. 2021. Cross-linguistic influences in word order. Effects of age, dominance and surface overlap. *Linguistic Approaches to Bilingualism* 11(6). 783–816.

Bot, Kees de. 2007. One theory for acquisition and attrition? *Linguistic Approaches to Bilingualism* 7(6). 678–681.

Bot, Kees de. 2019. Defining and assessing multilingualism. In John Schwieter (ed.), *The handbook of the neuroscience of multilingualism*, 3–18. Hoboken, NJ: John Wiley & Sons.

Chambers, Jack K. 1992. Dialect acquisition. *Language* 68(4). 673–705.

Chambers, Jack K. 1995. *Sociolinguistic theory*. Oxford: Blackwell.

Clements, J. Clancy. 2018. Speech communities, language varieties, and typology: What does acquisition have to do with it? *Journal of Pidgin and Creole Languages* 33(2). 413–414.

Coetsem, Frans van. 1988. *Loan phonology and the two transfer types in language contact*. Dordrecht: Foris Publications.

Coetsem, Frans van. 2000. *A general and unified theory of the transmission process in language contact*. Heidelberg: Winter.

Eckert, Penelope. 1997. Age as a sociolinguistic variable. In Florian Coulmas (ed.), *The handbook of sociolinguistics*, 151–167. Oxford: Blackwell.

Filipović, Luna. 2019. *Bilingualism in action: theory and practice*. Cambridge: Cambridge University Press.

Giles, Howard. 1980. Accommodation theory: Some new directions. *York Papers in Linguistics* 9. 105–136.

Gompel, Roger van & Manabu Arai. 2018. Structural priming in bilinguals. *Bilingualism: Language and Cognition* 21(3). 448–455.

Gregersen, Frans, Marie Maegaard & Nicolai Pharao. 2009. The long and short of (æ)-variation in Danish – a panel study of short (æ)-variants in Danish in real time. *Acta Linguistica Hafniensia* 41. 64–82.

Gussenhoven, Carlos & Rolf Bremmer. 1983. Voiced fricatives in Dutch: Sources and present-day usage. *North-Western European Language Evolution* 2. 55–71.

Hamann, Cornelia, Esther Rinke & Dobrinka Genevska-Hanke. 2019. Editorial: Bilingual development: The role of dominance. *Frontiers in Psychology* 10. 1–3.

Harbert, Wayne. 2007. *The Germanic languages*. Cambridge: Cambridge University Press.

Hayakawa, Sayuri & Viorica Marian. 2019. Consequences of multilingualism for neural architecture. *Behavioral and Brain Functions* 15(6). 1–24.

Heidlmayr, Karin, Emmanual Ferrange & Frédéric Isel. 2021. Neuroplasticity in the phonological system: The PMN and the N400 as markers for the perception of non-native phonemic contrasts by late second language learners. *Neuropsychologia* 156. 1–15.

Hendriks, Jennifer. 2018. The effects of complex migration trajectories on individual linguistic repertoires in the Early Modern Dutch urban context. *Neuphilologische Mitteilungen* 119(1). 121–144.

Hiramoto, Mie. 2010. Dialect contact and change of the northern Japanese plantation immigrants in Hawai'i. *Journal of Pidgin and Creole Languages* 25(2). 229–262.

Howell, Robert B. 1993. German immigration and the development of regional variants of American English: Using contact theory to discover our roots. In Joseph Salmons (ed.), *The German language in America*, 190–212. Madison, WI: Max Kade Institute.

Howell, Robert B. 2006. Immigration and koineization: the formation of Early Modern Dutch urban vernaculars. *Transactions of the Philological Society* 104. 207–227.

Hsin, Lisa, Géraldine Legendre & Akira Omaki. 2013. Priming cross-linguistic interference in Spanish–English bilingual children. In Sarah Baiz, Nora Goldman & Rachel Hawkes (eds.), *Proceedings of the 37th annual Boston University Conference on Language Development*, 165–177. Somerville, MA: Cascadilla.

Kerswill, Paul. 1996. Children, adolescents, and language change. *Language Variation and Change* 8. 177–202.

Kerswill, Paul. 2010. Contact and new varieties. In Raymond Hickey (ed.), *The handbook of language contact*, 230–251. Malden, MA: Wiley-Blackwell.

Kissine, Mikhail, Hans Van de Velde & Roeland van Hout. 2003. An acoustic study of standard Dutch /v/, /f/, /z/ and /s/. *Linguistics in the Netherlands* 20(1). 93–104.

Knotter, Ad. 1995. Vreemdelingen in Amsterdam in de 17e eeuw: groepsvorming, arbeid en ondernemerschap. *Historisch Tijdschrift Holland* 27. 219–235.

Koostra, Gerrit Jan & Willemijn J. Doedens. 2016. How multiple sources of experience influence bilingual syntactic choice: Immediate and cumulative cross-language effects of structural priming, verb bias, and language dominance. *Bilingualism: Language and Cognition* 19(4). 710–732.

Koostra, Gerrit Jan & Hülya Şahin. 2018. Crosslinguistic structural priming as a mechanism of contact-induced language change: Evidence from Papiamento-Dutch bilinguals in Aruba and the Netherlands. *Language* 94(4). 902–930.

Lenneberg, Eric. 1967. *Biological foundations of language*. New York: John Wiley & Sons.

Loey, Adolphe van. 1970. *Schönfelds Historische Grammatica van het Nederlands*. Zutphen: N.V. W. J. Thieme & Cie.

Mufwene, Salikoko. 2008. *Language evolution: Contact, competition, and change*. London: Continuum.

Nahkola, Kari & Maria Saanilahti. 2004. Mapping changes in real time: A panel study on Finnish. *Language Variation and Change* 16. 75–92.

Nycz, Jennifer. 2015. Second dialect acquisition: A sociophonetic perspective. *Language and Linguistics Compass* 9(11). 469–482.

Nycz, Jennifer. 2019. Linguistic and social factors favoring acquisition of contrast in a new dialect. In Sasha Calhoun, Paola Escudero, Marija Tabain & Paul Warren (eds.), *Proceedings of the 19th International Congress of Phonetic Sciences*, 1480–1484. Canberra, Australia: Australasian Speech Science and Technology Association.

Otheguy, Ricardo, Ana Celia Zentella & David Livert. 2007. Language and dialect contact in Spanish in New York: Toward the formation of a speech community. *Language* 83(4). 770–802.

Pavlenko, Anna & Scott Jarvis. 2002. Bidirectional transfer. *Applied Linguistics* 23(2). 190–214.

Pinget, Anne-France, René Kager & Hans Van de Velde. 2020. Linking variation in perception and production in sound change: Evidence from Dutch obstruent devoicing. *Language and Speech* 63(3). 660–685.

Putnam, Michael T., Tanja Kupisch & Diego Pascual y Cabo. 2017. Different situations, similar outcomes. Heritage grammars across the lifespan. In David Miller, Fatih Bayram, Jason Rothman & Ludovica Serratrice (eds.), *Bilingual cognition and language: The state of the science across its subfields*, 251–279. Amsterdam: John Benjamins.

Rijswijk, Remy van. 2016. *The strength of the weaker first language. Language production and comprehension by Turkish heritage speakers in the Netherlands*. Utrecht: LOT.

Salmons, Joseph. 2012. *A history of German. What the past reveals about today's language*. Oxford: Oxford University Press.

Sankoff, Gillian. 2005. Cross-sectional and longitudinal studies in sociolinguistics. In Ulrich Ammon, Norbert Dittmar, Klaus J. Mattheier, and Peter Trudgill (eds.), *An international handbook of the science of language and society*. Volume 2, 1003–1013. Berlin: De Gruyter Mouton.

Sankoff, Gillian. 2018. Language change across the lifespan. *Annual Review of Linguistics* 4. 297–316.

Sankoff, Gillian. 2019. Language change across the lifespan: three trajectory types. *Language* 95(2). 197–229.

Sankoff, Gillian & Hélène Blondeau. 2007. Language change across the lifespan: /r/ in Montreal French. *Language* 83(3). 560–588.

Sanz-Sánchez, Israel & Fernando Tejedo-Herrero. 2021. Adult language and dialect learning as simultaneous environmental triggers for language change. In Whitney Chappell & Bridget Drinka (eds.), *Spanish socio-historical linguistics: Isolation and contact*, 104–137. Amsterdam: John Benjamins.

Schmid, Monika. & Barbara Köpke. 2017. The relevance of first language attrition to theories of bilingual development. *Linguistic Approaches to Bilingualism* 7(6). 637–667.

Shockey, Linda. 1984. All in a flap: long-term accommodation in phonology. *International Journal of the Sociology of Language* 46. 87–96.

Siegel, Jeff. 2010. *Second dialect acquisition*. Cambridge: Cambridge University Press.

Solheim, Randi. 2009. Dialect development in a melting pot: The formation of a new culture and a new dialect in the industrial town of Høyanger. *Nordic Journal of Linguistics* 32(2). 191–206.

Stanford, James. 2008. Child dialect acquisition: New perspectives on parent/peer influence. *Journal of Sociolinguistics* 12(5). 567–596.

Stanford, James N. 2014. Language acquisition and language change. In Claire Bowern & Bethwyn Evans (eds.), *The Routledge handbook of historical linguistics*, 466–483. London & New York: Routledge.

Tagliamonte, Sali & Sonja Molfenter. 2007. How'd you get that accent?: Acquiring a second dialect of the same language. *Language in Society* 36. 649–675.

Treffers-Daller, Jeanine. 2019. What defines language dominance in bilinguals? *Annual Review of Linguistics* 5. 375–393.

Trudgill, Peter. 1986. *Dialects in contact*. Oxford: Blackwell.

Unsworth, Sharon, Vicky Chondrogianni & Barbora Skarabela. 2018. Experiential measures can be used as a proxy for language dominance in bilingual language acquisition research. *Frontiers in Psychology* 9. 1–15.

Van de Velde, Hans, Marinel Gerritsen & Roeland van Hout. 1996. The devoicing of fricatives in standard Dutch: A real-time study based on radio recordings. *Language Variation and Change* 8. 149–175.

Verspoor, Marjolijn, Wander Lowie & Kees de Bot. 2009. Input and second language development from a dynamic perspective. In Thorsten Piske & Martha Young-Scholten (eds.), *Input matters in SLA*, 62–81. Bristol, UK: Multilingual Matters.

Vries, Jan de. 1984. *European urbanization, 1500–1800*. Harvard, MA.: Harvard University Press.

Weijnen, Antonius A. 1966. *Nederlandse Dialectkunde*. 2nd ed. Assen: Van Gorcum.

Winford, Donald. 2020. Theories of language contact. In Anthony Grant (ed.), *The Oxford handbook of language contact*, 51–74. Oxford: Oxford University Press.

Yaeger-Dror, Malcah. 1989. Realtime versus apparent time change in Montreal French. *York Papers in Linguistics* 13. 141–153.

CHAPTER 5

Multilingual acquisition across the lifespan as a sociohistorical trigger for language change

Suzanne Aalberse
University of Amsterdam

Language contact implies more variation in language use, both in the individual and in the community. This increased variation can accelerate language change, but it can also halt it (Aalberse et al. 2019; Muysken 2013). Which parts of language do change, and which parts do not depends on cognitive and social factors: the change or non-change should be cognitively possible and socially acceptable. What is cognitively possible or cognitively likely partly depends on the age of the language user. What is socially desirable is also partly dependent on age. This chapter provides an overview of bilingual speaker optimization strategies inspired by Muysken (2013), relating preferences for a type of strategy to life stages. The chapter ends with a discussion on the challenges and opportunities of combining the lifespan acquisition perspective with the historical sociolinguistics of language contact.

Keywords: language contact, bilingual optimization strategies, acquisition across the lifespan, AoA (age of onset of acquisition), language change, language stability, cognitive factors, social factors

1. Introduction: Language contact outcomes as the result of bilingual optimization strategies

The central question of this chapter is whether language development can be affected by language contact and whether the age of onset of bilingualism matters in this development. The chapter explores how age interfaces with social factors, such as demography and communication patterns, to determine whether and how these individual developmental trajectories impact community grammars (see also Chapters 4 and 6 in this volume). I present an overview of types of contact-induced changes that research has related to age effects. I combine differ-

https://doi.org/10.1075/ahs.14.05aal
© 2024 John Benjamins Publishing Company

ent research traditions, such as language contact studies and language acquisition studies, from different theoretical perspectives ranging from usage-based theories to generative analyses. I present these different strands of research via the lens of the *bilingual optimization model* as articulated in Muysken (2013). This model is especially suitable for the present chapter because of two reasons: it aims at finding a unified account for different research traditions in language contact and bilingualism studies and it gives attention to cognitive, linguistic, and social factors. The model interprets outcomes of language contact and bilingualism via the lens of *bilingual optimization strategies*. It also supplements the research on bilingual acquisition of variation by children and adults outlined in Chapters 2 and 3, respectively, and helps to bridge differences in outcomes from different research traditions in seemingly similar situations by looking at how a specific mix of cognitive, linguistic, and social factors makes a certain outcome most likely.

The notion of optimization strategies is inspired by optimality theory. The idea underlying optimality theory is that language processing and production are forms of optimization. There is not one perfect outcome, but depending on the way social, cognitive, and linguistic factors interact a certain outcome becomes more likely. Language users can select various forms to convey a certain meaning, and the form they select is the one that best satisfies a set of ranked constraints. Constraints can include linguistic biases like 'be faithful to grammatical structure X', interactional biases like 'be explicit' and 'be transparent', cognitive biases like 'reduce processing load', and social biases like 'mark heritage identity'. Depending on the ranking of various constraints, a certain bilingual optimization strategy emerges as optimal in each situation.

Muysken (2013) distinguishes four distinct, if not always clearly separable bilingual optimization strategies in language contact situations, namely: (1) rely on universal principles of communication (UP); (2) rely on the first language (L1); (3) rely on the second language (L2); or (4) rely on both languages (L1/L2). He connects the relative likelihood of occurrence of each strategy to the typological differences between the languages in contact and to the sociolinguistics of the contact scenario, that is, the specification of the circumstances under which contact takes place. Factors like language prestige, numbers of language users per language, the length of contact and the level of shared bilingualism, among other factors, play a role in the selection of the optimal strategy. This chapter is inspired by these strategies, but they have been regrouped somewhat to fit the focus of the chapter on the role of age in acquisition. Table 1 presents an overview of the strategies in Muysken (2013) and the adaptation made for this chapter. I explain the adaptations below.

Table 1. Bilingual optimization strategies in Muysken (2013) and their counterparts in this chapter

Strategy in Muysken (2013)	Basic mechanism	Equivalent in this chapter	Process
UP	Improvised language based on universal principles of communication	Rely on one language	Reduction in form in the L1 or the L2 as the result of improvised language
L1	Stability or interference	Rely on one language	If the target language is the L1 and the speaker relies on the L1
		Rely on two languages	If the target language is the L2 and the speaker relies on parts of the L1
L2	Stability or interference	Rely on one language	If the target language is the L2 and the speaker relies on the L2
		Rely on two languages	If the target language is the L1 and the speaker relies on the L2
L1/L2	Congruence	Rely on two languages	The speaker chooses those forms that increase overlap between the two languages

As can be seen in Table 1, I distinguish between two strategies, namely (1) *rely on one language* and (2) *rely on more languages*, rather than the four strategies presented by Muysken (2013). The most substantial change to the original set of strategies as proposed by Muysken is the absence of the UP category ('universal principles of communication'). Muysken uses the UP strategy to refer to strategies of improvised language. This strategy is typical for situations where language users have no or little commonalities in their linguistic repertoire. Examples of UP-strategies include the use of topic-comment sequences narrating events in the order they occurred, and simplification strategies such as deflection. When reviewing the literature, many examples that were initially interpreted as a result from improvised language strategies have turned out to be relatable to specific languages in the local contact setting (Aboh 2015; Sharma 2017). For instance, processes like deflection or the use of a general locative marker at the expense of dedicated locative marker for specific locational relations (Indefrey et al. 2017) are labelled as UP because they are instantiations of form reduction, which in turn is associated with improvised language. Because these reduced forms do not come out of nowhere, but are clearly rooted in a specific language (for example, the generic locative case marker -*da* discussed in Indefrey et al. 2017 is part of Turkish), I consider these reductions as part of the strategy 'rely on one language' rather than as instantiations of UP.

I also regrouped the strategies involving reliance on the L1, the L2 and both L1/L2. Reliance on the first language can take two forms: speakers can rely on the first language targeting the first language (*stability*) or they can rely on the first language while targeting the second language (*contact-induced interference*). The same goes for relying on the second language, a form of stability when speakers target the second language and a form of interference when they target the first language. I refer to the cases of stability as 'rely on one language' strategies and the forms of interference 'rely on more languages'. In theory, *interference* (one language influencing the other) and *congruence* (two languages influencing each other, L1/L2 in the Muysken 2013 system) are clearly different: congruence is bidirectional (both languages adapt to each other), while interference is unidirectional (one language imposes itself on the other). Because many studies only report on one language, congruence and interference are not always easy to tease apart in practice, and therefore I include all under the label 'rely on more than one language'.[1]

The central question in this chapter is if and how the timing of the onset of bilingualism affects the choice and the working of these bilingual optimization strategies. Section 2 presents an overview of reasons why age sometimes matters in the direction and the speed of language change in general. Section 3 discusses the strategy to rely on one language in relation to age. What social and linguistic settings stimulate this strategy? Does life stage matter in the preference for this strategy and does life stage matter for the way in which the strategy is applied? Section 4 discusses some of the effects of relying on more languages on language development and again asks if the preference for this strategy is related to life stage and if life stages matter in how the strategy is implemented. Section 5 briefly discusses the challenges and opportunities in combining the field of acquisition across the lifespan with the field of historical sociolinguistics and language contact. Section 6 summarizes and concludes the chapter.

---

1. See Chapter 4 in this volume for a look at how some of these processes may apply to situations of dialect contact.

2. Life stages and language development

This section discusses possible outcomes of language contact in relation to age.[2] The central question in this chapter is if the age of onset of bilingualism matters for the outcome of language contact. The very short answer is that as individuals age, cognitive capacities and conceptual development are different. In addition, the age of onset of acquisition determines the levels of experience with the language, and more experience with a language leads to more *entrenchment*. Entrenchment refers to the strength of a form-function relation in memory based on the frequency and the reliability of evidence for this relation (see, for example, MacWhinney 2019 and references therein). Overall, late onset of acquisition of the second language increases the chance of strong entrenchment of the first language, while early onset of acquisition of the second language enhances the strong entrenchment of the second language at the expense of the first language (see Chapter 2 in this volume).

Let us first turn to cognitive factors. It is often assumed that young age is associated with more brain plasticity, which would facilitate both language learning and language forgetting whenever a language is no longer used (Montrul 2008). Moreover, young learners have smaller short-term memory, which might lead children to switch from declarative memory to procedural memory more quickly, yielding more rule-based learning in children and more item-per-item learning in adults (Ullman 2001). This difference is very pronounced in the domain of morphology. For example, research by Hudson Kam and Newport (2005) on the learning of morphology in an artificial language showed that adults probability-match their language input, whereas 6-year-olds maximize, always picking the most probable alternative. This difference in rule-based learning versus probability matching predicts that the outcome of the 'rely on one language' strategy is different in young learners than in older learners. Younger learners tend to regularize unsystematically variable morphological input, whereas adult learners show veridical learning of overall variable frequencies (see Chapters 2 and 3 in this volume). Note, however, that young children are sensitive to conditioned variation, which they typically learn veridically (Austin et al. 2022; Hudson Kam 2015).

Apart from exhibiting smaller memory capacities, children are less developed conceptually than older learners. Less conceptual development in combination with less short-term memory capacity might make young learners more focused on form. Adult learners already have a conceptual system in place, enabling them to focus more on meaning. Because of children's focus on form, Wexler (1998) has referred to young learners as 'inflection machines,' because of their talent to acquire form differences. Another reason why child learning differs from learning

---

2. See Chapter 1, Section 3 for an introduction to the role of age in language acquisition.

in adults is that very young children have a different intake from adults: infant phonetic discrimination is initially language universal, but a decline in phonetic discrimination occurs for non-native phonemes by the end of the 1st year (Kuhl et al. 2005). This decline in phonetic discrimination over time might make a difference in the intake of children and adults: if a phoneme is not part of the inventory of an adult learner, he/she might not perceive distinctions in the input and what is not perceived cannot be learned.[3]

Besides cognitive factors, the social embedding of language learning has also been shown to make a difference. A language user's network affects the type of input received, as well as the likelihood of adapting to or creating innovations. Some networks value conservative language behavior, while other networks value creativity (see Chapter 8 in this volume). In many societies, young children have an older generation as their main form of input whereas adolescents have a peer network. Baxter and Croft (2016) relate the change in network to the *adolescent peak*: during puberty, language change peaks in monolingual contexts. They suggest that this adolescence peak coincides with a time of heightened sensitivity about the potential for language use to signal personal identities in some parts of the world. Kerswill and Williams (2000) also show that pre-adolescents show features of a newly arising dialect, whereas the younger children in the same community are more home-oriented and hence produce language that is closer to the language of their parents.[4]

Many forms of multilingual creativity are also described as blooming during puberty (Dorleijn & Nortier 2012; Mensah 2016: 2), suggesting that the potential to signal identity can also result in forms of contact-induced change (see Chapter 6 in this volume). Creative language contact-induced innovations include exaggerated and consciously stereotyped features characteristic of second language learners (grammatical structures, pronunciation, prosodic features), insertions of (non-dominant language) formulaic expressions, greetings, discourse particles, interjections, and sometimes word reversion (Dorleijn & Nortier 2012). For instance, Wei (2011) notes that Chinese youth in England use the interjection 'cake sellers'. This interjection translates into Mandarin as *mai gao de* which sounds like the English *My God!* This type of bilingual play is only understandable for language users who know both languages and functions to express bilingual identity.

Yet another social factor that makes life stage important is access to education and exposure to print. In many societies, exposure to print and education increases with age, which can be expected to enhance the likelihood that certain forms of

---

[3] See Chapter 10 in this volume for an example from a heritage language community.
[4] For an example of the role of peer-based networks among older children and adolescents in the sociolinguistic incrementation of a change, see Chapter 9 in this volume.

grammatical variation associated with formal language registers will be acquired. Pires and Rothman (2009a) and Weerman et al. (2013) show that formal registers can include the reintroduction of previously lost markers, for example the inflected infinitive in Portuguese or genitive case in Dutch. Like the reuse of learner forms as identity markers in adolescents discussed in Dorleijn and Nortier (2012), the reintroduced case and inflected infinitives pattern differently than in previous stages of the language, which can be attributed to the different social triggers that motivated learners to acquire these forms in different historical periods.[5]

Both education and exposure to print shape how language can be manipulated (Read et al. 1986), how it is processed (Petersson et al. 2000) and how phonemic differences are perceived (Kolinsky et al. 2021). Petersson and colleagues report that "learning to read and write during childhood alters the functional architecture of the brain" (365). For instance, knowing an alphabetic system allows literates to process phonological segments (sublexical elements) of unknown words, whereas this is not possible for illiterates. Similarly, exposure to print is usually associated with more awareness of sociolinguistic norms, hence to a reduction in variation (Andringa & Dąbrowska 2019). If language users are socialized into the larger society in a language other than the language(s) used at home, the home language is likely to be more variable due to the absence of the homogenizing effects of literacy. Moreover, languages that are mostly used within the family are less likely to contain features associated with formal registers (Pires & Rothman 2009b) due to decreased access to formal registers.

Overall, the research reviewed in this section shows that age matters in which parts of the input become part of the intake and can thus become part of the grammar of the language user. Forms that a language user does not perceive (e.g., because of a decline in phonetic discrimination) cannot be learned. The way language users deal with unstructured variation also depends on age. Age-sensitive social factors like openness to linguistic creativity at specific ages or exposure to literacy and social norms can also affect how learners process and acquire specific forms. While much of the research reviewed in this section has analyzed monolingual contexts of language acquisition and change, its findings are also relevant to contact (bidialectal/bilingual) settings because they inform us on variability in cognitive and social openness to change and innovation, and they make us aware of the effects of diverging social networks across the lifespan. In short, possible outcomes of language contact are co-determined by the age at which language users of the bilingual community become bilingual, both because of age-dependent differences in acquisition and because of age-dependent transmission

---

5. See Chapter 7 in this volume for a case study of the influence of formal registers as an element in the emergence of a new grammatical norm.

strategies. These effects are surveyed in more detail in the next section, where the focus is on whether learners rely on one language or on more than one language, as advanced in Section 1.

3. Rely on one language

This section discusses the 'rely on one language' strategy. As we saw in Table 1, the main mechanism in this strategy is that the language user relies only on the language they are targeting. More specifically, the speaker relies on the L1 when targeting the L1 or on the L2 when targeting the L2. The central questions are in what circumstances this strategy is likely to be used (Section 3.1), which domains of language are most likely selected for this strategy (Section 3.2) and, from a lifespan perspective, whether the age of onset of bilingualism matters in the likelihood of this strategy and its effects (Section 3.3).

3.1 What social circumstances increase the likelihood of reliance on one language?

Short-term individual bilingualism in a society that values language separation increases the likelihood that language users may rely on one language. This is the case especially if the target language has prestige and its use is connected to specific situations that differ from the contexts where the other language is used (e.g., diglossic social contexts), or to different social groups. If one of the languages is not shared across a community, then the chance that interlocutors understand a form from the unshared language is lower. Lack of knowledge of the unshared language decreases the chance of a language user selecting forms from the non-shared language, and if a form from the non-shared language is nonetheless selected it is less likely to spread across the community because the form does not resonate in the addressee. The presence of monolingual interlocutors and a strong distribution of languages according to context can stimulate a *monolingual mode* (Grosjean 1998), where bilinguals suppress the use of features from other languages.

3.2 Which linguistic domains are most likely to be part of the 'rely on one language' strategy?

When one targets language X and only relies on the resources of language X, this results in a form of stability. Although much language contact research focuses on contact-induced change, the question of which parts of language resist contact-induced change is equally relevant (Aikhenvald 2003; Backus 2004; Kühl & Braunmüller 2014; Polinsky 2018; Silva-Corvalán 1994). In this literature, *categoricalness* is said to decrease permeability to contact effects: from a usage-based perspective, if something is always done in a particular way, alternatives are more easily precluded (i.e., they never come up in the mind of the speaker) than when they are already partly entrenched, even if weakly.[6] From a generative perspective, the stability due to categoricalness can be linked to a form being contained within one linguistic domain such as syntax rather than interfacing between different linguistic or extralinguistic domains such as semantics or pragmatics.

The effect of categoricalness is clear in the data on heritage Ambon Malay in the Netherlands presented in Moro (2016). In homeland Ambon Malay, nouns always precede adjectives. This order is retained in heritage Ambon Malay in the Netherlands despite the fact that it differs from the dominant language Dutch, where an adjective always precedes the noun. The same holds for the order of nouns and indefinite markers: the order that is dissimilar to Dutch (i.e., noun + indefinite marker) is retained in the heritage variant. In contrast, the positioning of numerals and demonstratives relative to the noun is variable in homeland Ambon Malay: the noun can both precede or follow the modifier. In contexts where homeland Ambon Malay is variable, the effect of Dutch is strong: the speakers in the Netherlands show an increase in the structures that overlap with the Dutch structure, with the modifier preceding the noun. This type of increase of the structure shared with the dominant language is referred to as a *system-preserving change* in Aikhenvald (2003).

Van Osch et al. (2017) find a similar effect of categoricalness in heritage Spanish in the Netherlands. The subjunctive is preserved in almost all heritage speakers when its use is obligatory, but it decreases in contexts where its use is variable. They also find that the type of variability matters. If the presence of the subjunctive is conditioned by a language-internal interface, like semantics, it is more stable than if it is conditioned by language-external interfaces, like pragmatics.

Apart from categoricalness and the type of interface, other factors that have been suggested as enhancing stability are *frequency*, *salience* and *transparency*. Although it makes sense that forms that are more frequent are more easily retained

---

6. I thank an anonymous reviewer for this observation.

than low frequent forms, O'Grady et al. (2011) show that it is never frequency alone that predicts retention or loss. Forms that are frequent but which have *fragile form–meaning* mappings due to *low acoustic salience* and *low transparency* might not be fully learned despite their high frequency. On the other hand, interpretations that are infrequent but easy to process are retained despite their low frequency. For instance, *acoustic salience* is related to audibility, which in turn may make a form easier to process. Kim et al. (2018) manipulate acoustic salience experimentally. They demonstrate that when the salience of the Korean accusative marker *-(l)ul* is enhanced in an experimental setting by manipulating volume, duration and pitch, heritage speakers perform better in a comprehension task.

If unclear form-meaning mappings make forms unstable, one would predict that transparent form-meaning mappings should be more stable. To be accurate, *transparency* does not only refer to form-meaning mappings, but also to the ways in which cognitive preferences are mapped onto structure. For instance, Culbertson et al. (2020) show that word orders that are *semantically transparent* (that is, in line with the relative strength of cognitive associations between the head and its modifiers) are crosslinguistically more frequent but also arise more frequently in improvised language. For example, adjectival properties (e.g., 'red') are on average more closely related to the objects they modify (e.g., 'wine') than numerosities are (e.g., 'two'), which are in turn more closely related to the objects they modify than demonstratives are (e.g., 'this'). Consequently, one may predict that if a language reflects this relative strength of cognitive association in its word order, this pattern will be more stable than if the word order deviates from these preferences.

In short, forms are more likely to be stable when they are used categorically in salient transparent and frequent mappings. Apart from the qualities of the target language, one could also relate stability to the force with which the other language imposes itself. Moro (2016), for example, shows that obligatory grammatical categories in Dutch such as finiteness and definiteness impose themselves on heritage Ambon Malay in the Netherlands. Resisting features from another language is more likely if the features in the other language are optional.

3.3 What is the role of age in the selection of the rely on one language strategy?

It has been claimed that young children separate their languages during language acquisition. If this is indeed true across the board, one would expect the 'rely on one language' strategy to be especially prevalent in young learners. Muysken (2008) notes that scholars like Genesee (1989) and the authors in Meisel (1994) found evidence for the *Autonomous Development Hypothesis*, which argues that the child's two languages develop separately, while Sánchez (2003) found evidence for functional interference and convergence in children. The question is whether these contact effects are due to an age preference or whether they are the effect of time depth and social circumstances. The Spanish-Quechua bilinguals Sánchez discusses come from a situation of long-term communal bilingualism, whereas the middle-class French-German children studied by Meisel and colleagues come from a situation where most of their surroundings are not bilingual and the start of bilingualism is recent (see also Chapter 2 in this volume).

Considering these different acquisition situations, we can see that the social situation of the children who seem to separate their languages is exactly the context where one would expect all age groups to rely on one language, which suggests that young learners are highly sensitive to the social patterns of use of each language in their communities. What is not completely clear is if it is only sensitivity to social patterns that makes the children reported in the studies in Meisel (1994) separate their languages or if there is also a cognitive aspect to language separation in young children. It is possible that relying on one language is more likely when there is no competition from a very entrenched language, allowing young learners to not show as much crosslinguistic influence because none of their languages are very entrenched yet, whereas adult learners might show less crosslinguistic influence of the L2 on the L1 if that L2 is not very entrenched. If so, the Quechua-Spanish children in Sánchez (2003) might show crosslinguistic influence because these forms were already part of their input, rather than being acquisitional innovations.

It is important to note that when language users rely on one language, this does not necessarily mean that they rely on the complete set of features in the feature pool. Both Aboh (2015) and Andringa and Dąbrowska (2019) note that any acquisition process is probably incomplete in some sense, meaning that not every form that was ever in the input is retained. It is therefore highly likely that the subset of the target language that is acquired does depend on age given the different age-based cognitive strategies described in Section 2. As it turns out, researchers comparing developmental paths in different age groups have indeed observed different applications of the 'rely on one language strategy' per age group.

A good example is Blom et al. (2008), a study that reports on the acquisition of adjectival inflection in Dutch by speakers in different age cohorts. Adjectival inflection in Dutch is organized as follows: predicative adjectives such as *mooi* 'beautiful' in (1a) are left bare, but in most cases the attributive adjective combines with a schwa [ə], such as *mooie* in (1b). If an attributive adjective is combined with an indefinite neuter singular noun like *gesprek* 'conversation', the adjective is again bare, as shown in (1c).

(1) Adjectival inflection in Dutch
    a. *De taal   is mooi*
        The language is beautiful
    b. *De mooie   taal*
        The beautiful language
    c. *Een mooi   gesprek*
        A beautiful conversation

Given the overall number of adjectives in discourse, the bare form is the most frequent, but within the class of attributive adjectives (i.e., the case in 1b), the form with [ə] is the most frequent. In this study, Blom et al. show that all learners, regardless of age, use the predicative adjective as targeted. However, the strategies with regard to the attributive adjectives differ. Young bilingual and monolingual children overgeneralize in one direction: they overuse the form with [ə]. Unlike the young learners, adult learners overgeneralize in both directions: they use bare forms and forms with [ə] in attributive position independent of definiteness or gender specifications of the noun. Critically, none of the bilingual learners acquire the rule that indefinite neuter singular nouns are bare in attributive position.

This difference between the developmental paths of young and older learners can be explained in various ways. For instance, adults might show more veridical learning in the sense that they replicate the overall distribution of forms with and without [ə] in the input (while ignoring grammatical conditions linked to this distribution), but children might be more sensitive to syntactic position and have a different statistical approach. Whatever the exact cause for this difference in acquisitional paths, age seems to shape the outcome of language contact. This effect is clear in Weerman (2002), who studies the acquisition of the [ə] rule in several contact varieties of Dutch. Surinamese Dutch and Iowa Dutch are acquired by young bilinguals, and they combine attributive adjectives with [ə]. Virgin Island Dutch, by contrast, is acquired mostly by adult learners, and has lost [ə]. Weerman explains the loss of [ə] as the result of intergenerational transmission. Specifically, the adults on the Virgin Islands who first used Dutch used attributive adjectives with and without [ə], and the distribution between these two forms was not grammatically conditioned. The next generation of child learners regularized this irregularity by using the bare form. The interaction of strategies of different types of learners across generations is referred to as a *cascade effect* by DeGraff (2009) and Aboh (2015), who compare the stages in language transmission to a waterfall, where the changes to the input enacted by one generation trigger determine how that input is processed and acquired by younger learners.

4. Rely on more languages

As advanced in Section 1, learners may also combine resources from more than one language as they build their grammars. This section discusses the 'rely on more languages' strategy. As we saw in Table 1, the 'rely on more languages' means that language users also incorporate parts of the L1 when targeting the L2 or parts of the L2 when targeting the L1. The central questions here are in what circumstances this strategy is likely to be used (Section 4.1), which domains of language are mostly likely selected for this strategy (Section 4.2) and whether the age of onset of bilingualism matters in the likelihood of this strategy and its effects (Section 4.3).

4.1 What social circumstances increase the likelihood of reliance on more languages?

Long-term communal bilingualism stimulates the co-activation of two (or more) languages in the same situation and, in turn, co-activation increases the likelihood of crosslinguistic influence (Moro 2016). If the same interlocutors share the same languages and use these languages in similar situations, language users are in a *bilingual mode* (Grosjean 1998) where all languages are active. Because language users share knowledge of multiple languages, the chance that one's interlocutors understand contact-induced innovations is higher, which in turn makes the spread of these innovations throughout the community more likely (Backus et al. 2011). Absence of a strict norm or a language ideology favoring language separation also increases the likelihood of reliance on more than one language (Muysken 2013; Chapter 8 in this volume).

4.2 Which linguistic domains are most likely to be part of the 'rely on more languages' strategy?

As explained in Section 3.2, categoricalness stimulates stability and relying on one language. On the flipside, *optionality* in combination with partial overlap with the other language encourages speakers to rely on two languages, as the shared option gets used more frequently. Partial overlap can be seen on a structural level, for example in the heightened use of demonstrative noun orders in heritage Ambon Malay in the Netherlands, but this enhanced overlap between the languages can also obtain on the conceptual level.

For example, Schoenmakers-Klein (1997) reports on speakers of heritage Dutch in Brazil who use the Dutch verb *pakken* ('to take') in a broader range of contexts than Dutch speakers in the Netherlands. In the Dutch spoken in the

Netherlands, the verb *pakken* ('take') is typically used in the sense that the subject acts intentionally and has control over the situation. Saying that someone *pakt de trein* ('takes the train') is fine, but *een ziekte pakken* ('taking an illness') is not, because one has no control over becoming ill. Schoenmakers-Klein relates the semantic extension of the verb *pakken* ('take') in heritage Dutch in Brazil to the influence of Brazilian Portuguese *pegar* ('take'), which is not limited to contexts of intention and control. Another example of enhancing the conceptual overlap in two forms is described in the work of Moro (2015). She describes the use of the verb *musti* ('must/have to') in heritage Ambon Malay. Whereas in homeland Malay, *musti* can only be used to encode external obligation such as *you must leave*, in the heritage variant *musti* can be used for internal obligations (e.g., 'I have to pee') just as in the contact language Dutch.

The combinatorial properties of the lexical items of one language can also be influenced by use in the other language (Johanson 2008). An example is presented by Backus et al. (2011), who study heritage Turkish in the Netherlands. In Dutch, the word *erg* ('bad') can be used as an intensifier, and this is also possible for the Turkish translational equivalent *kötü* ('bad') in this heritage Turkish variety, as shown in (2) (taken from Backus et al. 2011: 744). In such cases, an extension of combinatorial properties goes hand in hand with semantic expansion (see Chapter 11 in this volume for an additional example).

(2) Intensifiers in Turkish in the Netherlands, Dutch and Turkish in Turkey
   a. *acaip kötü sıcak-tı*   (Turkish in the Netherlands)
      very bad warm- PAST
      'incredibly warm'
   b. *heel erg warm*   (Dutch)
      very bad warm
      'incredibly warm'
   c. *acaip sıcak-tı*   (Turkish in Turkey)
      very warm- PAST
      'very warm'

Other forms of relying on more than one language can be classified as *contact-induced grammaticalization*, which involves the accelerated rise of grammatical markers under the influence of language contact. For example, Backus et al. (2011) show that the numeral *one* in Turkish in the Netherlands shows incipient signs of grammaticalization as an indefinite marker, and they relate this to contact with Dutch, which obligatorily encodes definiteness on nouns. The rise of overt morphological definiteness marking is also observed in Mandarin (Aalberse et al. 2017) and Ambon Malay in the Netherlands (Moro 2016). In addition to the rise of overt definiteness marking, Moro (2016) also observes the rise of overt finiteness marking in heritage Ambon Malay in the Netherlands. The author explains both changes as the result of obligatory marking of these grammatical features in Dutch. Overall, these examples show that obligatoriness of encoding of grammatical features in one language can thus enhance the likelihood of relying on more than one language, because the other language will develop a proxy to express this obligatory grammatical category also.

The role of the other language in the rise of a new structure is not always recognized because the relationship can be subtle. This is the case when the new structure already exists in the language but is used infrequently, which makes it harder for researchers to acknowledge it as the outcome of contact-induced grammaticalization. For example, van de Craats and van Hout (1997) interpret the hyperextension of the Dutch preposition *van* ('of' or 'from') in Turkish speakers of Dutch as a proxy for case marking inspired by the dominant language Turkish. Not every researcher would have recognized the role of Turkish in this structure (see Chapter 12 in this volume for a similar example).

4.3 What is the role of age in the selection of the 'rely on more languages' strategy?

The chance that a language user relies on more than one language clearly increases with age in the domain of phonology (Kerswill & Williams 2000; Piske et al. 2001). As described in Section 2.3, some language acquisition authors assume that young children are less likely to show crosslinguistic influence than adults in other domains of language as well. On the other hand, several authors (Matthews & Yip 2009; Thomason 2001; Trudgill 2011) have proposed that bilingual first language acquisition is an important source of contact-induced language change, including grammaticalization.

Most of the studies that suggest that young learners are the agents of contact-induced grammaticalization present indirect evidence. For instance, they may point out that language communities with evidence for contact-induced grammaticalization have many bilingual young learners, which makes them likely candidates as actuators of these changes. The increase of grammatical markers is interpreted as a form of complexification that is often associated with children. However, apart from having many young bilingual learners, these communities also exhibit long-term shared bilingualism, the exact circumstances that stimulate relying on more than one language regardless of age. Studies that rely on more direct observation of the action of children or adolescents in the creation of a new norm in a language contact situation, such as Chapter 8 in this volume, are few and far between.

To fully disentangle the role of age and the community, more research is needed, but some researchers have already addressed this question. For example, Matthews and Yip (2009) make a connection between developmental patterns in a Cantonese-English bilingual first language learner and patterns found in Singapore colloquial English. For instance, the use of the verb *give* as a dative marker or the use of the adverb *already* as a perfective marker is inspired by how their equivalents are used in Chinese languages like Mandarin and Cantonese. These forms of contact-induced grammaticalization are found both in the contact language (Singapore English) and among young English-Cantonese learners. Hence, young learners can be a source of contact-induced grammaticalization, but it is not always clear if the age of onset of bilingualism is also a crucial factor. Whereas there is some in-depth comparative work acquisitional patterns across different age groups on the 'rely on one language' strategy, there is not much comparative research on age effects in the 'rely on more languages' strategy outside the domain of phonology.

A study that indirectly does look at the role of age in the preference for a particular bilingual optimization strategy in conceptualization is Indefrey et al. (2017). The authors researched the use of locative markers in Dutch-Turkish speakers and found an effect of language dominance: in comparison to Turkish speakers in Turkey, Turkish-dominant speakers in the Netherlands overgeneralize the general neutral Turkish locative case marker *-da* at the expense of specifically dedicated markers for different locational relations. By contrast, Dutch-dominant speakers of Turkish map their Turkish locative markers on the Dutch system. In the study, dominance strongly correlates with the age of onset of bilingualism, so one could interpret this as a possible age effect. In this case, speakers with an early onset of Dutch rely on their two languages, mapping the conceptualization pattern of Dutch on Turkish forms, whereas learners with a later age of onset only rely on their L1 (albeit a reduced form of it). In this case, the deeper entrenchment of Dutch could be the reason for the learners who are Dutch-dominant and who acquired Dutch at a young age to use the conceptual mapping of Dutch. Alternatively, the longer experience with Turkish in Turkish-dominant speakers who were late bilinguals might also have constrained using Dutch conceptual groupings: by using general locative markers, the Turkish speakers do not violate Turkish nor Dutch constraints. Overall, the observed changes in the Turkish of the Turkish-dominant group are in line with possible structures in Turkish spoken in Turkey (although not the preferred form), whereas the Dutch-dominant group shows more innovative uses not found in non-heritage Turkish.

Another study that suggests an age effect in the selection of a bilingual optimization strategy is Aalberse et al. (2017). This study finds that both young and old Mandarin-Dutch bilinguals use more overt definiteness markers in their

Mandarin than monolingual Mandarin speakers. However, they differ in their strategy for finding a proxy for definiteness marking. Bilinguals who acquired Dutch after puberty selected the proximal demonstrative *zhege* as a proxy for definiteness (in line with Mandarin usage), whereas bilinguals who learned Dutch before puberty selected the more Dutch-like distal demonstrative *nage*. One could interpret observations in Indefrey et al. (2017) and Aalberse et al. (2017) as support for the idea that one language imposes itself more strongly on the other language if that other language is less entrenched (i.e., acquired later). This interpretation is in line with MacWhinney (2019).

In short, strong and opposing claims have been made about the relation between age and crosslinguistic influence. Ideas range from the Autonomous Development Hypothesis, suggesting that young learners separate their languages, to the idea that bilingual first language acquisition is the main source of contact-induced complexification in language contact. Additionally, entrenchment of a language (correlated with age of bilingual onset) might affect the level of crosslinguistic influence. Most likely, the more entrenched language will impose itself more on the less entrenched language than vice versa (MacWhinney 2019). Lastly, the chance of imposition of one language on the other is higher when a category is obligatorily expressed in the source language, regardless of age.[7]

5. Acquisition across the lifespan and the historical sociolinguistics of language contact: Challenges and opportunities

The previous sections have reviewed possible instantiations of two main bilingual optimization strategies: 'rely on one language' or 'rely on more languages'. We looked for evidence for the role of age in the choice between these strategies and in the application of these strategies. The clearest age effects were found in the domain of selective reliance on the L1, e.g., when a subset is acquired, children select differently than adults, at least in the case of inflection (see Section 3.1).

Although many strong claims have been made about the role of age in the occurrence of crosslinguistic influence in young learners, evidence is less clear here. It is likely that age effects are strongly mediated by demographic and other social factors (Clements 2009; Kerswill & Williams 2000; Labov 2007; Trudgill 2011). Therefore, a challenge for future research is to disentangle age effects from social effects. One could imagine experimental work where language users of the

---

[7] For further discussion of the role of crosslinguistic influence in language acquisition, see Chapter 2 in this volume.

same language pair with different ages of onset are compared with regards to a phenomenon (see Tsimpli 2014 for an example of this line of research).

Historical sociolinguistic studies can also be helpful in the process of disentangling the age factor from demographic factors: for example, by investigating bilingual acquisition in more diverse populations in different sociohistorical settings (for instance, see Schneider 2007 and Sharma 2017 on English in various (post)colonial contexts, or Clements 2009 or the studies in Schwegler et al. 2016 on Spanish and Portuguese in various contexts of contact) or by comparing ego documents in different generations of family members from one family (for instance, Hoffman & Kytö 2019 on contact between Swedish and English in Kansas; Martineau 2013 on shift from French to English in a Michigan family; or Stolberg 2019 on heritage German across three generations in Canada).

Another challenge for future research is unentangling the effect of *vertical* vs. *horizontal transmission* paths of contact-induced innovations: in a vertical path, innovations are transmitted across generations, from older to younger language users. In a horizontal path, innovations are transmitted among peers (Bryden et al. 2018). In Section 3 we saw that Weerman (2002) postulates a change across multiple generations. The first generation of adult second language learners probability-matches the input while ignoring grammatical conditioning. The following generation of young learners regularizes this input by omitting the unconditioned inflection all together. This chronological sequence has potential importance for sociohistorical studies of contact contexts. Along this vein, Sharma (2017: 16) asks why only some contact-induced innovations become more established hallmarks of a given variety over time. She argues that, when language users undergeneralize a certain form, for example using the *-ed* suffix in English only for perfectives, access to standard English (when socially available) will lead to implicit feedback, because language users will perceive the suffix *-ed* in other contexts than only with the perfective. In contrast, in cases of hyperextension, language users will not perceive such implicit feedback, and hence such hyperextensions are more likely to persist (see also Chapter 6 in this volume for a more detailed discussion of this principle).

A question that has been insufficiently researched is how innovations are transmitted when users rely on more than one language. In the case of intergenerational transmission, it is an open question if it is always the form selected by the youngest generation that is transmitted to an even younger generation. For example, in Section 4 we saw that younger Chinese generations in the Netherlands overuse the more Dutch-like distal form *nage* as proxy for definiteness in Mandarin in the Netherlands whereas the older generation uses the proximal distal *zhege*, which is more in line with Mandarin used in China. Will the form of the younger generation win out or does the form selected in the first generation stand a chance of being transmitted and if so under what circumstances? Sociohistorical studies can shed light on this question by offering diachronic evidence.

Besides the effects of acquisition age within bilingual communities, historical sociolinguistic studies of contact must also consider the possibility of horizontal transmission. Hall-Lew (2014) suggests that heritage Chinese social and linguistic practices might be available resources for place authentication in contemporary San Francisco beyond speakers of Chinese descent, suggesting that horizontal transmission outside the group is a possibility. Historical sociolinguists are uniquely positioned to investigate such patterns of horizontal and vertical transmission.

Moreover, historical sociolinguists are also in the position to take advantage of the opportunity to integrate ideas on agency and ability. Acquisition studies often explain differences from a hypothesized monolingual target in terms of a transmission failure: language users have not (yet) acquired a form because of lack of input or lack of access to certain learning strategies. The idea that learners have agency and are creative and thus might intentionally deviate from the norm or are perhaps steering towards a new norm is often not considered. In Section 2 we saw that learner forms can be used as identity markers in the second generation of a language heritage community. From a historical sociolinguistic perspective, the diachronic dimension may be particularly helpful to study how these innovations are treated in a community over time, and which social conditions favor the preservation of innovations emerging from bilingual language learning.

6. Conclusion

To summarize, age effects are a factor in contact-induced language change, which can be studied from the perspective of bilingual acquisition strategies ('rely on one language' vs. 'rely on more languages'). Age of onset of bilingualism affects what language users are likely to perceive and learn, and how they learn it. Age also affects the likelihood that language users value conservative or innovative behavior. A challenge is to disentangle age effects from social and demographic factors when studying the 'rely on more languages strategy' and to understand vertical and horizontal transmission paths. Historical sociolinguists are in a unique position to explore these questions whenever various transmission paths are documented in the archival record, especially if different contact settings can be compared in detail. The chapters in this volume propose various strategies to apply many of these strategies to specific cases of multilingual or multidialectal contact and change.

References

Aalberse, Suzanne, Ad Backus & Pieter Muysken. 2019. *Heritage languages: A language contact approach*. Amsterdam: John Benjamins.

Aalberse, Suzanne, Yiwen Zou & Sible Andringa. 2017. Extended use of demonstrative pronouns in two generations of Mandarin Chinese speakers in the Netherlands: Evidence of convergence? In Elma Blom, Jeannette Schaeffer & Leonie Cornips (eds.), *Studies in bilingualism*, 25–48. Amsterdam: John Benjamins.

Aboh, Enoch Oladé. 2015. *The emergence of hybrid grammars: Language contact and change*. Cambridge: Cambridge University Press.

Aikhenvald, Alexandra. 2003. Mechanisms of change in areal diffusion: New morphology and language contact. *Journal of Linguistics* 39. 1–29.

Andringa, Sible & Ewa Dąbrowska. 2019. Individual differences in first and second language ultimate attainment and their causes. *Language Learning* 69(1). 5–12.

Austin, Alison, Kathryn Schuler, Sarah Furlong & Elissa Newport. 2022. Learning a language from inconsistent input: Regularization in child and adult learners. *Language Learning and Development* 18(3). 249–277.

Backus, Ad. 2004. Convergence as a mechanism of language change. *Bilingualism: Language and Cognition* 7(2). 179–181.

Backus, Ad, Seza Doğruöz & Bernd Heine. 2011. Salient stages in contact-induced grammatical change: Evidence from synchronic vs. diachronic contact situations. *Language Sciences* 33(5). 738–752.

Baxter, Gareth & William Croft. 2016. Modeling language change across the lifespan: Individual trajectories in community change. *Language Variation and Change* 28: 129–173.

Blom, Elma, Daniela Polišenská & Fred Weerman. 2008. Articles, adjectives and age of onset: The acquisition of Dutch grammatical gender. *Second Language Research* 24(3). 297–331.

Bryden, John, Shaun Wright & Vincent Jansen. 2018. How humans transmit language: horizontal transmission matches word frequencies among peers on Twitter. *Journal of the Royal Society Interface* 15. 20170738.

Clements, J. Clancy. 2009. *The linguistic legacy of Spanish and Portuguese: Colonial expansion and language change*. Cambridge: Cambridge University Press.

Culbertson, Jennifer, Marieke Schouwstra & Simon Kirby. 2020. From the world to word order: Deriving biases in noun phrase order from statistical properties of the world. *Language* 96(3). 696–717.

DeGraff, Michel. 2009. Language acquisition in creolization and, thus, language change: Some cartesian-uniformitarian boundary conditions. *Language and Linguistics* Compass 3/4. 888–971.

Dorleijn, Margreet & Jacomine Nortier. 2012. Bilingualism and youth language. In Carol Chapelle (ed.), *The encyclopedia of applied linguistics*, 1–7. Hoboken, NJ: Wiley-Blackwell.

Genesee, Fred. 1989. Early bilingual development: One language or two? *Journal of Child Language* 16(1). 161–179.

Grosjean, François. 1998. Transfer and language mode. *Bilingualism: Language and Cognition* 1: 175–176.

Hall-Lew, Lauren. 2014. Chinese social practice and San Franciscan authenticity. In Veronique Lacoste, Jakob Leimgruber & Thierno Breyer (eds.), *Indexing authenticity: Sociolinguistic perspectives*, 55–77. Berlin: De Gruyter Mouton.

Hoffman, Angela & Merja Kytö. 2019. Varying social roles and networks on a family farm: Evidence from Swedish immigrant letters, 1880s to 1930s. *Journal of Historical Sociolinguistics* 5(2). 20180031.

Hudson Kam, Carla. 2015. The impact of conditioning variables on the acquisition of variation in adult and child learners. *Language* 91(4). 906–937.

Hudson Kam, Carla & Elissa Newport. 2005. Regularizing unpredictable variation: The roles of adult and child learners in language formation and change. *Language Learning and Development* 1(2). 151–195.

Indefrey, Peter, Hülya Şahin & Marianne Gullberg. 2017. The expression of spatial relationships in Turkish–Dutch bilinguals. *Bilingualism: Language and Cognition* 20(3). 473–493.

Johanson, Lars. 2008. Remodeling grammar: Copying, conventionalization, grammaticalization. In Peter Siemund & Noemi Kintana (eds.), *Language contact and contact languages*, 61–79. Amsterdam: John Benjamins.

Kerswill, Paul & Ann Williams. 2000. Creating a new town koine: Children and language change in Milton Keynes. *Language in Society* 29. 65–115.

Kim, Kitaek, William O'Grady & Bonnie Schwartz. 2018. Case in heritage Korean. *Linguistic Approaches to Bilingualism* 8(2). 252–282.

Kolinsky, Régine, Ana Luzia Navas, Fraulein Vidigal de Paula, Nathalia Ribeiro de Brito, Larissa de Medeiros Botecchia, Sophie Bouton & Willy Serniclaes. 2021. The impact of alphabetic literacy on the perception of speech sounds. *Cognition* 213. 104687.

Kuhl, Patricia, Barbara Conboy, Denise Padden, Tobey Nelson & Jessica Pruitt. 2005. Early speech perception and later language development: Implications for the "critical period". *Language Learning and Development* 1(3–4): 237–264.

Kühl, Karoline & Kurt Braunmüller. 2014. Linguistic stability and divergence. In Kurt Braunmüller, Steffen Höder & Karoline Kühl (eds.), *Stability and divergence in language contact: Factors and mechanisms*, 13–38. Amsterdam: John Benjamins.

Labov, William. 2007. Transmission and diffusion. *Language* 83. 344–387.

MacWhinney, Brian. 2019. Language attrition and the competition model. In Monika Schmid & Barbara Köpke (eds.), *The Oxford handbook of language attrition*, 5–17. Oxford: Oxford University Press.

Martineau, France. 2013. Written documents: What they tell us about linguistic usage. In Marijke van der Wal & Gijsbert Rutten (eds.), *Touching the past: Studies in the historical sociolinguistics of ego-documents*, 129–148. Amsterdam: John Benjamins.

Matthews, Stephen & Virginia Yip. 2009. Contact-induced grammaticalization: Evidence from bilingual acquisition. *Studies in Language* 33(2). 366–395.

Meisel, Jürgen (ed.). 1994. *Bilingual first language acquisition French and German grammatical development*. Amsterdam: John Benjamins.

Mensah, Eyo. 2016. The dynamics of youth language in Africa: An introduction. *Sociolinguistic Studies* 10(1). 1–14.

Montrul, Silvina. 2008. *Incomplete acquisition in bilingualism: Re-examining the age factor*. Amsterdam: John Benjamins.

Moro, Francesca. 2015. Modal categories in contact: The case of heritage Ambon Malay in the Netherlands. *Heritage Language Journal* 12 (3). 271–291.

Moro, Francesca. 2016. *Dynamics of Ambon Malay: Comparing Ambon and the Netherlands*. Utrecht: LOT dissertation series.

Muysken, Pieter. 2008. Traces of contact: Language contact studies and historical linguistics. *ERC-overview*. Nijmegen, The Netherlands.

Muysken, Pieter. 2013. Language contact outcomes as the result of bilingual optimization strategies. *Bilingualism: Language and Cognition* 16(4). 709–730.

O'Grady, William, Hye-Young Kwak, On-Soon Lee & Miseon Lee. 2011. An emergentist perspective on heritage language acquisition. *Studies in Second Language Acquisition* 33(2). 223–245.

Osch, Brechje, Aafke Hulk, Petra Sleeman & Suzanne Aalberse. 2017. Knowledge of mood in internal and external interface contexts in Spanish heritage speakers in the Netherlands. In Kate Bellamy, Michael Child, Paz González, Antje Muntendam & María del Carmen Parafita Couto (eds.), *Multidisciplinary approaches to bilingualism in the Hispanic and Lusophone world* 13. 67–92. Amsterdam: John Benjamins.

Petersson, Karl Magnus, Alexandra Reis, Simon Askelöf, Alexander Castro-Caldas & Martin Ingvar. 2000. Language processing modulated by literacy: A network analysis of verbal repetition in literate and illiterate subjects. *Journal of Cognitive Neuroscience* 12(3). 364–382.

Pires, Acrisio & Jason Rothman (eds.) 2009a. *Minimalist inquiries into child and adult language acquisition: Case studies across Portuguese*. Berlin: De Gruyter Mouton.

Pires, Acrisio & Jason Rothman. 2009b. Disentangling sources of incomplete acquisition: An explanation for competence divergence across heritage grammars. *International Journal of Bilingualism* 13(2). 211–238.

Piske, Thorsten, Ian MacKay & James Flege. 2001. Factors affecting degree of foreign accent in an L2: A review. *Journal of Phonetics* 29(2). 191–215.

Polinsky, Maria. 2018. Bilingual children and adult heritage speakers: The range of comparison. *International Journal of Bilingualism* 22(5). 547–563.

Read, Charles, Zhang Yun-Fei, Nie Hong-Yin & Ding Bao-Qing. 1986. The ability to manipulate speech sounds depends on knowing alphabetic writing. *Cognition* 24. 31–44.

Sánchez, Liliana. 2003. *Quechua-Spanish bilingualism: Interference and convergence in functional categories*. Amsterdam: John Benjamins.

Schneider, Edgar. 2007. *Postcolonial English: Varieties around the world*. Cambridge: Cambridge University Press.

Schoenmakers-Klein, Gunnewiek. 1997. Dutch language loss in Brazil and the conceptual hypothesis. In Jetske Klatter-Folmer & Sjaak Kroon (eds.), *Studies in maintenance and loss of Dutch as an immigrant language*, 99–119. Tilburg: Tilburg University Press.

Schwegler, Armin, John McWhorter & Liane Ströbel (eds.). 2016. *The Iberian challenge: Creole languages beyond the plantation setting*. Madrid: Iberoamericana/Vervuert.

Sharma, Devyani. 2017. A dynamic typology of syntactic change in Postcolonial Englishes. Presentation at the Societas Linguistica Europea. September 12, 2017.

Silva-Corvalán, Carmen. 1994. *Language contact and change: Spanish in Los Angeles*. Oxford: Clarendon Press.

Stolberg, Doris. 2019. Canadian heritage German across three Generations: A diary-based study of language shift in action. *Journal of Historical Sociolinguistics* 5(2). 20190005.

Thomason, Sarah. 2001. *Language contact: An introduction*. Washington D.C.: Georgetown University Press.

Trudgill, Peter. 2011. *Sociolinguistic typology: Social determinants of linguistic complexity*. Oxford: Oxford University Press.

Tsimpli, Ianthi. 2014. Early, late or very late? Timing acquisition and bilingualism. *Linguistic Approaches to Bilingualism* 4(3). 283–313.

Ullman, Michael. 2001. The declarative/procedural model of lexicon and grammar. *Journal of Psycholinguistic Research* 30. 37–63.

Van de Craats, Ineke & Roeland van Hout. 1997. De nieuwe kleren van de keizer: VAN als venster op de T2-verwerving van turkse leerders. *Gramma* 6(2–3). 151–167.

Weerman, Fred. 2002. *Dynamiek in taal en de explosie van de neerlandistiek*. Amsterdam: Amsterdam University Press.

Weerman, Fred, Mike Olson & Robert Cloutier. 2013. Synchronic variation and loss of case: Formal and informal language in a Dutch corpus of 17th-century Amsterdam texts. *Diachronica* 30(3). 353–381.

Wei, Li. 2011. Moment analysis and translanguaging space: Discursive construction of identities by multilingual Chinese youth in Britain. *Journal of Pragmatics* 43(5). 1222–1235.

Wexler, Ken. 1998. Very early parameter setting and the unique checking constraint: A new explanation of the optional infinitive stage. *Lingua* 106. 23–79.

CHAPTER 6

Language acquisition across the lifespan and the emergence of new varieties

Devyani Sharma
Queen Mary University of London

This chapter examines the role of acquisitional processes in the emergence of new language varieties, exploring the question in two ways. We first consider how different age groups and generations contribute to the emergence of new multi-ethnolects in Europe and in comparable contemporary contact situations. Age of exposure and the social context of acquisition are both shown to alter the course of a given variety. We then look at cases of post-colonial dialect emergence, which we exemplify with cases stemming from British colonialism. These examples are used to show that theories of second language acquisition can account for the development of specific grammatical features over generations, and indeed that those theories can in turn be evaluated by such examples. Overall, these cases show that new varieties are key contexts to understand the role of language acquisition in historical sociolinguistics.

Keywords: new dialect formation, language acquisition, lifespan, historical sociolinguistics, immigration, post-colonial Englishes

1. Introduction

Natural languages are never still. Social and cognitive flux is pervasive in any language, and this fundamental variability – in both society and cognition of language – leads to continual cycles of new dialect (or language) formation. Initial variability is followed by social embedding, and eventually a focused dialect system emerges over generations. The process is repeated regularly, each time these systems are disrupted.

The generational embedding of these cycles means that processes of individual acquisition throughout the lifespan are at the heart of this process of language variety formation. Although lifelong acquisition has been less prominent than social and structural analysis in the literature on the emergence of new varieties, this section of the book highlights its indispensable role in the study of this process. As will be seen below (and throughout this volume), the study of the ways in which individuals of various ages process their linguistic input and use it to construct or modify their personal grammars is critical to an understanding of language change in specific social environments. Therefore, our knowledge of these age-specific acquisitional trajectories can do a lot to inform historical sociolinguistic approaches to the emergence of new language varieties. This application of acquisitional theory to historical sociolinguistics can in turn start to integrate cognitive and social dynamics of language over time.

The discussion in this chapter is framed around three broad themes, each covered in a separate section. Section 2 articulates the need to understand processes of acquisition at different life stages when looking at new dialect emergence. Section 3 elaborates on how these ages of acquisition over the lifespan correspond to generational change in migrant or contact communities. Section 4 introduces examples of theories of acquisition that may be relevant to language change, and Section 5 turns specifically to how these models, and relatedly language dominance, can inform the study of new variety formation and sociohistorical change. Section 6 summarizes and concludes this chapter. Throughout the chapter, trends and examples from the literature of these proposals are used to illustrate these themes. Case studies from immigrant urban contexts (e.g., London, Stockholm) and non-Western societies (e.g., Iran, Australia, India, Singapore, Hong Kong) are emphasized, in order to expand the more traditional focus of sociolinguistic studies on non-immigrant Western communities. However, throughout the discussion of these 'high-contact' cases, I emphasize the intersection of acquisitional factors with social contact in determining outcomes. In short, whether intensive contact happens in childhood, adolescence, or adulthood can crucially affect linguistic outcomes.

2. Acquisition across life stages, social meaning, and emergent varieties

Research on new dialect formation in Western urban contexts has begun to show that acquisitional effects on sociohistorical change arise across all life stages. Although acquisition has historically not had a central role in variationist analyses of change and new dialect formation, it has long been implicated in such studies. Recent studies have taken acquisition of linguistic variation as a more central question and shed light on the ways in which individuals at various ages can contribute to the emergence of new varieties. This section examines the role of language acquisition in new variety formation at three broad life stages: younger childhood, later childhood and adolescence, and adulthood (see Chapters 2 and 3 in this volume). Using a range of empirical examples, we will see that differences in acquisition at each of these life stages can influence the form and speed of new variety formation in very different ways.

A particular focus in this section is on the *social* reinterpretation of linguistic forms at different ages, which can lead to wholesale change in usage. The study of new varieties emerging through social re-valuation and quantitative shifts in use has been largely centred in Western urban contexts, and so most examples in this section are from such settings. In the section that follows, we turn to the role of acquisition in long-term *structural* reorganization of language, with examples from the post-colonial development of new varieties of English.

The role of different age groups in language change is the subject of major theoretical debates in linguistics. Both formal and sociolinguistic research has demonstrated the role of child language acquisition in certain processes of language change (Kerswill 1996; Holmes-Elliott 2021; Lightfoot 1999; Oxbury & McCarthy 2019). Particularly in sociolinguistics, the later linguistic and acquisitional development of adolescents has also been widely discussed as instrumental in dialect change (Eckert 1997; Kerswill & Williams 2000). And finally, the diffusion of linguistic usage amongst adults who are past the critical period for dialect acquisition has also been argued to be a fundamental acquisitional distinction that accounts for distinct types of change and loss or preservation of complex rules (Payne 1980; Labov 2007). In this section we explore these three major acquisitional phases over the lifespan, with a focus on their contribution to the emergence of new varieties.[1]

2.1 The role of acquisition in childhood

At the youngest stage, children can fundamentally propel change in two ways, through *linguistic reorganization* and through *reindexing of social meaning*. I discuss each of these in turn.

Systematic linguistic reorganization – reanalysis, levelling, regularization – by children has been observed for mainstream language change (Lightfoot 1999) and for language and dialect formation in contact settings too (Winford 2003). In language change that does not involve what Thomason and Kaufman term *disruption*, i.e., in situations of sustained parent-child transmission of language (Labov 2007; see also *normal transmission* in Thomason & Kaufman 1988: 9–12), relatively faithful acquisition of the linguistic system occurs from child-directed input provided by adults. Lightfoot (1999) has nevertheless proposed that children are

---

1. For a discussion of the cognitive basis of some of these age-based differences elsewhere in this volume, see Chapter 1 (Section 3) and Chapter 2.

the locus of certain kinds of language change, particularly reanalysis and other forms of grammatical restructuring. In what Thomason and Kaufman termed 'disrupted' transmission, i.e., where the inter-generational input from carers to children in the given language is significantly disrupted, much more radical change can take place.

The most famous of these situations is the creation of creole languages by the first local-born children of speakers of an initial pidgin variety.[2] This was originally described in idealized terms as a single-generation creation of a new language or variety by the first generation of children to use the language natively. *Abrupt creolization* (see, for instance, Thomason & Kaufman 1988: 147–166) and child Universal Grammar were described as the cognitive driving forces of creole formation (Bickerton 1984). The degree to which this is the case is contested, however. For instance, Roberts (2000; see also Singler 2006 among others) has shown persuasively, using painstaking longitudinal historical data, that the quintessential example of this proposal, Hawaiʻian Creole, was not in fact formed in a single generation through the transformation of a pidgin into a creole by the first native-speaker children; rather, the Creole system found today developed over several generations in correspondence to moments of heightened demographic density of adolescents from particular ethnic groups over time. Even in recent cases of language emergence where the role of children seems key (as in the case of Nicaraguan Sign Language, see Kocab et al. 2016; Senghas & Coppola 2001; see also Chapters 7 and 8 in this volume), new grammars have been seen to develop from the action of consecutive cohorts of children, rather than from a single generation. We examine the role of adolescents and multi-generational change below.

In terms of social meaning, children can also play a central role in the wholesale re-indexing of standard speech forms. Labov (2001: 86) has described this process as *stylistic reinterpretation*: "Groups of speakers who are in contact with the community but are still excluded from its main rights and privileges will often participate in the use of linguistic variables with altered stylistic patterns. This applies to minority ethnic groups [...], children of the mainstream community, and geographic neighbors of smaller size."

We will examine minority ethnic groups and geographic neighbors later; our focus first is on Labov's mention of children of the mainstream community. In the quote above, Labov clarifies how children occupy centre stage in language change from the point of view of social meaning. A given form may be widespread and unremarkable in an adult population. However, from a child's perspective, in which *age* is a particularly salient social property, this form can gain an indexical

---

2. For an example of pidginization not involving creolization, see Chapter 12 in this volume.

association of 'old', regardless of whether the child has yet developed shared peer group indexicalities or identifications.

While child language acquisition plays an important part in systematic social re-indexing, and in some forms of syntactic and phonological analogy or reallocation, the extent to which they drive change is somewhat circumscribed. This is evident when we look at their acquisition of phonetic variation. Here, we see that children can very adeptly match caregiver input (Foulkes et al. 2005; Smith & Durham 2019). It is later ages, e.g., pre-teen and adolescence, that are more strongly associated with an increase in vernacularization and incrementation away from prevailing usage (Tagliamonte & D'Arcy 2009; Holmes-Elliott 2021). It must be noted, however, that the incrementation of vectors of change in vernacular norms by adolescents is predicated upon the existence of such established norms in the community: in cases of more unfocused variation or pervasive contact, younger learners have been shown to play an active role as leaders of change (e.g., O'Shannessy 2005; Sanz-Sánchez & Moyna 2023; see also Chapters 7 and 8 in this volume).

2.2 The role of acquisition in adolescence

When we turn to later childhood and teenage years, the nature of acquisition of linguistic systems and re-organization of the social meanings of forms changes somewhat. A key distinction is that between *transmission* and *diffusion*, introduced here primarily to distinguish between the impact of child and adult adoption of new forms, whether in high-contact or low-contact situations. Labov defines transmission as the "unbroken sequence of native-language acquisition by children" and relates this acquisitional process to diachronic relatedness of languages: "The continuity of dialects and languages across time is the result of the ability of children to replicate faithfully the form of the older generation's language, in all of its structural detail, with consequent preservation of the distances of the branches of the family tree" (2007: 346). By contrast, he defines diffusion as the spread of language forms "largely between and among adults", with much greater potential for loss or change in structure, on the assumption that "adults do not learn and reproduce linguistic forms, rules, and constraints with the accuracy and speed that children display" (349). Naturally, this distinction rests on accepting some form of a critical period for native-like language learning. While this assumption has been extensively debated, the present discussion accepts that there is an approximate critical period for native-like acquisition of language systems (see Newport 2002; Scovel 2000). In terms of acquiring new accent and dialect forms too, there is some evidence that the ability to fully acquire new forms (as compared to L1 native speakers) declines around this life stage (Payne 1980; Sharma 2018).[3]

For reasons of both acquisition and socialization, then, adolescence is a period of transition, at least in certain Western industrial societies. From the point of view of linguistic structure, if a variety develops primarily among adolescents, the more 'faithful' patterns of childhood transmission may be increasingly disrupted. From the point of view of social processes and social networks, the pre-teen and adolescent phase of life has been argued to contribute the most to new dialect formation (Tagliamonte & D'Arcy 2009). As noted, Roberts (2000) has convincingly shown that this was likely true even in what was originally described as the prototypical case of child-driven creole formation, Hawai'ian Creole. I describe two examples of new dialect formation here to emphasize the importance of pre-adolescence and adolescence in new variety formation (see also Chapter 9 in this volume).

Looking at the formation of new dialects through koinéization, when large numbers of people moved to English New Towns such as Milton Keynes after World War II, Kerswill and Williams (2000) found that the novel features of the new dialect were most noticeable among the older children, those approaching adolescence, and not among the more home-oriented younger children. Four-year-olds' social networks are still home-based, and so in the Milton Keynes data, these children were still overwhelmingly matching their home variety, participating in faithful transmission and acquisition of their parents' variety (see Foulkes et al. 2005; Smith & Durham 2019). It was the 8-year-olds and 12-year-olds who were shifting their social networks to be more peer-based, once embedded in school, and who were starting to koineize the distinct phonetic forms their families had brought to Milton Keynes from diverse regions, to create a new variety (see Chapter 4 in this volume).

Multicultural London English (MLE) is another new variety of British English but showcases a distinct mode of new dialect formation. It emerged in East and South London over the past 30–40 years in dense multi-ethnic enclaves within the original East London domains of Cockney (Kerswill & Torgersen 2020). It is spoken by young, working-class people of different ethnicities. Though led by non-White speakers, MLE has spread to speakers of all ethnicities in East London and is now more defined by class than ethnicity. Notably, its phonetic, grammatical, discourse, and lexical features stem from a very rich feature pool combining numerous heritage languages, L2 speech, creoles, post-colonial Englishes, and vernacular British forms (Cheshire et al. 2011). In this case, rather than

---

3. But see Chapter 3 in this volume for a discussion of the conditions in which adults may learn native-like variation in their L2.

the sustained transmission and koinéization observed in Milton Keynes, Cheshire et al. (2011) argue that the variety emerged out of group second language acquisition, whereby high levels of migration into parts of London led to a 'feature pool' (Mufwene 2001) of linguistic forms from vernacular British English, post-colonial varieties of English and L2 English together, with primarily 'lateral' peer-to-peer diffusion-like acquisition among children, adolescents and young adults.

Within this context, Cheshire et al. (2011: 186) offer a vivid case study of how the social context of adolescent acquisition at the individual level can drive change at the community level. They describe Abigail, a 13-year-old Albanian girl who moved to London aged 11 but who is a hyper-user of innovative phonetic and grammatical forms found in MLE. Her usage, which 'overshoots' that of her peers, may similarly reflect a need to show British belonging and authenticity (perhaps intensified by migrating just before adolescence), with a greater focus on the 'British' meaning of these innovative forms than their place in the class ecology of London. In the bigger picture, this individual dynamic, repeated across thousands of in-migrating children and teenagers, may systematically boost the use of new MLE forms in the peer group, speeding up processes of change underway.

2.3 The role of acquisition in adulthood

Finally, turning to adulthood, acquisition among first- and second-generation adults in situations of migration can similarly alter socio-indexical fields and intensify the rate and direction of change in a community. For example, Kerswill (1994) documented a classic example of rural migrants acquiring a new variant when arriving in a city, and re-interpreting this form – ə-lowering in the Norwegian spoken in Bergen – as urban rather than non-standard. For rural migrants coming to the city, the rural-urban divide was more salient in their personal frame of reference, and they used this form to signal urbanness, rather than non-standardness or informality.

In an earlier study, Modaressi-Tehrani (1978) observed a very similar process for a vernacular Persian phonetic form in Tehran, (aN)-raising, whereby rural migrants from the peripheral town of Ghazvin (about 140 km from Tehran) showed a novel use of this variant as prestigious rather than non-standard, due to the novel urban or cosmopolitan meaning that new adult acquirers associated it with.

More recently, Sharma (2021) has observed the same process among first generation South Asian adult migrants to London. Glottal replacement of /t/ is a classic vernacular London form that is well-known to correlate with casual speech in Britain. However, first-generation Asian migrants – individuals who moved to the UK as adults and lacked this dialect feature pre-migration – reserved their sparse use of glottal replacement of /t/ for *formal* speech ("I've go[ʔ] British passport now."). They tended to switch to /t/ or an Asian-style retroflex or retracted /ʈ/ in more engaged, relaxed speech ("He said throw glass of wa[ʈ]er eh outside- fron[ʈ] of- on top of me!"). When encountering this new British phonetic form, these adult migrants had little access to its usual British class meanings. The salient social meaning for them was a new cultural or ethnic meaning (Britishness), and so they used it to signal polite, formal accommodation to a British interlocutor. As we saw in the case of Abigail and diverse other cases above, when this acquisitional re-interpretation occurs on a large scale, it can potentially shift local meanings and give rise to change.

Finally, although not covered in detail here for reasons of space, it goes without saying that these processes of adult-to-adult diffusion lead to structural simplification and levelling of many kinds (e.g., loss of fine-grained phonological constraints or regularization of verb paradigms), not just social reindexing (see Chapters 10 and 11 in this volume for examples). The process accounts for widespread structural change in situations of contact among native speakers of a language too (see Labov 2007 for examples from numerous languages). Regardless of whether these structural innovations involve social reindexing, an important question is how these innovations emerging from individual acquisition spread throughout the community. This is examined next.

3. Age of acquisition and generational community change

The three life stages of acquisition outlined in the previous section – childhood, adolescence, and adulthood – often underpin a systematic macro-social pattern that has been observed in numerous multi-generational studies. In many of studies of contact and change, and in support of Roberts' critique of the original single-generation model, a *three-generation* timeframe for the establishment of a new variety has been observed. In abstract terms, it is possible to describe the first three generations of a migrant or contact community in terms of adult acquisition (Gen 1), adolescent acquisition (Gen 1.5/2), and childhood acquisition (Gen 3+). In this way, age of acquisition *intersects* with social environment to influence outcomes.

A few examples help to illustrate how the three life stages fit into the three-generational picture of new variety formation. Kerswill and Williams (2000), commenting on the observed speed of norm emergence in Milton Keynes, compare it to the data from the Høyanger variety of Norwegian studied by Omdal (1977):

> Yet there is strong evidence that focusing took place only in the third generation (the grandchildren of the migrants). Omdal states: "The first generation who were born and grew up in Høyanger [...] do not speak a unified dialect. Their speech bears the imprint of their parents' dialects [...]. To find a unified dialect, one must look to the next generation" (73)

They add:

> To explain these examples, we must look not only to the adults' speech accommodation [...] but also, in the light of the Milton Keynes children's linguistic behavior, to the young children's strategies. Taking first the failure of focusing to apply in the second generation, we must seek explanations both in social factors – such as the lack of opportunity for the formation of child peer groups in which the focusing can take place – and in linguistic factors, e.g., great linguistic differences. As for simplification, it is necessary to take account of the contribution of children, simply because they are demonstrably the main agents of focusing in Milton Keynes and elsewhere. (110)

There is evidence that other situations of contact closely replicate the incremental generational pattern observed in Milton Keynes. For instance, Sharma and Sankaran (2011) observed this same incremental emergence of a variety over generations of South Asians in London. They compare this pattern to parallels in Trudgill's analysis of the first generations of English speakers in New Zealand (and it is also reminiscent of Roberts' sociohistorical reanalysis of the genesis of Hawai'ian Creole). Their analysis focused on variants of /t/, mentioned earlier, in the English used by Punjabis in the London suburb of Southall. The data were studied through a generational lens, comparing the (India-born) G1 generation with both older and younger members of the (UK-born) G2 cohort. They found evidence of an emerging distribution of these two variants across members of the second generation. The older G2 participants combined the non-native use of the retroflex variant typical of the G1 with the native use of the glottal variant in a bidialectal pattern, maintaining the received phonological conditioning for both variants. By contrast, the younger G2 participants reorganized the phonetic constraints on the retroflex variant and also reallocated it, using it only sporadically to index ethnic allegiance as members of the immigrant group, but otherwise exhibiting the same use of /t/ variants as non-Punjabi L1 speakers of British English. The authors explain these incremental changes within the G2 in terms of the changing social experiences in the community over time:

> For the older group [of British-born Asians], surviving at school and in public involved an ability to downplay Indianness and to pass as British. This could be achieved both by acquiring nativelike use of British variants and possibly by beginning to "weaken" Asian variants phonetically, for instance, by favoring postalveolar variants. However, social survival also meant deep ties to their Asian world. Many went into their fathers' businesses and had direct transnational ties with family in India, conduits for the acquisition of Indian retroflexion and other forms. For this group, therefore, very strong and very distinct incentives existed for signaling authentic membership in both British and Indian groups, in different settings [leading to full bidialectal acquisition].

> [For the younger British Asian group] fewer direct ties account for their lack of fluent bidialectal ability in Indian English, and the lack of physical threat, hostility, or even substantial contact with non-Asians, reduced the need to pass as "purely" British as well. Both factors encouraged the use of occasional emblematic markers of Punjabiness integrated into British English, clearly distinct in form and function from what they see as "freshie" Indian English.
>
> (Sharma & Sankaran 2011: 423–424)

The sensitivity of the speakers' linguistic behavior to their changing social environment of acquisition also explains why the emergence of these new patterns may take some time: "[c]rucially, the younger Gen 2 group's modified retentions of foreign traits [...] did not develop immediately. [S]ystematic structural and social reallocation shows considerable lag in this community, focusing toward a new norm only two generations later" (424). This chronological progression is further proof of the generational staggering proposed for the focusing of other new varieties in historical and sociolinguistic studies: "[o]ur results bear a striking abstract resemblance to Trudgill's (2004) analysis of new-dialect formation in New Zealand, in which he argued that a focused variety only emerged at Stage III [i.e., the children of the first local born generation]" (424).

Young (2019) found a similar multi-generational shift in speech rhythm in the Swedish multiethnolect used by men in Rinkeby, a neighborhood of Stockholm with a high percentage of immigrant population. As in the case of British South Asians, the Swedish situation includes first generation migrants but then two different Stockholm-born generations. These working-class speakers with migrant heritage backgrounds had lower intervocalic alternation in their prosody than speakers from other groups, resulting in a so-called 'staccato' rhythm. However, speakers born before 1987 have much higher and more mainstream alternation than speakers born after 1987, very much like the bidialectal acquisition of the local British vernacular by older British Asians. The younger cohort achieved a staccato rhythm effect through very different phonetic means. When participants' school attendance was examined in relation to annual data on the ethnic and socioeconomic makeup of Stockholm schools, a discrete break in school systems was found that coincided closely with the change in phonetic systems. All speakers' schools were relatively diverse until 2001, after which a significant divergence in school types developed, with younger speakers born after 1987 attending predominantly ethnic-minority schools for most of their pre-teen and teen years, just at the time that linguistic innovation intensified. Once again, Young's findings point to immigrant groups as potentially propelling language change within the broader community.

Outside the Western context too and within a very different social embedding, this type of multi-generational restructuring has been described for mixed languages such as Light Warlpiri (O'Shannessy 2005), examined in more detail in Chapter 8 in this volume. Together, these examples offer a diachronic template for how different ages of acquisition and their respective social contexts relate to the distinct generational stages of a community undergoing new dialect formation. Cognitive theories on language acquisition also shed light on the sociohistorical dynamics in the emergence of new varieties; we turn to these in the next section.

4. Theories of language acquisition and new dialect formation

The final theme of this chapter turns to the cognitive underpinnings of acquisition, and their role in sociohistorical change. The section moves away from Western urban centres and focuses instead on the emergence of post-colonial contact varieties around the world over a longer time span, through generations of largely adult informal acquisition. While most of the examples in this section concern the expansion of English, the themes explored here can also apply to post-colonial varieties of other languages (e.g., Silva-Corvalán 1994). Particularly for the cognitive and processing dimension of acquisition (as opposed to social indexicality), specific theories of first and second language acquisition can illuminate long-term outcomes of language contact and change. In what follows, I show how several theories in second language acquisition (SLA) are potentially relevant to long-term dialect outcomes and the emergence of new varieties. The discussion in this section dovetails with several other chapters in this volume, including the presentation of L2 acquisition of variation in Chapter 3, the role of acquisition in dialect contact in Chapter 4, and the application of bilingual acquisition strategies in Chapter 5.

SLA models have traditionally been concerned with classroom learning, placing speakers on a trajectory towards a fixed, usually idealized, native target system. Longer-term naturalistic usage that diverged from the target over time was acknowledged but nevertheless seen as a fossilized, incomplete stage of learning. For instance, new varieties of English in post-colonial settings were thus initially described in terms of fossilization (Selinker 1972) and pedagogical concerns (Agnihotri & Khanna 1994; Quirk 1990).

Scholars soon countered that the full cognitive and social life of these communities could not be depicted simply as failed SLA (e.g., Kachru 1983; see Canagarajah 2013 for a similar, more recent critique). This observation is particularly relevant to contexts of language contact where schooling or other forms of exposure to standardized L1 models are not a part of the sociolinguistic ecology for most speakers. In this vein, Sridhar and Sridhar (1992) pointed to the absence of a native target, heterogeneous modes of transmission among non-native speakers, and a stable, functional role for English in multilingual settings. Unlike classroom SLA, the original (colonial) native target is generally absent in these English contexts, and transmission proceeds from one local (often L2) speaker to another. This process allows features that may have originated as transitory individual SLA features to become dialect features over time. A good example is Singapore, where this shift from individual SLA to a new variety is dramatically visible. Platt et al. (1984) cite the example of older Indian Singaporeans, who retain Indian features in their speech, in contrast to the younger generation of Indian Singaporeans who, according to an identification study, were indistinguishable from other Singaporeans. Younger Indian Singaporeans have acquired a dialect with Chinese-derived features even though they may not be speakers of Chinese languages themselves. Ultimately, the acquisition effect in these situations becomes historical rather than in the individual, but individual acquisitional trajectories across populations of speakers sharing similar social histories are at the root of this process.

After an initial rejection of SLA accounts of New Englishes, scholars began to reintroduce acquisitional factors, but in a more nuanced way than previous literature (e.g., Meriläinen & Paulasto 2014; Mukherjee & Hundt 2011). For instance, Hilbert (2008), examining interrogative inversion in Indian and Singapore English, finds robust parallels to intermediate stages of L2 acquisition, including a reliance on formulaic chunks and strikingly similar preferences for (non)-inversion with different auxiliaries. Mesthrie (2001) also showed the presence of each developmental stage claimed for L1 and L2 acquisition of negation in English in an elegant analysis of a subsample of Black South African English. Van Rooy (2011) has similarly identified stabilizing innovations in Black South African English that may have originated as SLA errors. Davydova (2011) uses a continuum of relative complexity and difficulty of acquisition of selected English forms adapted from Housen (2002) to argue that L2-easy and L2-difficult features emerge differently in New Englishes, irrespective of the L1. Finally, at a more global level, Szmrecsanyi (2009) has examined contrasts across varieties according to a hierarchy of morphosyntactic complexity and analyticity in Englishes across variety types, implicitly invoking an acquisitional and contact basis for structural simplification in certain types of English.

I turn next to a number of specific theoretical proposals in SLA and show their relevance for post-colonial new dialect formation (and potentially for other sociohistorical contact processes). The *Subset Principle* (Fodor & Sakas 2005; Pinker 1984; Wexler & Manzini 1987) was proposed as a model of how learners navigate towards a target grammar. The model has been critiqued as too strong to offer a global account of first language acquisition, but the fundamental contrast it describes is very likely to play some part in acquisition, perhaps even more so in second language acquisition, where a clear contrast arises between two grammars (Ayoun 1996; White 1989).

In this model, two possible relationships between a learner's hypothesized grammar for their second language (L2) and the actual target grammar are a subset relation and a superset relation. If a learner is starting from a grammar that generates a subset of the grammatical constructions of the target grammar, they can expand straightforwardly to the target because they will encounter naturally occurring positive evidence of further constructions used in the language. However, if their initial hypothesized grammar generates a superset of the constructions allowed by the target grammar (e.g., because their L1 has that superset system), then they are already generating all standard uses and will require explicit negative evidence in order to eliminate ungrammatical outputs. Naturally encountered data will not achieve this easily. The prediction is therefore that a learner will find it harder to accurately acquire an L2 if their L1 generates a superset of that system.

When we compare Indian English to British English (the historical target variety), we can see this effect in action (Sharma 2009). Because of the nature of perfectivity marking in Indo-Aryan languages like Hindi, Indian English speakers who have variable use of overt past tense marking in English tend to reserve it more for perfective past verbs, as in Hindi. This is a *subset* of actual standard English use of the past tense, as British English permits past morphology with both perfective verbs (*I finished*) and imperfective verbs (*I wanted*). Learners will quickly encounter explicit counterevidence in the form of past imperfective clauses in English and expand their learner grammar. By contrast, Indian English speakers often use of the progressive *-ing* form in English as an imperfective marker, also on analogy with the Hindi imperfective marker *-ta*. So they can use it with progressive meaning (*I was leaving*) but also stative meaning (*I was knowing*). This generates a *superset* of British English uses. Indian English speakers already produce the entire set of target constructions and more, and so would need explicit negative feedback to identify which constructions to eliminate. Sharma (2009) argues that this may explain why, over time, it is the over-use of the progressive that became established as a hallmark of Indian English, and not under-use of the past tense form, which tends to be used more like British English.

Another recent theory in SLA that may underpin long-term outcomes in new varieties is the *Interface Hypothesis*, which argues that syntactic properties that involve an interface with another cognitive domain, particularly the syntax-pragmatics interface, may be more difficult to fully acquire than narrow syntax (i.e., non-interface) properties due to the nature of input needed for acquisition and related processing loads (Sorace & Filiaci 2006; Sorace & Serratrice 2009; also Müller & Hulk 2001 for bilingual L1 acquisition). The claim, put simply, is that "narrow syntactic properties are completely acquirable in a second language, even though they may exhibit significant developmental delays, whereas interface properties involving syntax and another cognitive domain may not be fully acquirable" (Sorace & Filiaci 2006: 340). Once again, this model is fundamentally concerned with which features require more input to be resolved, and so is potentially relevant for post-colonial contexts of declining input from the lexifier language.

Once again, examining Indian and Singapore English, effects of this kind in dialect outcomes can be observed. For example, research has found that L1-L2 differences in the topic-sensitivity of subject drop (an interface syntax area) can lead to an erosion of featural requirements such as [+topic] or [+subject] in one or both languages. The erosion of these features leads to underspecification and ambiguity, which are often resolved in favor of universal discourse pragmatic licensing to optimize processing. Serratrice et al. (2004) showed that bilingual English-Italian children did this: as topic-drop rules for subjects differ in their two languages, the children resorted to an optimized discourse strategy. In both English and Italian, null subjects "were constrained by discourse pragmatics: null arguments were significantly more likely to be associated with uninformative than informative features" (p.199). This precise effect was found in Indian English and Singapore English use of articles, which were significantly more likely to be omitted in uninformative, or redundant, NPs (Sharma 2005).

Following a similar line of thinking, Ingham (2017) has argued that interface effects could account for why we see more change at the syntax-semantics interface than in narrow syntax in a different long-term contact situation, which he exemplifies with the case of Anglo-Norman French. For a more recent historical ecology, Yao (2016) has proposed that the Interface Hypothesis may also account for the use of cleft construction in Hong Kong English.

The two models described here all relate to how much input is needed by a learner. In the case of new post-colonial varieties, this input commonly shifts from native 'settler' speakers such as British English-speaking colonizers (Schneider 2007) to indigenous, often non-native or bilingual diffusion within the post-colonial region. Input is therefore very likely a crucial dimension of acquisition that is implicated in long-term post-colonial dialect outcomes.

Intriguingly, a wider typological comparison of grammatical change in New Englishes complicates the picture, and suggests that some features that do *not* require a lot of input nevertheless resist full acquisition in the long term. One example is persistent errors in the use of *he* and *she* by advanced L2 English speakers of languages such as Mandarin or Hungarian. Despite readily available evidence of a need to track the gender of the referent, learnability remains compromised for speakers of L1s that lack grammatical gender. This difficulty suggests that input is not the only factor in SLA-driven change (see DeKeyser 2020). The L1 grammar is an additional, possibly even stronger constraint, placing hard limits on learnability in some domains of grammar (see Chapter 5 in this volume). These observations in fact support a competing set of SLA models, all of which focus on core obstacles to perfect L2 acquisition, such as the *Failed Features Hypothesis* (Hawkins & Chan 1997), the *Feature Reassembly* and the *Bottleneck Hypotheses* (Lardiere 2009; Slabakova 2008), and the *Interpretability Hypothesis* (Tsimpli & Dimitrakopoulou 2007), and offer less support for models that L2 learners may, with sufficient input, rely on the same UG principle as L1 learners to guide their acquisition of a second language, such as the *Full Transfer/Full Access Hypothesis* (Schwartz & Sprouse 1994).

Besides consideration of specific L2 acquisition models, this brief discussion suggests a bidirectional benefit to bringing acquisition research to bear on the study of new variety formation. Not only can theories of SLA enhance our understanding of why certain contact features become entrenched more than others, but these cases of diachronic change can also feed back into debates within SLA theory. Overall, the studies reviewed here suggest that full sociohistorical elucidation of the circumstances in which new varieties emerge should include not only the acquisitional contribution of speakers of various ages and their sociolinguistic environment, but also the actual linguistic properties of the alternatives in the speakers' linguistic pools.[4]

5. Language acquisition and the emergence of new varieties: Challenges and opportunities

In closing, I reflect briefly on both challenges and opportunities in applying questions of language acquisition to the study of how new varieties emerge, and describe how the studies in this section of the book make headway in this regard.

Although acquisition has been an acknowledged component of language variation and change and the emergence of new varieties for a long time, the recent interest in incorporating a lifespan acquisition perspective into the sociohistorical study of change faces challenges in a few areas. First, analysis of acquisitional effects requires specific types of data – elicited judgements, language dominance, biographical detail – that may be scarce or entirely inaccessible in earlier stages of a community (i.e., an acquisitional version of the *bad data* problem typically faced by historical sociolinguists, Auer et al. 2015). Language dominance in particular has been shown in the previous section to be a key factor. Second, the need for fine-grained information about social context and individual dominance

---

4. See Chapter 4 in this volume for a model to integrate the speaker's full linguistic repertoire in acquisition-based historical sociolinguistic accounts.

or usage has direct implications for method and analysis. Certain comparative, elicited, or experimental methods and analysis may be ruled out for sociohistorical data, forcing analysts to find creative ways to infer acquisitional effects; some of these modifications and solutions were discussed in earlier sections. And finally, in terms of theoretical modelling too, models of classroom SLA do not apply straightforwardly to naturalistic historical or contemporary settings. This too is a long-standing challenge that creolists and language contact scholars have wrestled with for decades.

However, the preceding discussion has shown that these practical obstacles should not prevent us from looking at the role of acquisition in change, as it clearly is a fundamental, contributing element. All of the examples above have shown that historical patterns of social variation and change can be better understood with a wider lens that incorporates an analysis of not only linguistic structure and social indexicality, but also acquisition over the lifespan. Just as linguists cannot gain direct access to the brain to observe language processing, so too must scholars of language change find creative solutions to accessing and analysing acquisitional data, even if indirectly, to track its role in change.

The detailed case studies in this volume all relate directly to these challenges and opportunities as well as to the wider themes above. They richly demonstrate the operation of these principles in the formation of new varieties, as well as solutions to some of the practical challenges. Some of these solutions include the application of crosslinguistic comparisons and demographic reconstruction as a window into the sociohistorical evolution of the community (Chapter 11), the combination of sociophonetics corpora with more traditional written data (Chapters 9 and 10), the incorporation of L1 and L2 acquisitional data (Chapters 7 and 12), or the direct observation of generational differences in emergent language communities (Chapter 8).

The cases studies draw together the many themes outlined in this chapter: the cognitive and processing effects of language dominance, differences in language acquisition at different ages, and the sensitivity of social indexicality and social positioning to life stage. Across all these studies, we see that the socio-cognitive lens of language acquisition over the individual lifespan fundamentally expands our understanding of how new varieties take shape over generations.

6. Conclusion

This chapter has reviewed the role of acquisitional factors at different stages of the lifespan in longer-term emergence of new language varieties. To understand different dimensions of this process, we examined two broad types of cases. First, the emergence of new multiethnolects and similar contemporary contact situations showed fine differences in how the age of exposure and acquisition, as well as the social context of that acquisition, altered the course of a given variety in distinct ways. Second, case studies primarily from the context of the colonial imposition and expansion of English were used to look more closely at how specific theories of second language acquisition might retrospectively account for which grammatical features came to be most established within a particular linguistic ecology. Interestingly, this latter set of cases also indicated that such situations of emergence out of contact can in turn also inform theoretical claims in the acquisition literature. The discussion has shown that new variety formation, particularly in situations of migration and contact, is one of the most instructive contexts in which to study the interface between language acquisition and historical sociolinguistics.

References

Agnihotri, Rama Kant & Amrit Lal Khanna (eds.). 1994. *L2 acquisition: Sociocultural and linguistic aspects of English in India*. New Delhi: Sage.

Auer, Anita, Catharina Peersman, Simon Pickl, Gijsbert Rutten & Rik Vosters. 2015. Historical sociolinguistics: the field and its future. *Journal of Historical Sociolinguistics* 1(1). 1–12.

Ayoun, Dalila. 1996. The subset principle in second language acquisition. *Applied Psycholinguistics* 17(2). 185–213.

Bickerton, Derek. 1984. The Language Bioprogram Hypothesis. *The Behavioral and Brain Sciences* 7(2). 173–188.

Canagarajah, Suresh. 2013. *Translingual practice: Global Englishes and cosmopolitan relations*. London: Routledge.

Cheshire, Jenny, Paul Kerswill, Sue Fox & Eivind Torgersen. 2011. Contact, the feature pool and the speech community: The emergence of Multicultural London English. *Journal of Sociolinguistics*, 15(2). 151–196.

Davydova, Julia. 2011. *The present perfect in non-native Englishes: A corpus-based study*. Berlin: De Gruyter Mouton.

DeKeyser, Robert. 2020. Input is not a panacea. *International Journal of Bilingualism* 24(1). 79–81.

Eckert, Penelope. 1997. Age as a sociolinguistic variable. In Florian Coulmas (ed.), *The handbook of sociolinguistics*, 151–167. Oxford: Blackwell.

Fodor, Janet & William Sakas. 2005. The Subset Principle in syntax: Costs of compliance. *Journal of Linguistics* 41. 513–569.

Foulkes, Paul, Gerry Docherty & Dominic Watt. 2005. Phonological variation in child-directed speech. *Language* 81(1).177–206.

Hawkins, Roger & Cecilia Chan. 1997. The partial availability of Universal Grammar in second language acquisition: the 'failed functional features hypothesis'. *Second Language Research* 13(3). 187–226.

Hilbert, Michaela. 2008. Interrogative inversion in non-standard varieties of English. In Peter Siemund & Noemi Kintana (eds.), *Language contact and contact languages*, 261–289. Amsterdam: Benjamins.

Holmes-Elliott, Sophie. 2021. Calibrate to innovate: Community age vectors and the real time incrementation of language change. *Language in Society* 50(3). 441–474.

Housen, Alex. 2002. The development of tense-aspect in English as a second language and the variable influence of inherent aspect. In Rafael Salaberry & Yasuhiro Shirai (eds.), *The L2 acquisition of tense-aspect morphology*, 155–195. Amsterdam: John Benjamins.

Ingham, Richard. 2017. Maintenance and change in language contact: The case of Anglo-Norman. *Zeitschrift für Dialektologie und Linguistik* 84 (2–3). 383–402.

Kachru, Braj. 1983. *The indianization of English: The English language in India*. Oxford: Oxford University Press.

Kerswill, Paul. 1994. *Dialects converging: Rural speech in urban Norway*. Clarendon Press.

Kerswill, Paul. 1996. Children, adolescents and language change. *Language Variation and Change* 8. 177–202.

Kerswill, Paul & Eivind Torgersen. 2020. Tracing the origins of an urban youth vernacular: founder effects, frequency and culture in the emergence of Multicultural London English. In Karen Beaman, Isa Buchstaller, Sue Fox, Stephen Levey & James A. Walker (eds.), *Socio-grammatical variation and change: In honour of Jenny Cheshire*, 249–276. London: Routledge.

Kerswill, Paul & Ann Williams. 2000. Creating a new town koine: children and language change in Milton Keynes. *Language in Society* 29(1). 65–115.

Kocab, Annemarie, Ann Senghas & Jesse Snedeker. 2016. The emergence of temporal language in Nicaraguan Sign Language. *Cognition* 156. 147–163.

Labov, William. 2001. *Principles of linguistic change, Vol. 2: Social Factors*. Malden, MA: Blackwell.

Labov, William. 2007. Transmission and diffusion. *Language* 83(2). 344–387.

Lardiere, Donna. 2009. Some thoughts on the contrastive analysis of features in second language acquisition. *Second Language Research*, 25(2). 173–227.

Lightfoot, David. 1999. *The development of language: Acquisition, change, and evolution*. Oxford: Blackwell.

Meriläinen, Lea & Heli Paulasto. 2014. Embedded inversion as an angloversal: Evidence from inner, outer, and expanding circle Englishes. In Markku Filppula, Juhani Klemola & Devyani Sharma (eds.), *The Oxford handbook of world Englishes*, 191–216. Oxford: Oxford University Press.

Mesthrie, Rajend. 2001. Male workers' English in the Western Cape – interlanguage, code-switching and pidginisation. In Stanley Ridge, Elaine Ridge & Sinfree Makoni (eds.), *Freedom and discipline: Essays in applied linguistics from Southern Africa*, 85–104. New Delhi: Bahri.

Modaressi-Tehrani, Yahya. 1978. A sociolinguistic analysis of modern Persian. Lawrence, KS: University of Kansas PhD dissertation.

Mufwene, Salikoko. 2001. *The ecology of language evolution*. Cambridge: Cambridge University Press.

Mukherjee, Joybrato & Marianne Hundt (eds.). 2011. *Exploring second-language varieties of English and learner Englishes: Bridging a paradigm gap*. Amsterdam: John Benjamins.

Müller, Natascha & Hulk, Aafke. 2001. Crosslinguistic influence in bilingual language acquisition: Italian and French as recipient languages. *Bilingualism: Language and Cognition* 4(1). 1–22.

Newport, Elissa. 2002. Critical periods in language development. In Lynn Nadel (ed.), *Encyclopedia of cognitive science*, 737–740. London: Macmillan.

Omdal, Helge. 1977. Høyangermålet – en ny dialekt. *Språklig Samling* 18. 7–9.

O'Shannessy, Carmen. 2005. Light Warlpiri: A new language. *Australian Journal of Linguistics* 25(1). 31–57.

Oxbury, Rosie & Kathleen McCarthy. 2019. Acquiring a multiethnolect: the production of diphthongs by children and adolescents in West London. In Sasha Calhoun, Paola Escudero, Marija Tabain & Paul Warren (eds.), *Proceedings of the 19th International Congress of Phonetic Sciences*, 2208–2212. International Phonetic Association. https://www.internationalphoneticassociation.org/icphs-proceedings/ICPhS2019/papers/ICPhS_2257.pdf (15 October 2021).

Payne, Arvilla. 1980. Factors controlling the acquisition of Philadelphia dialect by out-of-state children. In William Labov (ed.), *Locating language in time and space*, 143–178. New York: Academic Press.

Pinker, Steven. 1984. *Language learnability and language development*. Cambridge, MA: Harvard University Press.

Platt, John, Heidi Weber & Ho Mian Lian. 1984. *The new Englishes*. London: Routledge.

Quirk, Randolph. 1990. Language varieties and standard language. *English Today* 6(1). 3–10.

Roberts, Sarah. 2000. Nativization and the genesis of Hawaiian Creole. In John McWhorter (ed.), *Language change and language contact in pidgins and creoles*, 257–300. Amsterdam: John Benjamins.

Sanz-Sánchez, Israel & María Irene Moyna. 2023. Children as agents of language change: Diachronic evidence from Latin American Spanish phonology. *Journal of Historical Linguistics* 13(3). 327–374.

Schneider, Edgar. 2007. *Postcolonial English: Varieties around the world*. Cambridge: Cambridge University Press.

Schwartz, Bonnie & Rex Sprouse. 1994. Word order and nominative case in nonnative language acquisition: A longitudinal study of (L1 Turkish) German interlanguage. In Teun Hoekstra & Bonnie Schwartz (eds.), *Language acquisition studies in generative grammar*, 317–368. Amsterdam: John Benjamins.

Scovel, Thomas. 2000. A critical review of the critical period research. *Annual Review of Applied Linguistics* 20. 213–223.

Selinker, Larry. 1972. Interlanguage. *International Review of Applied Linguistics in Language Teaching* 10. 209–241.

Senghas, Ann & Marie Coppola. 2001. Children creating language: How Nicaraguan Sign Language acquired a spatial grammar. *Psychological Science* 12(4). 323–328.

Serratrice, Ludovica, Antonella Sorace & Sandra Paoli. 2004. Cross-linguistic at the syntax-pragmatics interface: Subjects and objects in Italian-English bilingual and monolingual acquisition. *Bilingualism: Language and Cognition* 7(3). 183–205.

Sharma, Devyani. 2005. Language transfer and discourse universals in Indian English article use. *Studies in Second Language Acquisition* 27(4). 535–566.

Sharma, Devyani. 2009. Typological diversity in New Englishes. *English World-Wide* 30(2). 170–195.

Sharma, Devyani. 2018. Style dominance: Attention, audience, and the 'real me'. *Language in Society* 47(1). 1–33.

Sharma, Devyani. 2021. Biographical indexicality. In Lauren Hall-Lew, Emma Moore & Robert Podesva (eds.), *Social meaning and linguistic variation: Theorizing the third wave*, 243–264. Cambridge: Cambridge University Press.

Sharma, Devyani & Lavanya Sankaran. 2011. Cognitive and social forces in dialect shift: Gradual change in London Asian speech. *Language Variation and Change* 23. 399–428.

Silva-Corvalán, Carmen. 1994. *Language contact and change: Spanish in Los Angeles*. Oxford: Clarendon.

Singler, John. 2006. Yes, but not in the Caribbean. *Journal of Pidgin and Creole Languages* 21(2). 337–358.

Slabakova, Roumyana. 2008. *Meaning in the second language*. Berlin: De Gruyter Mouton.

Smith, Jennifer & Mercedes Durham. 2019. *Sociolinguistic variation in children's language: Acquiring community norms*. Cambridge: Cambridge University Press.

Sorace, Antonella & Francesca Filiaci. 2006. Anaphora resolution in near-native speakers of Italian. *Second Language Research* 22(3). 339–368.

Sorace, Antonella & Ludovica Serratrice. 2009. Internal and external interfaces in bilingual language development: Beyond structural overlap. *International Journal of Bilingualism* 13(2). 1–16.

Sridhar, Kamal & Shikaripur Sridhar. 1992. Bridging the paradigm gap: Second-language acquisition theory and indigenized varieties of English. In Braj Kachru (ed.), *The other tongue*, 91–108. Urbana, IL: University of Illinois Press.

Szmrecsanyi, Benedikt. 2009. Typological parameters of intralingual variability: grammatical analyticity versus syntheticity in varieties of English. *Language Variation and Change* 21(3). 319–353.

Tagliamonte, Sali & Alexandra D'Arcy. 2009. Peaks beyond phonology: Adolescence, incrementation, and language change. *Language* 85(1). 58–108.

Thomason, Sarah & Terrence Kaufman. 1988. *Language contact, creolization, and genetic linguistics*. Berkeley: University of California Press.

Trudgill, Peter. 2004. *New-dialect formation: The inevitability of colonial Englishes*. Edinburgh: Edinburgh University Press.

Tsimpli, Ianthi Maria & Maria Dimitrakopoulou. 2007. The Interpretability Hypothesis: evidence from wh-interrogatives in second language acquisition. *Second Language Research* 23(2). 215–242.

van Rooy, Bertus. 2011. A principled distinction between error and conventionalized innovation in African Englishes. In Joybrato Mukherjee & Marianne Hundt (eds.), *Exploring second-language varieties of English and learner Englishes: Bridging a paradigm gap*, 189–208. Amsterdam: John Benjamins.

Wexler, Kenneth & M. Rita Manzini. 1987. Parameters and learnability in binding theory. In Thomas Roeper & Edwin Williams. (eds.), *Parameter setting*, 41–76. Dordrecht: Reidel.

White, Lydia. 1989. *Universal grammar and second language acquisition*. Amsterdam: John Benjamins.

Winford, Donald. 2003. *An introduction to contact linguistics*. Oxford: Blackwell.
Yao, Xinyue. 2016. Cleft constructions in Hong Kong English. *English World-Wide* 37(2). 197–220.
Young, Nathan. 2019. Rhythm in late-modern Stockholm – Social stratification and stylistic variation in the speech of men. London: Queen Mary University of London. PhD dissertation.

PART III

Case studies

CHAPTER 7

Tracing the emergence of the *voseo/tuteo* semantic split in Río de la Plata second person subjunctives
The role of child language acquisition

María Irene Moyna & Pablo E. Requena
Texas A&M University | The University of Texas at San Antonio

This study documents the history of second person singular informal variation in Rioplatense Spanish. It focuses on the competition between *voseo* and *tuteo* forms in the subjunctive and proposes that the outcome of this variation can be linked to the acquisition of these forms by children. In contrast with other verb forms in the variety, which eradicated *tuteo* progressively, in the subjunctive *tuteo* prevailed in epistemic contexts, while *voseo* continued to be possible in deontic contexts. By combining data from the historical record (Study 1) with converging data from contemporary children acquiring the same structures (Study 2), we show that the subjunctive forms most likely to select *tuteo* are acquired later, making them more susceptible to normative influence. Because changes in the second singular present subjunctive coincided with the spread of public education in the region, we argue that the semantic split resulted from the interaction of linguistic, social, and developmental factors, and sketch a sociohistorical account for the actuation of this change.

Keywords: *voseo*, *tuteo*, Rioplatense Spanish, subjunctive, diachronic change, language acquisition, language variation

1. Introduction

This study documents the morphological evolution of Rioplatense Spanish (RPS) – the Spanish variety spoken in Buenos Aires and Montevideo, the capitals of Argentina and Uruguay on either side of the Río de la Plata estuary, and which spreads from there to other localities in the interior. The specific morphological change analyzed involves the competition between two second person singular (2SG) variants of the present subjunctive (standard *tuteo* vs. vernacular *voseo*) which resulted in changes to their overall frequencies, but, more importantly, in different rates of use by the modality expressed by the subjunctive (deontic vs. epistemic). We focus on changes spanning the period between the late 19th and the early 21st centuries, which have been previously documented (Fontanella de Weinberg 1979; Johnson 2016a, b; Johnson & Grinstead 2011; Siracusa 1972), but not accounted for satisfactorily. The process started under social conditions of great demographic upheaval, which led to the proliferation of competing forms. However, sociohistorical circumstances alone cannot account for the ensuing trajectory of change. Instead, the specialization of variants will be linked to their acquisitional properties, a hypothesis which we tested empirically in a complementary experiment with children from the same dialectal area.

We contend that, as proposed by the *cascade principle* (DeGraff 2009), both children and adults had a part in the change, but their roles were different. While adults were responsible for providing heterogeneous linguistic data, children did not merely replicate this heterogeneity, but instead, they made it systematic by eliminating variation (Hudson Kam 2015; Hudson Kam & Newport 2005, 2009) and using the difference to convey subtle semantic distinctions.[1] We show that the deontic subjunctive, typically acquired during the preschool years, was more likely to retain non-standard (*voseo*) forms. By contrast, the epistemic subjunctive, which requires sophisticated cognitive capacities and develops concurrently with formal education (Dracos et al. 2019; Pérez-Leroux 1998; Requena et al. 2017; Sánchez-Naranjo & Pérez-Leroux 2010), was more susceptible to prescriptive pressure. We propose that *tuteo* subjunctive adoption in epistemic contexts is linked to the generalization of mandatory schooling in the region during the late 19th and early 20th centuries. This chronology explains why the early-acquired deontic contexts of the subjunctive were less susceptible to normativization and retained higher levels of *voseo*, while the late acquisition of epistemic subjunctives made these forms more vulnerable to the influence of the standard forms presented in school classrooms, which led to *tuteo* generalization.

For this argument to be plausible, it must combine two types of evidence. First, it requires that we document the specific path of change in the available historical record. Second, we must present data from contemporary children as they acquire these same forms. Following the *uniformitarian approach* (DeGraff 2009; Labov 2001), according to which cognition follows universal age-specific

---

1. See also Chapters 2, 5 and 6 in this volume for further discussion of the acquisitional contributions of children and adults to the emergence of new dialectal norms. See Chapter 8 for another case study that reveals a similar interaction among speakers of various ages, including young children.

developmental stages, current acquisition data are relevant to the reconstruction of past change. As other chapters in this volume, we strive to articulate a more solid heuristics for the explanation of language change from a historical sociolinguistic perspective than studies that do not incorporate acquisitional correlates.

In what follows, we summarize the external and internal forces that shaped the 2SG verbal paradigm. First, we present a sociohistorical and demographic account of the Río de la Plata region (Section 2), followed by a description of the evolution of its address system, the features of the subjunctive, and the current structure of variation in 2SG subjunctive (Section 3). Study 1 reanalyzes available historical data to show the sequence of *voseo/tuteo* evolution in the subjunctive for the period of interest (Section 4). Then, Study 2 reports on experimental data from present-day children as they acquire subjunctives in the same dialect area (Section 5). Section 6 discusses how contemporary acquisition experimental data can help link past and present stages of the subjunctive from a sociohistorical perspective. Section 7 concludes the paper and points to future research.

2. A brief sociodemographic history of the Río de la Plata

Because *voseo/tuteo* variation in the address paradigm of RPS dates back to the earliest Spanish settlement in the 16th century, it is necessary to consider the demographics of the area since colonial times. Given the Spanish interest in precious metals in the Andean region, Spanish settlement in the Río de la Plata started inland, in Asunción (founded in 1537), and faced west. The early European contingents represented different Spanish varieties, as well as other Peninsular languages such as Portuguese and Basque (Boyd-Bowman 1985). The scarcity of women among the Spanish settlers led to intermarriage with the local population and to the subsequent emergence of *mestizos* (Sarreal 2014: 17, 21). These Hispano-Guaraní creole populations then spread their linguistic varieties southward, to Buenos Aires (1580) and Montevideo (1730), remote areas that few Europeans were willing to settle in. For most of the colonial period, these towns remained small and marginal, with limited reach into the surrounding countryside. Spanish thus never completely displaced indigenous languages, partly because large populations of Guaraní speakers lived in isolation in Catholic missions, and partly because seminomadic groups continued to inhabit the hinterland well into the 19th century.

After independence in the 1810s, Uruguay and Argentina both underwent rapid economic and demographic changes, as sources of raw materials for industrializing European nations, especially Britain. The process accelerated after the 1860s, leading to an improvement in the economic outlook for the region. Modern livestock management was made possible by the introduction of barbed wire (Nahum 1968), making it easier to control large herds with less labor. The resulting surplus rural workers were forced to migrate to towns and cities to eke out a living in incipient industries, bringing with them their vernacular speech.

There, these working-class rural populations encountered a second contingent crucial to the demographic transformation of the Río de la Plata, namely, European immigrants who were also lured to the region by the prospect of economic opportunities. These immigrants, mainly from Mediterranean countries (the Iberian Peninsula and Italy), together with their descendants, are estimated to have been responsible for over half of the total population growth of Argentina between 1869 and 1959 (Germani 1966: 167), and for the sevenfold demographic growth of Uruguay between 1850 and 1900 (Goebel 2010). The newcomers concentrated in the burgeoning capital cities, where they lived in tenements and neighborhoods alongside the local working class, and they soon mixed with them, as suggested by low rates of endogamy (Goebel 2010).

Because of the sustained high levels of immigration, there was no gradual assimilation: instead, a new hybrid culture emerged. One of its characteristics was linguistic contact between different native Spanish varieties and second language (L2) interlanguages, that is, an idiosyncratic variety developed by learners and characterized by transfer of features from their native language, incomplete acquisition, and overgeneralization of rules (Selinker 1972; see also Chapter 3 in this volume). In this context, the institutionalization of mandatory public education provided a crucial tool for social cohesion. Within five years (1877–1882) both Uruguay and Argentina had made primary school mandatory and free, leading to large drops in illiteracy by the early 20th century (Spalding 1972: 46; Sucazes & Andina n.d.). As a result, working-class children of different backgrounds were thrust together in an environment with competing linguistic varieties, whose contact contributed to the formation of a new urban RPS norm. In the next section, we focus on the development of the informal address paradigm of this variety, and in particular, on its peculiar present subjunctive split.

3. Address forms in RPS

3.1 The diachrony of informal address in RPS

Although we have scanty written evidence from either Buenos Aires or Montevideo, data from the rest of Spanish America suggest that the Spaniards who first arrived in the continent brought with them a complex and unstable 2SG system, including variation in informal address (pronominal/verbal paradigms etymologically associated with *vos* and *tú*) and formal address (*vos/usted/él~ella*) (Fontanella de Weinberg 1993). Given the very early date of Spanish settlement in the Río de la Plata, these must have been the forms that were first acquired by the original *mestizo* population and their descendants. Lack of normative pressure due to low literacy, isolation from Spain, and the absence of large urban areas that could encourage *koine* formation, made it possible for this original heterogeneity to persist over time. In what follows, attention will be paid to informal paradigms, which are both the most relevant to our argument and the most complicated to trace in the historical record.

Personal letters in the colonial Spanish CORDIAM database (Academia Mexicana de la Lengua 2022) show two 2SG informal pronouns, *tú* and *vos*, each with its verbal paradigm (*tuteo* and *voseo*), in use throughout the continent from the earliest periods. *Vos*, a second person plural (2PL) form in Classical Latin, evolved in Late Latin and Hispano Romance, first into a polite 2SG form, and later into a familiar 2SG that competed with *tú* for pragmatic contexts towards the end of the medieval period (Penny 1991: 123–125). Over the 16th and 17th centuries, *tuteo* became categorical in Peninsular Spanish and in those colonies that sustained frequent contacts with Spain (e.g., Mexico, Antilles, coastal Peru). By contrast, in the remote Río de la Plata, *vos* and *tú* continued to compete for centuries. Vernacular *voseo* was beyond the reach of prescriptive pressure, since it was used in intimate discourse and in a region with low social hierarchization and virtually no schooling (see Section 2). For a comparison of 2SG exponents in RPS, Table 1 includes the subject pronoun, imperative, present indicative, and present subjunctive forms for *tuteo* and *voseo*, distinguishable in regular verbs by their stress placement.

Table 1. *Tuteo/voseo* paradigms for subject pronoun and sample forms of *hablar* 'to talk'

	Tuteo	Voseo
Subject pronoun	*tú*	*vos*
Imperative	*habla*	*hablá*
	['aβla]	[aβl'a]
Present indicative	*hablas*	*hablás**
	['aβlas]	[aβl'as]
Present subjunctive	*hables*	*hablés**
	['aβles]	[aβl'es]

* Diphthongized forms (*habláis, habléis*) are also attested historically, but we have excluded them from consideration because they have no bearing on our main argument.

The evolution of *voseo/tuteo* variation in RPS has been reconstructed with evidence from personal letters, official documents, and plays (see Fontanella de Weinberg 1971, 1987:110, for Buenos Aires, and Bertolotti 2015, for Uruguay). These materials show that during the late 18th and early 19th centuries, *voseo* and *tuteo* forms could be mixed quite freely (see examples in Moyna & Sanz-Sánchez 2023: 14–15). Over the course of the first half (Argentina) or second half (Uruguay) of the 19th century, this variation started to resolve in favor of *voseo*, first in the imperative, and in rural varieties. By the late 19th century, *voseo* had also become virtually categorical in subject pronouns and present indicatives and looked very much like the present-day paradigm (Fontanella de Weinberg 1999). The generalized adoption of *voseo* flew in the face of educational attempts to prop up *tuteo*, used natively by the many Spanish-born educators (Goebel 2010:199; Zubillaga 1993:34) and prescribed to locally trained teachers (Oroño 2014). In light of the many successes of the RPS education systems in eradicating vernacular features, the failure to eliminate *voseo* stands out as exceptional (see Moyna & Sanz-Sánchez 2023 for an account).

More notably, perhaps, the reduction in address variation was taking place amidst the profound demographic transformations summarized in Section 2, as Buenos Aires and Montevideo teemed with domestic migrants and immigrants. Although the written record is not forthcoming with evidence of informal address, local drama does provide glimpses of high linguistic variability in the pool of 2SG forms available to children. Native Spanish speakers are represented as using urban, rural, Peninsular, and Latin American dialects with different 2SG paradigms, while immigrants are depicted as L2 interlanguage speakers (e.g., the Italian-Spanish interlanguage known as *cocoliche*), one of whose features is inconsistent use of address forms (see Moyna and Sanz-Sánchez 2023:17, for some examples).

With that variability as a backdrop, the complex evolution of the present subjunctive is difficult to trace. Fontanella de Weinberg (1979) attempted to do so, observing that the pervasive variation in the colonial Spanish 2SG paradigm continued in the RPS present subjunctive well after *voseo* had prevailed in the imperative. This, she claims, was followed by a split in *voseo/tuteo* selection based on the different meanings of 2SG subjunctive (negative imperative vs. subordinate). Moyna (2009) provides a more detailed and empirically supported sequence of events, combining data from plays written in the 1900s, which reflect the speech of those born after 1850, and the *Norma Culta de Buenos Aires* spoken corpus (Barrenechea 1987) analyzed by Siracusa (1972), which reflects 20th century speakers. These results confirm an increase in *voseo*, which had become categorical in the imperative for speakers born around 1900, and in the present indicative for speakers born around 1920 (Table 2).

Table 2. *Voseo* percentages in RPS after 1880, taken from Moyna (2009) and Siracusa (1972)

	Imperative %	Present indicative %	Present subjunctive %
Plays[*]			
Characters born before 1850	75.9 (536/706)	65.4 (390/596)	49.7 (82/165)
Characters born 1850–1880	80.9 (539/666)	77.4 (439/567)	44.5 (77/173)
Interviews[**]			
Participants born 1890–1915	99.4	92.9	25
Participants born 1916–1935	99.8	99	20.2
Participants born 1936–1945	99.1	99.9	16.9

[*] Data from Moyna (2009), based on publication dates of plays and estimates of characters' chronological age
[**] Totals unavailable in Siracusa (1972)

Table 2 also presents the earliest quantitative evidence of 2SG present subjunctive evolution, and thus constitutes an antecedent for the current study. It shows that subjunctives lagged in *voseo* adoption compared to the imperative and present indicative, barely reaching 50% in speakers born before 1900. This lag is not surprising in itself, considering that the subjunctive is typical of subordinate clauses, and could thus be predicted to be conservative (Bybee 2002). However, Table 2 also shows a second, unexpected tendency: the subjunctive becomes less, rather than more *voseante* over time, bucking the trend of the rest of the paradigm, and countering what might be expected based on the *constant rate effect* (Kroch 1989). While these data thus provide clues about the overall evolution of 2SG subjunctive, the analysis in incomplete, because it does not consider the semantico-pragmatic complexity hidden in the subjunctive. In what follows, we describe this internal complexity and its impact on L1 acquisition (Section 3.2) and provide evidence that modern-day RPS presents differences in the frequency of *voseo/tuteo* selection across subjunctive modality (Section 3.3).

3.2 The Spanish subjunctive

In order to consider the relationship between subjunctive and address, we need to take a step back and start with some basic notions. Verbal inflection can be used to mark the status of a proposition or its modality (Palmer 2001:1). From a semantic perspective, modality can be broadly synonymous with ways of qualifying states of affairs (Nuyts 2005). To exemplify, the Spanish subjunctive can express that a speaker is not committed to the truth of a proposition, as in non-assertive predicates (e.g., *Dudo que vos me* **quieras** 'I doubt that you like$_{sbjv}$ me'). In contrast, if the speaker commits to the truth of the proposition through a strongly assertive predicate, the subordinate verb will appear in the indicative (e.g., *Es obvio que vos me querés* 'It is obvious that you like$_{ind}$ me').

The semantic values of the Spanish subjunctive are very diverse (Fábregas 2014). Here we focus on two contexts where subjunctive morphology expresses different modalities (following Palmer 2001: 8–9). First, subjunctive forms used in imperatives under the scope of negation can be considered expressions of *deontic* modality, which relates to obligation or permission emanating from an external source about events that are not yet actualized.[2] For example, in (1) the speaker is directing what the addressee is not to do.

(1) No **coma-s** apurad-o.
no eat-2SG.T.[3]PRS.SBJV hurry.PTCP.M
'Don't eat in a rush.'

Second, the subjunctive is also used to express *epistemic* modality, which relates to the speaker's assessment of the truth value or factual status of the proposition. Where deontic modality deals with events, epistemic modality is concerned with propositions. For example, in temporal adjunct clauses with *cuando* 'when' in the present, Spanish speakers can signal the epistemic status of the proposition as habitual or future by using indicative or subjunctive, respectively. When the proposition is construed as habitual, the indicative is used (see (2)). By contrast, when it is construed only as a future possibility, the subjunctive is categorically used (see (3)).

(2) *Conduce-s cuando* **tiene-s** *gana-s*.
drive-2SG.T when have-2SG.T.PRS.IND desire-PL
'You drive whenever you want to.'

(3) *Podrá-s conducir cuando* **tenga-s** *dieciséis año-s*.
can-2SG.FUT drive.INF when have-2SG.T.PRS.SBJV sixteen year.PL
'You will be able to drive when you are sixteen.'

---

2. We are aware of analyses that consider these forms "syncretic with subjunctive, but morphosyntactically different from it" (Fábregas 2014: 46). For simplicity, in keeping with traditional grammars (2014: 8), we will refer to negative commands as subjunctive forms that involve modal meanings (2014: 79).

3. In this paper, address glosses include T for *tuteo*, V for *voseo*, and U for *ustedeo*.

Syntactically, the two contexts above also differ because the subjunctive appears in the main verb in negative commands, whereas it appears in embedded clauses in adverbials with *cuando* 'when'.

The internal semantic complexity of the subjunctive is also reflected in its acquisition. Crosslinguistic evidence points to a progression in the expression of modality by children, where epistemic modality is acquired after deontic modality (Deen 2016; Lozano 1995; Peréz-Leroux 1998). This is clear from the order in which monolingual and bilingual Spanish-speaking children master subjunctive use with deontic modality: volitional verbs such as *querer* are acquired by age 5;0, before mastery of subjunctive in epistemic contexts, which happens between the ages of six and seven (Dracos et al. 2019; Pérez-Leroux 1998; Requena et al. 2017; Sánchez-Naranjo & Pérez-Leroux 2010). Therefore, the acquisition of modality is assumed to proceed from deontic to epistemic (Palmer 2001). In what follows, we show that the deontic/epistemic distinction also has morphological reflexes in RPS.

3.3 The *voseo/tuteo* subjunctive split in RPS

In contemporary RPS, the distinctive subjunctive semantico-pragmatic values mentioned earlier have contributed to a *voseo/tuteo* split in 2SG forms, because subjunctive *voseo* is more frequent in deontic than in epistemic modality (Di Tullio 2010; Fontanella de Weinberg 1979), and its deontic use changes the pragmatic force of a negative command. For example, in a brief questionnaire that asked twelve informants from Buenos Aires to rate the politeness/rudeness of a written command in *tuteo* and *voseo* versions (1 = most polite; 5 = most forceful), Fontanella de Weinberg (1979) found an average difference of more than one point in politeness ratings (2.3 for *tuteo*, 3.7 for *voseo*). Similarly, García Negroni & Ramírez Gelbes (2004) proposed that the prosodic features of negative imperative *voseo* are those of intensification. According to those authors, *voseante* negative imperatives correspond to situations of "discursive imposition".

Pursuing further the distinctions in semantico-pragmatic values of *voseo/tuteo* forms, Johnson and Grinstead (2011) explored the subjunctive dichotomy in Argentine television data from the early 21st century. They found that *tuteo* negative imperatives were acceptable in all contexts, but *voseo* was restricted to urgency, including not just angry commands but also consolation (i.e., not impoliteness). The researchers found support for this initial observation with an online survey that asked 151 participants to select *voseo/tuteo* negative commands in hypothetical situations. Here too, *voseo* was used more in urgent than non-urgent contexts.

Johnson (2016a) followed Haverkate (1979) in distinguishing among prohibitive directives, i.e., speech acts meant to tell the interlocutor not to do something.

Of these, two are pertinent to the current study, namely, *cessatives*, which order an interlocutor to stop performing an action in progress (as in (4)) and *preventives*, which attempt to make an addressee refrain from starting an action (as in (5)).

(4) No me   lo   recuerde-s   más.
    no me.1SG.DAT it.3SG.M.ACC remind-2SG.T.PRS.SBJV more
    'Stop reminding me of that!'

(5) No **vayas**   a salir   sin   abrigo.
    no go-2SG.T.PRS.SBJV to leave.INF without jacket
    'Don't you go out without your jacket.'

Johnson (2016a) reanalyzed data from an earlier survey of *voseo/tuteo* selection in negative imperatives by reclassifying items as immediate or neutral, depending on whether the addressee has already started the action. In addition, immediate contexts were subdivided into angry and non-angry. Johnson found that *voseo* was used significantly more in immediate contexts, i.e., to stop the addressee from performing an action in progress. In addition, angry immediate contexts exhibited higher odds of *voseo*. Johnson also found an effect for sociolinguistic factors such as location, but no cross-generational differences.

Johnson (2016b) extended her analysis to the perceptual effects of *voseo/tuteo* negative imperatives on the certainty that an event has already occurred. The study concluded that the difference between 2SG negative imperatives was due to distinct "levels of speaker commitment" to the proposition, and that other interpretations (e.g., greater accusatory value of *voseo* negative imperatives) were a consequence of this greater certainty (2016b: 49).

To summarize, the present situation in the RPS 2SG subjunctive reflects its complex semantics. Of the two options, *tuteante* forms are almost categorical in non-deontic subordinate clauses, i.e., those introduced by non-volitional verbs (e.g., *no creo que* **vengas** 'I don't think you'll come$_{sbjv}$'). By contrast, when used with deontic value, such as negative imperatives and volitional subordinate clauses, subjunctive *voseo* is possible. While regional and gender differences create nuances, the semantic distinction is robust and general to all RPS dialects.

Although the present-day semantico-pragmatic correlates of differential *voseo/tuteo* use in the subjunctive are well established, we are still missing a timeline for the emergence of this distinction, as well as an account of the factors leading to it. Johnson's findings of relative stability in the early 21st century (2016a: 147) contrast with the intergenerational gradient found in historical data (Table 2). This difference suggests that analyzing the 20th century in detail may be crucial in ascertaining the trajectory of this change. Once a timeline is established, the semantic complexity of the subjunctive, in particular as it pertains to child acquisition, may explain the outcome attested in 21st-century RPS.

4. Study 1: History of the *voseo/tuteo* subjunctive split

In this section, we analyze in detail the historical trajectory of *voseo/tuteo* competition in the subjunctive. In order to do so, we reclassify the pertinent data from previous studies (Moyna 2009; Siracusa 1972) by considering modality (i.e., epistemic vs. deontic) as a separate variable. We are guided by the following questions:

1. Did the relative frequency of *voseo/tuteo* subjunctives change over time in epistemic contexts? Did it change in deontic contexts (negative commands)?
2. Were there differences in the rates of *voseo/tuteo* subjunctive between epistemic and deontic contexts in any given period? If so, how did these differences evolve over time?
3. Did the relative frequency of *voseo/tuteo* subjunctives differ in preventive and cessative negative commands in any given period and over time?

We predict that over the period analyzed, subjunctive *voseo* went down across the board, for both epistemic and deontic contexts. Additionally, in line with previous research, we predict that subjunctive *voseo* forms decreased more markedly in epistemic than in deontic contexts, increasing the gap between the two modalities over time. Moreover, given the alignment of *voseo* with cessatives, we predict that *voseo* rates decreased more in preventive commands.

4.1 Data sources

To map the evolution of the *voseo/tuteo* split in the subjunctive for the period of interest, we selected available datasets representative of three points in time: the late 19th and early 20th centuries, the mid-20th century, and the early 21st century. For the first period, we considered a database of plays used previously in a sociohistorical study (Moyna & Ceballos 2008), whose subjunctive data have only been considered globally (Moyna 2009). For the second period, we analyzed subjunctive forms in the *Norma Culta de Buenos Aires* spoken corpus (Barrenechea 1987; Siracusa 1972). For the third period, we considered the responses of a survey carried out in Montevideo between 2012 and 2018. The specific responses analyzed here are part of a larger questionnaire of 2SG usage, other portions of which have been analyzed previously (Moyna 2020).

4.2 Data coding

For the plays and speech transcripts (i.e., first and second periods), we manually extracted each occurrence of 2SG subjunctive verbs. Apart from coding 2SG forms (*tuteo* or *voseo*), data were classified using semantico-pragmatic criteria. We first classified forms according to deontic or epistemic value. Deontics included negative commands (*No comas* 'Don't eat$_{sbjv}$') and indirect commands, i.e., expressions of volition or threat embedded within a lower clause (*No quiero que vengas* 'I don't want you to come$_{sbjv}$'). Epistemic forms included adverbials (e.g., *para que tengas* 'so that you have$_{sbjv}$'); conditionals (e.g., *siempre que consintás* 'as long as you consent$_{sbjv}$'); and concessives (e.g., *aunque no querás* 'even if you don't want$_{sbjv}$ to'); adjectival relative clauses (e.g., *tomá lo que quieras* 'take what you would like$_{sbjv}$'); presupposition phrases, which assume the truth of the embedded clause by expressing an attitude towards it (e.g., *Es útil que sepas* 'It is useful that you know$_{sbjv}$'); and subordinate doubt clauses (e.g., *Dudo que seas...* 'I doubt that you are$_{sbjv}$...'). Subjunctives that did not fit into the above categories were identified as 'other'.

In turn, negative commands were classified into two subcategories, preventives vs. cessatives. The former included commands meant to dissuade the interlocutor from beginning an action, whereas the latter included prohibitions uttered in reaction to events in progress, including reproaches (following Johnson 2016a; see Section 3.3). The pragmatic force of negative commands was determined through several types of evidence, including the linguistic and situational context of utterance and/or stage directions.

For the last period, data came from six items in a written survey administered to 367 adult speakers from Montevideo. The items were part of a 34-question instrument used and described in detail in Moyna (2020). The six items selected presented participants with hypothetical situations with possible 2SG subjunctive answers. Two items tested epistemic contexts (*Es raro que....* 'It's strange that...' and *No me parece que* 'I don't think that...') and the remaining four tested deontic contexts of negative command. Two were preventive (e.g., *No te olvides, por favor.* 'Don't forget, please.') and two were cessative (e.g., *¡No me rompas más cosas!* 'Stop breaking my stuff!'). Participants were asked to select the form (*voseo, tuteo,* or *ustedeo*) they would naturally use in each situation. A different response could be written in if none of those provided reflected participants' preferences. A sample trial is shown in Figure 1.

Of the total responses, 1868 selected either *tuteo* or *voseo* exclusively, and are thus reported below.

4.3 Results and discussion

Figure 2 shows *voseo/tuteo* rates in deontic and epistemic contexts in the three periods. There is an overall drop in the frequency of *voseo* subjunctive in both epistemic and deontic contexts over time. In addition, within the first two periods considered, there were no significant differences in *voseo/tuteo* subjunctive rates

Su primo y usted tienen que encontrarse en una oficina pública para hacer un trámite. Usted sabe que él suele ser impuntual. Usted le dice:
'Your cousin and you need to meet at a public building to run an errand. You know that he is often late. You tell him:'

a. *No llegues tarde, por favor.* 'Don't be$_{sbjvT}$ late, please.'
b. *No llegués tarde, por favor.* 'Don't be$_{sbjvV}$ late, please.'
c. *No llegue tarde, por favor.* 'Don't be$_{sbjvU}$ late, please.'
d. *Otra forma* 'Another form': _____

Figure 1. Sample survey trial

by context. Thus, in the early period, *voseo* made up 47% of deontic uses and 50% of epistemic uses. In the intermediate period, *voseo* was used in 19% of deontic contexts and 14% of epistemic contexts. In other words, the overall drop in *voseo* 2SG subjunctives was substantial, but there was little observable difference between contexts. This finding is tentative, given the different nature of the corpora for the two periods. The earliest corpus includes plays, while the second period includes naturalistic data, where subjunctives are less frequent. By contrast, in the last period, *voseo* subjunctives continue to drop, but do so more steeply in epistemic than deontic contexts. Specifically, in deontic contexts they fall from 19% to 11%, while in epistemic contexts, the drop is from 14% to 3%. The difference between the two contexts in the 21st century is quite considerable (i.e., 11% vs. 3%), confirming a larger drop in *voseo* forms for epistemic uses.

To examine the *voseo/tuteo* frequencies in preventive and cessative commands, we then focused solely on the two deontics. Figure 3 suggests that *voseo* rates differ between both types of commands. Statistical analyses are not possible for the middle period due to scarce data. However, analyses of the first and the last periods indicate a significant difference in *voseo* use only in the latter ($F(1, 1236) = 5.034$, $p < .05$),[4] with participants selecting *voseo* forms more in cessative commands (14%) than in preventive commands (10%). While the rates of *voseo* are very low for both cessative and preventive commands in this period, the slightly (and statistically significant) higher rates of *voseo* in cessatives offer support for the specialization of *voseo* for cessatives proposed by Johnson (2016a, b).

To summarize, the evidence points to a marked decrease in *voseo* frequency relative to *tuteo* in the subjunctive between the turn of the 20th century and the early 21st century. This is true for both epistemic and deontic contexts. While

---

4. The model results showed that the odds for using *voseo* in cessative is 1.49 times greater than the odds for using *voseo* in preventive negative commands, with a 95% confidence interval (1.05, 2.11).

Chapter 7. *voseo/tuteo* semantic split in Río de la Plata second person subjunctives 163

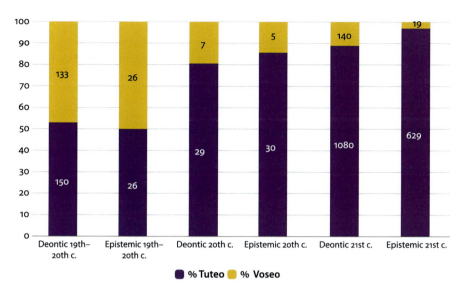

Figure 2. Rate of *tuteo* and *voseo* in deontic and epistemic contexts in the three periods (totals included in data labels)

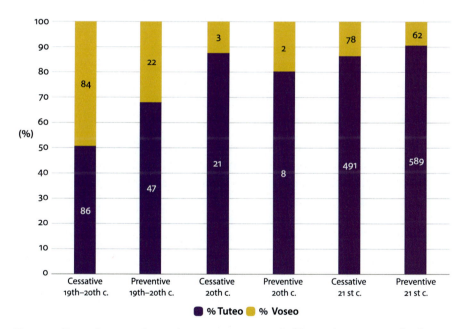

Figure 3. Rate of *tuteo* and *voseo* in negative commands (deontic) contexts in the three periods (totals included in data labels)

in the two earlier periods there are few observable differences between these forms by context, in the last period *tuteo* becomes almost categorical for epistemic contexts, while *voseo* is considerably more frequent in deontic contexts than in epistemic contexts. Within deontic modality, *voseo* forms were found to have specialized for cessative meaning towards the 21st century.

Could the differences in *voseo/tuteo* frequencies between deontic and epistemic contexts described in this Section owe their impetus and trajectory to the acquisitional timing of the subjunctive? Study 2 explores this hypothesis empirically by considering the acquisition of 2SG subjunctive forms by contemporary children born to parents who speak a dialect where *voseo* and *tuteo* continue to compete in the subjunctive.

5. Study 2: The acquisition of subjunctive split

To the best of our knowledge, no study has addressed the acquisition of 2SG *voseo/tuteo* forms across semantico-pragmatic modalities in RPS. Study 2 fills this void by addressing whether the timing of acquisition of 2SG subjunctive forms by children could contribute to their diachronic development. We specifically address the following:

1. Are 2SG subjunctive forms mastered earlier in deontic contexts than in epistemic contexts?
2. Do children exhibit any specialization of *voseo* 2SG forms with cessative deontic contexts when acquiring RPS?

Based on previous research on the acquisition of subjunctive in children, we predict that 2SG deontic contexts will be acquired before epistemic contexts (Deen 2016; Lozano 1995; Peréz-Leroux 1998). Johnson (2013: 159) made specific predictions about the age of acquisition of the pragmatic distinction between *voseo* and *tuteo* subjunctive around the age of 4–5. Therefore, we predict that children acquiring RPS will show evidence of the specialization of 2SG *voseo* forms by age 5.

5.1 Participants

Fifty-two Spanish monolingual children were recruited from Córdoba, an interior province of Argentina included in the RPS macroregion, and where *voseo* is the main informal address form (Prevedello 1989). Twenty-four children were about to complete kindergarten (ages 5;5–6;5, $M=6;0$) and twenty-eight were about to complete second grade (ages 7;3–8;5, $M=7;11$). The younger group represented children with limited influence from the prescriptive and formal language uses that characterize the school context. Their age also typically corresponds with mastery of the subjunctive with deontic modality (Dracos et al. 2019), while their mastery of epistemic modality is under way. The older group had already been in the school system for a couple of years and were expected not only to have command of core deontic and epistemic subjunctive contexts, but also to have some experience with the prescriptive forces of formal education. Nine adults from the same region were also tested.

5.2 Stimuli and procedure

A sentence completion task was used, following best practices for eliciting mood selection in subordinate clauses (Dracos et al. 2019). Ten situations were constructed where a mother was scolding a child because of something the child was doing (deontic modality – negative command) or about to do (epistemic modality – adverbial clause). In the case of the direct negative command condition, the five trials consisted of situations where a mother came into the room to find the child doing something they were not supposed to do. Then the mother uttered a cessative negative command (see Figure 4a for a sample trial). Cessative negative commands were selected because they categorically select subjunctive, and previous literature points to their greater *voseo* use (see Section 3.3). The other five trials consisted of situations where a child was known to habitually misbehave, and the mother reminded them not to misbehave when in the same situation again. In this second situation, the mother would use an adverbial clause with *cuando* 'when' with future reference (see Figure 4b for a sample trial). Adverbial clauses with future reference were chosen because they also select subjunctive categorically, and because epistemic modality is acquired later than deontic modality, at an age that coincides with greater influence of the school system. Therefore, *tuteo* was predicted to surface in this condition, especially among the older children.

Note that our model did not test for the entirety of the predicted variation in *tuteo/voseo* subjunctive. Although our theoretical model and our historical data would have predicted significant differences in *voseo* across the board (i.e., increasing from epistemic, to preventive deontics, to cessative deontics), constraints of the experimental model (sample size, respondent fatigue, developmental limitations) led us to choose only the two endpoints in this scale. Thus, to maximize the possibility of statistically significant effects, of the two possible deontics, only cessative subjunctives were selected to contrast against epistemic subjunctives.

a. *A Sarita na le gusta perder cuando juega a las cartas. Por eso siempre hace trampa. Ahora está jugando a las cartas con su vecino y ya empezó a hacer trampa (¿ves cómo se esconde una carta para después?). Su mamá se da cuenta de que Sarita está haciendo trampa y le dice: "Sarita! No …"* (*hagas*-T/*hagás*-V *trampa*)
'Sarita doesn't like to lose when she plays cards. So, she always cheats. Now she's playing cards with her neighbor and she's already started cheating (see how she's hiding a card for later?). Her mom realizes that Sarita is cheating and tells her: "Sarita! Don't…." (cheat)'

b. *A Leo le gusta ayudar a la abuela a hacer milanesas. Pero cada vez que hace milanesas con la abuela, se ensucia toda la ropa. Hoy Leo va a ir de vuelta a lo de la abuela y van a hacer milanesas otra vez. Entonces, la mamá le dice: "Leo, escuchame lo que te voy a decir. Ponete un delantal cuando…"* (*hagas*-T/*hagás*-V *milanesas*)
'Leo likes to help grandma prepare milanesas. But every time he cooks milanesas with grandma, he gets his clothes all dirty. Today Leo will go to grandma's and they will cook milanesas again. So, his mom tells him: "Leo, listen to what I say, put on an apron when…" (you make milanesas)'

Figure 4. Sample trials for sentence completion task

Five verbs were prompted by the experimenter through the preambles. Each verb was prompted twice, once in a negative command trial and once in an adverbial trial. Four of the verbs (*hacer* 'do', *poner* 'put', *sacar* 'take out', *ver* 'see') are among the most frequent verb lemmas (> 20 times) in two longitudinal corpora representing Latin American Spanish (Montes, Remedi) in CHILDES (MacWhinney 2000). The last verb (*gritar* 'scream') was among the most frequent verb lemmas in only one of those corpora. All five verbs evoked actions familiar to children and frequent in parental reprimands (e.g., don't put on your new shoes, don't watch another episode on TV…). Recall that *voseo* subjunctives of these verbs differ from *tuteo* subjunctives in that the former are stressed on the last syllable (e.g., *hagás* vs. *hagas*, *veás* vs. *veas*; see Table 1). Although the *voseo* variant sometimes reduces irregularities, such as diphthongization in *tuteo* (e.g., *poder* 'to be able to' → *podás* for *voseo* vs. *puedas* for *tuteo*), this did not apply to the verbs selected.

Children whose parents provided written permission and who assented were tested in a quiet area at school. Presentation of the stimuli took place in the same order across participants to avoid two consecutive trials with the same verb.

Adults were tested online through videoconference. Data were transcribed by a native speaker of the dialect.

5.3 Results and discussion

Responses other than subjunctive were coded as "Other." These included use of indicative (as in *"Sarita! No... tenés que/debés hacer$_{inf}$ trampa"* 'Sarita, you should/must not cheat$_{inf}$') and cases where the participant used an impersonal expression instead of 2SG forms (as in *"Ponete un delantal cuando... sea la hora de cocinar con la abuela"* 'Put on an apron when it's time to cook with grandma'). "Other" also included unclear or missing responses, as well as cases where the 2SG subjunctive verb used by the participant is invariable in *tuteo* or *voseo* (e.g., *dar* 'pass' in *le des la pelota a todos* 'that you pass the ball to everyone'). A total of 443 responses by the children and 63 responses by the adults contained 2SG subjunctive.

Figure 5 shows the distribution of subjunctive forms (*tuteo, voseo*) as well as other forms by condition and group. We first observe that the adults underused subjunctive forms in the deontic but not in the epistemic condition. While it has been previously observed that caregivers can use fewer negative imperatives than children (see Gathercole et al. 1999: 182; 2002), in the present experimental task negative commands were the target form of half the trials. Careful examination of adult responses reveals a strong tendency to avoid direct negative commands in favor of positively phrased commands. This could originate in advice to parents and educators in favor of the use of 'do' commands as opposed to 'stop' commands when giving instructions to children (e.g., McMahon & Forehand 2005). This behavior was almost exclusive to parents and did not seem to impact children's performance in the task, since the latter did not hesitate to provide negative commands. When it comes to the 2SG, the adults did not produce *voseante* forms at all. This was surprising, especially in the epistemic condition, where adults produced more subjunctive responses. In the absence of another explanation, this would imply that the adult grammar does not select *voseo* in such contexts. However, in line with the observation that they may have been avoiding direct negative commands overall, adults may also be avoiding the pragmatic force added by *voseo*. In the epistemic contexts, adults did not produce *voseo* forms either.

For the children, subjunctive responses (obtained by combining *tuteo* and *voseo*) were higher in the deontic condition (negative commands) than in the epistemic condition (with adverb *cuando* 'when'). Moreover, we find that the younger group uses more *voseo* than the older group in both conditions. This is especially noticeable in the epistemic context, where *voseo* exhibits a marked decrease with age. As *voseo* use drops between kindergarten and second grade, *tuteo* use increases, more noticeably in the epistemic than in the deontic condition.

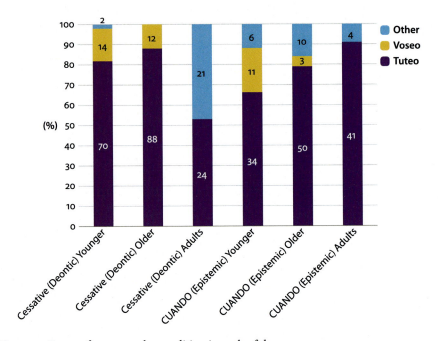

Figure 5. Types of responses by condition in each of the groups

To test whether subjunctive use differed by condition in the child participants,[5] we combined all subjunctive forms (*voseante* and *tuteante*) into a "Subjunctive" category, while all non-subjunctive responses were grouped into an "Other" category. We ran a Generalized Linear Mixed Model (GLMM) in SPSS using response (Subjunctive vs. Other) as an outcome variable, and Condition and Age group as predictor variables, with the Condition × Age group interaction. The random effect structure included a random intercept for Participant and a crossed random effect for Trial. To determine the best-fit model, we removed the non-significant interaction. The results (see Table 3 for complete model output) revealed significant effects of Condition ($F(1,10) = 15.87$, $p = .002$) and Age group ($F(1,47) = 4.64$, $p = .036$). The children tested produced significantly more subjunctive with negative commands than with adverbial clauses with *cuando* 'when'. Specifically, the estimated odds ratio (OR) indicates that children were nine times more likely to produce the subjunctive overall with negative commands as compared to adverbial clauses with *cuando*. The effect of Age indicates that age groups differed in the degree to which they selected the subjunctive. The estimated odds

---

5. There were only nine adult participants and, as described in the text, they behaved very differently from the children in the deontic condition. Therefore, they were not included in the statistical analyses.

ratio indicates that the odds of producing subjunctive were 62% lower in children in the younger group compared to children in the older group.

Table 3. Complete model output: Estimates for multi-level logit mixed model of use of subjunctive versus other responses, with Age Group as between-participants factors and condition as a within-participant factor ($N = 520$; AIC = 2,885; BIC = 2.893; Log likelihood = 2,881)

Fixed effect	Odds ratio	SE	t	p	CI Lower	CI Upper
Intercept	6.042	.4450	4.042	.001	2.335	15.635
Condition (negative command)*	9.369	.5615	3.985	.002	2.701	32.506
Age group (younger)**	.383	.4454	−2.156	.036	.156	.938

Random effect covariance	Estimate	SE	Z	p	CI Lower	CI Upper
Participant (intercept)	1.376	.508	2.707	.007	.667	2.838
Trial (intercept)	.453	.343	1.323	.186	.103	1.994

* Adverbial clauses with *cuando* was the baseline level. ** Older was the baseline level.

Finally, to test whether Condition and Age impact the type of subjunctive form used (*tuteo* vs. *voseo*), we analyzed only subjunctive responses through another GLMM, where *voseo* was the response variable. Condition and Age were entered as predictor variables and the same random structure as the previous model was used. The results revealed non-significant effects of Condition ($F(1,7) = .263$, $p = .623$) and Age group ($F(1,59) = 3.795$, $p = .056$) as well as a non-significant interaction between the two ($F(1,439) = 1.442$, $p = .230$).

To summarize, these results show that Spanish-speaking children use more 2SG subjunctive forms in the deontic context than in the epistemic context, an effect that mirrors the order of mastery of these modal meanings. Additionally, 2SG subjunctive use increased with age in our sample. When it comes to the specialization of *voseo* 2SG forms, we did not find an effect of subjunctive form by condition. However, descriptive data indicate that while the *voseo:tuteo* ratio remains stable between age groups for the deontic condition, *voseo* use decreases dramatically for the older children in the epistemic condition.

6. Language acquisition and the historical sociolinguistics of *voseo/tuteo* variation in the 2SG subjunctive

The acquisition-based perspective adopted in this chapter has shed new light on the sociolinguistic and structural factors that may explain the evolution of 2SG subjunctive forms in RPS. Sociohistorical data on the *voseo/tuteo* alternation reveal a protracted period of instability and competition between forms which lasted until the first decades of the 20th century. This was followed first by an increase in *tuteo* frequency across the board, and later by a further reduction in *voseo*, especially in epistemic contexts, which has led to the current lopsided distribution of forms, with markedly less *voseo* in epistemic than in deontic contexts.

However, historical data to reconstruct subjunctive evolution is scant, because it compounds three problems: (a) *methodological*: sparse written record in an area of low literacy; (b) *structural*: infrequency of subjunctive compared to the indicative in naturalistic samples; and (c) *pragmatic:* dearth of informal 2SG forms in early data. Thus, subjunctive evolution cannot be clarified solely with the ego documents typical of historical research. This chapter has resorted to alternatives, such as drama and naturalistic conversations, which narrow down the timing of the change to between the late 19th and the early 21st centuries. In fact, most evidence points to the 20th century as our period of interest. By doing this, we were able to match up the linguistic change to a demographic and social context of massive immigration and rapid spread of institutionalized education that took place in the Río de la Plata in the late 19th century.

Elsewhere it has been argued that the loosening of social networks due to massive domestic and international migration into dense urban areas increased the linguistic variability in the dialect, while at the same time disrupting the norms that would have assigned different social value to these forms (Moyna & Sanz-Sánchez 2023). The children of turn-of-the-century Montevideo and Buenos Aires thus faced the daunting task of systematizing the unfocused variability of their input in order to acquire it. While in the imperative and the present indicative they eliminated *tuteo*, in the present subjunctive *voseo* forms did not replace their *tuteo* counterparts. Instead, it was *tuteo* that gradually gained ground, in a more protracted process that spanned the 20th century, as we have shown in Study 1. In other words, something about the present subjunctive led to different outcomes. We argued that this something can be found in the process of subjunctive development in children, as shown in Study 2. Considering what we know about the sociolinguistic history of RPS and about the acquisitional trajectories of today's RPS speaking children, we can now address the following question: How did children contribute to shaping the dialect variety they were acquiring?

The data from Study 2 (Section 5) can be invoked to shed light on this question. There are statistically significant differences in the overall preference for subjunctive form by age group and context. Both effects replicate previous studies of the emergence of subjunctive use in children. The subjunctive is firmly established in 2SG negative commands well before its use generalizes to the simplest epistemic contexts mastered. In epistemic contexts, the children produced non-subjunctive responses, a finding that is in line with variation reported in previous studies of adult speakers and with accounts of how modal complexity impacts the protracted development of mood selection in children.

We also found (non-statistically significant) differences in the rate of *voseo/tuteo* subjunctive use between age groups. The differences were negligible for deontic contexts, but they increased in epistemic uses, since the older children – i.e., those with two years of formal schooling – opted for *tuteo* subjunctive almost to the exclusion of *voseo* in these contexts. In fact, the older children presented a difference in relative frequencies of *tuteo* and *voseo* approximating those of contemporary statistically validated studies for RPS adult speakers (Johnson 2016a, b). Some subjunctive uses (e.g., epistemic) are mastered later than others (e.g., deontic), at an age that coincides with formal education and higher exposure to school-sanctioned *tuteo*. The acquisition data have suggestive parallels in the receding historical trajectory of *voseo* subjunctive in epistemic contexts (Section 4).[6]

Let us now flesh out our hypothesis by connecting the dots between our historical and acquisitional results. The historical evidence shows an extensive latent period of *voseo/tuteo* competition in RPS across the verbal paradigms, between colonization and the early 19th century. Then, around the time of independence in the early 19th century, informal *voseo* started to gain ground across the verbal paradigm, rather than receding, as it had done in other varieties. The available historical data (Fontanella de Weinberg 1971, 1987) proves that the process started in the imperative, and anecdotal evidence provides additional information about the progression of this change, since contemporaneous witnesses identified children as its source (for instance, grammarian Juan Cruz Varela, cited by Fontanella de Weinberg 1971: 497). This may be tied to the phonological salience of *voseo* imperatives (syllable-final stress) and greater regularity vis-à-vis *tuteo* (Moyna 2009).

---

[6]. As one reviewer states, the growing preference for *tuteo* in the older group could be a consequence of 'age grading' (Wagner 2012) and of the incorporation of those children into a linguistic marketplace that favors the standard. However, we believe that it is not advisable to conflate changes over the span of a grownup's life, and those that happen during child acquisition. Changes in adult usage are related to strategic preferences in performance, while those in child usage are connected with different levels of linguistic competence (see Chapter 2 in this volume).

Thus, a child born in the second half of the 19th century in either Buenos Aires or Montevideo encountered a highly variable 2SG paradigm, with doublets in many frequent verbs (present indicative, present subjunctive), and an incipient preference for *voseo* imperatives. Let us recall that this child had a good chance of having at least one immigrant parent, and/or rural migrant parents and grandparents, all of whom added to an unsystematic input of urban, rural, and immigrant L2 forms. However, once *voseo* started making inroads in the imperative, this raised the ratio of oxytonic *voseo* (see Table 1) forms in the feature pool, tilting the balance overall, and accelerating the selection of oxytonic *voseo* forms in the present indicative. Elsewhere it has been argued that dense urbanization, collective child-care arrangements, and early participation in mandatory schooling created the conditions for the existence of children peer groups (Moyna & Sanz-Sánchez 2023). These were responsible for the rapid generalization of *voseo* in the imperative and present indicative paradigms, as children acquired language from other children, before school could have any role in shaping their input.

As a result, by the early 20th century only the subjunctive continued to exhibit considerable variability in 2SG. If the changes had progressed apace, *voseo* would have been expected to advance in this context, too. However, at this point, the complex pathway of subjunctive acquisition and the prevailing social circumstances interacted to bring about a different outcome. As a result of earlier mastery of subjunctive with deontic uses (as demonstrated by the children in the present study), we argue that turn-of-the-century children must have exhibited a greater preference for subjunctive in negative imperative contexts than in epistemic contexts by the time they reached school age. This difference in the strength of the association between subjunctive and particular modal uses (greater with deontic than epistemic) could have created a sort of "protective barrier" for subjunctive forms already in use in deontic contexts, resulting in divergent pathways of change for subjunctives in epistemic contexts.[7] As literacy became universal as a consequence of education legislation (Section 2), increasing numbers of children were subjected to normative pressure to use standard *tuteo*. Indeed, we know from contemporary data that the passage from pre-school to school age matches a decrease in *voseo* use in epistemic contexts today, which provides a glimpse into this historical scenario. In other words, while it had been thoroughly routed in the left periphery (imperative) and the main clause (indicative present), *tuteo* found a way to fight back in the lower clause (subjunctive), and to a lesser extent, in the

---

7. We thank an anonymous reviewer for suggesting the term 'protective barrier' to encapsulate our idea.

negative imperative, because it was propped up by the educational system during a crucial time in child subjunctive development.[8]

Note that the evidence we have analyzed in this chapter questions the common argument that children cannot actuate languages changes. In this particular case, we argue, it was indeed the children who led the change. Although the same normative pressures were at work on parents and children, adult grammars were a great deal more fixed – in the case of native speakers of non-normative dialects – and a great deal more variable – in the case of adult L2 Spanish speakers. Adults were thus much less likely to actuate this change, although it was their linguistically and socially unsystematic input that fed it. In this sense, this data point at the combined historical action of speakers of various ages and linguistic backgrounds in the emergence of this dialectal norm (see Chapter 6), as has been pointed out for other contexts of contact and change in this volume.

7. Conclusion

Our study is the first to combine historical and acquisitional perspectives to explain the most crucial – and unaccounted for – circumstances that led to the semantico-pragmatic split of RPS 2SG subjunctive forms, namely, why it may have happened. More generally, it is a window into the complexities of language change in messy contexts. Elsewhere it has been proposed (Sanz-Sánchez & Moyna 2023; Moyna & Sanz-Sánchez 2023) that for children to change language following their own acquisitionally determined routes, several conditions must be met, namely: (1) a highly variable input; (2) the possibility of peer influence among small children; and (3) weak normative pressures (see also Chapter 8 in this volume). The present study is a corollary to these studies, showing how language evolution fares when one of those components is missing. Indeed, *voseo/tuteo* variation in the 2SG subjunctive developed in a context of extreme variability similar to the imperative and the present, but its evolution lagged compared to those other forms, not just historically, but also acquisitionally. This offered just enough time and opportunity for the normative forces of school to revert the seemingly inevitable progress of the *voseo* innovation started by previous cohorts of RPS child learners.

There is a larger analytical point to be made here. Lack of data is an endemic problem in historical research. For periods before the generalization of literacy, we are well aware that the record only reflects the written and often formal uses of a sliver of the population, so researchers celebrate the rare occasion when they

---

8. See Chapter 5 for a reflection of the importance of normative pressures on child language acquisition.

get glimpses of other social classes. However, very few historical linguists decry the complete erasure of children from the record, which can make us forget that their influence on language change may have been distinct from that of their parents. This skews our perceptions, a bit like those medieval paintings that depict children as miniature adults. We propose a different starting point: that adults and children each had different roles with significant effects on language change (DeGraff 2009). For this proposal to move beyond mere unprovable speculation, we need to broaden the universe of our data collection to include modern children, who can be assumed to have been cognitive analogues to their historical counterparts.

The findings of the present study can and should be supported with additional data, obtained through different techniques. For example, diachronic changes should be documented with data of comparable robustness for all periods, even if the sources and methods must be adjusted for the limitations of each one. Other chapters in this volume offer additional examples of how data beyond the written corpora can be incorporated to shed light on the sociohistorical interface between individual acquisitional trajectories and community change, such as historical audio recordings (Chapters 9 and 10) or crosslinguistic comparison (Chapters 11 and 12). Like the authors of these other case studies, we believe that both historical and contemporary data can be expanded with additional sources, such as mid-20th century plays or films. Additionally, it may be possible to obtain a more complete picture of the trajectory of *voseo/tuteo* present subjunctive acquisition if we add older children. Still, this study demonstrates empirically that expanding the sources for historical linguistics with contemporary children (and adults) can provide a clearer picture of the actuation of past changes.

Finally, it may be necessary to rethink some of the methods used to elicit *voseo* forms, which seem to be taboo in certain social situations and result in avoidance. For instance, respondents seemed reluctant to choose *voseo* options in the survey for Study 1, given that it is felt to be impolite. Similarly, adults tested in Study 2 did not produce *voseo* subjunctives in direct commands. However, the fact that children did produce these forms in their negative commands strongly suggests that these forms must occur in their input at home. This is a challenge for future researchers interested in eliciting language that only appears when speakers make no effort to mitigate the illocutionary force of their commands.

Acknowledgments

We would like to thank the administrators, teachers, students, and parents at Escuela Dr. Dalmacio Vélez Sarsfield in the city of Arroyito (Córdoba, Argentina) for their assistance and participation and Ariadne Pacheco for her assistance processing historical data.

Abbreviations

1	first person	PL	plural
2	second person	PRS	present
3	third person	PTCP	participle
ACC	accusative	RPS	Río de la Plata Spanish
DAT	dative	SBJV	subjunctive
FUT	future	SG	singular
GLMM	Generalized Linear Mixed Model	T	*tuteo* form
IND	indicative	U	*usted* form
INF	infinitive	V	*voseo* form
M	masculine		

References

Academia Mexicana de la Lengua. 2022. *Corpus Diacrónico y Diatópico del Español de América (CORDIAM)*, www.cordiam.org (27 February, 2022)

Barrenechea, Ana (ed.). 1987. *El habla culta de la ciudad de Buenos Aires: Materiales para su estudio*. Buenos Aires: Universidad Nacional de Buenos Aires.

Bertolotti, Virginia. 2015. *A mí de vos no me trata ni usted ni nadie: Sistemas e historia de las formas de tratamiento en la lengua española en América*. Mexico City: Universidad Nacional Autónoma de México/Universidad de la República, Uruguay.

Boyd-Bowman, Peter. 1985. *Indice geobiográfico de más de 56 mil pobladores de la América Hispánica*. Volume 1. Mexico City: Instituto de Investigaciones Históricas, UNAM.

Bybee, Joan. 2002. Main clauses are innovative, subordinate clauses are conservative. Consequences for the nature of constructions. In Joan Bybee & Michael Noonan (eds.), *Complex sentences in grammar and discourse: Essays in honor of Sandra A. Thompson*, 1–17. Amsterdam: John Benjamins.

Deen, Kamil. 2016. Mood alternations. In Jeffrey Lidz, William Snyder & Joe Pater (eds.), *The Oxford handbook of developmental linguistics*, 367–385. Oxford: Oxford University Press.

DeGraff, Michel. 2009. Language acquisition in creolization and, thus, language change: Some cartesian-uniformitarian boundary conditions. *Language and Linguistics Compass* 3/4. 888–971.

Di Tullio, Angela. 2010. El voseo argentino en tiempos del Bicentenario. *RASAL Lingüística* 1–2. 47–72.

Dracos, Melisa, Pablo E. Requena & Karen Miller. 2019. Acquisition of mood selection in Spanish-speaking children. *Language Acquisition* 26. 106–118.

Fábregas, Antonio. 2014. A guide to subjunctive and modals in Spanish: questions and analyses. *Borealis–An International Journal of Hispanic Linguistics* 3. 1–94.

Fontanella de Weinberg, María Beatriz. 1971. El voseo en Buenos Aires en las dos primeras décadas del siglo XIX. *Thesaurus* 26. 495–514.

Fontanella de Weinberg, María Beatriz. 1979. La oposición "cantes/cantés" en el español de Buenos Aires. *Thesaurus* 34. 72–83.

Fontanella de Weinberg, María Beatriz. 1987. *El español bonaerense. Cuatro siglos de evolución lingüística (1580–1980)*. Buenos Aires: Hachette.

Fontanella de Weinberg, María Beatriz. 1993. Usos americanos y peninsulares de segunda persona singular. In Ana María Barrenechea, Luis Martínez Cuitiño & Elida Lois (eds.), *Actas del III Congreso Argentino de Hispanistas*, 144–153. Buenos Aires: Asociación Argentina de Hispanistas.

Fontanella de Weinberg, María Beatriz. 1999. Sistemas pronominales de tratamiento usados en el mundo hispánico. In Ignacio Bosque & Violeta Demonte (eds.), *Gramática descriptiva de la lengua española*. Volumen 1, 1401–1425. Madrid: Espasa Calpe.

García, Negroni, María Marta & Silvia Ramirez Gelbes. 2004. Politesse et alternance *vos/tú* en espagnol du Río de la Plata. *Le cas du subjonctif*. In *Actes du colloque "Pronoms de deuxième personne et formes d'adresse dans les langues d'Europe"*. Paris: Instituto Cervantes.

Gathercole, Virginia, Eugenia Sebastián & Pilar Soto. 1999. The early acquisition of Spanish verbal morphology: Across-the-board or piecemeal knowledge? *International Journal of Bilingualism* 3(2–3). 133–182.

Gathercole, Virginia, Eugenia Sebastián & Pilar Soto. 2002. Negative commands in Spanish-speaking children: No need for recourse to Relativized Minimality (a reply to Grinstead 2000). *Journal of Child Language* 29(2). 393–401.

Germani, Gino. 1966. Mass immigration and modernization in Argentina. *Studies in International Comparative Development Studies* 2. 165–182.

Goebel, Michael. 2010. *Gauchos, gringos*, and *gallegos*: The assimilation of Italian and Spanish immigrants in the making of modern Uruguay 1880–1930. *Past and Present* 208(1). 191–229.

Haverkate, Henk. 1979. *Impositive sentences in Spanish: Theory and description in linguistic pragmatics*. Amsterdam: North Holland.

Hudson Kam, Carla. 2015. The impact of conditioning variables on the acquisition of variation in adult and child learners. *Language* 91(4). 906–937.

Hudson Kam, Carla & Elissa Newport. 2005. Regularizing unpredictable variation: The roles of adult and child learners in language formation and change. *Language Learning and Development* 1(2). 151–195.

Hudson Kam, Carla & Elissa Newport. 2009. Getting it right by getting it wrong: When learners change languages. *Cognitive Psychology* 59(1). 30–66.

Johnson, Mary. 2013. The pragmatic alternation between two negative imperatives in Argentinian Spanish. Unpublished PhD dissertation. The Ohio State University.

Johnson, Mary. 2016a. Pragmatic variation in *voseo* and *tuteo* negative commands in Argentinian Spanish. In María Irene Moyna & Susana Rivera-Mills (eds.), *Forms of address in the Spanish of the Americas*, 127–148. Amsterdam: John Benjamins.

Johnson, Mary. 2016b. Epistemicity in *voseo* and *tuteo* negative commands in Argentinian Spanish. *Journal of Pragmatics* 97. 37–54.

Johnson, Mary & John Grinstead. 2011. Variation in the *voseo* and *tuteo* negative imperatives in Argentine Spanish. *University of Pennsylvania Working Papers in Linguistics* 17. 99–104. Article 12.

Kroch, Anthony. 1989. Reflexes of grammar patterns of language change. *Language Variation and Change* 1. 199–244.

Labov, William. 2001. *Principles of linguistic change. Volume 2: Social factors.* Oxford: Blackwell.

Lozano, Anthony. 1995. Cognitive development, deontic and epistemic subjunctives. *Hispanic Linguistics* 6/7. 93–115.

MacWhinney, Brian. 2000. *The CHILDES project: The database.* Volume 2. Mahwah, NJ: Lawrence Erlbaum.

McMahon, Robert & Rex Forehand. 2005. *Helping the noncompliant child: Family-based treatment for oppositional behavior.* New York: Guilford.

Moyna, María Irene. 2009. Child acquisition and language change: *Voseo* evolution in Río de la Plata Spanish. In Joe Collentine, Barbara Lafford, MaryEllen García & Francisco Marcos Marín (eds.), *Proceedings of the 2007 Hispanic Linguistics Symposium*, 131–142. Somerville, MA: Cascadilla.

Moyna, María Irene. 2020. Formas de tratamiento y mitigación en el español de Montevideo. In Tatiana Maranhão de Castedo & Ana Berenice Peres Martorelli (eds.), *El voseo en América, Origen, usos y aplicación*, 165–197. Curitiba: Appris.

Moyna, María Irene & Beatriz Ceballos. 2008. Representaciones dramáticas de una variable lingüística: Tuteo y voseo en obras de teatro del Río de la Plata (1886–1911). *Spanish in Context* 5(1). 64–88.

Moyna, María Irene & Israel Sanz-Sánchez. 2023. Out of the mouths of babes: The role of children in the formation of the Río de la Plata address system. *Journal of Historical Sociolinguistics* 9(2). 189–210.

Nahum, Benjamín. 1968. *La estancia alambrada.* Montevideo: Arca.

Nuyts, Jan. 2005. The modal confusion: On terminology and the concepts behind it. In Ales Klinge, Henrik Hegel Müller (eds.), *Modality: Studies in form and function*, 5–38. London: Equinox.

Oroño, Mariela. 2014. La escuela y la lengua en la construcción de la identidad nacional uruguaya: Los libros de lectura usados en la escuela pública en los años 40 del siglo XX. *Boletín de Filología* 49(2). 215–236.

Palmer, Frank. 2001. *Mood and modality.* Cambridge University Press.

Penny, Ralph. 1991. *A history of the Spanish language.* Cambridge: Cambridge University Press.

Pérez-Leroux, Ana. 1998. The acquisition of mood selection in Spanish relative clauses. *Journal of Child Language* 25(3). 585–604.

Prevedello, Nora Lilí. 1989. El voseo en el habla de Córdoba: Dos fuerzas en pugna. In Luz Arrigoni de Allamand (ed.), *Actas del II Congreso Argentino de Hispanistas*, Volume 1, 287–300. Mendoza: Facultad de Filosofía y Letras.

Requena, Pablo E., Dracos, Melisa, & Miller, Karen. 2017. Acquisition of Spanish mood selection in complement clauses. In Maria LaMendola & Jennifer Scott (eds.), *Proceedings of the 41st Boston University Conference on Language Development*, Volume 2, 563–575. Somerville, MA. Cascadilla.

Sánchez-Naranjo, Jeannette, & Ana Pérez-Leroux. 2010. In the wrong mood at the right time: Children's acquisition of the Spanish subjunctive in temporal clauses. *Canadian Journal of Linguistics/Revue canadienne de linguistique* 55(2). 227–255.

Sanz-Sánchez, Israel & María Irene Moyna. 2023. Children as agents of language change: Diachronic evidence from Latin American Spanish phonology. *Journal of Historical Linguistics* 13(3). 327–374.

Sarreal, Julia. 2014. *The Guaraní and their missions: A socioeconomic history*. Stanford: Stanford University Press.

Selinker, Larry. 1972. Interlanguage. *International Review of Applied Linguistics in Language Teaching* 10. 209–241.

Siracusa, María Isabel. 1972. Morfología verbal del voseo en el habla culta de Buenos Aires. *Filología* 16. 201–213.

Spalding, Hobart. 1972. Education in Argentina, 1890–1914: The limits of oligarchical reform. *The Journal of Interdisciplinary History* 3(1). 31–61.

Sucazes, Daniel & Orual Andina. Undated. *Indicadores demográficos: Variables estadísticas relevantes durante el siglo XX. Área sociodemográfica*. Fascículo 4: Educación y Capacitación. Montevideo: Instituto Nacional de Estadística.

Wagner, Suzanne Evans. 2012. Age grading in sociolinguistic theory. *Language and Linguistic Compass* 6. 371–382.

Zubillaga, Carlos. 1993. *Hacer la América: Estudios históricos sobre la inmigración española al Uruguay*. Montevideo: Fin de Siglo.

CHAPTER 8

The influences of adult and child speakers in the emergence of Light Warlpiri, an Australian mixed language

Carmel O'Shannessy
The Australian National University

Many analyses of language change are only able to draw on data from adult speech and therefore cannot empirically motivate a connection between an origin of a potential change and the actuation of that change throughout a community of speakers. The case study of the recent emergence of Light Warlpiri (O'Shannessy 2005), a mixed language spoken in northern Australia, provides new perspectives on the roles of different age groups of adults and children in the emergence of the mixed language, and suggests an empirically motivated model of how a mixed language can emerge from practices of code-switching between languages, in a two-stage process (O'Shannessy 2020). This case also has important implications for the sociohistorical study of the potential role of young learners in other cases of language change and the emergence of new languages.

Keywords: Warlpiri, Light Warlpiri, acquisition, child language, Australia, mixed language, language contact, innovation

1. Introduction

Most analyses of language change, including contact-induced change, are only able to draw on adult speech examples to identify and then motivate a given change. There are two main reasons for this. One is that most studies of language change have taken place well after the change has been actuated, partly because it is not always apparent that a change has been in progress until it is embedded in the community of speakers. The other is that it is usually the case that child language is documented only by researchers who are specifically interested in child language development, and this field is relatively new. In contrast, written records of adult speech and writing have been collected for centuries. There is therefore much more data available on adult language, reaching back further in time. The consequence of the bias in sampling and recording adult language data is that it allows little insight into the roles different age groups may play in language change, and why. This ultimately restricts our understandings of human social cognition, in terms of what kinds of language analytic processes are possible in what kinds of social configurations.

Exceptions to the bias of evidence have been steadily increasing in recent decades, especially in contact-induced language change, the focus of this chapter. School-aged children lead change in contexts where they are speakers of different dialects of a language (Amery 1993; Kerswill & Williams 2000), including where they are from different language backgrounds (e.g., Cheshire et al. 2011). Children have been hypothesized to select some features from variable input and reproduce them more often than others, or to the exclusion of others (Aboh 2009; McConvell 2008; Mufwene 2001). Children have also been observed to regularize grammatical subsystems so that their production differs from that of adults (Jourdan 1989, 2009; Sankoff 1991; Shnukal & Marchese 1983; see also Chapters 2 and 6).

What would evidence for a child-influenced change be? The data would need to show that child speakers brought an innovation into a local way of speaking that has remained in that way of speaking as the children grew to adulthood and was passed on to the next generation of speakers. The only way to know if children initiated a change is to compare the speech production of child and adult speakers in a single community at one point in time – specifically, the time that child speakers are actuating the change among their own age cohort, but adult speakers are not. Evidence of child-initiated change so far suggests that an innovation first spreads among the children's own age cohort, and that adults are slower to take it up (O'Shannessy 2020).

Across all language learning situations individual children typically produce speech that differs from the input they receive in the course of language acquisition, especially in the earliest years. These differing productions do not result in language change, because they do not remain in a child's speech as the child grows up, and they do not spread through a community of speakers. In other words, they are purely *developmental* (e.g., Brown 1973: 373–375; Bybee & Slobin 1982; Cazden 1968; Clark 2009: 105–112, 179–180). Rather, each child in time conforms to the input they hear in the community. Theories about how a child comes to make productions that differ from the adult input in the first place, and then how a child learns to conform to the input, are the theories of child first language acquisition.

The ways in which children's developmental productions differ from those of adults show some similarity across languages. The most common strategies relevant to this paper are regularization of aspects of morphology and syntax, and re-analysis of aspects of the input. For example, children regularize irregular paradigms, e.g., *brang* or *bringed* for 'brought', and undertake grammatical re-analysis, e.g., *can I avocado* (analysing the first two syllables of the name of a fruit, 'avocado', as the words 'have a', and seeing the name of the fruit as 'cado').

The most common child language acquisition context, that of growing up bilingually or multilingually, is also the least well understood academically. In these contexts, children employ the language processing strategies just mentioned, and the strategies may involve aspects of both languages (de Houwer 2005, 2009). In this process, there is the possibility of crosslinguistic transfer, and this is seen in the earliest years of speech production (Döpke 2000; Müller & Hulk 2001; Serratrice et al. 2004). Some contexts are even more complex, as there are two or more languages or linguistic systems, and there may be a change in progress in the community of speakers.

Children can play differing roles in different situations. The most dramatic outcome of influence children can have is that in specific circumstances they can create a new linguistic system (e.g., Nicaraguan Sign Language, see Kegl et al. 2001). Children can influence more subtle changes too. For example, they can regularize variable input, seen in phonology (Amery 1993; Kerswill & Williams 2000), morphosyntax (e.g., Jourdan 1989; O'Shannessy 2013; Shnukal & Marchese 1983), and word order (Kotsinas 1998; Quist 2008).[1] Crucial to the discussion is understanding the input the children receive at a specific time range, the changes they putatively make to that input in their own production, and how such a change could spread throughout a community of speakers.[2]

Many of the language processing strategies where change takes place are the same as those that occur in contexts where there is ultimately no language change (see Chapter 5; for a uniformitarian view of the historical effect of language learning strategies, see DeGraff 2009). In those contexts, changes brought in by individual child learners typically do not spread among the speakers in the community, and the child learners later return to the speech patterns of the community. What is different in instances of language change is that the innovations do take hold among a community of speakers and are transmitted to the next generations. The differences are not in the type of language processing by a child learner, but in the social configurations in which the child learners are growing up (O'Shannessy & Davidson 2020). This part of the puzzle, about how a putative change initiated by children might have spread through a population, is not often addressed. In the rest of this chapter, I present a case study of the emergence of Light Warlpiri and show how child learners built on the input they

---

1. For a discussion of language changes influenced by children in complex contexts see O'Shannessy & Davidson (2020).
2. See also Chapter 6 for a similar claim, and Chapter 7 for an additional case study of a sociohistorical context where young children operated as social agents of language change.

heard to internalize mixed input as a single system, add grammatical innovations, and conventionalize the new linguistic system within their community so that it became their primary everyday way of speaking.

The chapter is organized as follows. In Section 2, I sketch the sociohistorical situation in which this new language emerged, showing how it is directly linked to processes of colonization. In Section 3, I detail the roles of adult and child speakers, illustrating a two-stage process of language emergence – adult input, and child learners acting on that input. Section 4 explores the role of child speakers in the development and regularization of the new way of speaking since its emergence. Section 5 focuses on the need to bring together language acquisition and sociohistorical perspectives for increased understandings of the processes involved. Section 6 concludes the chapter.

2. The sociohistorical context for the emergence of Light Warlpiri

Data for this study were collected in Lajamanu, an Indigenous and multilingual community in Australia's Northern Territory. In Lajamanu today, older adults speak Warlpiri as their main everyday language, and also code-switch between Warlpiri and English and/or Kriol. Younger adults and children speak Light Warlpiri as their main everyday language, also learn Warlpiri from birth, and learn English and aspects of Kriol as they grow up. Light Warlpiri speakers frequently code-switch between Light Warlpiri and Warlpiri and see this as part of their sociolinguistic repertoire (O'Shannessy 2021). Although Kriol and varieties of English spoken by Aboriginal people in the area are separate languages with distinct social histories, there are features of varieties of Aboriginal ways of speaking English that overlap with those of Kriol, so for some features it can be difficult to identify the source language.

The sociohistorical context of Light Warlpiri relates directly to colonization, specifically to the forced relocation of Warlpiri people to establish a new community and their adaptation to introduced sociocultural practices. The community of Lajamanu has a population of approximately 600, and is situated 557 km from the nearest town, Katherine, and about 600 km from the other Warlpiri communities. The community is the product of forced relocation of Warlpiri from their traditional lands to the current site, then called Hooker Creek, in 1948–1949 (Berndt & Berndt 1987: 264; Rowse 1998: 147). The relocation meant that the people in the community were quite distant from their extended families and kin, and at that time communication by phone was very limited. The road south to the other Warlpiri communities is unsealed and can only be driven for about 7–8 months per year due to monsoonal rains. The Lajamanu community, then, is isolated from the other Warlpiri communities. In addition, the road north to the regional centre of Katherine is mostly sealed, making travel to Katherine for health and administration reasons much easier than to other distant centres. Katherine is a meeting place for Indigenous people speaking many different traditional languages, and the *lingua franca* spoken there is an Indigenous contact language, Kriol (an English-lexified creole), which is also the L1 for many people in the area. In the only community close to Lajamanu, 107 kms away, a new mixed language, Gurindji Kriol, is spoken (McConvell & Meakins 2005). All of this means that the relocation of Warlpiri people to the community now called Lajamanu reduced their access to their Warlpiri-speaking kin, and created a need for interaction with speakers of Kriol and likely L2 learner varieties of English.

Colonization brought cattle stations, mining, and at the time of the establishment of the Lajamanu community, World War II army camps. People from Lajamanu worked in cattle stations often far from Warlpiri country, in the mines and in the army camps. In each of these contexts they interacted with speakers of other Indigenous languages, probably using the emerging Kriol or what has been called 'station pidgin' as common languages (McConvell 2008). It's reasonable to think that code-switching between speakers' own primary languages and the *lingua franca* languages occurred. Even though the speakers were likely multilingual, they were in situations where they needed to interact with speakers of other languages, often from distant places, without time for more language learning.

Language documentation in Lajamanu and other Warlpiri communities shows that adults continued to speak Warlpiri as their main language (e.g., Hale 1967, 1982; Meggitt 1954; Reece 1971; Rockman & Cataldi 1994; Swartz 1982, 1991). However, based on the speech of now older speakers in Lajamanu, it seems that speakers also code-switched between Warlpiri and the *lingua franca* speech styles on their return to Lajamanu. By 1979 children were incorporating English into their Warlpiri and there was some variation in their Warlpiri (Leeding & Laughren 1979: 10). At that point the innovative features of Light Warlpiri do not appear to have been present, so the process at that time was likely code-switching. The social history briefly outlined here shows how the relocation of people to establish a new community far from their kin, and their need to work in contexts with speakers of many languages, has led to the emergence of the new mixed language.

These days, there is a bus service for travel to Katherine, and there are limited flight services. Families often travel by car to the other Warlpiri communities to interact with family and participate in sports, education meetings and traditional ceremonies. Children attend the local government primary school, where English is the main language of instruction. There have been English–Warlpiri bilingual education programs for periods of time since the early 1980s, but there are also periods when there is very little time given to instruction in Warlpiri, despite the struggle by Warlpiri people for this instruction to be maintained. There is some post-primary education available, and most young people spend some time at high school in Darwin, about 900 km away. Light Warlpiri is not spoken in the other Warlpiri communities. Within the community, children spend time with peers and extended family of all ages, and multi-age interactions are typical. Children also spend considerable amounts of time playing in multi-age peer groups.

3. The roles of adults and children in the emergence of Light Warlpiri

Previous chapters in this volume (e.g., Chapter 6) have reflected on the relative weight of the contribution of speakers of various ages to the emergence of new local norms. In a similar vein, the present case study in Australia has also taken several perspectives on the roles of adults and children in a dramatic change, the emergence and development of a relatively new mixed language, Light Warlpiri, and these perspectives are the focus of this chapter.

Light Warlpiri shows a nominal-verbal structural split. It combines nominal structure from Warlpiri with verbal structure mostly from Kriol. In addition, an innovative verbal auxiliary structure draws on all three sources – Kriol, English and Warlpiri. The source languages contribute to the new way of speaking in different ways across domains (O'Shannessy 2013; O'Shannessy & Brown 2021), as shown in (1a–c) (from O'Shannessy 2020: 459).

(1) a. Light Warlpiri
 Ngajarra-ng wi=m bai-im dress-pawu kurdu-pawu-k.
 1DL.EXCL-ERG 1PL.S-NFUT buy-TR dress-DIM child-DIM-DAT
 'We two bought a little dress for the child.'
 b. Warlpiri, constructed
 Ngajarra=rlujarra-rlu payi-manu warrpa-pardu kurdu-pardu-ku.
 1DL.EXCL-1DL.EXCL.S-ERG buy-CAUS dress-DIM child-DIM-DAT
 'We two bought a little dress for the child.'
 c. Kriol, constructed[3]
 minbala bin baiy-am lil-wan dres ba det lilgel
 1DL.EXCL PST buy-TR little-NOM dress PURP DET young.girl
 'We two bought a little dress for the girl.'

Example (1a) is from Light Warlpiri and shows Warlpiri structure in the presence of the ergative case suffix *–ng* 'ERG', the diminutive suffix *–pawu* 'DIM', and the dative case suffix *–k* 'DAT'. Warlpiri vocabulary appears in the free first person dual

---

3. Many thanks to Denise Angelo for this Kriol example.

Chapter 8. The influences of adult and child speakers in the emergence of Light Warlpiri 185

exclusive pronoun, *ngajarra* '1DL.EXCL', and the noun *kurdu* 'child'. The verb *bai/payi* 'buy' is from both English and Kriol, and a Kriol transitive suffix *–im* 'TR' is attached. The innovative auxiliary form, *wi-m* '1PL.NFUT', appears before the verb, and draws on the English and Kriol pronoun form *we*, and attaches the new temporal element, *-m* 'NFUT'. The word *dress* is from English. The new auxiliary structure draws on the source languages that contribute to the mixed language, but is not the same as either of them (O'Shannessy 2020).

Although three languages are named as the source languages of Light Warlpiri, they can be categorized into two groups: Warlpiri, on the one hand, and Kriol and varieties of English on the other. I use the term 'varieties of English' because more than one variety of English is used in the community; minimally, Standard Australian English and varieties of English as often spoken by Aboriginal people, for instance with elements derived from Kriol present. The two groups are distinct in a few ways. Warlpiri is an agglutinating Pama-Nyungan language, and is the ancestral language of the speakers. English and Kriol are both English-lexified isolating languages, and the Warlpiri people encountered them as a result of Australia's colonization, and only within approximately the last 80 years, as explained above (Section 2). Table 1 summarizes the source languages and their relevant features.

Table 1. How the three source languages of Light Warlpiri are categorized into two groups

	Warlpiri	English	Kriol
Lexifier language	Warlpiri-lexified	English-lexified	English-lexified
Ancestral language?	Ancestral	introduced	introduced
Language typology	Agglutinating	isolating	isolating

Kriol and varieties of English are separate languages with distinct social histories (see Section 2), yet by being English-lexified they have some overlapping properties, for example they share some pronouns (e.g., *you/yu* '2SG') and verb stems (e.g., 'get', 'bring'). When some of these elements appear in Light Warlpiri it is not always clear if they were derived from English or Kriol, so the notation 'English/Kriol' is used.

Empirical data gathered since 2002, spanning age groups from two years to 70 years old, allow an apparent-time based hypothesis about the code-switching antecedents of the new way of speaking, how it conventionalized, and crucially, which age groups are likely to have most influenced the innovative features. More specifically, the study of Light Warlpiri suggests that very young children may play an active role in contact-induced language change by participating in social practices of marking overlapping identities. They may also, through the same sets of language processes seen in other child language acquisition contexts, initiate a potential change that is actuated throughout the age cohort through sociolinguistic practices (O'Shannessy 2020).

One important point shown in the case of Light Warlpiri is that the child learners built on the adult input directed to them. The new language arose through a two-stage process. First, adults spoke to young children in a child-directed speech register that involved consistently code-switching between the two groups of source languages: Warlpiri, and English and/or Kriol. Adults used a code-switching pattern that involved inserting English and/or Kriol pronouns and verbs into an otherwise Warlpiri string, as shown in (2) (from O'Shannessy 2012, 325).

(2) *yakarra nyanya* WI HAB-IM *nyanya wana ngalipa nyanya*
    DIS   food 1PL have-TR food DIS 1PL.INCL food
    'Gosh, we have food, food, you know, us, food.'

In (2), the speaker inserts a pronoun (*wi*) and verb, including verbal morphology (*hab-im*), into a Warlpiri string. This patterning is the basis of what then became the structure of Light Warlpiri.

In the second stage, the young children internalized this patterning as a single linguistic system and conventionalized it among their peers. As this happened, the children also added grammatical innovations in the verbal auxiliary subsystem, and these innovations are key to distinguishing Light Warlpiri as a conventionalized system. The evidence that the children built on the input they received is important theoretically because it contrasts with a theory that children would add complexity to input that was impoverished (Bickerton 1984). This case study shows clearly that there was no impoverishment or deficit in the input, the input was in a sense not far from the children's innovative productions. The cycle is a little like that of the *cascade principle* (DeGraff 2009), where adult L2 learner features are passed on to a next generation of learners and become part of that group's L1.[4] A difference in the Light Warlpiri situation is that the input involved adult L1 and L2 (specifically, Warlpiri and elements of Kriol).

In structural terms, the innovation is that a pronoun paradigm in the English/Kriol input (*im* '3SG' and *dem* '3PL') was reanalyzed as a pronoun-plus-TMA structure. For example, *im* '3SG' > *i-m* '3SG-NONFUTURE', *dem* '3PL' > *de-m* '3PL-NONFUTURE'. This pattern was regularized across all pronouns, creating new forms and structure that do not exist in either English, Kriol or Warlpiri. The new structure is evidenced by the presence of *wi-m* '1PL-NONFUTURE' and *yu-*

---

4. See also Chapter 5 for further discussion of the distinction between *vertical* transmission from adults to children, and *horizontal* transmission in peer-to-peer communication and acquisition.

m '2SG-NONFUTURE', which only exist in Light Warlpiri, not in its sources.[5] The structure was likely influenced by English 'I'm', which has a pronoun-plus-TMA structure, and the Warlpiri auxiliary system, here illustrated by the 1SG form, *ka=rna* 'PRES-1SG' (O'Shannessy 2013). The young speakers created a structure of pronoun-plus-TMA that is absent from the input languages, in which past and present tense together contrast structurally with future tense (or a realis – irrealis modal contrast). In the process, a Kriol past tense marker in the input, *bin* 'PAST', was to a large extent replaced by the new structure. The Kriol past marker can still occur in Light Warlpiri but mostly does not (O'Shannessy 2020).

The reanalysis was applied to and regularized across the verbal auxiliary subsystem, as illustrated in Table 2. It is not known which part of the reanalysis occurred first.

Table 2 compares the auxiliary structures of Kriol with those of Light Warlpiri, showing how the Light Warlpiri system involves reanalysis of the Kriol system, followed by regularization of the reanalysis across the whole paradigm.

To identify the contribution of young children versus adults, the verbal complex in Light Warlpiri is compared to the productions of speakers in the generation older than the Light Warlpiri speakers, who have not adopted the innovations in the auxiliary (O'Shannessy 2012, 2020). (3) shows an utterance from the parent of a young child, and the parent is older than the Light Warlpiri-speaking generations.

(3) Light Warlpiri   (O'Shannessy 2020)
see Piko-*ng*   im faind-im *jurlpu*...
look name-ERG 3SG find-TR bird
'Look! Piko found the bird'

This example shows vocabulary and grammar from both Warlpiri and English/Kriol. The referent, Piko, is identified as the transitive subject and semantic agent of the action by the use of the Warlpiri ergative case marker, *-ng* 'ERG', and the transitive object, *jurlpu* 'bird' is in absolute case, realized as null marking. The English/Kriol phrase *im faind-im* '3SG find-TR' is inserted within the Warlpiri string, and there is a 3rd person pronoun, *im* '3SG', preceding a transitive verb, marked with transitive marking from Kriol. Interestingly there is no Kriol past tense marker *bin* 'PST', as there is in (1c), above. This suggests that the Kriol past tense marker, often present in the code-switching speech of adults in the community older than the Light Warlpiri speakers, was not always present in speech directed to young children. It follows that the young children did not themselves delete the Kriol past tense marker independently of the speech directed to them, it

---

5. See Dahmen (2022), on a similar structure used by Jaru speakers in a neighboring community.

Table 2. Light Warlpiri auxiliary paradigm and its sources (adapted from O'Shannessy 2020: 464)[a]

Forms	1SG	1PL	2SG	2DL/PL	3SG	3PL
Light Warlpiri nonfuture	a-m	wi-m	yu-m	yudu/yumob bin	i-m	de-m
Kriol past	ai bin	wi bin	yu bin	yudu/yumob bin	i bin	dei bin
Light Warlpiri future	a-rra a-l	wi-rra wi-l	yu-rra _	yudu/yumob garra	i-rra i-l	de-rra _
Kriol future	ai garra/a-rra[*]	wi garra/wi-rra	yu garra/yu-rra	yudupala/ yumob garra	i garra/i-rra	dei garra/de-rra
Light Warlpiri desiderative	a-na[**]	wi-na	yu-na	yudu/yumob wanaxs	i-na	de-na
Kriol desiderative	ai wandi/ wani/ wana	wi wandi/ wani/ wana	yu wandi/ wani/ wana	yudu/yumob wandi/wani/ wana	i wandi/ wani/ wana	dei wandi/ wani/ wana
English contracted desiderative	I wana	we wana	you wana	you wana	he/she/it want/s to	they wana

a. Kriol data from Schultze-Berndt et al. (2013). Kriol varieties have more pronoun forms and person and number distinctions than are shown here, e.g., inclusive-exclusive distinctions in the 1st person. Here I show only those most likely to have been sources for Light Warlpiri.
* The contracted future auxiliary forms have been reported for some varieties of Kriol (Schultze-Berndt et al. 2013; Cutfield, S. p.c.), and for Gurindji Kriol (Meakins 2011).
** The contracted a-na auxiliary forms are also attested in Gurindji Kriol (Meakins 2011).

was already only variably present. This deletion suggests that conventionalization entailed the elimination or reduction in the frequency of at least some variable elements present in the sources.

It is important to note that, from an age perspective, the children made only a small change in the adult speech patterns that they heard, but the small change has a dramatic effect on the overall structure of the system. The changes to the children's way of speaking as a conventionalized system show that they regularized and extended morpho-syntactic paradigms, and in doing so, created new structure and new semantics.

Evidence that it was young children, and not adult speakers, who brought the innovation into the auxiliary system can be found in the fact that it is only the Light Warlpiri-speaking cohorts, speakers now aged 40 years and below, who use the innovative *yu-m* and *wi-m* constructions. Older speakers, who code-switch between Warlpiri and English/Kriol, do not produce the *yu-m* and *wi-m* constructions. They tend to use the more Kriol-like construction including a Kriol pronoun, *im* '3SG', or for instance, *you/yu* '2SG', and the Kriol past tense marker, *bin* 'past', not the new construction *wi-m* or *yu-m*. These usage patterns show that the new, conventionalized pronoun-plus-TMA system was brought into the innovating cohort's style in time for it to be well-conventionalized among themselves, and before they began transmitting the new system to their own children.

Young children make a similar kind of re-analysis to the one seen in Light Warlpiri in other language acquisition contexts, but in those other environments, they typically later conform to the surrounding community grammar and the new construction doesn't remain in their individual grammar. Based on this it seems likely that speakers aged around three to four years old created the new pattern (O'Shannessy 2020). Monolingual English-speaking children have been observed to produce the same kind of re-analysis of auxiliary forms as appears in Light Warlpiri. For instance, they may reanalyze 'I wana' (from 'I want to') to 'a-na', then alter return to 'I wana', but in the English context this has not spread or conventionalized among English speakers, likely because of social factors (O'Shannessy 2020). English is a widely spoken, socially powerful and often dominant language, with clear written norms reinforced through schooling and literacy practices and strong social senses of what is the 'correct' way to speak it in each community of speakers. As we will see below, these factors differ from those in the small community in which Light Warlpiri emerged. This research has shown that young children process language input in the same ways in both monolingual and multilingual contexts, but this leads to different outcomes in the wider community ways of speaking because of differing sociolinguistic properties.

Bilingual and multilingual children are aware of the separate systems of their input from an early age, and maintain separation of the two or more systems as they grow up (de Houwer 1990, 2005, 2009; Genesee 1989; Genesee et al. 1995; Lanza 1992, 1997). So why did the children in this case study internalize the mixed input as a single system? It is not the case that the cohort of innovating Light Warlpiri-speaking children simply mixed all of their input into one system. Rather, the children identified differences between Warlpiri input and the mixed input they heard in the child-directed speech register (O'Shannessy 2020). As they grew up, they spoke the newly conventionalized system as their primary everyday language, as well as traditional Warlpiri, as a separate linguistic system, and they still do. They did maintain separation of the input systems, and the systems were the mixed input on the one hand, and unmixed Warlpiri on the other. Since bilingual and multilingual children usually do not internalize mixed input into a new mixed system, we need to look for reasons why this would happen in this context and other similar contexts where a mixed language has emerged from conventionalized code-switching practices.

Four main factors that are present when child learners influence the emergence of a new linguistic system have been identified (O'Shannessy 2019). The first is that the child learners spend a considerable amount of time interacting with each other in multi-age peer play groupings. This is likely a common social situation in the world (Cheshire et al. 2011; Cheshire et al. 2015; Cheshire & Gardner-Chloros 2018; Quist 2008), but it has not received as much research attention as the less-common middle-class situations in which child language acquisition research has more often been conducted. Second is that the children grow up in a community with strong social ties, what Milroy and Milroy (1985) call *dense, multiplex* social networks, where most people know each other and interact with each other in many ways on an everyday basis. A community like this would also often have a clear social boundary (or, in the case of Light Warlpiri, a geographical boundary), but any kind of social network boundary would be as relevant. Third, the children appear to have considerable independence in their speech behaviour, free from overt normative prescriptivism in terms of how they should speak (see Kerswill & Williams 2000). The fourth factor, so far identified only in the Light Warlpiri context, is a "culture of linguistic creativity" (O'Shannessy 2019: 332), where different registers and styles of speech production are present and valued in the community of speakers. None of these factors is in principle exclusive to any area of the world or time period (see Chapter 7 in this volume), so young children might have played an active role in the emergence of new community norms in any sociohistorical setting where these factors co-occur.

While young children can be hypothesized to have conventionalized some aspects of the grammar of Light Warlpiri when it first emerged in the 1980s, other innovations appear to be more recent. This raises the question of whether new cohorts of young children have contributed to these innovations.

4. The role of child speakers in the development of Light Warlpiri since its emergence

As explained in Section 3, the emergence of Light Warlpiri had occurred by the time the current age group of speakers who are now approximately 25–40 years old, who can be called Generation 1, were late teenagers, estimated because it was then that they began to pass the new conventionalized way of speaking on to the next generation, their children. In some instances, the group of children who can be called Generation 2 are now approximately 20 or so years old and are passing

Light Warlpiri on to their own children, Generation 3. There are so far several Generation 3 child learners in the community.

Has any change occurred in Light Warlpiri since its emergence? If so, has it been influenced by child speakers? To explore this question a comparison is needed between adult and child speakers where speakers in both age groups are speakers of Light Warlpiri. Adult speakers of Light Warlpiri can belong to either Generation 1 or 2, since a generation spans about 20 years. Light Warlpiri speakers also speak Warlpiri and English and typically have some knowledge of Kriol, so they are in a complex language environment, and Warlpiri, English or Kriol could influence their ways of speaking Light Warlpiri. In addition, Light Warlpiri itself shows internal variation in some domains, so there is the potential for further regularization and perhaps re-analysis (O'Shannessy 2016a).

In the remainder of this section, I will first present some comparisons of relevant aspects of Warlpiri and Light Warlpiri. Following this I provide examples that illustrate where child speakers tune in to the variation in adult speech and reproduce it in a similar way to the adults, and, in contrast, where child speakers tune in to the variation in adult speech but produce the variants with quantitative differences.

Warlpiri and Light Warlpiri exhibit clear differences, for instance in the verbal complex of each language, but also similarities. Notably, they share nominal structure, with Warlpiri nominal case-marking retained in Light Warlpiri. The marking of ergative and dative case in both languages shows variation. Ergative marking optionally[6] indicates a transitive subject in both Warlpiri and Light Warlpiri, shown in (4) and (5), and occurs in both ergative-absolutive and ergative-dative case arrays (Hale 1982).

(4) Warlpiri (O'Shannessy 2016b)
Kamina-rlu jinta-ngku ka=ø=ø jarntu ma-ni yard-jangka.
girl-ERG one-ERG PRES=3SG.S=3SG.O dog get-NPST yard-ABL
'The girl got the dog from the yard by herself.'

Example (4), of Warlpiri, shows two forms of the ergative marker on stems of differing lengths, the form *-rlu* on a stem of three syllables and *-ngku* on a stem of two syllables. Both stem length and harmony with the preceding vowel condition the allomorphy of the ergative case marker in Warlpiri. The allomorphy of these case markers in Warlpiri is undergoing change, and new forms *-ngu/ngi* and *-ng*, derived from *-ngku/ngki*, have emerged (O'Shannessy 2016a).

---

6. For the conditions of the optionality see O'Shannessy (2005, 2013, 2016a, 2016b).

(5) Light Warlpiri (O'Shannessy 2016a)
jinta-kari-ng na i-m ged-im *kanta*
one-other-ERG DIS 3SG.S-NFUT get-TR bush.coconut
'Now the other one is getting the bush coconut.'

Example (5), of Light Warlpiri, shows the newer Warlpiri contracted form, *-ng*, on a word stem of four syllables. In Light Warlpiri the ergative marker also has allomorphy, but increasingly the contracted forms *-ng/-ing* are used to the exclusion of other forms. The ergative allomorphs in both Warlpiri and Light Warlpiri are shown in Table 3.

Table 3. Allomorphy of the ergative case marker in Warlpiri and Light Warlpiri

Final vowel of stem	Classic Warlpiri		Contemporary Warlpiri		Light Warlpiri	
	Back vowel	Front vowel	Back vowel	Front vowel	Back vowel	Front vowel
Stems have 2 morae	-ngku	-ngki	-ngku, -ngu, -ng	-ngki, -ngi, -ng	-ng	-ing, -ng
Stems have 2+ morae	-rlu	-rli	-rlu	-rli	-ng	-ing, -ng

In the case of the dative, case marking appears in ergative-dative, ergative-absolutive-dative and absolutive-dative case arrays, and in these arrays dative case is registered in the auxiliary as well as marked on the nominal (Hale 1982). It may also appear on an adjunct noun phrase, on the nominal only. In Warlpiri, the dative case marker has forms conditioned by vowel harmony, *-ku/ki*, and these can be contracted to *-k*, as in (6).

(6) Warlpiri (Laughren et al. 1996)
Wati-ngki ka=ø=rla kurdu-ku warri-rni.
man-ERG pres=3SG.S=DAT child-DAT search-NPST
'The man is looking for the child.'

In Example (6) the dative case function is marked on the auxiliary by *-rla*, and on the nominal by *-ku*.

In contrast, in Light Warlpiri dative case does not appear on the auxiliary, it is only marked on a nominal, as in (7).

(7) Light Warlpiri (O'Shannessy 2016b)
Kurdu-kurdu wita i=m shaut-ing *jarntu-k.*
child-REDUP small 3SG.S-NFUT shout-PROG dog-DAT
'The little children are shouting to the dog.'

Chapter 8. The influences of adult and child speakers in the emergence of Light Warlpiri

The dative allomorphs in both Warlpiri and Light Warlpiri are shown in Table 4.

Table 4. Allomorphy of the dative case marker in Warlpiri and Light Warlpiri

	Classic Warlpiri		Contemporary Warlpiri		Light Warlpiri	
Stems end with:	Back vowel	Front vowel	Back vowel	Front vowel	Back vowel	Front vowel
	-ku	-ki	-ku, -k	-ki, -k	-ku, -k	-ki, -k, -ik

The use of ergative case marking can be thought of as a vulnerable domain, due to the pressure from English and contact with Kriol, both of which use word order to indicate core grammatical functions. If word order came to be used more for this function, then ergative case marking would be needed less. Dative case marking could also be vulnerable, as English and Kriol have periphrastic means of marking this function. The question of how these functions are realized by children is raised.

The marking of the two case functions, ergative and dative, by child speakers (mean ages 7, 9, 12) of Light Warlpiri and Warlpiri over two time periods has been examined (O'Shannessy 2016a, b). The studies analyzed recordings of the children telling narratives from picture prompts (O'Shannessy 2004) in 2005 and 2010. In that time Light Warlpiri speakers increased their use of subject-verb word order, but also increased their use of ergative case marking on overt transitive subjects, from 51% in 2005 data to 79% in 2010 data, making it more in line with the amount of marking in Warlpiri (O'Shannessy 2016b). Second, when the word order was not subject-verb order, in 2010 the transitive subject hosted an ergative case-marker much more often – 63% of transitive subjects in post-verbal position had a case-marker in 2005, increased to 96% in 2010 (O'Shannessy 2016b). In the children's Warlpiri narratives, the amount of ergative case marking remained constant between 2005 and 2010, but the proportion of ergative marking increased when the transitive subject was in postverbal position (O'Shannessy 2016b).

In terms of allomorphy, the degree of variation in allomorphy in Light Warlpiri decreased over time. In the 2005 data, all the allomorphs present in Warlpiri were present in Light Warlpiri, although some occurred less often than others: the *-rlu/rli* forms that occur in Warlpiri on longer word stems occurred very infrequently in Light Warlpiri. In the 2010 data only two forms appear in Light Warlpiri, the contracted form, *-ng* and its grammaticalized variant *-ing* that occurs on consonant-final stems, as shown in Table 5.

In summary, Light Warlpiri ergative case marking over time became more like that in Warlpiri in that it was used more often on overt transitive subjects, but it became less like that in Warlpiri because the allomorphy was regularized so that only two, newer allomorphs occur.

Table 5. Ergative allomorphs in each language, 2005 and 2010 (O'Shannessy 2016b)

	Warlpiri	Light Warlpiri
2005	-rlu/i, -ngku/i, -ngu/i, -ng	-rlu/i, -ngku/i, -ngu/i, -ng
2010	-rlu/i, -ngku/i, -ngu/i, -ng	-ing -ng

Turning to dative case marking, differential use of allomorphy in each language is also seen. Between 2005 data and 2010 data, in both languages fewer dative case forms with a vowel (*-ku/-ki*) were used, showing a rise in use of *-k*. Yet dative case forms with a vowel were used more often in Warlpiri texts than in Light Warlpiri texts (O'Shannessy 2016b). In the Light Warlpiri data, a case form with an epenthetic vowel before the case marker (*-ik*) occurs, the dative counterpart to the ergative form (*-ing*).

In the analysis of ergative and dative case-marking, children show similar patterning in both Warlpiri and Light Warlpiri in some areas, yet create greater differences between the two languages in others. Both Warlpiri and Light Warlpiri show changes in the allomorphy of both types of affixing, with newer allomorphs being added in both languages, but the two languages differ in the extent to which the older and newer allomorphs occur. In Warlpiri, all the older allomorphs still occur frequently, and more frequently than the newer ones. Light Warlpiri differs in that the newer allomorphs occur much more frequently than the older ones, almost to the exclusion of the older allomorphs. In addition, in Light Warlpiri, a transitive clause with verb-subject (VS) word order will almost always have an ergative-marked transitive subject. In other words, the correlation between word order and ergative case marking in Light Warlpiri has been regularized more than it is in Warlpiri.

A direct comparison between the productions of child and adult speakers of Light Warlpiri in terms of lexical and phonological choices has also been made (O'Shannessy 2015). The two languages share vocabulary from Warlpiri: for instance, the Warlpiri word *watiya* 'tree' occurs in both languages, and the English word *tree* only occurs in the specific noun phrase *palm tree*. But there are other referents where speakers make different choices depending on the language spoken. For example, for the referent 'fire', when speaking Warlpiri only the Warlpiri word *warlu* 'fire' occurs, but in Light Warlpiri the word *warlu* 'fire' and English *fire* both occur. In the case of *warlu/fire* the children and adults use both choices to similar extents. Similarly, the referent of 'dog' has near-synonyms in Warlpiri, *jarntu* 'dog' and *maliki* 'dog', but they have different sociocultural connotations, in that *jarntu* 'dog' has an added meaning of 'companion'. Light Warlpiri speakers use both words when speaking Light Warlpiri and use *jarntu* more often than *maliki*. But when speaking Warlpiri, *maliki* is used more often than *jarntu*, by both adults and children. A community of practice construct (Lave & Wenger 1991; Wenger 1998) is invoked to explain this, where child speakers show themselves to be members of both the Warlpiri and Light Warlpiri speaking communities. They show that they can tune in to subtle variation in the speech of adults (O'Shannessy 2015).

Some other items show different patterning, where children's productions lead those of adults. These are Warlpiri nominal suffixes that occur in both languages, the diminutive suffix, with forms -*pardu* and –*pawu*, and the intensifier suffix, with forms -*nyayirni* and -*nyayirn*. All age groups use both forms of both suffixes. The –*pawu* pronunciation of the diminutive suffix occurs more often in Light Warlpiri than in Warlpiri, and there are differences between age groups: children use this form the most often of all age groups in the study, young adults use it the next most often and older adults use it least often. Similarly, the contracted form of the intensifier suffix -*nyayirn*, is used more often by children than by adults. The conclusion is that some aspects of change-in-progress in a language may progress at equal rates by both child and adult speakers, and others may be pushed further, and led by child speakers (O'Shannessy 2015).

Language variation appears before language change occurs. The Light Warlpiri case study shows that young children can be very tuned in to language variation. The final example is about language knowledge that children have that they do not typically produce. When recording the children, we talked in terms of different styles of speaking in the community. A few children wanted to be recorded speaking a style, in fact a different language, Gurindji Kriol (see McConvell & Meakins 2005), that is spoken in a neighboring community. They did so, and although they were not able to speak the neighboring language completely accurately, they did produce features that are characteristic of that language and different from their own. Although they do not speak the neighboring language, they know aspects of it and are aware of some of its features.

5. Language acquisition and the historical sociolinguistics of Light Warlpiri

The case study of Light Warlpiri shows that there is a benefit to combining the perspectives of child language acquisition and historical sociolinguistics, increasing our understandings of the mechanisms of how a new language can emerge and how innovations can be brought in. Child language acquisition research usually asks about the language processing mechanisms children employ to learn the target system grammar. Similarly, most bilingual L1 acquisition research examines children's production from the perspective of child language processing, in contexts where the input languages are fairly clearly different in types and separated in domains of input, for instance with each parent mostly speaking a different language to the child, even if not strictly adhered to (e.g., de Houwer 1990, 2005, 2009; Döpke 2000; Genesee 1989; Genesee et al. 1995; Lanza 1992, 1997). A prominent question in this research has been about the age at which children are aware that they are learning two distinct systems.

Studies of how koinés and multi-ethnolects emerge (Cheshire et al. 2011; Quist 2008; see also Chapters 4 and 6 in this volume) and of how children acquire sociolinguistic variation present in the community (e.g., Roberts 1997a, b; see Chapter 2) do pay close attention to the speech of children and how innovations are brought into the community in the time frame being studied. These usually involve differences within overall similar, mutually intelligible ways of speaking, and what emerges is a new dialect, or a continuing change that was already in progress within a dialect (e.g., Roberts 1997a, b). In the case of historical work, however, there is rarely the kind of data available to trace the influences of each age group at across a specific time period.

Given that the emergence of mixed languages from typologically quite distinct sources is uncommon, we must ask what is specific about the contexts in which they emerge, as opposed to other contexts. If we were only to study adult speech data, it would be difficult to respond to this question. Many groups of bilingual and multilingual speakers code-switch, but a conventionalized fusion of languages of this type does not usually eventuate (e.g., Toribio 2002). Similarly, bilingual children are well able to separate the grammars and vocabulary of the two languages spoken separately in a community (e.g., de Houwer 1990, 2005, 2009; Döpke 2000; Genesee 1989; Genesee et al. 1995; Lanza 1992, 1997). Why then have some conventionalized languages, like Light Warlpiri, emerged in such contexts, and how have they been internalized by the following generations? We can only respond to these questions by bringing together several intersecting theories and empirical observations – the actual speech patterning of the adult cohort, who were code-switching; the likely input to the then-children, which was a mixed system; acquisition processes that children undertake, including reanalysis, regularization and language separation; and the sociolinguistic context at the time of language emergence. The contribution of each subdiscipline is crucial in constructing an empirically based theory of how a new mixed language can emerge.

There is a significant methodological point to note, drawing on Mufwene (2001), about better understanding a sociolinguistic situation at the time that a new way of speaking emerges. On learning that the source languages of Light Warlpiri are Warlpiri on the one hand, and Kriol and English on the other, one might ask why the child generation did not keep these languages separate as they grew up. The reason is that they were not hearing these languages in the input as separate systems. They were hearing Warlpiri and a mixed system. They did indeed keep these two systems (i.e., Warlpiri and a mixed system) separate, and have continued to do so: but the mixed system has been conventionalized as a new mixed language. If such details of the sociolinguistic situation at the time of language emergence are not known, we cannot accurately identify the social and cognitive mechanisms involved.

A lifespan perspective on language acquisition also adds insight into the mechanisms involved. By following adult and child speakers of Light Warlpiri and Warlpiri over time, a nuanced picture emerges of the ways in which the age groups contribute to changes and regularization in the two languages. Child speakers of Light Warlpiri appear to regularize innovations in their primary way of speaking more than they do in Warlpiri. In this way, some areas of both languages that overlap, for instance case marking morphology, become more differentiated. In other areas both child and adult speakers are more like each other. As shown in other sociohistorical contexts elsewhere in this volume, tracing speakers across time allows a window onto the lifespan of the language as well as the speakers.

6. Conclusion

The case study of Light Warlpiri shows that children can be agents of language change in specific social situations. There is a clear link between the social environment in which Warlpiri children develop multilingual competencies and the emergence of Light Warlpiri as a new mixed language. The kinds of changes children bring into a language are those that could also appear in any child's speech production during the language acquisition process. The difference between child language development productions that later recede as the child conforms to the community way of speaking, and children influencing language change, is the sociolinguistic configuration of the community of speakers at the time, influenced by its social history.

When identifying historical language changes, it is worth considering if they are similar to those that are evidenced as having been made by children acquiring their L1(s) in other contexts, and considering if there may have been a role for child speakers in the particular context that we are working with. The whole socio-historical arena needs to be taken in account. It may be that children have played a greater role in language change in some contexts than is generally thought.

Acknowledgements

Many thanks to the Warlpiri and Light Warlpiri speakers who taught me their languages and participated in research activities, and all members of Lajamanu Community, especially Tanya Hargraves, Deandra Burns, Eva Ross, Leah Johnson, Sabrina Nelson, Lily Hargraves, Elaine Johnson, Gracie White, Marlkirdi Rose, Elizabeth Ross, Valerie Patterson, and the families of children who were recorded. Many thanks to reviewers and the editor of the volume. This paper was written as part of the Australian Research Council grant FT190100243.

Abbreviations

1	1st person	NOM	nominative
3	3rd person	NPST	nonpast
ABL	ablative case	O	object
CAUS	causative	PL	plural
DAT	dative case	PRES	present
DET	determiner	PROG	progressive
DIM	diminutive	PST	past
DIS	discourse marker	PURP	purposive
DL	dual	REDUP	reduplication
ERG	ergative case	S	subject
EXCL	exclusive	SG	singular
INCL	inclusive	TR	transitive
NFUT	nonfuture		

References

Aboh, Enoch Oladé. 2009. Competition and selection. That's all! In Enoch Oladé Aboh & Norval Smith (eds.), *Complex processes in new languages*, 317–344. Amsterdam: John Benjamins.

Amery, Rob. 1993. An Australian Koine – Dhuwaya, a variety of Yolnu Matha spoken at Yirrkala in North-East Arnhem Land. *International Journal of the Sociology of Language* 99. 45–64.

Berndt, Ronald & Catherine Berndt. 1987. *End of an era – Aboriginal labour in the Northern Territory*. Canberra: Australian Institute of Aboriginal Studies.

Bickerton, Derek. 1984. The Language Bioprogram Hypothesis. *The Behavioral and Brain Sciences* 7(2). 173–188.

Brown, Roger. 1973. *A first language: The early stages*. Cambridge, MA: Harvard University Press.

Bybee, Joan & Dan Slobin. 1982. Rules and schemas in the development and use of the English past tense. *Language* 58(2). 265–289.

Cazden, Courtney. 1968. The acquisition of noun and verb inflections. *Child Development*. 39(2). 433–448.

Cheshire, Jenny & Penelope Gardner-Chloros. 2018. Introduction. Multicultural youth vernaculars in Paris and urban France. *Journal of French Language Studies* 28(2). 161–164.

Cheshire, Jenny, Paul Kerswill, Sue Fox & Eivind Torgersen. 2011. Contact, the feature pool and the speech community: The emergence of Multicultural London English. *Journal of Sociolinguistics* 15(2). 151–196.

Cheshire, Jenny, Jacomine Nortier & David Adger. 2015. Emerging multiethnolects in Europe. *Queen Mary's Occasional Papers Advancing Linguistics* 33. https://www.qmul.ac.uk/sllf /media/sllf-new/department-of-linguistics/33-QMOPAL-Cheshire-Nortier-Adger-.pdf (15 January 2022).

Clark, Eve. 2009. *First language acquisition*. 2nd edition. Cambridge: Cambridge University Press.

Dahmen, Joshua. 2022. Bilingual speech in Jaru–Kriol conversations: Codeswitching, codemixing, and grammatical fusion. *International Journal of Bilingualism* 26(2). 198–226.

DeGraff, Michel. 2009. Language acquisition in creolization and, thus, language change: Some cartesian-uniformitarian boundary conditions. *Language and Linguistics Compass* 3/4. 888–971.

de Houwer, Annick. 1990. *The acquisition of two languages from birth: A case study*. Cambridge: Cambridge University Press.

de Houwer, Annick. 2005. Early bilingual acquisition: focus on morphosyntax and the separate development hypothesis. In Judith Kroll and Annette de Groot (eds.), *Handbook of bilingualism: Psycholinguistic approaches*, 30–48. Oxford: Oxford University Press.

de Houwer, Annick. 2009. *Bilingual first language acquisition*. Bristol: Multilingual Matters.

Döpke, Susanne. 2000. *Cross-linguistic structures in simultaneous bilingualism*. Amsterdam: John Benjamins.

Genesee, Fred. 1989. Early bilingual development: One language or two? *Journal of Child Language* 16(1). 161–179.

Genesee, Fred, Elena Nicoladis & Johanne Paradis. 1995. Language differentiation in early bilingual development. *Journal of Child Language* 22(3). 611–631.

Hale, Kenneth. 1967. Lessons in Walbiri, I-VII. *Mimeo*. Cambridge, MA: M.I.T. Prepared with the assistance of Sam Japangardi Johnson.

Hale, Kenneth. 1982. Some essential features of Warlpiri verbal clauses. In Stephen Swartz (ed.), *Papers in Warlpiri grammar: In memory of Lother Jagst*, 217–314. Darwin: Summer Institute of Linguistics-Australian Aborigines Branch.

Jourdan, Christine. 1989. Nativization and anglicization in Solomon Islands Pijin. *World Englishes* 8(1). 25–35.

Jourdan, Christine. 2009. Complexification or regularization of paradigms: The case of prepositional verbs in Solomon Islands Pijin. In Enoch Oladé Aboh & Norval Smith (eds.), *Complex processes in new languages*, 159–170. Amsterdam: John Benjamins.

Kegl, Judy, Ann Senghas & Marie Coppola. 2001. Creation through contact: Sign language emergence and sign language change in Nicaragua. In Michel DeGraff (ed.), *Language creation and language change: Creolization, diachrony and development*, 179–237. Cambridge: MIT Press.

Kerswill, Paul & Ann Williams. 2000. Creating a new town koine: Children and language change in Milton Keynes. *Language in Society* 29. 65–115.

Kotsinas, Ulla-Britt. 1998. Language contact in Rinkeby, an immigrant suburb. In Jannis Androutsopoulos & Arno Scholz (eds.), *Jugendsprache. Langue des jeunes. Youth language*, 125–148. Frankfurt am Main: Peter Lang.

Lanza, Elizabeth. 1992. Can bilingual two-year-olds code-switch? *Journal of Child Language* 19(3). 633–658.

Lanza, Elizabeth. 1997. Language contact in bilingual two-year-olds and code-switching: language encounters of a different kind? *International Journal of Bilingualism* 2(1). 135–162.

Laughren, Mary, Robert Hoogenraad, Kenneth Hale & Robin Granites. 1996. *A learner's guide to Warlpiri*. Alice Springs: Institute for Aboriginal Development Press.

Lave, Jean & Etienne Wenger. 1991. *Situated learning: Legitimate peripheral participation*. Cambridge: Cambridge University Press.

Leeding, Valerie & Mary Laughren. 1979. *A report on research of the children's speech at Hooker Creek (Lajamanu)*. Technical report. Darwin: Northern Territory Education Department.

McConvell, Patrick. 2008. Mixed languages as outcomes of code-switching: Recent examples from Australia and their implications. *Journal of Language Contact* 2. 187–212.

McConvell, Patrick & Felicity Meakins. 2005. Gurindji Kriol: A mixed language emerges from code-switching. *Australian Journal of Linguistics* 25(1). 9–30.

Meakins, Felicity. 2011. *Case-marking in contact: The development and function of case morphology in Gurindji Kriol*. Amsterdam: John Benjamins.

Meggitt, Mervyn. 1954. Sign language among the Walbiri of Central Australia. *Oceania* 25 (1–2). 2–16.

Milroy, Lesley & James Milroy. 1985. Linguistic change, social network and speaker innovation. *Journal of Linguistics* 21. 339–384.

Mufwene, Salikoko. 2001. *The ecology of language evolution*. Cambridge: Cambridge University Press.

Müller, Natascha & Aafke Hulk. 2001. Crosslinguistic influence in bilingual acquisition: Italian and French as recipient languages. *Bilingualism: Language and Cognition* 4(1). 1–21.

O'Shannessy, Carmel. 2004. *The monster stories: A set of picture books to elicit overt transitive subjects in oral texts*. Unpublished series. Nijmegen, The Netherlands: Max Planck Institute for Psycholinguistics.

O'Shannessy, Carmel. 2005. Light Warlpiri: A new language. *Australian Journal of Linguistics* 25(1). 31–57.

O'Shannessy, Carmel. 2012. The role of code-switched input to children in the origin of a new mixed language. *Linguistics* 50(2). 328–353.

O'Shannessy, Carmel. 2013. The role of multiple sources in the formation of an innovative auxiliary category in Light Warlpiri, a new Australian mixed language. *Language* 89(2). 328–353.

O'Shannessy, Carmel. 2015. Multilingual children increase language differentiation by indexing communities of practice. *First Language* 35(4–5). 305–326.

O'Shannessy, Carmel. 2019. Why do children lead contact-induced language change in some contexts but not others? In Edit Doron, Malka Rappaport Hovav, Yael Reshef & Moshe Taube (eds.), *Linguistic contact, continuity and change in the genesis of Modern Hebrew*, 321–335. Amsterdam: John Benjamins.

O'Shannessy, Carmel. 2016a. Distributions of case allomorphy by multilingual children. *Linguistic Variation* 16(1). 68–102.

O'Shannessy, Carmel. 2016b. Entrenchment of Light Warlpiri morphology. In Felicity Meakins & Carmel O'Shannessy (eds.), *Loss and renewal: Australian languages since colonisation*, 217–251. Amsterdam: John Benjamins.

O'Shannessy, Carmel. 2020. How ordinary child language acquisition processes can lead to the unusual outcome of a mixed language. *International Journal of Bilingualism* 25(2). 458–480.

O'Shannessy, Carmel. 2021. Code-switching as a way of speaking: From language shift to language maintenance. In Anna Babel & Mark Sicoli (eds.), *Contact, structure, and change: A festschrift in honor of Sarah G. Thomason*, 36–42. Ann Arbor: Michigan Publishing.

O'Shannessy, Carmel & Connor Brown. 2021. Reflexive and reciprocal encoding in the Australian mixed language, Light Warlpiri. *Languages* 6(2), 105.

O'Shannessy, Carmel & Lucinda Davidson. 2020. Language contact and change through child first language acquisition. In Raymond Hickey (ed.), *The handbook of language contact*, 67–91. New York: Wiley-Blackwell.

Quist, Pia. 2008. Sociolinguistic approaches to multiethnolect: Language variety and stylistic practice. *International Journal of Bilingualism* 12(1–2). 43–61.

Reece, Laurie. 1971. As Wailbri children learn Wailbri. *Mankind* 8(2). 148–150.

Roberts, Julie. 1997a. Acquisition of variable rules: A study of (-t,d) deletion in preschool children. *Journal of Child Language* 24(2). 351–372.

Roberts, Julie. 1997b. Hitting a moving target: Acquisition of sound change in progress by Philadelphia children. *Language Variation and Change* 9. 249–266.

Rockman, Peggy Napaljarri & Lee Cataldi. 1994. *Yimikirli: Warlpiri dreamings and histories: Newl recorded stories from the Aboriginal elders of Central Australia*. San Francisco: HarperCollins.

Rowse, Tim. 1998. *White flour, white power*. Cambridge: Cambridge University Press.

Sankoff, Gillian. 1991. Using the future to explain the past. In Francis Byrne & Thom Huebner (eds.), *Development and structures of Creole languages: Essays in honor of Derek Bickerton* 61–74. Amsterdam: John Benjamins.

Schultze-Berndt, Eva, Felicity Meakins & Denise Angelo. 2013. Kriol. In Susanne Michaelis, Philippe Maurer, Martin Haspelmath & Magnus Huber (eds.), *The Survey of Pidgin and Creole languages: Volume 1: English-based and Dutch-based languages*, 241–251. Oxford: Oxford University Press.

Serratrice, Ludovica, Antonella Sorace & Sandra Paoli. 2004. Crosslinguistic influence at the syntax–pragmatics interface: Subjects and objects in English–Italian bilingual and monolingual acquisition. *Bilingualism: Language and Cognition* 7(3). 183–205.

Shnukal, Anna & Lynell Marchese. 1983. Creolization of Nigerian Pidgin English: A progress report. *English World-Wide* 4(1). 17–26.

Swartz, Stephen. 1982. Syntactic structure of Warlpiri clauses. In Stephen Swartz (ed.), *Papers in Warlpiri Grammar: In memory of Lothar Jagst*, 69–127. Darwin: Summer Institute of Linguistics-Australian Aborigines Branch.

Swartz, Stephen. 1991. *Constraints on zero anaphora and word order in Warlpiri narrative text*. Darwin: Summer Institute of Linguistics.

Toribio, Almeida Jacqueline. 2002. Spanish-English code-switching among US Latinos. *International Journal of the Sociology of Language* 158. 89–119.

Wenger, Etienne. 1998. *Communities of practice: Learning, meaning, and identity.* Cambridge: Cambridge University Press.

CHAPTER 9

Child and adolescent transmission and incrementation in acquisition in historical sociophonetic data from English in Missouri, 1880–2000

Christopher Strelluf
University of Warwick

> Phonological conditioning of allophones of /æ/ is typologically important for American Englishes and a site of ongoing sound change. Combining historical and present-day data, this chapter traces productions of /æ/ in the US state of Missouri from the 1880s to 1990s. It reveals a transition to a nasal /æ/ system that progressed via children's probabilistic calculations, as children initially acquired the /æ/ of their speech community (transmission) and then introduced innovations as they approached adulthood (incrementation). It also posits roots for the actuation of modern-day /æ/-backing in turn-of-the-century associations with high socioeconomic status and/or metropolitan Kansas City, which may have initiated incrementation. These findings highlight the value of historical sociophonetic explorations of sound changes as consequences of cognitive processes of language acquisition.

> **Keywords:** sound change, nasal system, /æ/, TRAP, pre-nasal, priors, probabilistic, transmission, incrementation, historical sociophonetics

1. Introduction

This chapter explores transmission and incrementation in sound change through a historical sociophonetic lens. I use the label *historical sociophonetics* to describe work that extends the time-depth of sociophonetics through focused application of sociophonetic methods and theories to datasets that cannot be collected from language users via modern surveys and elicitations. Though historical sociophonetics is a novel label, many important studies have used archival recordings of speakers born before the advent of sociolinguistic fieldwork to reach back in linguistic time (e.g., the many projects on New Zealand Englishes built from NZ National Broadcasting Service recordings, such as Gordon et al. 2004; studies collected in Hickey 2017a; see also Chapter 10 for an example in this volume).

Historical sociophonetics relies on data that happens to have been recorded at some point in the past, archived and preserved, and discovered as a linguistic resource. Such data will often be imperfect. Compared with data collected in a modern survey, historical sociophonetic datasets are unlikely to be balanced for macro-level social categories and will often be relatively poor in audio quality (Denis 2016; Hickey 2017b: 1–2). Specific to this volume's focus on language acquisition across the lifespan, among potential sources for historical sociophonetic datasets (e.g., oral histories, recorded broadcasts, old linguistic surveys), only a few are likely to contain recordings of children and adolescents or members of families across generations. The data I work with in this chapter cannot explore transmission and incrementation with the precision of huge surveys that contain many interviews with children and adolescents (e.g., Denis et al. 2019; Labov 2001; Labov et al. 2013; Tagliamonte & D'Arcy 2009). Nor can it offer the direct view of transmission and incrementation afforded by corpora that were purpose-built to examine intergenerational language change (e.g., Hall & Maddeaux 2020; Kerswill 1996; Kerswill & Williams 2000) or panel studies with the same children at different developmental stages (e.g., Holmes-Elliott 2021; Sankoff & Blondeau 2007).

Nevertheless, this chapter will show that aspects of historical and modern sound changes can be revealed through historical sociophonetic explorations of those sound changes as processes of transmission and incrementation. Conversely, it will also show that historical sociophonetic explorations can shed light on those processes of transmission and incrementation. Indeed, despite the familiar limitations that historical sociolinguists face in "making the best use of bad data" (Labov 1994: 11), this chapter will demonstrate that bringing historical sociophonetics and acquisition theory together can generate new – likely otherwise undiscoverable – explanations for sound change. In addition, by examining the age-based acquisitional component of language change in a social context not characterized by large-scale demographic rearrangement or pervasive language contact, this chapter offers a counterpoint to the more unstable sociohistorical contexts studied by other case studies in this volume (e.g., immigration in Chapters 7 and 10, forced resettlement in Chapter 8, or colonial expansion in Chapters 11 and 12).

By combining a dataset built from archival recordings with data from modern sociolinguistic interviews, I will examine changes in acoustic qualities of the vowel /æ/ in the US state of Missouri from the 1880s to 2000. I briefly summarize a portion of the literature on /æ/ in North American Englishes in Section 2, describe the Labovian model of transmission and incrementation through a sociophonetic lens in Section 3, and present this chapter's historical sociophonetic dataset in Section 4. Section 5 traces the emergence of a "nasal" /æ/ configuration in Englishes spoken by white Missourians, where allophones that occur before nasal consonants (henceforth labeled, TAN) are produced higher and fronter in vowel space than allophones before oral obstruents (TRAP), and illustrates the advancement of this sound change through transmission and incrementation. Section 6 then explores interactions between this sound change and macro-level social categories, connecting historical developments to recent sound change in metropolitan Kansas City, Missouri and identifying sociolinguistic meanings that may have initiated incrementation. Together, these findings highlight the value of historical sociophonetic examinations of sound change as acquisitional processes, as summarized in Section 7, which concludes this chapter.

2. /æ/ in American Englishes

Labov et al. (2006: 121) position the configuration of /æ/ as one of "two pivot points of North American English vowel structure," and use /æ/ configurations as a primary diagnostic for defining North American English dialect regions. Labov (2007: 353–354) categorizes five types of /æ/ system.

1. Nasal: TAN is tense and TRAP is lax.
2. Raised: /æ/ is always tense.
3. Continuous: /æ/ is produced along a continuum from relatively lax to relatively tense, generally according to phonetic effects of consonant codas.
4. Breaking: /æ/ is triphthongal.
5. Complex: /æ/ is lax or tense according to idiosyncratic, variety-specific rules.

/æ/ has been studied extensively in many speech communities. Chapter 3 of Labov et al.'s (1972) seminal study is primarily devoted to describing /æ/ configurations in American and British Englishes. Labov (2007) extensively reviews the diffusion of New York City's complex /æ/ system to Cincinnati, New Orleans, and other speech communities, as well as diffusion of Chicago's raised system to St. Louis and other cities along the I-55 corridor. Philadelphia's complex system has featured prominently in the work of Labov and his students at University of Pennsylvania, and projects like Payne's (1980) study of the acquisition of Philadelphia's /æ/ by children have provided foundational data for Labov's conceptualizations of transmission and incrementation (e.g., Labov 2001: 429–432). Labov (e.g., 2007: 372; Labov et al. 2006: 190) also posits /æ/-raising as the initiating event in the Northern Cities Shift and locates the beginning of the Northern Cities Shift in the construction of the Erie Canal, which brought together workers with different

/æ/ configurations that subsequent generations leveled to a raised system (Labov 2010: 114–118).

With intensive scholarly attention, /æ/ has also been revealed to be a site of dynamic sound change. The most common /æ/ configuration in North American English according to Labov et al. (2006: 180) is the continuous system, and nasal systems also occur widely (174). Many of the same speech communities where analyses of complex or raised /æ/ systems were foundational to Labovian theories of sound change and language acquisition have more recently been found to be retreating from their traditional configurations to adopt continuous or nasal systems. Boberg and Strassel (2000) identify a shift from a complex to a nasal system in Cincinnati, and Carmichael (2020) reports the same in New Orleans. Haddican et al. (2021) describe New York City's complex system retreating, too. Labov et al. (2016) describe a reorientation to a nasal system in Philadelphia but associate the nasal system with graduates of elite high schools, while graduates of Catholic schools retain the traditional complex system. Friedman (2014) documents the retreat from raised /æ/ along the I-55 corridor. The impression across North American Englishes is of widespread leveling of /æ/ toward pan-continental continuous or nasal systems.

In addition to phonological and typological issues of the configuration of /æ/ in speech communities, the phonetic quality of /æ/ is also undergoing change. In particular, the lowering and backing of TRAP has been identified as a change-in-progress in Englishes across North America (see Becker 2019 for examples from Canada, California, the Pacific Northwest, the Midwest, and Michigan). Like the widespread realignment to continuous and nasal /æ/ configurations, TRAP lowering and backing appears to be happening in almost every North American speech community where researchers look for it. Moreover, TRAP lowering and backing seems to be something of a destroyer of local and regional sound systems, as in speech communities in Michigan (e.g., Nesbitt et al. 2019) and New York (e.g., Thiel & Dinkin 2020) where the Northern Cities Shift is being undone by TRAP lowering and backing.

In short, developments in the phonetic qualities and phonological rules for /æ/ are pervasive in North American Englishes. The case is no different in Missouri, where several configurations for /æ/ have either been documented or might be expected following historical settlement patterns. Large portions of Missouri were settled by migrants from the South Midland and Appalachia, and surveys of lexis (Carver 1987; Faries 1967; Faries & Lance 1993) and sound systems (e.g., Labov et al. 2006: 257) attest to the alignment of central, eastern, and southern Missouri to the modern South. Labov (2007: 354) associates the /æ/ breaking system with the South, so – to the extent that areas of Missouri are phonologically aligned with the South – triphthongal productions of /æ/ might be expected.

Complicating this expectation is St. Louis, which has been described as a "northern enclave in the Midland area" for its participation in the Northern Cities Shift (Labov et al. 2006: 276). Accordingly, as noted above, a raised /æ/ system has been identified in St. Louis to varying extents across the metropolitan area's history (see Duncan 2018 for a recent perspective).

Furthermore, areas of Missouri were settled by substantial populations from the North Midland. Strelluf (2018: 1–4) describes competition around modern-day metropolitan Kansas City between settlers from the South and North Midland through the second half of the nineteenth century. Population dynamics included efforts by Kansas City businesses to attract investment from northeastern banks and railroads, and pre-Civil War abolitionist efforts to flood the area just west of Kansas City with anti-slavery settlers so that Kansas would be admitted to the Union as a free state. Tensions were manifest in brutal Civil War battles and genocidal raids. Local histories apocryphally claim events such as Kansas City being stripped of municipal authority by the pro-secessionist Missouri state government, and the Kansas City mayor responding by accepting a Union commission and organizing a local force to suppress Confederate activities in the city (Brown & Dorsett 1978: 26).

These conflicts corresponded to the most dramatic period of growth in Missouri's population, which grew from about 65,000 people at Missouri's admission to the Union in 1821 to approximately 1.5 million at the end of the Civil War and more than 3 million in 1900 (Gibson & Jung 2002: Table 40). The fundamental underpinnings of these conflicts in social and cultural differences belie any notion that there was a monolithic settler population to provide a single historical phonetic quality or phonemic configuration for /æ/ in Missouri.

More recently, based on data from modern sociolinguistic interviews, metropolitan Kansas City has been described as participating in the pan-continental sound changes affecting TAN and TRAP. For instance, Strelluf (2018: 70–71) reports that TAN had undergone "moderate" raising between the 1950s and 1980s, and then either stabilized or perhaps began to retract. It also identifies social differentiation, with males producing TAN slightly lower and fronter than females. More dramatically, TRAP lowering and backing is described as a "vigorous change in progress" in the late twentieth century (2018: 74). Females strongly led this change, with regression estimates suggesting that males trailed females by about 34 years (2018: 69). This gap closely matched the 30-year lead of females over males that Labov (2001: 312) reported for vocalic changes-in-progress in Philadelphia, corresponding to about one generation, and aligned with Labov's (2001: 457) position that male "participation in the change is due to the increment inherited from their female caretaker, not from the incrementation process."

While these patterns aligned with broader recent sound changes across North America, they also cast doubts on typical explanations for the sound change. Gordon (2004) is often cited as proposing the merger of the low back vowels /ɑ/ (LOT) and /ɔ/ as the initiating event of TRAP lowering and backing, with the backing of LOT as part of that merger creating an opening in vowel space into which TRAP is dragged. However, in Kansas City, Strelluf (2018) found that TRAP lowering and backing preceded LOT backing, making it more likely that TRAP was pushing LOT than LOT dragging TRAP. Working from historical sociophonetic data, he subsequently described more complex interactions across apparent time where LOT sometimes dragged TRAP and TRAP sometimes pushed LOT (Strelluf 2019a: 137). Strelluf also continued to find, though, that structural relationships among vowels could not fully account for TRAP lowering and backing in Kansas City, and that social factors which had not yet been fully identified were also driving TRAP lowering and backing. He further noted that, despite commonality in the sound change between Kansas City and speech communities in Canada and the western United States, there was not an obvious social mechanism like migration or contact by which TRAP lowering and backing would have been imported from those speech communities into Kansas City (Strelluf 2018: 166). Implicitly, then, whatever social factors are motivating TRAP lowering and backing in Kansas City at the end of the twentieth century, they likely arose from within the local speech community.

The developments of and questions around /æ/ across North America and in Missouri and Kansas City specifically show that /æ/ is a valuable area of vowel space to explore. A combined perspective of historical sociophonetics and models of transmission and incrementation will help make sense of that space historically and in the present.

3. Probabilistic processing of sociophonetic inputs in transmission and incrementation

As advanced elsewhere in this volume (see Chapters 1, 2 and 6), *transmission* refers to young children acquiring the language norm of the speech community they grow up in (especially the sociolinguistic norm of their adult caregivers), and *incrementation* refers to older children and adolescents changing this norm, specifically by advancing innovations that exist within their speech community beyond the levels they acquired through transmission. Labov (1994: 580–588; 2001: 446–497; 2010: 140–145) advanced a probabilistic model to account for the analyses of phonemic and phonetic targets by children and adolescents during transmission, and their subsequent reanalyses of targets during incrementation.

Figure 1 visualizes the phonetic environment that surrounds children during language acquisition (cf. Labov 1994: 586–587; 2010: 143). It plots single-point estimates of F1 and F2 for tokens of TRAP and LOT spoken by John, who was born in Kansas City in 1887. Mixed-effects estimated means of F1 and F2 for each vowel are also plotted, and an arrow is overlaid to highlight one TRAP token that occurs among LOT tokens.

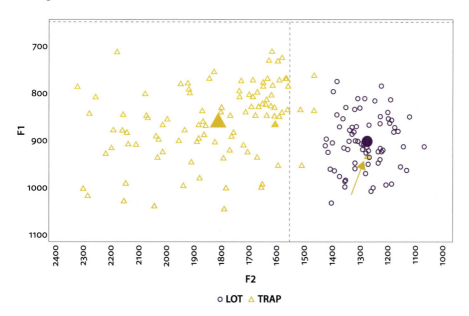

Figure 1. TRAP and LOT tokens and means for John, b. 1887

John's productions of TRAP and LOT reflect the variability that children encounter during acquisition. Children growing up in John's speech community in the late 1800s would not hear a single consistent phonetic target for /æ/ or /ɑ/, but rather would hear allophones being produced across a range of acoustic values. Children would identify tendencies within this variability for the vowels to occur within more constrained acoustic ranges. From these tendencies, they would identify phonemic and phonetic targets for /æ/ and /ɑ/ (see also Pierrehumbert 2003).

Thomas (2019: 459–460) provides a succinct overview of the connections between this model and exemplar theory and related theories of language cognition. Following Thomas's summary, children also store social information about people who use the different phonetic variants they are tracking and draw upon this social information in determining phonemic categories and interpreting phonetic productions. Cournane (2019: 139) suggests that children may use such social information to calculate the rate of incrementation by associating more conservative variants with older people and more innovative variants with younger people. Labov (2001: 463) implies the same in saying that when a girl leaves the exclusive influence of her caregivers, she "must quickly perceive that girls older than she is use more advanced forms of changing linguistic variables."

As children encounter these multiple layers of radical variability, they will encounter some tokens being produced with atypical qualities, such as John's backed TRAP token. The handling of such aberrant tokens by children and adolescents drives incrementation. If productions like John's backed TRAP token are rare, or if children have previously and more frequently encountered the type being produced with a vowel more acoustically like other TRAP types, then children will register John's backed TRAP token as an outlier. They will exclude the outlier from calculations of the type's phonemic assignment, and of the phonemic and phonetic targets of /æ/ and /ɑ/.

If the backed token is not dismissed, however, then children will enter the aberrant production as a valid prior into their modeling of phonemic and phonetic targets. Most straightforwardly, if children analyze John's backed TRAP token as containing /ɑ/, then it will "be subtracted from the pool of tokens that determine the mean target" of /æ/ (Labov 1994: 587). Or, if children and adolescents continue to analyze the underlying vowel in the token as TRAP, then they will include the token's low F2 in their calculation of the mean acoustic value of /æ/. John's aberrant token would then exert a slight backward pull on the phonetic target of TRAP, and on the range of acoustic values of productions that map to /æ/ perceptually.

Holmes-Elliott (2021: 467) concludes her panel study of incrementation among adolescents by warning that it remains challenging to understand why adolescents increment, and speculates that the answer might lie in children's desires to "keep up" with older peers. However, Labov's probabilistic model provides an entirely mechanical motivation for incrementation irrespective of the motivations of language users. Indeed, in computational modeling of a cross-generational chain shift, Stanford & Kenny (2013) found that speaker-level probabilistic analysis of phonetic targets within a speech community was sufficient to effect a unidirectional vocalic chain shift. Moreover, their model predicted that children would increment sound change forward even without assumptions that children's processes for language acquisition were biologically different from those of adults. Instead, childhood incrementation occurred because (as a natural consequence of being alive and encountering the surrounding speech community for less time than adults) children's models for vowels contained fewer priors, causing innovative variants to exert greater influence on their language models (e.g., Stanford & Kenny 2013: 147).

The fact that children are biologically different from adults in terms of their language processing and production likely magnifies the effects of children's probabilistic phonemic and phonetic modeling. Cournane (2019: 128, 134–143) summarizes that during acquisition children characteristically innovate divergent inputs, are highly sensitive to variation, and overshoot inputs. These characteristics make it likely that children will naturally assign more weight to aberrant phonetic productions than they will to productions that fall closer to a mean. Indeed, Cournane (2019: 134) argues that "children start by overshooting rather than matching the innovative pattern." In her view, transmission and incrementation are actually not sequential processes but simultaneous ones, and by showing the consequences of incrementation, adult language is a sum of radical innovation during childhood followed by retreat toward more conservative variants during adolescence (2019: 141–143). Accordingly, Cournane's (2019: 143–144) *Reverse-U model of incrementation* shows two peaks of innovation in acquisition: an earlier peak caused by childhood over-generalization, and a later peak corresponding to socially driven adolescent innovation, as quantified in studies like Tagliamonte & D'Arcy (2009; see also Chapter 2).

The total effect of children's and adolescents' probabilistic calculations of phonemic and phonetic targets provides a robust mechanism not only for incrementation, but for the logistic incrementation that Labov associates with females (e.g., Labov 2001: 447–460; see also Denis et al. 2019; Tagliamonte & D'Arcy 2009). First, while the inputs provided to children are their caregivers' language systems, caregivers' systems would have been built from an older stage of the language which would have been exposed to a greater proportion of conservative priors. By being exposed to fewer conservative priors, children might replicate their caregivers' systems, but will experience less of the inhibiting effect of non-innovative variants. Second, children and adolescents are biologically primed to overshoot inputs, which would also push them toward increased weighting of innovative priors. Third, children and adolescents may be calculating cross-generational differences in their productions and building their own language models based on appropriate productions for someone their age (see Cournane 2019: 139). Fourth, Labov (2001: 445) acknowledges that transmission can continue as children enter school and begin to receive inputs from older children. He clarifies specifically: "This is transmission in the simplest sense of transmitting forms, but it does not yet account for the regular and linear increment." In other words, children and adolescents continue to build their initial model of language from exposure to other children, and older children engaged in incrementation will provide innovative priors to the younger children's transmitted language. Then the younger children will subsequently engage in incrementation from a starting point that is already more advanced than their caregivers' inputs.

Methodologically, Labov's model of probabilistic calculation of phonemic and phonetic targets aligns neatly with data that sociophoneticians routinely use to study vocalic sound changes. To the extent that speech in a recording provides a representative sample of a speaker's normal productions, and to the extent that data from a few speakers provides a representative sample of a speech community, then the datasets derived from large sociophonetic datasets mirror the language environment that surrounds children and adolescents throughout language acquisition. As Figure 1 illustrates, clouds of formant measurements derived from sociophonetic datasets illustrate mean phonetic qualities, ranges of phonetic variation, and occurrences of aberrant productions in inputs to transmission and incrementation. In doing so, sociophonetic data helps understand the intersections between productions, transmission and incrementation, and sound change. And historical sociophonetic data specifically can shed light on these processes in the past and present, as will be shown in the following sections.

4. The dataset

The data in this study come from two corpora of Missouri English: a historical sociophonetic corpus of recordings and a modern corpus of sociolinguistic interviews. For the historical corpus, I collected archival recordings of 45 speakers who were born in Missouri and spent the entirety of childhood and adolescence there. The oldest speaker in this historical corpus was born in 1884, and the youngest in 1938. The interviews are skewed toward males, with 39 males and 6 females. The largest source of historical recordings is a set of 39 interviews from the Missouri Mule History Project, an oral history project of individuals connected with mule breeding, trading, and farming in the early twentieth century. This collection is the focal point of a book-length historical sociophonetic project (Strelluf & Gordon 2024), which will include an extended overview.

Since the mule project was naturally weighted toward interviewees from rural areas of Missouri, I supplemented the corpus with additional sources of recordings from urban Kansas City and St. Louis. Interviews with two St. Louisans were included from the USS Schley Oral History Project and the Kirkwood, Missouri, Oral History Project. Three recordings of Kansas Citians were digitized from the Arthur B. Church KMBC Radio Collection, which features radio broadcasts from the 1940s with contemporarily prominent Kansas Citians. Data in this chapter is taken from speeches by President Harry S. Truman, Kansas City mayor John Gage, and the Roger T. Sermon, mayor of Independence, Missouri. An interview with a fourth Kansas Citian was taken from the American English Dialect Recordings in the Center for Applied Linguistics Collection at the Library of Congress (see Gordon & Strelluf 2017: 233–236 for discussion of these sources).

This historical corpus was combined with a corpus of 71 modern sociolinguistic interviews of people who lived throughout childhood and adolescence in Missouri in the Kansas City Metropolitan Statistical Area. Fifty-five of these came from sociolinguistic interviews I conducted from 2012 to 2016 with Missourians born between 1955 and 1999. Sixteen additional recordings of Kansas Citians born during the 1970s and 1980s were included from interviews conducted by Matthew J. Gordon and his students between 2002 and 2008. Extended descriptions of these interviews appear in Strelluf (2016, 2018, 2019a). Of relevance to the present study, 19 Missourians in this modern corpus were 18 years old or younger when they were interviewed, with a few interviewees as young as 13. These adolescents were likely still in the process of advancing language change through incrementation. The modern corpus includes 34 females and 37 males.

All Missourians in both corpora are white. I have assigned each person a socioeconomic index (SEI) score based on the combined occupational prestige and SEI ratings in Nakao and Treas (1994; also used in Labov 2001: 60, 477–478; Labov et al. 2006: 30). I assign SEI based on speaker's occupation or the occupation of their household's "breadwinner" (see Labov et al. 2006: 30 for this usage). SEI scores in the corpora range from scores in the 50s for professions such as beautician, farrier, and parking attendant, to scores around 160 for professions like attorney or politician.

Interviewees were assigned to one of nine Missouri regions following Gordon (2006), based on the location where they spent childhood and adolescence. For inter-speaker comparability between the historical and modern corpora, I categorized Kansas City as a region based on the current US Census Kansas City Metropolitan Statistical Area, even though many small towns that are now part of Kansas City were small rural communities during the language acquisition periods of Missourians in the historical corpus. (I did build models that separated the small rural communities in the historical dataset from modern Kansas City and St. Louis, but this coding did not affect results.)

Together, these codings make it possible to model the historical and modern corpora according to a set of macro-level social categories conventional to sociophonetic research: biological sex, year (and decade) of birth, city (and region) where language acquisition took place, and SEI. I identify speakers following naming conventions I have used in previous projects with the same datasets. People in the historical corpus drawn from publicly available sources are not pseudonymized, while those in the modern corpus are. People related to other people in the corpus are assigned a surname initial.

In studies that follow Labov's focus on single-point estimates of the first two vowel formants, phonological tenseness of /æ/ is associated with lower F1 (raised in vowel space) and higher F2 (fronter in vowel space), and laxness is associated with higher F1 and lower F2. For the present study, I transcribed recordings in ELAN (2022; Wittenburg et al. 2006) and used FAVE (Rosenfelder et al. 2014) to automatically align recordings and transcripts and extract formant estimates at one-third of vowel duration via FAVE's FAAV setting. Formant estimates are reported from the normalized values returned by FAVE's built-in Lobanov (1971) routine. I followed quality-control procedures for working with FAVE data that were previously described in Strelluf (2018: 33), including removing high-frequency "stop words" subject to phonetic reduction and only reporting vowels marked in the CMU Dictionary (Lenzo 2014) as bearing primary stress. Additionally, I excluded tokens where estimates for their F1 or F2 fell more than 1.5 times outside the interquartile range of either formant in all other tokens of the vowel produced by the speaker (Tukey 1977). I have recommended this procedure to eliminate measurements that are likely to be erroneous in very large corpora of machine-extracted formants (Strelluf 2019b). However, in the current project where aberrant productions feature importantly, I acknowledge that some valid measurements of actual aberrant productions may be excluded. Here, 547 TRAP tokens and 292 TAN tokens were removed from the dataset.

These procedures generated a corpus of 10,678 TRAP tokens and 5057 TAN tokens produced by 116 Missourians. I worked with these measurements in R (R Core Team 2021) using custom scripts.[1] I describe analytic procedures below as I explore changes in /æ/ in Missouri as processes of transmission and incrementation.

5. Transmission and incrementation in multi-generational speech community sound changes

Despite an absence of unified external motivations for language change in Missouri (see Section 2), /æ/ underwent uniform changes in Missouri from the 1880s to 1990s. Figure 2 plots mean "diagonal" measurements for all 116 Missourians by birth year for TAN (Figure 2a) and TRAP (Figure 2b). Diagonal, calculated as $F_2 - 2*F_1$, is used following Labov et al. (2013: 40; see also Labov 1994: 458, 505; 2010: 145–150) to capture the simultaneous raising and fronting or lowering and backing of front vowels. Mean values for F1 and F2 are estimated by mixed-effects regression using the lme4 package (Bates et al. 2015) in R, with "word" entered as a random intercept for all speakers, and "interview task" also entered as a random intercept for speakers in the modern corpus. Males and females are differentiated to display gendered differences in uptake of sound changes. Smoothed

---

[1] These scripts are freely available at https://files.warwick.ac.uk/cstrelluf/browse/faveR.

non-parametric locally weighted regression (LOESS) lines are overlaid to suggest general patterns.

TAN diagonals in Figure 2a increase steadily from the nineteenth to late-twentieth centuries. In such cases of uniform change across multiple generations in the absence of external sources of language change, transmission and incrementation must necessarily be drivers of change. For TAN, from a standpoint of transmission, each Missourian is born into a speech community where previous generations have already raised and fronted TAN, and therefore acquires a TAN target that is higher and fronter than the one the previous generation acquired. Through adolescence, Missourians subsequently increment their own productions of TAN even higher and fronter, generating apparent-time increases in diagonal. As adults, these Missourians have children and pass their further raised and fronted TAN to the next generation of Missourians.

In Figure 2b, TRAP diagonals vary unsystematically in the historical corpus. Transmission is of course taking place as children acquire language, but because there is not a change taking place in the speech community, there are no changes for children to advance through incrementation. In the modern corpus, Kansas City females tend to produce TRAP with smaller diagonal measurements than males. The lowered and backed TRAP of females in the 1950s is transmitted to subsequent generations of Missourians, and these subsequent generations (especially females) increment TRAP further lower and backer. Females born during the 1980s and 1990s produce TRAP with substantially smaller diagonal measurements than other speakers. Males born in the 1980s and 1990s also seem to be beginning to lower and back TRAP, and a cluster of male diagonal measurements in the 1990s appears to be at roughly the same level as a cluster of females born around the 1960s. These results align with analyses in Strelluf (2018, 2019a).

Figure 3 zooms in on these sound changes to show transmission and incrementation operating in the setting where they most directly take place: interactions between caregivers and children. It plots mixed-effects estimated mean values of TRAP and TAN for members of the D Family from the modern corpus. When I interviewed them in 2012, Scott and Lori had both lived from birth in the 1960s through adulthood in the Kansas City suburb of Independence. Their children, Peyton and Elly, were born in the 1990s and had also only lived in Independence (the dashed line in the plot at 650 Hz in F1 represents the middle of vowel space in height. This line, along with another at 1550 Hz in F2, provides a common reference point across vowel plots in this chapter).

All four family members produce a raised and fronted TAN. Consistent with Strelluf (2018: 70), males Scott and Peyton produce TAN slightly lower and fronter than females Lori and Elly. More broadly, consistent with the analysis that TAN raising and fronting was no longer a change-in-progress, Elly's and Peyton's TAN

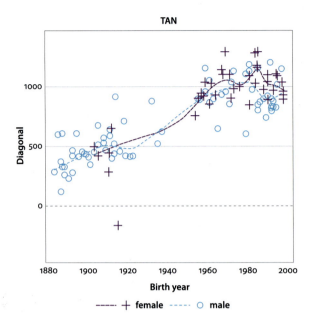

a. TAN

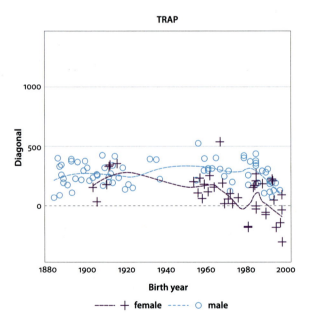

b. TRAP

Figure 2. Mean diagonal measurements of /æ/ among Missourians born between 1880 and 2000

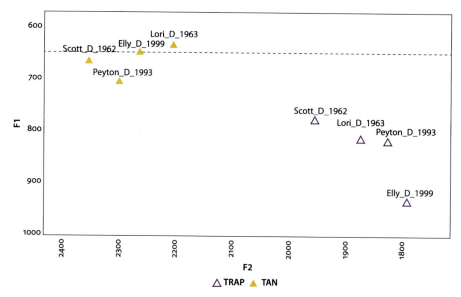

Figure 3. TRAP and TAN means members of the D Family

productions do not appear to be systematically different from those of their parents. Elly's TAN, in particular, appears to be an average of her parents'.

The family's TRAP productions likewise reflect community-level changes in progress. Scott's TRAP vowel is most conservative. Lori has incremented her TRAP backer and lower relative to Scott's in line with the community. Peyton produces a slightly backer TRAP than Lori, but matches his mother's TRAP quality in F1. Elly produces the most innovative TRAP.

The distribution of TRAP qualities across members of the D Family matches Labov's (2001) models of the roles of age and biological sex in transmission and incrementation, with a mother being more innovative than a father, a son basically matching his mother, and a daughter matching and then further innovating her mother's productions. As such, the D Family provides a direct view of transmission and incrementation at the level where they are taking place. Scott and Lori transmitted qualities of their allophones of /æ/ to Peyton and Elly. Peyton's and Elly's productions then evolved according to patterns in the broader speech community. In the case of TAN (a historical change that had stabilized) Peyton and Elly matched their parents' productions, which in turn matched patterns in the speech community. In the case of TRAP, which was undergoing change in the speech community, Peyton and Elly matched their mother's productions, and then Elly especially incremented her vowel further in the direction of the community sound change.

Multi-generational, apparent-time sound changes at the macroscopic level of a speech community or microscopic level of a family necessarily reflect outcomes of transmission and incrementation. Large collections of acoustic measurements of individual utterances, though, also provide a glimpse of the inputs that children and adolescents are exposed to during language acquisition, and which they use to probabilistically determine phonemic and phonetic targets.

Figure 4 visualizes changes in overlap among all tokens of TRAP and TAN uttered by each Missourian, as overlap among tokens will feature prominently in children's processing of aberrant productions as outliers or valid priors. Overlap is reported as Bhattacharyya's coefficient (see Johnson 2015; Strelluf 2016) calculated with the adehabitatHR package (Calenge 2006). A coefficient of 1 indicates complete overlap among two sets of points on a plane, and 0 indicates no overlap. As in Figure 2, Missourians are plotted by birth year and symbols indicate biological sex. LOESS lines suggest general trends among the datasets.

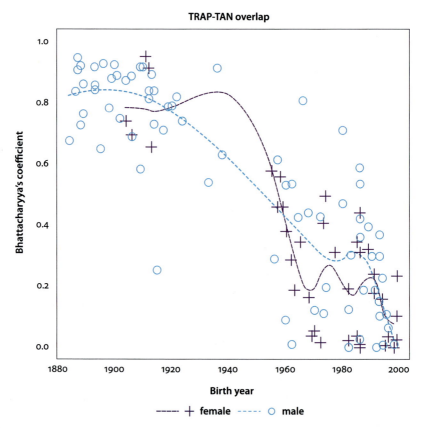

Figure 4. TRAP-TAN overlap among Missourians born between 1880 and 2000

The decreasing Bhattacharyya's coefficients from the 1880s to 2000 reflect the growing allophonic split between TRAP and TAN in apparent time. High coefficients among Missourians born before 1900 show TRAP and TAN being produced in effectively identical vowel space, while coefficients approaching 0 toward the end of the twentieth century indicate that the allophones occupied distinct portions of vowel space.

The apparent-time decrease in overlap in Figure 4 directly reflects the data that children would use to probabilistically build language models during acquisition, according to the process outlined in Section 3. Across the twentieth century, each generation of Missouri children encountered fewer phonetically overlapping tokens of TRAP and TAN than had previous generations. Accordingly, when they did encounter overlapping TRAP and TAN tokens, each generation of Missouri children would have been increasingly likely to dismiss these variants as outliers. Conversely, non-overlapping tokens, including those on the high-front periphery of TAN or low-back periphery of TRAP, would be increasingly likely to be accepted as valid priors. The combined effect would be that each generation of Missouri children's targets for TRAP and TAN would be shifted "toward the salient outliers in the direction of the change" (Labov 2001: 496). In terms of mean formant values, the phonetic consequence of this processing of outliers would be, as seen in Figure 2, to drag TAN higher and fronter in apparent time and, potentially, to drag TRAP lower and backer. But the underlying mechanism for these changes would be the way that overlap among TRAP and TAN affected children's processing of individual tokens as outliers or valid priors.

The changes in the relative overlap of TRAP and TAN that children encountered in Missouri from the 1880s to 1990s is illustrated at the speaker-level in the plots in Figure 5. These show the TRAP and TAN tokens in the recordings of four males from Kansas City. Mixed-effects estimated mean values for each set of tokens are also plotted.

At the start of the sample, John's TRAP and TAN tokens show no allophonic separation, quantified as a Bhattacharyya's coefficient of 0.905. Guyton's tokens also overlap substantially with a coefficient of 0.688, but the beginnings of separation are visible, as Guyton's TAN tokens occur relatively higher and fronter and his TRAP tokens relatively lower and backer. A half-century later, Robert's TRAP and TAN tokens visually suggest two distinct allophones, and their overlap is measured at just 0.287. Finally, at the end of the apparent-time sample, Eric's TRAP and TAN tokens are widely separated in vowel space, with no actual overlap displayed and a negligible Bhattacharyya's coefficient of 0.011. Together, these four Kansas Citians show a progression from an undifferentiated or continuous /æ/ system in the 1880s to a nasal system by the 1990s. Across Missouri, the reduced system of overlap exemplified by these four Kansas Citians that was transmitted to

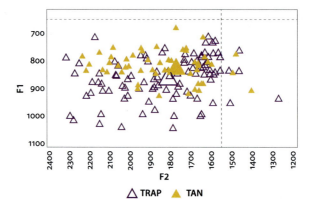

a. John, b. 1887

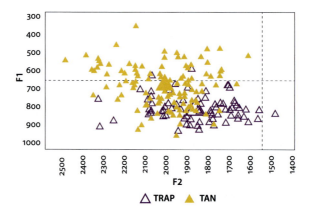

b. Guyton, b. 1906

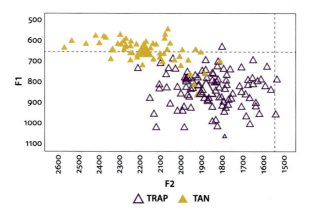

c. Robert Z., b. 1956

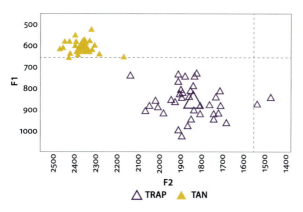

d. Eric J., b. 1998

Figure 5. Apparent time changes in TRAP-TAN overlap among four Kansas City males

each generation would have led to children assigning more weight to inputs that further reduced overlap, causing TRAP and TAN to further separate through incrementation.

An important question concerns the degree to which parental input shaped the systems acquired by their children, and how much the latter deviated from the former through incrementation. The historical corpus of this study unfortunately contains few parent-child pairs to afford direct views of this relationship. Moreover, among the few females in the corpus, none is a daughter to any other speaker, so female contributions to incrementation will not be visible in this dataset. Nevertheless, the historical corpus offers a few examples of Missourians who follow patterns predicted by Labovian models of transmission and incrementation.

Twin brothers Elmer and Elwood H., for instance, demonstrate the similarity of systems acquired in the same family at the same time. Elmer and Elwood were born in 1893 on a farm in the central Missouri town of Boonville. Both continued to live in Boonville throughout their adult lives. Their nearly identical configurations of TRAP and TAN tokens are plotted in Figure 6. Elmer's tokens return a Bhattacharyya's coefficient of 0.915 and Elwood's a coefficient of 0.854. While transmission and incrementation cannot be disentangled in their data, the similarities of their productions suggest that they acquired the same /æ/ system through transmission and any incrementation that took place occurred at identical rates.

In Figure 7, mother and son Elizabeth and George B. align with Labov's (2001: 306–307, 463) contention that sons match the variety they receive from their mothers through transmission. Elizabeth was born in 1912 and grew up on

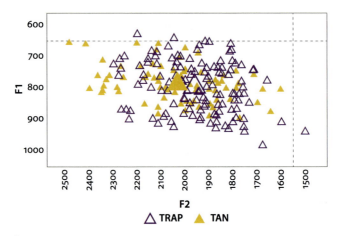

a. Elmer H., b. 1893

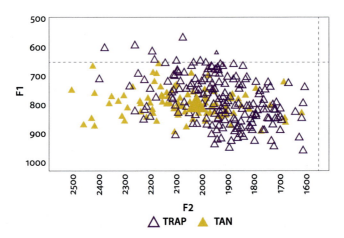

b. Elwood H., b. 1893

Figure 6. TRAP-TAN vowel plots of twin males born in Boonville, Missouri

a farm in the south-central Missouri town of Licking. She raised George from his birth in 1936 on a farm in Lake Spring about 20 miles away. Their highly overlapping TRAP-TAN configurations are so remarkably similar that they each produce a Bhattacharyya's coefficient of 0.911. While large empirical studies of incrementation (e.g., Tagliamonte & D'Arcy 2009: 99) have challenged the essentialized role of biological sex in Labov's incrementation model by showing that boys advance (rather than match) the language systems they inherit by transmission from their caregivers, George has adopted his mother's TRAP-TAN system exactly.

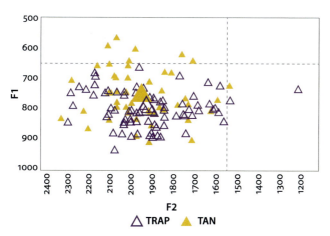

a. Elizabeth B., b. 1912

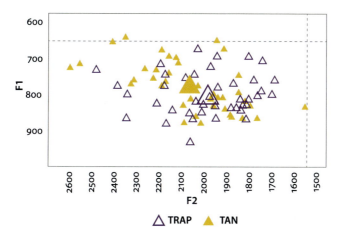

b. George B., b. 1936

Figure 7. TRAP-TAN vowel plots of a mother and son from south-central Missouri

Finally, Figure 8 illustrates that female-led incrementation will result in females' language systems being more advanced in the direction of speech community innovations than the systems of contemporary males. Ben A. was a fruit farmer in the central Missouri city Columbia, where he was born in 1910. His wife, Lillian A., was born in 1913 and grew up on a farm in Callaway County about 20 miles to the east. Each of them produces TRAP and TAN tokens that overlap but show evidence of an emerging allophonic distinction. Reflecting a female lead in incrementation, though, Lillian's system shows greater evidence of the emerging TRAP-TAN split than does Ben's. Her tokens generate a Bhattacharyya's coefficient of 0.653. While Ben's TAN tokens are visually weighted toward the fronter and higher end of /æ/ vowel space, a fair number of higher-fronter TRAP tokens result in a coefficient of 0.913, suggestive of a conservative TRAP-TAN configuration.

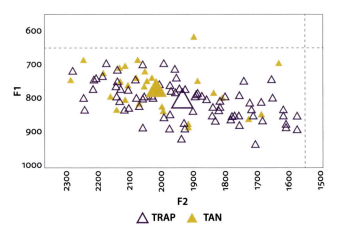

a. Ben A, b. 1910

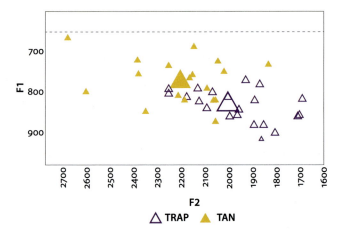

b. Lillian A, b. 1913

Figure 8. TRAP-TAN vowel plots of a husband and wife from central Missouri

Overall, these cases appear to conform to the predictions of the Labovian model of transmission and incrementation regarding the role of input from caregivers to children, and the importance of gender in the progression of changes via incrementation.

6. Language acquisition and the historical sociolinguistics of /æ/ in Missouri English

While imperfect for providing a direct view on the primary loci of transmission and incrementation, the historical corpus nevertheless provides snapshots of the language inputs that generations of Missouri children would have used to build their language models. From these snapshots, we can see how children would have calculated phonemic and phonetic targets, and how differences in the inputs children received across time would have resulted in differences in their processing tokens as either outliers or valid priors. Finally, we can see that differences in children's probabilistic calculations of targets resulted in sound changes being incremented forward, which over a century resulted in a state-wide shift in Missouri from an undifferentiated or continuous /æ/ system in the late 1800s to a nasal system in the late 1900s. Still, the fact that these changes may have advanced through transmission and incrementation does not explain how they were actuated.

Labov's models for transmission and incrementation via processing of phonetic inputs provide mechanisms that are technically sufficient to account for multi-generational sound changes independent of speaker-external influences (such as the macro-level social categories that traditionally serve as independent variables in quantitative sociolinguistics) or speaker-internal motivations (such as children switching their social alignment from caregivers to peers and older children). However, while transmission and incrementation advance sound changes in the absence of social or individual motivations, they are not inherently independent of such motivations. Labov (2001: 462) posits that incrementation accelerates "when the incipient change is attached to or is associated with a particular style or social group." He notes that "this association is an arbitrary, almost accidental event."

Two observations make it apparent that some factor beyond the self-perpetuating mechanism described above must have been operating on /æ/ in Missouri across the apparent-time sample. First, while TAN raising and fronting progressed naturally via transmission and incrementation after the 1880s, the fact that TRAP and TAN were produced in overlapping configurations in the historical corpus means that something needed to initiate the process of them allophonically separating. Second, while the lowering and backing of TRAP at the end of the apparent-time sample is a viable consequence of incrementation as children accept low-back priors that decrease overlap, lowering and backing is not the only viable consequence. Clearly separated systems like Eric J's (Figure 5d) would create space between TRAP and TAN tokens, where TRAP tokens could be produced without overlapping with TAN, and these could be accepted during transmission as valid priors for TRAP, which would potentially lead to moderate raising and fronting of TRAP. Nor is it clear why TRAP lowering and backing only began in the second half of the twentieth century. Accordingly, in this section I will briefly explore whether macro-level social categories can reveal factors that might have initiated incrementation.

As an inductive approach, every Missourians' measurements for TRAP and TAN diagonals and Bhattacharrya's coefficients were entered into a series of conditional inference trees with social categories as predictors. Conditional inference trees model a dataset by testing a dependent variable against each independent variable to identify statistically significant binary splits in the dataset. If significant effects are found, the algorithm selects the independent variable with the lowest *p*-value and divides the dataset into two nodes. The process then repeats at each node until no more significant predictors are found (see Tagliamonte & Baayen 2012). I created trees with the party package (Hothorn et al. 2006) in R. Sex, birth year, city of language acquisition, and SEI were included as independent variables. Decade of birth and region were also modeled.

For the full corpus, outputs of these models aligned with the analyses that have already been presented. TRAP diagonal is predicted by biological sex ($p < 0.001$), and females are further split between those born in 1969 or earlier who produce larger TRAP diagonals and those born after who produce smaller diagonals ($p = 0.03$). TAN diagonal is split at 1938 ($p < 0.001$), corresponding to the break between the historical and modern corpora. The historical corpus node is further split at 1902 ($p = 0.013$), with Missourians who were born earlier of course producing the smallest TAN diagonals. Bhattacharyya's coefficients decrease in apparent time. All Missourians in the historical corpus are clustered together with the largest coefficients ($p < 0.001$). Modern corpus speakers are further divided ($p = 0.003$), with Missourians born after 1990 having a median coefficient of just 0.109.

Modeling the historical corpus alone to identify social predictors that might have initiated incrementation in /æ/ results in no additional predictors being selected for either Bhattacharyya's coefficient or TAN diagonal. This is surprising, given that TAN clearly underwent change within this corpus. A tree for TRAP diagonal, however, selects SEI as a significant predictor ($p = 0.022$), with indexes above 96 being associated with lower TRAP diagonals and indexes of 96 and below associated with higher diagonals. It is a tenuous link, but in the search for Labov's "accidental" and "arbitrary" associations, this at least raises the possibility that lower and backer TRAP might have taken on some degree of social prestige in Missouri through association with higher socioeconomic status. Labov (2001: 462) states that when incipient changes become associated with styles or social groups, the sound changes that survive to advance in a speech community "are mostly associated with female speakers of an upwardly mobile class." The female lead during the second half of the twentieth century in TRAP lowering and retraction aligns with TRAP being relatively more prestigious. The possibility of a connection between higher socioeconomic status and lower and backer TRAP in Missouri in the first half of the twentieth century offers a possible initiating association to cause TRAP lowering and backing to advance via incrementation.

Alternatively, even though neither city nor region of language acquisition is selected by conditional inference tree modeling as a significant predictor of any of the measurements examined in this chapter, the correlation between SEI and TRAP diagonal may reflect areal differences within Missouri. Among the Missourians who are ranked highest in terms of SEI are several Kansas Citians, including the extreme of US President Harry S Truman. It is possible that the association between higher SEI and lower TRAP diagonal may actually reflect a fact about vowel quality in Kansas City in the late 1800s and early 1900s.

There is support for this possibility. A Kruskall-Wallis rank sum test measures region as a significant predictor of TRAP diagonal among speakers in the historical corpus ($\chi^2 = 18.251$, $p = 0.019$). Modeling Kansas City separately from all other Missouri regions shows that Kansas Citians in the historical corpus tend to produce TRAP with a smaller diagonal measurements than other Missourians, as shown in Figure 9. This is true not only for the Kansas Citians with the highest SEIs in the sample, but also for the Kansas Citians with lower SEIs of 77 and 92.

Additionally, the Kansas Citians show a relatively linear relationship between increasing SEI and decreasing TRAP diagonal. The thick dashed line plotted in Figure 9 represents a linear model of the relationship between TRAP diagonal and SEI for the Kansas Citians, which estimates a decrease in TRAP diagonal of 1.8 Hz for every 1-point increase in SEI (TRAP diagonal = −1.833 * SEI + 388.159; $R^2 = 0.449$, $p = 0.014$). The thin dashed line calculated for all other Missourians is not significant nor predictive (TRAP diagonal = −0.664 * SEI + 350.715; $R^2 = 0.011$, $p = 0.254$). As such, in Kansas City at the turn of the twentieth century, both locality and socioeconomic status might have interacted with the lowering and backing of TRAP to plant a seed for TRAP lowering and backing to advance rapidly through incrementation at the end of the twentieth century.

This proposition offers new directions for understanding a modern sound change that I have previously argued is not fully explained by proposed social or structural causes. It suggests that seemingly recent sound changes might have their origins in sociolinguistic realities of speech communities several generations ago, and to have advanced via transmission and incrementation across multiple generations of children and adolescents to the point where they become apparent in modern sociophonetic surveys.

This new explanation for a modern change in TRAP is complemented by the identification of the phonological reconfiguration of /æ/ over multiple generations across Missouri through the fundamental social interactions of parents raising children and children emerging into society. The sociolinguistic associa-

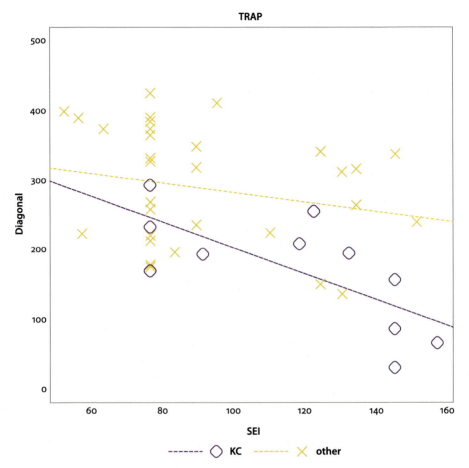

Figure 9. Comparison of relationships in Kansas City and other Missouri regions between socioeconomic index and TRAP diagonal in the historical corpus

tions or other factors that initiated the incrementation of TAN fronting and raising remain to be discovered, but the initiation and advancement of the change itself (revealed by the historical sociophonetic approach illustrated in this chapter) is itself noteworthy. As summarized in Section 2, changes from complex and raised /æ/ systems to continuous and nasal ones have been widely documented, but I am not familiar with other communities where a transition from a continuous to a nasal system has been traced. Because continuous and nasal systems are lowest-common-denominator /æ/ configurations in North American Englishes, it is possible that this is an aspect of sound change that is flying under the radar in other speech communities. Alternatively, it might be that such transitions have occurred farther back in time than can be surveyed in modern sociophonetic datasets.

In either case, historical sociophonetic analyses may reveal yet more dynamism in /æ/ in American Englishes. In this chapter, this dynamism has emerged only through intentional examination of past phonetic and phonological systems complemented by probing these past systems from the perspective of the cognitive processes of older children and adolescents engaging in language acquisition.

7. Conclusion

The quality of /æ/ changed dramatically in Missouri between 1880 and 2000. From a starting point of a continuous or undifferentiated /æ/ in low-front position, TAN raised and fronted, resulting in an allophonic separation from TRAP characteristic of a nasal system. This change took place over a relatively large geographic space, across ruralities and urbanities, despite differences in the cultural allegiances and phonological systems of settler populations across the state. Additionally, in the large Missouri metropolitan area of Kansas City, TRAP lowered and backed, especially in the last third of the twentieth century.

This chapter has demonstrated that both sound changes can be understood as having advanced through transmission and incrementation via children's and adolescents' processing of TRAP and TAN tokens as either outliers or valid priors (see Chapters 2 and 6 in this volume). It has elucidated some aspects of the origins of those changes through historical sociophonetic analysis, including positing social status and localness in the historical corpus as initiators of the incrementation that led to TRAP lowering and backing in the modern corpus. In addition, the data in this study shed light on the dynamics of sociolinguistic change as the consequence of various age-based forms of acquisition in this community, including transmission from older speakers and incrementation in peer-to-peer networks. In this sense, it adds to the evidence of how forms of *vertical* and *horizontal* communication contribute to individual acquisition trajectories and, ultimately, to change at the level of the community (see Chapter 5 in this volume).

As other contributions in this volume make clear, historical sociolinguists have much to gain from the incorporation of data beyond more written corpora. The findings in the present study demonstrate that, even where corpora are not ideally built to study transmission and incrementation in a speech community, approaches to historical sociophonetic datasets informed by the processes children use to build language from caregiver and speech community inputs can shed new light on conditions for language acquisition and, ultimately, for the progression and actuation of historical and modern sound changes.

References

Archival sources

American English Dialect Recordings, Center for Applied Linguistics Collection, Library of Congress. Project description: https://www.loc.gov/item/afccal000255/

Arthur B. Church KMBC Radio Collection, Marr Sound Archive, University of Missouri-Kansas City. Project description: https://library.umkc.edu/spec-col/KMBC/index.html

Kirkwood, Missouri, Oral History Project, State Historical Society of Missouri. Project description: https://files.shsmo.org/manuscripts/columbia/C3962.pdf

Missouri Mule History Project, State Historical Society of Missouri. Project description: https://collections.shsmo.org/manuscripts/columbia/c3954

USS Schley Oral History Project, in the Alex Primm Oral History Collection, State Historical Society of Missouri. Project description: https://files.shsmo.org/manuscripts/springfield/SP0054.pdf

Secondary sources

Bates, Douglas, Martin Maechler, Ben Bolker & Steve Walker. 2015. Fitting linear mixed-effects models using lme4. *Journal of Statistical Software* 67(1). 1–48.

Becker, Kara (ed.). 2019. *The low-back merger shift: Uniting the Canadian vowel shift, the California vowel shift, and short front vowel rotations across North America*. Durham, NC: Duke University Press.

Boberg, Charles & Stephanie Strassel. 2000. Short-a in Cincinnati: A change in progress. *Journal of English Linguistics* 28(2). 108–126.

Brown, Theodore & Lyle Dorsett. 1978. *K.C.: A history of Kansas City, Missouri*. Boulder, CO: Pruett.

Calenge, Clément. 2006. The package adehabitat for the R software: A tool for the analysis of space and habitat use by animals. *Ecological Modelling* 197(3–4). 516–519.

Carmichael, Katie. 2020. (æ)fter the storm: An Examination of the short-a system in Greater New Orleans. *Language Variation and Change* 32. 107–131.

Carver, Craig. 1987. *American regional dialects*. Ann Arbor, MI: University of Michigan Press.

Cournane, Ailís. 2019. A developmental view on incrementation in language change. *Theoretical Linguistics* 45(3–4). 127–150.

Denis, Derek. 2016. Oral histories as a window to sociolinguistic history and language history: Exploring earlier Ontario English with the Farm Work and Farm Life Since 1890 oral history collection. *American Speech* 91(4). 513–516.

Denis, Derek, Matt Hunt Gardner, Marisa Brook & Sali Taglimonte. 2019. Peaks and arrowheads of vernacular reorganization. *Language Variation and Change* 31. 43–67.

Duncan, Daniel. 2018. Language variation and change in the geographies of suburbs. New York: New York University PhD dissertation.

ELAN (Version 6.3) [Computer software]. 2022. Nijmegen: Max Planck Institute for Psycholinguistics, The Language Archive. https://archive.mpi.nl/tla/elan (15 January 2022).

Faries, Rachel. 1967. A word geography of Missouri. Columbia, MO: University of Missouri PhD dissertation.

Faries, Rachel & Donald Lance. 1993. Regional variation in Missouri. In Timothy Frazer (ed.), *"Heartland" English: Variation and transition in the American Midwest*, 245–256. Tuscaloosa, AL: University of Alabama Press.

Friedman, Lauren. 2014. *The St. Louis corridor: Mixing, competing, and retreating dialects.* Philadelphia: University of Pennsylvania. PhD dissertation.

Gibson, Campbell & Kay Jung. 2002. Historical Census statistics on population totals by race, 1790 to 1990, and by Hispanic origin, 1970 to 1990, for the United States, regions, divisions, and states [Working paper 56]. Washington: US Census Bureau. Accessed 13 May 2022.

Gordon, Elizabeth, Lyle Campbell, Jennifer Hay, Margaret Maclagan, Andrea Sudbury & Peter Trudgill. 2004. *New Zealand English: Its origins and evolution.* Cambridge: Cambridge University Press.

Gordon, Matthew. 2004. The West and Midwest: Phonology. In Bernd Kortmann & Edgar Schneider (eds.), *A handbook of varieties of English: A multimedia reference tool, volume 1, Phonology*, 338–350. Berlin: Mouton de Gruyter.

Gordon, Matthew. 2006. Tracking the low back merger in Missouri. In Thomas Murray & Beth Lee Simon (eds.), *Language variation and change in the American Midland*, 57–68. Philadelphia: John Benjamins.

Gordon, Matthew & Christopher Strelluf. 2017. Evidence of American regional dialects in early recordings. In Raymond Hickey (ed.), *Listening to the past: Audio records of accents of English*, 232–256. Cambridge: Cambridge University Press.

Haddican, Bill, Michael Newman, Cecelia Cutler & Christina Tortora. 2021. Aspects of change in New York City English short-a. *Language Variation and Change* 33(2). 135–163.

Hall, Erin & Ruth Maddeaux. 2020. /u/-fronting and /æ/-raising in Toronto families. *University of Pennsylvania Working Papers in Linguistics* 25(2). 51–60. https://repository.upenn.edu/pwpl/vol25/iss2/7

Hickey, Raymond (ed.). 2017a. *Listening to the past: Audio records of accents of English* [Studies in English Language]. Cambridge: Cambridge University Press.

Hickey, Raymond. 2017b. Analysing early audio recordings. In Raymond Hickey (ed.), *Listening to the past: Audio records of accents of English*, 1–12. Cambridge: Cambridge University Press.

Holmes-Elliott, Sophie. 2021. Calibrate to innovate: Community age vectors and the real time incrementation of language change. *Language in Society* 50(3). 441–474.

Hothorn, Torsten, Kurt Hornik & Achim Zeileis. 2006. Unbiased recursive partitioning: A conditional inference framework. *Journal of Computational and Graphical Statistics* 15(3). 651–674.

Johnson, Daniel Ezra. 2015. Quantifying overlap with Bhattacharyya's affinity. Paper presented at NWAV 44, Toronto, ON. https://danielezrajohnson.shinyapps.io/nwav_44 (15 January 2022).

Kerswill, Paul. 1996. Children, adolescents, and language change. *Language Variation and Change* 8. 177–202.

Kerswill, Paul & Ann Williams. 2000. Creating a new town koine: Children and language change in Milton Keynes. *Language in Society* 29(1). 65–115.

Labov, William. 1994. *Principles of linguistic change, volume 1: Internal factors.* Oxford: Blackwell.

Labov, William. 2001. *Principles of linguistic change, volume 2: Social factors*. Oxford: Blackwell.

Labov, William. 2007. Transmission and diffusion. *Language* 83(2). 344–387.

Labov, William. 2010. *Principles of linguistic change, volume 3: Cultural and cognitive factors*. Oxford: Blackwell.

Labov, William, Sharon Ash & Charles Boberg. 2006. *Atlas of North American English: Phonetics, phonology, and sound change*. Berlin: De Gruyter Mouton.

Labov, William, Sabriya Fisher, Duna Gylfadottír, Anita Henderson & Betsy Sneller. 2016. Competing systems in Philadelphia phonology. *Language Variation and Change* 28(3). 273–305.

Labov, William, Ingrid Rosenfelder & Josef Fruehwald. 2013. One hundred years of sound change in Philadelphia: Linear incrementation, reversal, and reanalysis. *Language* 89(1). 30–65.

Labov, William, Malcah Yaeger & Richard Steiner. 1972. *A quantitative study of sound change in progress*. Philadelphia: US Regional Survey.

Lenzo, Kevin. 2014. *The CMU pronouncing dictionary* v. 0.7b. http://svn.code.sf.net/p/cmusphinx/code/trunk/cmudict. (Feb. 7 2022)

Lobanov, Boris. Classification of Russian vowels spoken by different speakers. *Journal of the Acoustical Society of America* 49(2). 606–608.

Nakao, Keiko & Judith Treas. 1994. Updating occupational prestige and socioeconomic scores: How the new measures measure up. *Sociological Methodology* 24(1). 1–72.

Nesbitt, Monica, Suzanne Evans Wagner & Alexander Mason. 2019. A tale of two shifts: Movement toward the low-back-merger shift in Lansing, Michigan. In Kara Becker (ed.), *The low-back merger shift: Uniting the Canadian vowel shift, the California vowel shift, and short front vowel rotations across North America*, 144–165. Durham, NC: Duke University Press.

Payne, Arvilla. 1980. Factors controlling the acquisition of the Philadelphia dialect by out-of-state children. In William Labov (ed.), *Locating language in time and space*, 143–178. New York: Academic Press.

Pierrehumbert, Janet. 2003. Phonetic diversity, statistical learning, and acquisition of phonology. *Language and Speech* 46(2–3). 115–154.

R Core Team. 2021. *R: A language and environment for statistical computing*. R Foundation for Statistical Computing, Vienna, Austria. URL https://www.R-project.org/

Rosenfelder, Ingrid, Josef Fruehwald, Keelan Evanini, Scott Seyfarth, Kyle Gorman, Hilary Prichard & Jiahong Yuan. 2014. *FAVE (Forced Alignment and Vowel Extraction) Program Suite* v1.2.2 10.5281/zenodo.22281.

Sankoff, Gillian & Hélène Blondeau. 2007. Language change across the lifespan: /r/ in Montreal French. *Language* 83(3). 560–588.

Stanford, James & Laurence Kenny. 2013. Revisiting transmission and diffusion: An agent-based model of vowel chain shifts across large communities. *Language Variation and Change* 25. 119–153.

Strelluf, Christopher. 2016. Overlap among back vowels before /l/ in Kansas City. *Language Variation and Change* 28. 379–407.

Strelluf, Christopher. 2018. *Speaking from the Heartland: The Midland vowel system of Kansas City*. Durham, NC: Duke University Press.

Strelluf, Christopher. 2019a. Structural and social correlations with the Low-Back Merger Shift in a US Midland community. In Kara Becker (ed.), *The Low-Back Merger Shift: Uniting the Canadian Vowel Shift, the California Vowel Shift, and short front vowel rotations across North America*, 120–143. Durham, NC: Duke University Press.

Strelluf, Christopher. 2019b. Machine-automated vowel measurement, old sound recordings, and error-correction procedures. Presented at the First Annual Meeting of the North American Research Network in Historical Sociolinguistics, New York, USA.

Strelluf, Christopher & Matthew Gordon. 2024. *The origins of Missouri English: A historical sociophonetic analysis*. Lanham, MD: Lexington.

Tagliamonte, Sali & Alexandra D'Arcy. 2009. Peaks beyond phonology: Adolescence, incrementation, and language change. *Language* 85(1). 58–108.

Tagliamonte, Sali & Harald Baayen. 2012. Models, forests, and trees of York English: *Was/were* variation as a case study for statistical practice. *Language Variation and Change* 24. 135–178.

Thiel, Anja & Aaron Dinkin. 2020. Escaping the TRAP: Losing the Northern Cities Shift in real time. *Language Variation and Change* 32. 373–398.

Thomas, Erik. 2019. Innovations in sociophonetics. In William Katz & Peter Assmann (eds.), *The Routledge handbook of phonetics*, 448–472. London: Routledge.

Tukey, John. 1977. *Exploratory data analysis*. London: Addison-Wesley.

Wittenburg, Peter, Hennie Brugman, Albert Russel, Alex Klassmann & Han Sloetjes. 2006. ELAN: A professional framework for multimodality research. In *Proceedings of LREC 2006, Fifth International Conference on Language Resources and Evaluation*, 1556–1559.

CHAPTER 10

Language dominance across the lifespan in Wisconsin German and English varieties
Voice onset time and final obstruent neutralization, 1863–2013

Samantha M. Litty
Europa-Universität Flensburg

Large-scale German immigration to Wisconsin began in the first half of the 19th century and continued until about World War I. These immigrants built German-speaking institutions alongside English and other immigrant language institutions, allowing for the presence of German in many Wisconsin communities over several generations, along with a desire to preserve local history and heritage in the region. These practices are reflected in an archival record that allows for the study of features of local German and English over a period of 150 years. This chapter focuses on two such features, namely variation of voice onset time and final obstruent neutralization. A combination of historical written sources (spanning between the 1860s and the 1940s) and audio recordings from the 1940s and 2013 shows the existence of these features, as well as different periods along their development over time. This study looks at how language acquisition in heritage language communities and shifts in language dominance may have played a role in the emergence and development of these features in Wisconsin German and Wisconsin English varieties.

Keywords: heritage language, adult L2 acquisition, language dominance, voice onset time, final obstruent neutralization, bilingualism

1. Introduction

German has been spoken in Wisconsin for over 175 years and has also helped shape the regional variety of English. The local form of German has developed distinctly from the places of origin of the immigrants who brought it with them, meaning it does not sound exactly like the German spoken anywhere in German-speaking Europe today. This is likely due to several reasons, including contact not only with English and multiple non-mutually intelligible German varieties, but also with other 'older' immigrant languages such as Norwegian, Polish, Czech, and Finnish.

By combining written sources (1863–1940) from German immigrants to the Upper Midwest in the 19th century and their descendants and audio recordings made in German and English in the 1940s and 2013, we can observe usage in individuals and at the community level over a longer span of time than would be possible with just one data source. This helps to show the historical development of specific features. In this case study, I show how changing patterns of language dominance played a role in individual feature variation.[1] This chapter focuses on two such features, namely variation of voice onset time and final obstruent neutralization. For both syllable-initial and syllable-final forms, 'unexpected' variants (i.e., variants atypical in non-contact varieties of German or English) in laryngeal distinctions[2] reflect language contact. While variation in both syllable-initial and syllable-final forms may vary by individual, there are trends based on regional (for example, German from different areas, and also English from different areas) and language differences (German varies from English). These trends show us how these forms are expected to vary in monolingual settings, and give some indication that these distinctions in bilingual, contact settings may differ from those typical of either language in monolingual settings.

The rest of this chapter is structured as follows. In Section 2, I describe the sociohistorical information of German immigration and German speakers in Wisconsin, before moving on to the data sources in Section 3. In Section 4, I describe the phonetic analysis of voice onset time and how written representations indicate variation therein. In Section 5, I describe the phonetic analysis of final obstruent neutralization and how written representations indicate variation in final obstruent neutralization. Section 6 introduces and discusses how these

---

1. I thank an anonymous reviewer for suggesting the possibility that opportunities for *co-activation*, not just language dominance, may have potentially also played a role in cross-linguistic interference in this bilingual community. This possibility must for now remain the topic of future studies. See also Chapter 4 in this volume for a proposal on how to incorporate language dominance levels in the sociohistorical study of language contact and change, and Chapter 5 for a discussion of the role of dominance in various forms of bilingual acquisition.

2. In laryngeal realism, distinctions regarding neutralization, or representations of the contrast in features (see Iverson & Salmons 1995, 2011) are indicated by [voice], [spread glottis], and [constricted glottis]. A blank space [ ] indicates the absence of a phonological specification. In laryngeal realism, both German and English are aspirating languages, where, for example, laryngeal mergers take place finally between aspirated and passively voiced obstruents, commonly referred to as *Auslautverhärtung*, or final devoicing, when this is final fortition, not 'devoicing' (see Iverson & Salmons 2011: 4–6).

audio and written data can be seen to vary based (at least partially) on language dominance. Section 7 ties this research to acquisition and change, and Section 8 summarizes and concludes this chapter.

2. Sociohistorical background

German immigration to the United States can be classified into three time periods: a first period from colonial times to the American Revolutionary War (1776–1781), a second period from the early 1800s to World War I, and a third period post WWI to today (Litty forthcoming). The German-speaking immigrants and their descendants relevant to this research came to the United States during the second period. They left their homelands for several reasons, with push factors ranging from lack of availability of land to an attempt to escape military conscription, and pull factors such as the broad availability of land in the United States or following family who had previously immigrated (Litty forthcoming).[3]

In Wisconsin, German immigration began in the 1830s and continued through the early 20th century peaking around 1890 (Eichhoff 1971: 46–47). In 1910, in some areas of eastern Wisconsin, the population of German descent made up 35% of the total (Eichhoff 1971: 49). Seifert estimates the number of German speakers to have been about 400,000 at that time (1993: 334). Frey (2013: 172) and Wilkerson and Salmons (2008, 2012) found that some individual towns remained 24–28% monolingual German speaking, and Hustisford (a small town in Dodge County) is estimated to have been as much as 42% bilingual German-English speaking, with another 31% estimated to have been possibly bilingual. While the shift to English is currently advanced throughout the region, Purnell et al. (2005a, b) estimate that 1.5% of the population of Dodge County still spoke German at home in 2000.

This major immigration wave brought a multitude of both High and Low German varieties. Previous research on Wisconsin German has shown several varieties including Oderbrüchisch, Ripuarian, Mosel Franconian, Westphalian, Pomeranian, Ostfälisch, and Kölsch (Litty 2017a: 85). The continued presence of German across public and home domains allowed for many of these varieties to continue being used beyond the traditional 3-generation model of language shift to the dominant language (see Alba 2004; Alba et al. 2002; Fishman 1972). German-speaking immigrants were settling Wisconsin at the same time as non-German speakers who were also organizing and building institutions such as schools, churches, recreation

---

3. For more details on the historical and demographic characterization of Wisconsin German varieties and German immigrants, see Litty (2017b, forthcoming); Litty et al. (2015, 2019).

(theaters, cultural clubs), and media (newspapers, magazines, bulletins). Consequently, these German institutions were not competing against already existing institutions, but rather developed around the same time. These institutions, coupled with the extended influx of German-speaking immigrants, contributed to the maintenance of a German-speaking social space for several generations.

The combination of different varieties, particularly regional varieties and dialects which were spoken in the home initially, and Standard German, which was introduced through schools, churches, and the media, may have led to the emergence of the standard-like Heritage German variety we see in Wisconsin speakers today via dialect contact (see Chapter 4 in this volume). Even so, many of these speakers exhibit a mix of features uncharacteristic of any German-speaking region in Europe. This mix of features not only includes lexical choices and morphosyntactic variation but also phonetic-phonological variation. Given the correlation between generational cohort and the language use patterns found in other heritage language settings (Alba et al. 2002; Nove 2021, among others; see also Chapter 6 in this volume), a legitimate sociohistorical question is whether these correlations also obtained in Wisconsin German, and whether they helped shape the emergence of a unique variety of English influenced by the articulatory patterns typical of bilinguals.

3. Data sources

Where traditional sociohistorical studies focus on either written or spoken data, and either historical or modern sources (see i.e., Auer et al. 2015: 1–2; Hickey 2017; Trudgill 2004; Wright 2006), this project expands current standards in historical sociolinguistics by combining written and spoken data from historical and modern sources (see Chapters 7 and 9 in this volume for similar approaches). While the data presented on here were first collected and analyzed in my 2017 dissertation (Litty 2017b), the analysis of the features from a language acquisition perspective is new.

The written data are dated 1863–1940 and they were produced by a total of 89 authors from five Wisconsin communities. The collections themselves were found in the Wisconsin Historical Society Library and Archives, the Max Kade Institute (MKI) archive in Madison, Wisconsin, and from historical societies throughout Wisconsin.[4] As written sources, ego-documents – i.e., personal, unpublished documents, such as letters, diaries, memory albums – often reflect variation more similar to the creators' spoken language than other text types (Elspaß 2012), the data here are predominantly from personal letters. Most of these writers were lit-

---

4. The full description of the texts and their collections is available in Litty (2017b: 40–43).

erate in German, but those who moved to the U.S. as adults were not subjected to any English-language education and most had not received any formal training in writing English. Consequently, their English is likely to have been impacted by their L1 phonologies (German). This also means that fewer instances of non-standard or unexpected features are anticipated in the texts authored by those who are more educated or who are more practiced in writing Standard German. However, as Litty (2017a, b, 2019, 2022, among others) has shown, even in otherwise Standard German writings of the time period, regional and dialectal indicators are often evident.

The audio data come from recordings of both male and female speakers in German and English in the late 1940s and 2013. The English recordings from the 1940s are part of the Helene Stratman-Thomas Collection, stored in the Mills Music Library at the University of Wisconsin in Madison. These recordings were created as part of the Wisconsin Folksong Collection, 1937–1946, in which the intent was to record the songs, not the spoken language of the individuals presenting. However, brief segments at the beginning of each recording are spoken, and from this spoken part the English data is drawn. The German audio recordings are housed in the sound archives of the Max Kade Institute for German-American Studies in Madison. The older recordings, made 1945–1949, are part of the Lester W. J. "Smoky" Seifert Collection and were made with the intent of recording speakers of all varieties of German spoken in Wisconsin (see Bousquette 2020). As each of the speakers recorded were at least bilingual German/English speakers (if not trilingual in a non-standard German variety, often a Low German variety), the intended collection data was German (of all varieties), but the recordings also frequently include segments of spoken English, which are included in this analysis. The 2013 German recordings are part of the Litty-Evans collections, which was compiled as part of the Wisconsin German Project, supervised by Joseph Salmons (University of Wisconsin – Madison). This collection is much more extensive than the previous collections, due to the ease of creating longer recordings with modern technology. Speakers include German-English bilinguals from Dodge County, and English monolinguals from Richland County. Data is drawn (where possible) in both German and English from the bilinguals in Dodge County.

To allow for comparison between the written and audio data, I have analyzed the audio recordings using Praat (Boersma & Weenink 2022) as described in Sections 4 and 5. Only after it has been determined whether the results from the audio data are comparable to previous research, and therefore "standard like", or whether the values are unexpected and therefore "non-standard like", can these be compared with results from the written data. Written data are simplified along a simple binary: either the writer exhibits non-standard forms indicative of variation in voice onset time (VOT) or final obstruent neutralization (FON), or they do not. The process of determining which variants are suggestive of variation in VOT or FON is described in Sections 4.1 and 5.1.

4. Voice onset time

Voice onset time (VOT) is the "interval of time, measured in milliseconds, between the stop gap and the onset of vocal fold pulsing" (Thomas 2011), that is, between the closure (the amount of time during which articulatory occlusion occurs) and the beginning of when the vocal folds are engaged. Very simply put, for example, when considering an American English /t/, VOT is the interval of time corresponding to the puff of air in words like 'tooth' or 'tap'. This interval is visible in phonetic analysis (for example, in Praat). VOT is an expected area to see bilingual acquisition effects, as demonstrated by previous research in other language communities (see Khattab 2002; Olson 2013; Stoehr et al. 2017, among others). To summarize this research, bilingual production of VOT in each language is often unlike that of monolinguals in each language: for instance, bilinguals often produce VOT values in one of their languages that are intermediate between those typical of monolinguals. How much and in the direction of which language bilingual VOT is affected depends on many factors, including the type of task, the phonological position of the stop segment in question, each speaker's age at onset of bilingualism and relative levels of language dominance.

Syllable initially, VOT has been shown to vary across Wisconsin (Litty 2014). Geiger and Salmons (2006) show that some Wisconsin English speakers exhibit lower VOT than reported for General American English (henceforth GAE) (Lisker & Abramson 1964). Although VOT values from previous studies are known, speakers in this study are mostly bilingual speakers of both German and English, so according to Thomas (2011) and other studies of bilingual VOT we might expect to find intermediate or changing VOT, rather than VOT that just resembles either German or English. While it is useful to compare VOT to previous research, it is equally important to compare speakers within their groups to account for trends and patterns, including possible changes due to shifts in language dominance across the lifespan.

In this project, I compare VOT values for the speakers with other documented VOT values.[5] Some previous studies group all spread obstruents together

---

5. Measuring VOT for /p^h, t^h, k^h/ starts from the beginning of the burst until the wave form becomes regular or sinusoidal or until voicing sets in and until Formant 2 is level; this is usually about halfway through the first small wave of the vowel. Voicing is considered "set in" when the voicing line is fully dark, not the first shadows of voicing. This is usually 1–2 pulses into Formant 1.

and all unmarked obstruents together, others keep averages or average ranges separate for each obstruent. Because VOT is shown to vary quite widely even on an individual basis, ranges for tokens can then also be especially broad, especially if a speaker exhibits pre-voicing. What is comparable, however, is the generally expected pattern for both Standard German and GAE values, namely the duration of VOT for /pʰ/ < /tʰ/ < /kʰ/[6] and /p/ < /t/ < /k/.

There is also some variation on what is considered an acceptable threshold for *spread* vs. *unmarked* obstruents. For example, 40 ms is given as a statistical threshold between spread and unmarked stops (Ali et al. 2001:82; Niyogi & Ramesh 1998:13). Tokens perceived as 'within-category' are 10–30 ms from token value, while 20 ms is considered a 'boundary-value stimulus' (Blumstein et al. 2005:1354). Given that values for just noticeable differences of obstruent categories also vary, conservatively 20–30 ms between categories is considered acceptable here (see Hirsh 1959:767; Lisker & Abramson 1964:399; Stevens & Klatt 1974:653, among others).

The values for previous studies of VOT in GAE are shown in Table 1.[7]

Table 1. GAE VOT (in ms) from previous studies

Source	/pʰ/	/tʰ/	/kʰ/	/p/	/t/	/k/
Lisker & Abramson 1964: 395	58	70	80	-100–1	-102–5	-88–21
Lisker & Abramson 1964: 410, running speech	10–45	15–70	30–85	-65–15	-90–25	-45–13
Stevens & Klatt 1974: 653		>50			<20–30	
Allen et al. 2003				69–119		

4.1 VOT in audio data

Because the data drawn from historical recordings is limited and token totals for individual obstruents are low, data here is grouped to reflect [spread] vs [unmarked] obstruent categories for each of the collections of English speakers in Wisconsin. The averages are shown in Table 2.

Only one speaker produced English tokens in the Seifert collection, whereas tokens are taken from four speakers each for each of the other collections. While

---

6. As German and English are [spread], not [voice] languages, I follow the transcription convention in Iverson & Salmons (1995) of /pʰ, tʰ, kʰ/ to indicate [spread] tokens and /p, t, k/ for [unmarked].

7. In this table, the long hyphen (–) indicates a range, while the short hyphen (-) indicates a negative value.

Chapter 10. Language dominance across the lifespan in Wisconsin German and English   241

Table 2. English values (in ms) from Wisconsin

Source	/pʰ/	/tʰ/	/kʰ/	/p/	/t/	/k/
Seifert English		55			32	
Stratman-Thomas English		51			29	
Litty-Evans English, bilinguals		58			11	
Litty-Evans English, monolinguals		49			12	

previous studies show so much variation, these values appear to fall generally with the expected ranges given in Table 1. In all the Wisconsin English groups, tokens categorized as [spread] exhibit longer VOTs than [unmarked] tokens, and all have thresholds of >22 ms, indicating that as a group, each of these follows patterns within expected ranges.

However, when considered on an individual basis, it is evident that personal averages are quite variable. Litty has compared each speaker recorded in English from these four collections, finding no speakers that produce expected patterns of obstruent category distinction falling within previously given ranges for all categories (2017b: 134–135). There are several reasons why this might be the case, including study design and speaker sex. However, for present purposes of considering language dominance as a factor in variation, it is enough to note that these speakers individually are considered outside the norm for GAE.

For German speakers, VOT values can be compared with previous studies for German, shown in Table 3.

Table 3. Standard German VOT (in ms) from previous studies, as reported in Jessen (1998)

Sources	/pʰ/	/tʰ/	/kʰ/	/p/	/t/	/k/
Taylor 1975		50			<20	
Keating 1984		60–70			<20	
Angelowa & Pompino-Marschall 1985	36	39	47	6	11	16

Table 3 shows that VOT exhibits some variation in standard German, although two studies group tokens by obstruent category, both of which exhibit categorical distinctions of >30 ms. Both show that the average VOT for [unmarked] tokens should be lower than 20 ms. When data from German recorded in Wisconsin is grouped according to obstruent category, as shown in Table 4, we see that [spread] tokens exhibit longer VOT than [unmarked] tokens, as expected. However, the earlier recordings (Seifert) exhibit average VOT of only 17 ms difference, indicating that there is no categorical distinction between [spread] vs [unmarked] tokens. The Litty-Evans recordings from 2013, on the other hand, exhibit a much larger categorical distinction with an average threshold of 66 ms.

Table 4. German VOT (in ms) from Wisconsin

Sources	/pʰ/	/tʰ/	/kʰ/	/p/	/t/	/k/
Seifert German		59			42	
Litty-Evans German		61			-5	

Litty (2017b: 133) also analyzes these speakers individually and according to individual tokens, and finds more variation among the German data than among the English. Again, several possible explanations such as study design and data collection and speaker sex may account for these distinctions, but here it is enough to note that these speakers are considered outside expected norms when compared with previous German studies.

4.2 VOT in written sources

While the measurement of VOT in audio recordings is quite straightforward, "measuring" VOT in written sources is not. Orthographic representations signify phonological, not phonetic features, however non-standard variation syllable-initially (which could suggest phonetic variability) can be identified according to non-standard orthographic representations in the text, as shown in (1–2).

(1) Korn 2 Acker Kardofel 25 bis 30 Tonne
 Heu und ein bar schwere braune
 Pferde 7 Jahr alt so groß als man
 '…corn, 2 acres of potatoes, 25–30 tons
 hay and a couple of heavy brown
 horses, 7 years old as big as one…'
 Personal letter, Max Kade Institute Archives, Goth Collection, 1869

In (1), there are two non-standard orthographic forms possibly indicative of *lenition*, i.e., a shorter VOT than expected: the variants *Kardofel* 'potato' and *bar* 'couple' rather than the expected *Kartoffel* and *Paar*, which possibly signal shorter

VOT in /tʰ/ > /t/ appearing written as <d> rather than <t>, and /pʰ/ > /p/ written as <b> rather than the expected <p>.

In (2), on the other hand, we see what appears to suggest *fortition*, or a longer VOT than expected.

(2) how they press the feet of the women. Some six
different ministers were there the Paptist + Methodist
and some others they sat on the Kanzel to listen to
Personal letter, Wisconsin Historical Society Library,
Krueger Collection, 1897

In (2), where we expect *Baptist* to be written with a <b> to indicate a shorter VOT, the writer uses <p>, suggesting /p/ > /pʰ/. These orthographic variations may be seen occasionally in writers from other regions as a sign of lack of familiarity with spelling standards, but due to Wisconsin's history of language contact and to the frequency of these spellings in these written sources, I interpret this variation in my corpus as likely indicative of variations in speech (see Howell 1993 for a similar argument). Because the frequencies of varying or unexpected non-standard forms are different for each group (German and English sources), I do not attempt to measure to what extent each exhibits these forms, rather I am simply determining whether the unexpected non-standard forms showing syllable-initial variation are exhibited.

In an earlier study of this same written corpus, Litty (2017b: 130–131) found that of the 89 writers examined, 27 exhibit orthographic forms indicative of variation in VOT. These are relatively evenly split, with 14 producing these variations in English and 13 in German.[8] None of the writers produced non-standard forms indicative of variation in VOT in both languages. Only three writers produced non-standard orthographic representations showing syllable-initial variation only. The other 24 writers also exhibited non-standard orthographic representations indicative of final obstruent neutralization. This feature is analyzed in more detail in the next section.

---

8. Some English examples with the non-standard form listed first: *get > yet, put > but, recards > regards*. Some German examples with the non-standard form listed first: *tauert < dauert, dod < Tod, Paracke > Baracke, Glayton > Clayton*.

5. Final obstruent neutralization

Final obstruent neutralization (FON) is also known under other names. In relation to German, this feature is usually called *final devoicing, final obstruent devoicing*, or *final fortition* (in German: *Auslautverhärtung*). However, because German and English are [spread glottis] and not [voice] languages, I use the term *neutralization* to describe all processes associated with the change from lenis to fortis features. As with VOT (see Section 4), FON is a common area for bilingual acquisition effects: L2 and heritage speakers dominant in FON languages have been observed to apply this process to languages that do not commonly exhibit it among monolinguals (Dmtrieva et al. 2010; Özaslan & Gabriel 2019).

Generally, in everyday spoken language, German neutralizes the distinction between [spread] and [unmarked] obstruents word- and often syllable-finally too, so that words like *Rad* 'bicycle' and *Rat* 'advice, or council' are pronounced the same. By contrast GAE, apart from the use of glottal stops,[9] maintains a distinction, so the English words *rad* and *rat* are pronounced differently. In the English word *rad*, for example, this distinction may be made with more glottal pulsing and a longer vowel. In GAE the length of the preceding vowel is widely seen as the most important factor of 'voicing', whereas in *rat* there is no pulsing, and the vowel is shorter. In eastern Wisconsin English, we also see final /s/ realized as /s^h/, where a word like *beers* or a name like Van Hise would be produced with final /s^h/ rather than the expected /s/. Purnell et al. (2005a, b) show that the way Southeastern Wisconsin speakers distinguish final obstruents is unlike German, but also different than GAE, where they are distinguished via cues of lengthened preceding vowel or final pulsing.[10] To recap: there are three general patterns: first, in standard German the distinction between final obstruents is neutralized; second, in GAE, the distinction is maintained, most frequently with perceptual cues such as vowel duration and glottal pulsing as a percent of consonant duration; and third, the pattern previously seen in eastern Wisconsin English, which shows that the distinction between final obstruents is not maintained, but the manner in which this is done mirrors neither patterns in German nor GAE.

---

9. Even in speakers who use glottal stops, the distinction is often carried by preceding vowel duration.

10. Other cues may be used to distinguish voicing in GAE, but vowel length and glottal pulsing are the determinants used here.

5.1 FON in audio data

More research has been conducted on FON than on VOT in this region, including in Watertown (Dodge County), where several recordings were made, as well as where written data was gathered for this project. Because we have previous data from the same region, from speakers of a similar demographic background, we might expect to see similar results in data for the Watertown English speakers. The overview of FON measurement values used to determine how distinctions are made between final obstruents is shown in Table 5.

Table 5. Mean FON values for GAE and Watertown English; Purnell et al. (2005a, b)

Language	Token type	Vowel duration in ms	Consonant duration in ms	Vowel to consonant ratio	% pulsing to consonant ratio
GAE	Spread /p^h, t^h, k^h, f^h, s^h/ = <p, t, k, f, s>	101	100	1.41	0.36
	Unmarked /p, t, k, f, s/ = <b, d, g, v, z>	157	102	1.80	0.69
Watertown English	Spread	110	n/a	0.26	n/a
	Unmarked	162	n/a	0.77	n/a

Litty (2017b: 145–146) describes the set of expectations that applies to this data. The first is that the preceding vowel's duration should be increased before [unmarked] tokens for English. Second, for GAE, the ratio of vowel-to-consonant duration should be approximately 1.5 times longer for [unmarked] obstruents than for [spread] obstruents (Chen 1970; Purnell et al. 2005a, b). Litty analyzes data for individual speakers of both German and English and finds that all English speakers recorded in the 1940s follow the pattern that the vowel duration is longer before [unmarked] than [spread] tokens. An overview of the averaged collection results for Wisconsin English is shown in Table 6.

Table 6 shows that all three English groups exhibit longer average vowel duration before an unmarked consonant than for spread consonants, which matches previously reported patterns. We also expect the duration of the vowel to be longer than the consonant for both spread and unmarked obstruents. This holds true in the Stratman-Thomas collection, but not in the Seifert collection, which may be due to the small number of tokens. However, the mean vowel and consonant duration for spread consonants is equal in the Litty-Evans collection, which

Table 6. Mean FON values of Wisconsin English

Language	Token type	Vowel duration in ms	Consonant duration in ms	Vowel to consonant ratio	% pulsing to consonant ratio
Seifert English	Spread	70	92	0.75	0.32
	Unmarked (1 token)	(144)	(86)	(1.67)	0
Stratman-Thomas English	Spread	102	90	1.14	0.21
	Unmarked	147	67	2.20	0.59
Litty – Evans English	Spread	97	97	1.00	0.15
	Unmarked	131	122	1.08	0.38

is unexpected. Not only are the English data for each group unexpected: the German data also do not follow expected patterns, as shown in Tables 7 and 8.

Table 7. Mean FON values for Standard German, Purnell et al. (2005b)

Language	Token type	Vowel duration in ms	Consonant duration in ms	Vowel to consonant ratio	% pulsing to consonant ratio
German	Spread	89	76	1.33	0.43
	Unmarked	115	77	1.83	0.49

Compared with the values shown in Table 7, Litty (2017b: 183–184) finds several variations among the German and English data. In all cases the mean vowel-to-consonant ratios for the German data from German-English bilinguals in Wisconsin are smaller than expected, but are similar to one another (for a more detailed analysis, see 145–186).

Table 8. Mean FON values for Wisconsin German

Language	Token type	Vowel duration in ms	Consonant duration in ms	Vowel to consonant ratio	% pulsing to consonant ratio
Seifert German	Spread	107	97	1.10	0.22
	Unmarked	n/a	n/a	n/a	n/a
Litty-Evans German	Spread	105	105	1.00	0.15
	Unmarked	n/a	n/a	n/a	n/a

The data from Wisconsin German speakers in Table 8 show that the mean of percent pulsing to consonant ratio is also lower than expected for German as summarized in Table 7. The data here only sometimes pattern with previous studies: in other words, the difference in the typical pattern appears to indicate that vowel length is not the main indicator in distinguishing between final obstruents for all groups of Wisconsin English as has previously been suggested elsewhere (see Purnell et al. 2005b).

Because the FON values are variable and appear to be undergoing change in both German and GAE/Watertown English, we must consider these values but also any patterns that follow across the language data. For example, all three varieties have longer mean vowel durations than consonant durations, regardless of [spread] or [unmarked]; the mean vowel to consonant ratio is larger for unmarked tokens than spread tokens; and finally, the duration of the unmarked vowel is greater than the spread vowel. Interestingly, these three patterns hold true for most but not for all the speakers analyzed here individually. Table 9 shows the number of individual speakers in each corpus that conform to these general patterns:

Table 9. Expected patterns for FON from Wisconsin recordings

Expected pattern	German	English
spread: vowel > consonant	6/8	6/11
unmarked: vowel > consonant	n/a	8/11
mean vowel-to-consonant ratio: unmarked > spread	n/a	8/11
unmarked vowel > spread vowel	n/a	10/11

Of the German speakers, six of eight follow the expected patterns. Of the English speakers, expected patterns vary, with five of the eleven following all four patterns. Of those who do not pattern as expected, most exhibit unexpected patterns in no more than two categories. Only one exhibits unexpected patterns in three categories, and none in all four. Given that these differences in the community may reflect individual acquisitional trajectories, they are particularly relevant to an investigation into the relationship between the circumstances in which these speakers acquired language and long-term trends of change in communal norms.

5.2 FON in written sources

As was the case with VOT, using written variation to locate possible variations in FON is complicated. When L1 German speakers learn English, this feature is often evident in orthography, as Bagwell et al. (2019: 32) show in 19th-century correspondence, e.g., *twelf* and *thinks* instead of "twelve" and "things".[11] It is necessary to note that it is not always easy to distinguish between orthographic variation indicative of variation in FON or simply due to varied spelling norms,[12] or due to orthographic representations which designate oral pronunciations in English. These examples tend to be more variable than the VOT examples, and intra-writer variation is a strong indicator of the writer producing spelling variations mirroring pronunciation. We can see these patterns of German-like final fortition in the English letters, as shown in (3).

(3) Max was there to and Mr Swere tolt
him that I was there but he wou
dend bleve it he told Mr Swear that
he was a liar then Max went to
the post office and there he just
got the dispatch what Fritz send
away wen I started

'Max was there too, and Mr. Swere told him that I was there, but he wouldn't believe it. He told Mr. Swere that he was a liar. Then Max went to the post office and there he just got the dispatch what [which] Fritz sent away when I started.'
Personal Letter, Max Kade Institute Archives, Goth Collection, 1889

---

11. Howell (1993: 91–193) gives a broader overview of phonetic/phonological effects resulting from the imposition of German features onto English, sampling studies of German-influenced English from Eastern Pennsylvania; St. Clair County, Illinois; and Milwaukee, Wisconsin, showing remarkable consistency across the American regional variants. While only a few illustrative examples are depicted here, this data is in line with that from previous studies.

12. For example, in the case of the spelling of /s/ vs /s^h/, there are some variations in British vs American usage – such as the alternation between -*ise* and -*ize* – which do not reflect a difference in pronunciation. This makes it impossible to use any orthographic variation in such instances to denote possible variations in pronunciation. An example from the corpus is *frose/froze*. However, where <z> is used orthographically according to American conventions where there is a clear expectation for <z> only in American English, this orthographic variation may indicate variation in pronunciation.

What we have in Example (3) is variation in word-final position ("tolt" for *told*, "woudend" for *wouldn't*, "send" for *sent*). (3) comes from a letter written by a first-generation immigrant, who was 64 at the time of writing. Given the writer's age, this variation may be due to exposure to English and an awareness of German final fortition, which may have caused the writer to vary in the forms she produced, or it may be because the writer was unexperienced with writing in English. Be that as it may, this writer did vary between writing final <t> and <d>, which may be suggestive of variation in FON. An example possibly indicating hypercorrection is shown in (4).

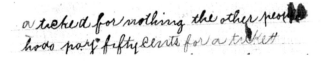

(4) a ticked for nothing. the other people
    hado[13] pay fifty cents for a tickett
    '[...] a ticket for nothing. The other people had to pay fifty cents for a ticket.'
                                    Personal Letter, Wisconsin Historical Society Library,
                                                              Krueger Collection, 1892

What is particularly striking about (4) is the variation in the two orthographic representations of the English word *ticket*. The first time the writer used it in line 1, it was realized with a final <d>, which supports the view that this author spoke German and realized both final <t> and <d> as /tʰ/. In the second line, however, the writer wrote *tickett*, possibly indicating an intended strengthening of the final obstruent.

To summarize, the evidence presented in Sections 4 and 5 has shown that there is a considerable amount of variation in both audio and written data. Illustrative examples from the written data are intended to showcase patterns which occur frequently in otherwise standard language texts, not to be in any way exhaustive of all orthographic inconsistencies or possible explanations thereof. However, because the authors were writing in the standard language – and do more frequently than not – follow standard written orthographic guidelines, the instances where these orthographic errors occur suggest that these errors may be of phonologic significance. Due to our presumption that the writers intended to produce texts in the standard orthography, and that the types of orthographic

---

13. While it may appear that "hado" for "had to" is a lenition of the /tʰ/ in <to>, this is more likely an orthographic representation of an oral feature, where the /t/ in *had* and the /tʰ/ in *to* assimilate and so are often produced this way in spoken speech.

variation which occur are consistent across writers and geographic regions, I interpret these variations as indicative of potential variation in or imposition of German phonologic systems on the writers' English (see Howell 1993). In the audio data, the differences in where variation is found – both in German and English, and in different factors of each feature – indicate that the variation may be due to individual differences, or due to a trading relationship in the communities where the data was collected from a German-like pattern to an English-like pattern, or rather something possibly not fully resembling either.

Now that I have given examples of the data from both audio and written sources showing variation in VOT and/or FON, I turn to a comparison of how language dominance may impact a speaker or writer's produced data. In this comparison, the sociohistorical context of lifelong exposure and acquisition of German and/or English plays a central role.

6. Language dominance

Each writer or speaker has been categorized for *language dominance* at the time of recording or writing. For the modern speakers, this was easily done, based on data presented in the recordings themselves. Without exception, all bilingual speakers recorded in 2013 report a switch in their language dominance from German to English in or prior to adolescence. For most this was in response to direct questions regarding which languages they used in different domains at different times of their lives. Several consultants report learning English from older siblings who had entered school already, while others describe beginning to use English only after entering school themselves. Others continued to use German in various domains, albeit often infrequently. One consultant, for example, recalls using German into her 20s where she worked at a local hotel. Another describes working in a hospital and being mostly English dominant herself, but occasionally having to use German with older patients. Most also reported not having used German at all in several years, indicating that they were English (L2) dominant at the time of recording in 2013, which is then the final distinction of how these speakers were categorized as belonging to group 2b as either known or presumed bilingual, English dominant individuals (see this section below).

Because language dominance may vary over the lifespan (see Chapters 4 and 5 in this volume), attempting to determine language dominance for a specific point in one's lifespan posthumously is challenging. Factors such as where the speaker or writer lived, with whom they interacted, their education location and level, and the period in which they lived, among others, make classification complicated. For the audio recordings from the 1940s, if language dominance was not explicitly stated in their recordings, information regarding language use was cross checked with census records where available. For several speakers from the Stratman-Thomas collection, full names were not given and so this information is unavailable. Where speakers note they learned a song from their parent or grandparent and remember it from childhood, they are classified as "assumed English dominant". For speakers from the Seifert collection, as significant metalinguistic data was collected on the speakers, this information has been corroborated where possible. Finally, for the authors of written documents, language dominance data is drawn from their texts (occasionally there is indication of preference for writing one language over another, or struggles with writing in German, or writing courses attended, etc.) and from other data in the collection, as well as census data where possible.

With these limitations in mind, based on the available information I have classified each speaker or writer from the historical corpora (i.e., the Seifert and Stratman-Thomas collections) into one of the following categories (adapted from Wilkerson & Salmons 2012: 13).

1. Pre-shift monolingual; here, German monolingual
2. a. (Known or presumed) bilingual; German dominant
   b. (Known or presumed) bilingual; English dominant
3. Post-shift monolingual; here, English monolingual

Those considered presumed bilingual are classified according to their correspondence with known German speakers, for example by receiving letters in German, or from relationships to German monolinguals. For those classified as category 2, German or English dominance is simplified and determined by the language in which the speaker or writer produced the most data samples. If they produced data in both languages, the language in which they produced the most data samples is used as the distinguishing factor. If a writer, for example, wrote seven letters, two in German and five in English, this writer would be classified as belonging to 2b. In practice, most writers produced data in only one language, or in both languages simultaneously or alternating, in which case best judgement according to content, generation, family language or census data was applied.

6.1 Language dominance and non-standard VOT and FON forms in spoken and written data

In total, 89 writers and 16 speakers are considered here ($N=105$). Years of birth span 1819–1944, with the earliest recorded speaker born in 1861 and the latest born writer born in 1906. Of those 46 are women, and 59 are men. Where Wilkerson and Salmons (2012) classified writers and speakers according to their general *lan-*

guage status (i.e., which languages they spoke and whether they acquired them as children or as adults), here I focus on language dominance, which can shift across the lifespan and affect phonological awareness.

The data for language status may give a good overview of how many writers and speakers from each group produced non-standard-like forms, but it may not reflect the effect of changes in language dominance throughout the lifespan (see Chapter 4 in this volume). Therefore, we can get a more transparent idea of how language dominance may play a role by considering the distribution in forms possibly indicative of non-standard VOT and FON variation shown in Table 10. Of the 105 speakers initially analyzed, two English bilinguals from the Stratman-Thomas Collection were removed from the analysis at this point as they were determined to be bilingual English-French and bilingual English-Ho-Chunk/Winnebago, and the rest of the analysis focuses only on German and English.

Table 10. Language dominance of speakers and writers; adapted from Litty (2017b)

	Total number of speakers and writers	Speakers and writers exhibiting non-standard-like forms indicative of variation (both VOT and FON)	Percent
1. Pre-shift monolingual, German	9	9	100
2a. Bilingual, German dominant	17	11	65
2b. Bilingual, English dominant	46	30	65
3. Post-shift monolingual, English	31	15	48
Total	103	65	63

65 of the 103 writers and speakers produced forms exhibiting non-standard-like variation. These data show how the prevalence of non-standard forms changes as writers and speakers shift from monolingual German, to bilingual, to monolingual English. All monolingual German writers and speakers produce non-standard-like forms, where only 65% of the bilinguals do (regardless of whether they are German or English dominant), and finally, of those who are post-shift monolingual English speakers, only 48% produced non-standard-like forms indicative of variation in VOT or FON.

Of the 103 speakers/writers considered here, 38 did not produce any non-standard forms indicative of variation in VOT or FON. The distribution of their language dominance is shown in Table 11.

Chapter 10. Language dominance across the lifespan in Wisconsin German and English   253

Table 11. Speakers and writers exhibiting only standard-like forms, by language dominance

	Language of data collection			Total
	German	English	Both	
1. Pre-shift monolingual, German	0	0	0	0
2a. Bilingual, German dominant	3	2	1	6
2b. Bilingual, English dominant	0	14	2	16
3. Post-shift monolingual, English	0	16	0	16
	3	32	3	38

Unexpectedly, there are no writers in the "pre-shift monolingual, German" group who exhibit only standard-like forms. In other words, all the pre-shift monolingual Germans, who would not be expected to experience variation due to change in personal language shift, exhibit non-standard orthographic representations. This may indicate that German orthographic conventions are more likely to show variation, perhaps more so in this particular setting, where heritage communities are far from the standardizing/homogenizing forces in Europe and where competing spelling norms are present in a variety of settings other than just schools (see Section 2).

The following considers the distribution of non-standard forms by language. Speakers and writers exhibiting non-standard like forms in German by level of language dominance and type of feature are shown in Table 12.

Table 12. Speakers and writers exhibiting non-standard-like forms in German, by type of feature and language dominance

	Non-standard-like forms indicative of:			Total
	VOT	Both	FON	
1. Pre-shift monolingual, German	1	6	2	9
2a. Bilingual, German dominant	0	4	7	11
2b. Bilingual, English dominant	1	9	1	11
3. Post-shift monolingual, English	n/a	n/a	n/a	n/a
	2	19	10	31

Of the speakers and writers who do exhibit non-standard-like forms indicative of VOT or FON, nine belong to the pre-shift monolingual German speaking group, and eleven each to the bilingual groups. This distribution shows that those who are bilingual and German dominant are just as likely to exhibit non-standard-like forms in their German writing or speech as those who are bilingual and English dominant. While non-standard-like representations of variation in VOT only are very rare (happening only three times in this data), two of those are found in the German data. Nineteen speakers and writers exhibit variation in both VOT and FON, with six belonging to the pre-shift monolingual German group, four to the bilingual, German dominant group, and the largest belonging to the bilingual, English dominant group. While non-standard-like representations of variation in FON alone are not rare, of the ten speakers and writers exhibiting variation in FON only, seven are bilingual, German dominant.

The following shows the use of non-standard forms in English. The distribution by type of feature and level of language dominance is shown in Table 13.

Table 13. Speakers and writers exhibiting non-standard-like forms in English, by language dominance*

	Non-standard-like forms indicative of:			Total
	VOT	Both	FON	
1. Pre-shift monolingual, German	n/a	n/a	n/a	n/a
2a. Bilingual, German dominant	0	0	0	0
2b. Bilingual, English dominant	1	17	7	25
3. Post-shift monolingual, English	0	7	8	15
Total	1	24	15	40

* Six speakers and writers produced non-standard-like forms in both German and English, and they are included in the overall count twice. This is why the combined total of speakers and writers listed in Tables 11, 12, and 13 is 109, rather than 103.

Table 13 reveals several interesting findings. First, although there are relatively few speakers or writers classified as bilingual, German dominant, three produced data in both German and English. Therefore, it is possible in principle for non-standard forms to exist in this category. That there are none in this corpus may be due to there only being 3 writers who fit the category and therefore having produced fewer data points, for example, or that these writers were more aware of their German dominance and therefore spent special attention on filtering out non-standard forms (see Özaslan & Gabriel 2019 for a similar description of the effect of metalinguistic awareness on phonological production in bilinguals). The largest amount of variation shows up in the group categorized as bilingual, English dominant. As this group is made up of writers and speakers who are post-shift from L1 to L2, this might explain why so many exhibit variations in this category.

As the shift is completed, the group of monolingual English speakers exists in a community where English is the dominant language both at home and in society (education, media, etc.). These sociolinguistic changes seem to correlate with fewer speakers and writers exhibiting variation than in the bilingual groups.

6.2 A closer look at the written data

Because the expanse and duration of the written data is spread more evenly across more people and a longer time frame, this section takes a closer look at the written data only.

89 writers produced data considered here. Of 51 writers who produced non-standard orthographic forms indicative of variation in VOT or FON, only one produced non-standard-like forms in both German and English, although eight produced data in both languages. Three produced orthographic representations of VOT only, 24 produced orthographic variants suggesting FON only, and 24 produced orthographic representations suggesting both VOT and FON, as shown in Table 14.

Table 14. Number of writers producing non-standard orthographic variations by language and type of feature

Language	\multicolumn{3}{c	}{Non-standard-like forms indicative of:}	Total
	VOT	Both	FON	
German	2	11	14	27
German & English	0	0	1	1
English	1	13	9	23
Total	3	24	24	51

Of the 24 who produced orthographic variation of both VOT and FON, 13 exhibited orthographic variations in English only, and eleven in German only. Among these, is a subset of six writers who produced data in both German and English, but who exhibit non-standard-like orthographic forms produced in one language only. Of these six, three produced orthographic representations in English and three in German. However, none produced non-standard orthographic representations in more than one language, despite having produced texts in both languages, which indicates that language dominance, duration of contact, or age of onset of bilingualism may play an important role. Of the other 18 writers of this group who produced data in one language only, 8 produced non-standard orthographic representations only in German, 10 only in English.

What is notable about the group that produced non-standard orthographic forms suggesting both VOT and FON in German is that six are categorized as pre-shift monolingual German speakers. Therefore, for these writers, there was likely no bilingual component or language dominance component involved. Of the ten who produced nonstandard orthographic forms only in English, eight are categorized as bilingual, English dominant speakers, and the remaining two are as monolingual English speakers. Seven of the eight, born between 1864 and 1880, produced their texts while classified as young adults, which may indicate a shift in language dominance, or at least in preferred or practiced language use. While having grown up German dominant, these bilinguals or presumed bilinguals are writing and producing non-standard orthographic representations of L2 phonology indicative of VOT and FON in their L2, English, an expected effect of bilingual acquisition after childhood (see Chapter 5 in this volume).

Returning to the writers who produced non-standard orthographic representations only either syllable-finally or syllable-initially, three exhibited word initial forms, and 24 syllable finally. This tells us that word initial variation is less frequent than word final.[14] Of the 3, one exhibits this variation in English (categorized as bilingual, English dominant), the other two in German (one categorized as pre-shift monolingual German, the other as bilingual, English dominant). There appear to be no other commonalities (age, sex, generation) among this group.

Of the 24 who produced non-standard orthographic representations indicative of FON only, nine do so in German, fourteen in English, and one does in both German and English.

If we consider language dominance for this group, of those producing non-standard-like orthographic representations syllable-finally in German, two are categorized as pre-shift monolingual German, seven as bilingual, German dominant, and the last – who is also the only writer to produce non-standard-like forms in both languages – is categorized as bilingual, English dominant. Of those who produced syllable-final non-standard-like orthographic representations in English, seven are categorized as bilingual, English dominant (including the writer who also produced forms in German), and eight as post-shift monolingual, English. Those who were bilingual, English dominant or monolingual English speakers would have been educated in English schools and therefore had more experience with expected orthographic norms.

To summarize the evidence presented in this section, the overall prevalence of non-standard forms follows the community shift from monolingual German to bilingual to monolingual English. As a percentage, more of the monolingual German writers produced non-standard forms than any other group, which then

---

14. See Chapter 3 in this volume for a discussion of variability in L2 production.

decreases for those identified as bilingual (regardless of language dominance) and then decreases again with the shift from bilingual to monolingual English. This indicates that the most variation was found first among monolinguals who were themselves immigrants and living in a country where their L1 was not the societally dominant language (although perhaps dominant in their individual communities). The speakers/writers who were bilingual may have been less likely to produce nonstandard forms than German monolinguals, but they were more likely to produce nonstandard forms than English monolinguals (who were post shift and living in society dominated by English). This evidence suggests that these bilingual speakers were in a period of shift, navigating variation in their language use just as their communities were navigating a shift from German to English. From a bilingual acquisition perspective that sees language dominance across the lifespan as a dynamic dimension, the distribution of spellings suggestive of VOT or FON appears to respond to community trends shaped by bilingual acquisition after childhood. Most of the bilingual, English dominant group that produced nonstandard orthographic forms in English only were young adults, who may have had relatively little contact with English at that time, may have recently shifted or were undergoing the transition from German dominant to English dominant.

7. Language acquisition and the historical sociolinguistics of VOT and FON in Wisconsin German and English

Historical sociolinguistic research often builds on the *uniformitarian principle*, or the assumption adapted from the natural sciences that forces producing change today are the same as those of the past (see Labov 1972: 275). Therefore, historical sociolinguistics frequently use modern analysis techniques or data from modern studies as comparanda for historical evidence. For example, while modern sociophonetic studies might be designed for a particular group of consultants, or to illicit a particular set of tasks, they can also be applied to the analysis of historical recordings.

The present study illustrates how historical researchers can be informed by modern studies on VOT or FON in present-day bilingual communities. While we might not expect to find the same values in these communities as in historical data, we might expect to find similar patterns, such as bilingual speakers producing VOTs which are like neither language when spoken by a monolingual, but rather taking up some middle ground (Thomas 2011). For instance, Nagy et al. (2014) studied VOT in several heritage language communities in Toronto. They found that Italian speakers did not differ from homeland speakers over three generations, but for Russian and Ukrainian speakers VOT got longer over each generation, becoming more similar with English. These types of variation among languages and heritage groups opens many new avenues in historical sociolinguistics, particularly relevant for the study of Wisconsin German and English over time. The fact that these historical recordings and documents exist makes the work possible, but it also means researchers are faced with some challenges as well. In the case of these Wisconsin data, the overall picture that emerges is that bilingual speakers who were exposed to English during their childhood or whose dominance shifted to English in adulthood often still exhibit nonstandard forms in both languages well after their language dominance had shifted (especially evident in the spoken data). On the other hand, bilingual speakers who were exposed to English late or who remained dominant in German as adults tend to be more likely to exhibit variation of nonstandard forms in the L1, but not in their L2 (German), which may be due to language shift in the broader community or less availability of contact to German outside of their local communities. This form of phonological variability in speakers of various bilingual profiles and with different acquisitional histories is reminiscent of the conditions leading to the emergence of local varieties in other immigration heritage communities (see Chapter 6 in this volume).

Many of the challenges involved in incorporating a lifespan acquisition perspective in the sociohistorical study of language variation and change are very similar here as in other chapters of this volume: transparent acquisitional data for historical periods are lacking, extant archival materials are of limited social representativeness, and written materials do not capture the degree of linguistic (here, phonetic) detail that audio recordings may afford. As regards these historical communities of Wisconsin German and English speakers, an added difficulty in reconstructing language acquisition contexts and gauging individual levels of language dominance posthumously comes into play. For the modern recordings, made in 2013, the speakers were asked specifically about their language use and shifts in preferred usage over their lifetimes. For the older recordings, these questions were not recorded, meaning that both language status (monolingual, bilingual, bilingual post community shift, etc.) and language dominance (German vs. English) must be determined in other ways. For some, language status as a bilingual was easily determined because the speaker or writer produced language samples in both languages. In other cases, bilingual status could be assumed based on interactions with known monolinguals. Overall, these classification protocols show that historical sociophoneticians, as well as other historical researchers, must get creative in order to replicate the categories used in current research to analyze their data.

Language acquisition research, particularly as applies to heritage speakers, is an additional factor which can be expected to influence future historical sociolinguistic studies. For example, dominance shift is described as leading to lower confidence and therefore less usage of the heritage language (Sevinç & Backus 2017). While not considered as a factor in this study on Wisconsin German and English speakers, it is conceivable that less usage of the heritage language could impact VOT or FON.

8. Conclusion

Combining written with audio data offers a much deeper historical picture than one data type alone, allowing us to integrate historical sociolinguistics with sociophonetics in a new way. As suggested elsewhere in this volume (e.g., Chapters 2 and 4), language dominance can be used as a factor to tease out variation in written and spoken data across different groups of German and English speakers in Wisconsin and to shed new light on the development of these regional features.

Sixty-three percent of the speakers and writers analyzed here produce data showing variation in VOT/syllable-initial tokens and FON/syllable-final tokens. Accounting for language used and language dominance shows the greatest variation occurs among pre-shift monolingual German speakers, with 100% of those analyzed producing non-standard-like forms. This decreases to 65% for bilingual speakers, and to 48% for monolingual English speakers. This overall decrease in variation from monolingual German-speaking immigrants to subsequent generations becoming bilingual in German and English and finally to the last generations completing the shift to English mirrors the societal shift from German-speaking immigrants existing in monolingual domains, to bilingual communities, and finally to monolingual English dominant communities. In addition, the largest number of speakers and writers who produced non-standard-like forms in English belong to the bilingual, English dominant group, suggesting that variation is most common in speakers and writers who are completing the shift from language dominance in their L1 to their L2.

Finally, results show that variation in VOT/syllable-initial forms alone is rare, regardless of language or language dominance. Overall, non-standard-like forms suggesting variation both syllable-initially and syllable-finally are most prevalent among bilinguals who are English dominant in the audio and written data used in the present study. Speakers and writers exhibiting non-standard-like forms only syllable-finally increases with the shift from monolingual German, to bilingual, to monolingual English. This shift suggests that other features were more noticed across a community level, and perhaps even community externally, resulting in widespread adaption to English norms, whereas syllable-final variation/final obstruent neutralization more broadly went unnoticed or unstigmatized within Wisconsin, allowing for this variation to increase as Wisconsin communities shifted from German to English dominant.

Funding

This research is supported by a Postdoctoral Research Fellowship through the Alexander von Humboldt Foundation.

Acknowledgements

In addition to the audiences at the Historical Sociolinguistics Network (HiSoN) Conference held at the Universidad de Murcia in June 2022, I thank two anonymous reviewers, and the editor of this volume for discussions and suggestions. Any remaining shortcomings are my own.

References

Archival sources (written)

Krueger Collection. Wisconsin Historical Society Library and Archives. Madison, WI.
Goth Collection. Max Kade Institute for German-American Studies. Madison, WI.

Archival sources (audio)

Helene Stratman-Thomas Collection. 1937–1946. Wisconsin Folksong Collection, Mills Music Library, University of Wisconsin-Madison. Madison, WI.
Lester W.J. "Smoky" Seifert Collection. 1945–1949. Sound Archives of the Max Kade Institute for German-American Studies. Madison, WI.
Litty-Evans Collection. 2013. Wisconsin German Project, Sound Archives of the Max Kade Institute for German-American Studies. Madison, WI.

Secondary sources

Alba, Richard. 2004. Language assimilation today: Bilingualism persists more than in the past, but English still dominates. https://escholarship.org/uc/item/0j5865nk (21 December 2022).
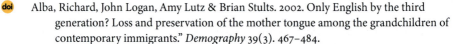Alba, Richard, John Logan, Amy Lutz & Brian Stults. 2002. Only English by the third generation? Loss and preservation of the mother tongue among the grandchildren of contemporary immigrants." *Demography* 39(3). 467–484.

Ali, Ahmed Abdellaty, Jan Van der Spiegel & Paul Mueller. 2001. Robust classification of stop consonants using auditory-based speech processing. In *Acoustics, Speech, and Signal Processing: Proceedings ICASSP'01*, 81–84.

Allen, Sean, Joanne Miller & David DeSteno. 2003. Individual talker differences in voice–onset–time. *The Journal of the Acoustical Society of America* 113(1). 544–552.

Angelowa, Tanja & Bernd Pompino-Marschall. 1985. Zur akustischen Struktur initialer Plosiv-Vokal-Silben im Deutschen und Bulgarischen. *Forschungsbericht des Instituts für Phonetik und Sprachliche Kommunikation der Universität München* 21. 83–96.

Auer, Anita, Catharina Peersman, Simon Pickl, Gijsbert Rutten & Rik Vosters. 2015. Historical sociolinguistics: the field and its future. *Journal of Historical Sociolinguistics* 1(1). 1–12.

Bagwell, Angela, Samantha Litty & Mike Olson. 2019. Wisconsin immigrant letters: German influence and imposition on Wisconsin English. In Raymond Hickey (ed.), *Keeping in Touch. Emigrant Letters across the English-speaking World*, 27–41. Amsterdam: John Benjamins.

Blumstein, Sheila, Emily Myers & Jesse Rissman. 2005. The perception of voice onset time: an fMRI investigation of phonetic category structure. *Journal of Cognitive Neuroscience* 17(9). 1353–1366.

Boersma, Paul & David Weenink. 2022. Praat: doing phonetics by computer [Computer program]. Version 6.2.09. http://www.praat.org/ (20 February 2022).

Bousquette, Joshua. 2020. From bidialectal to bilingual: Evidence for two-stage language shift in Lester W. J. 'Smoky' Seifert's 1946–1949 Wisconsin German Recordings. *American Speech* 95(4). 485–523.

Chen, Matthew. 1970. Vowel length variation as a function of the voicing of the consonant environment. *Phonetica* 22(3). 129–159.

Dmtrieva, Olga, Allard Jongman & Joan Sereno. 2010. Phonological neutralization by native and non-native speakers: The case of Russian final devoicing. *Journal of Phonetics* 38(3). 483–492.

Eichhoff, Jürgen. 1971. German in Wisconsin. In Glenn Gilbert (ed.), *The German language in America: A symposium*. Austin: University of Texas Press, 43–57.

Elspaß, Stephan. 2012. The use of private letters and diaries in sociolinguistic investigation. In Juan Manuel Hernández-Campoy & Juan Camilo Conde-Silvestre (eds.), *The handbook of historical sociolinguistics*, 156–169. Malden, MA: Wiley-Blackwell.

Fishman, Joshua. 1972. *The sociology of language*. Rowley: Newbury.

Frey, Benjamin. 2013. Toward a general theory of language shift: A case study in Wisconsin German and North Carolina Cherokee. Madison, WI: University of Wisconsin. PhD dissertation.

Geiger, Stephen & Joseph Salmons. 2006. Reconstructing variation at shallow time depths.: The historical phonetics of 19th century German dialects in the U.S. In Thomas Cravens (ed.), *Variation and reconstruction*, 37–58. Amsterdam: John Benjamins.

Hickey, Raymond (ed.). 2017. *Listening to the past: Audio records of accents of English*. Cambridge: Cambridge University Press.

Hirsh, Ira. 1959. Auditory perception of temporal order. *The Journal of the Acoustical Society of America* 31(6). 759–767.

Howell, Robert. 1993. German immigration and the development of regional variants of American English: Using contact theory to discover our roots. In Joseph Salmons (ed.), *The German language in America: 1683–1991*, 188–212. Madison, WI: Max Kade Institute.

Iverson, Gregory & Joseph Salmons. 1995. Aspiration and laryngeal representation in Germanic. *Phonology* 12(3). 369–396.

Iverson, Gregory & Joseph Salmons. 2011. Final devoicing and final laryngeal neutralization. In Marc Van Oostendorp, Colin Ewen, Elizabeth Hume & Keren Rice (eds.), *The Blackwell companion to phonology*, 1622–1643. Malden, MA: Wiley-Blackwell.

Jessen, Michael. 1998. *Phonetics and phonology of tense and lax obstruents in German*. Amsterdam: John Benjamins.

Keating, Patricia. 1984. Phonetic and phonological representation of stop consonant voicing. *Language* 60(2). 286–319.

Khattab, Ghada. 2002. VOT production in English and Arabic bilingual and monolingual children. In Dilworth Parkinson & Elabbas Benmamoun (eds.), *Perspectives on Arabic linguistics: Papers from the Annual Symposium on Arabic Linguistics*, 1–37. Amsterdam: John Banjamins.

Labov, William. 1972. *Sociolinguistic patterns*. Philadelphia: University of Pennsylvania Press.

Lisker, Leigh & Arthur Abramson. 1964. A cross-language study of voicing in initial stops: Acoustical measurements. *Word* 20(3). 384–422.

Litty, Samantha. 2014. Stop. Hey, what's that sound? Initial VOT in Wisconsin German and English. Paper presented at the 20th Annual Germanic Linguistics Annual Conference (GLAC), May 2–3, 2014. Purdue University, West Lafayette, Indiana.

Litty, Samantha, Christine Evans & Joseph Salmons. 2015. Gray zones: The fluidity of Wisconsin German language and identification. In Peter Rosenberg (ed.), *Linguistic construction of ethnic borders*, 183–205. Frankfurt: Peter Lang.

Litty, Samantha. 2017a. A turn of the century courtship. *Sociolinguistica* 31(1). 83–100.

Litty, Samantha. 2017b. We talk German now yet: The sociolinguistic development of voice onset time and final obstruent neutralization in Wisconsin German and English varieties, 1863–2013. Madison, WI: University of Wisconsin. PhD dissertation.

Litty, Samantha. 2019. Letters home: German-American Civil War soldiers' letters 1864–1865. *Journal of Historical Sociolinguistics* 5(2). 1–34.

Litty, Samantha, Jennifer Mercer & Joseph Salmons. 2019. Early immigrant English: Midwestern English before the dust settled. In Sandra Jansen, Markus Huber & Lucia Siebers (eds.), *Processes of change in English: Studies in Late Modern and present-day English*, 115–137. Amsterdam: John Benjamins.

Litty, Samantha. 2022. Historical sociolinguistic contexts: Networks and feature availability in 19th-century German letter collections. In Kelly Biers & Joshua Brown (eds.), *Selected Proceedings of the 11th Annual Workshop on Immigrant Languages in the Americas (WILA 11)*, 40–47. Somerville, MA: Cascadilla.

Litty, Samantha. Forthcoming. The German Midwest. In Jon Lauck (ed.), *The Oxford Handbook of Midwestern History*. Oxford: Oxford University Press.

Nagy, Naomi, Joanna Chociej & Michol Hoffman. 2014. Analyzing ethnic orientation in the quantitative sociolinguistic paradigm. *Language & Communication* 35. 9–26.

Niyogi, Partha & Padma Ramesh. 1998. Incorporating voice onset time to improve letter recognition accuracies. In *Proceedings of the 1998 IEEE International Conference on Acoustics, Speech and Signal Processing, 1998.* Volume 1, 13–16.

Nove, Chaya. 2021. Outcomes of language contact in New York Hasidic Yiddish. In Christian Zimmer (ed.), *German(ic) in language contact: Grammatical and sociolinguistic dynamics*, 43–71. Berlin: Language Science Press.

Olson, Daniel. 2013. Bilingual language switching and selection at the phonetic level: Asymmetrical transfer in VOT production. *Journal of Phonetics* 41(6). 407–420.

Özaslan, Merve & Christoph Gabriel. 2019. Final obstruent devoicing in English and French as foreign languages: Comparing monolingual German and bilingual Turkish-German learners. In Christoph Gabriel, Jonas Grünke & Sylvia Thiele (eds.), *Romanische Sprachen in ihrer Vielfalt: Brückenschläge zwischen linguistischer Theoriebildung und Fremdsprachenunterricht*, 177–209. Stuttgart: ibidem.

Purnell, Thomas, Joseph Salmons & Dilara Tepeli. 2005a. German substrate effects in Wisconsin English: Evidence for final fortition. *American Speech* 80(2). 135–164.

Purnell, Thomas, Joseph Salmons, Dilara Tepeli & Jennifer Mercer. 2005b. Structured heterogeneity and change in laryngeal phonetics Upper Midwestern final obstruents. *Journal of English Linguistics* 33(4). 307–338.

Seifert, Lester. 1993. The development and survival of the German language in Pennsylvania and Wisconsin. In Joseph Salmons (ed.), *The German language in America*, 322–337. Madison, WI: Max Kade Institute for German-American Studies, University of Wisconsin-Madison.

Sevinç, Yeşim & Ad Backus. 2017. Anxiety, language use and linguistic competence in an immigrant context: a vicious circle? *International Journal of Bilingual Education and Bilingualism* 22(3). 706–724.

Stevens, Kenneth & Dennis Klatt. 1974. Role of formant transitions in the voiced-voiceless distinction for stops. *The Journal of the Acoustical Society of America* 55(3). 653–659.

Stoehr, Antje, Titia Benders, Janet Van Hell & Paula Fikkert. 2017. Second language attainment and first language attrition: The case of VOT in immersed Dutch-German late bilinguals. *Second Language Research* 33(4). 483–518.

Taylor, Dennis. 1975. The inadequacy of bipolarity and distinctive features: the German "voiced/voiceless" consonants. In Peter Reich (ed.), *Second LACUS forum*, 107–119. Chicago: Chicago Linguistic Circle.

Thomas, Erik. 2011. *Sociophonetics: An introduction*. London: Palgrave Macmillan.

Trudgill, Peter. 2004. *New-dialect formation: The inevitability of colonial Englishes*. Oxford: Oxford University Press.

Wilkerson, Miranda & Joseph Salmons. 2008. "Good old immigrants of yesteryear," who didn't learn English: Germans in Wisconsin. *American Speech*. 83(3). 259–283.

Wilkerson, Miranda & Joseph Salmons. 2012. Linguistic marginalities: Becoming American without learning English. *Journal of Transnational American Studies* 4(2). https://escholarship.org/uc/item/5vn092kk

Wright, Laura (ed.). 2006. *The development of Standard English, 1300–1800: Theories, descriptions, conflicts*. Cambridge: Cambridge University Press.

CHAPTER 11

The contact origin(s) of 'hand' and 'foot' > 'limb' in Antioquian Spanish
Tracing historical adult L1 transfer

Eliot Raynor
Princeton University

This study examines the semantic extension of *mano* 'hand' and *pie* 'foot' to their contemporary senses of 'upper limb' and 'lower limb' in Spanish varieties of Antioquia, Colombia. This dialectally idiosyncratic pattern, hitherto unexplained in the literature, is accounted for here as the combined outcome of adult acquisition among various groups. First, Chocoan languages predominating in the region throughout the early colonial period show a congruent pattern in the lexemes for 'upper limb' (e.g., Embera Chamí *húa*) and 'lower limb' (e.g., Embera Catío *hḗrṹ*), and their speakers plausibly initiated the change via L1 transfer. Chroniclers' accounts also reveal that Antioquia's earliest Europeans relied heavily upon enslaved African(-descendants), and records of ships carrying enslaved peoples to the nearby port cities demonstrate that much of the African-born population in 16th-century Antioquia spoke languages with congruent patterns also (e.g., Kikongo *kóoko* 'upper limb' and *kúulu* 'lower limb'). It is proposed that adult Spanish learners with these L1s reinforced the innovative variant.

Keywords: Spanish, language contact, naturalistic second language acquisition, transfer, Chocoan, Bantu, Caboverdianu, Kriyol

1. Introduction

The present study explores the sociohistorical and acquisitional conditions that led to the restructuring of body part reference in the Spanish of Antioquia, Colombia. The pattern under analysis consists of the use of lexical items *mano* 'hand' and *pie* 'foot' for the entire limbs, which would typically be expressed with the lexemes *brazo* 'arm' and *pierna* 'leg', as exemplified in (1)–(4), extracted from the *Corpus Sociolingüístico de Medellín* (PRESEEA 2014):

(1) Me   quebré la **mano** derecha y   me   pusieron yeso.
     REFL.1s broke the **hand** right   and DAT.1s put.3P cast
     'I broke my right **hand/arm** and they put a cast on it for me.'[1]

(2) Se   me partió la carne del **pie** izquierdo al   lado de la rodilla.
     REFL DAT opened the skin of.the **foot** left   to.the side of the knee
     'The skin of my left **leg** was cut open along the side of my knee.'

This variant co-occurs with the canonical Spanish lexemes for the limbs *brazo* 'arm' and *pierna* 'leg', which appear in the same corpus.

(3) Ya   la tenía   en mis **brazos** una bebé.
     already her had.1s   in my **arms** a   baby
     'I already had her in my arms, a baby.'

(4) Las **piernas** a mí no me   respondían.
     the **legs**   to me not DAT.1s respond
     'My legs weren't responding to me.'

Here I propose that the extension of *mano* and *pie* in Antioquia, uncharacteristic of other Spanish varieties, emerged diachronically through language contact – specifically L1 transfer during adult language acquisition (see Chapters 4 and 5 in this volume) – as opposed to a language-internal mechanism such as metonymy, the latter having been proposed in a few similar cases (see Wilkins 1996: 275ff on Proto-Austronesian > Palauan, among others). The details provided below of the sociohistorical-acquisitional context of Antioquia provide a window into the development of an idiosyncratic pattern arising from a previously undescribed historical language contact scenario.[2]

---

1. Here an ambiguous reading is given, though the full context of the utterance illustrates more clearly that this reference is to the upper limb in its entirety. The transcript is as follows, my translation, with parenthesis to clarify which Spanish lexeme was used in each context:

(i) A: I broke my **hand/arm** (*mano*), I broke my **hand/arm** (*mano*) and they put a cast on it for me [...]

B: What would have happened if you had broken both **legs** (*piernas*), both **hands/arms** (*manos*)?

A: Uh, what would have happened? Well I'd be in the hospital for longer not able to do anything, without moving, there in the beds, laying there, even more bored because without being able to move my **arm** (*brazo*) now not able to move anything.

A's reference to the same injured limb with both *mano* and *brazo*, we see that the former has extended its typical referential denotation.

2. 'Idiosyncratic' here is not intended to mean unique, since this feature is generalized among Spanish varieties across northwestern Colombia beyond the department of Antioquia (see

Demographic and sociohistorical data is available for early colonial Antioquia via Spanish chroniclers' accounts of the earliest settlements in the region in the 16th century (Cieza de León 1864 [1553]; Núñez de Balboa 1864 [1515]; Robledo 1864 [1539]), as well as from the *Transatlantic Slave Trade Database* (Voyages Database 2009). The picture painted by these materials is further strengthened by 18th-century census data from Antioquia, which demonstrate that *blancos* 'whites' – European-descendant L1 Spanish speakers – were vastly outnumbered demographically by *esclavos de varios colores* 'enslaved people of all colors', *libres de varios colores* 'free people of all colors', and *indios* 'people of Amerindian origin' (Tovar Pinzón et al. 1994: 102–123). Overall, these sources paint a history of socially pervasive adult language learning throughout the colonial period.

Evidence points to a scenario leading to *substratum transfer through shift* (Thomason & Kaufman 1988: 38–43), a subtype of the general process of pattern replication or transfer in adult second language acquisition (Matras & Sakel 2007; Odlin 1989). In this scenario, congruent body partonomies from relevant substrate languages – Amerindian languages such as Embera, and West African languages including Kikongo – were replicated in Antioquian Spanish by way of community-wide language shift(s) during the colonial era. Linking the synchronic data from Antioquia to the development of new varieties through diverse contexts of naturalistic second language acquisition, as discussed in Winford (2020), the present chapter demonstrates that substrate influence may originate via the interaction of speakers of genetically and/or typologically diverse languages that nonetheless share a congruent pattern absent in the L1 colonial variety.

Theoretically, this chapter applies the reasoning that, under certain social circumstances, adult L2 learners may be critical agents in the emergence of a new language variety.[3] Methodologically, approaching language change in the past requires selecting a set of theoretically-sound principles and methods. In this case study, research on language contact and L2 acquisition is combined with sociohistorical insights derived from chroniclers' accounts and other rich archival materials. This chapter offers a first attempt to account for the semantic pattern described above, painting a picture of language usage and learning in colonial Antioquia. The chapter also provides a plausible hypothesis for the derivation of 'hand' / 'arm' > 'limb', an otherwise unattested feature of contemporary Antioquian Spanish, the origins of which point to language contact and L1 transfer through shift in 16th-century New Granada (present-day Colombia).

Raynor 2017, 2021). It has not, however, been discussed by other authors nor is it attested in any varieties outside of the immediately contiguous area.

3. See Chapters 3, 5 and 6 in this volume for further discussion of theory supporting this approach, as well as Chapters 10 and 12 for other case studies in this volume that study the action of adult L2 speakers in other cases of language contact and change.

This chapter is structured as follows: Section 2 weighs the evidence concerning the languages spoken by the Amerindian population of Antioquia at the time of Spanish colonization. Section 3 uses archival accounts to portray first-hand depictions of early colonial Antioquia. Section 4 considers the data regarding the West African(-descendant) population in Antioquia in the 16th century and broader demographic trends carrying on through the 18th century. Section 5 provides lexical data on limb partonomy for the relevant Amerindian and West African substrate languages. Section 6 combines the perspectives of language acquisition and historical sociolinguistics to re-analyze the context of variation and change in which the variant under discussion originated. A brief conclusion is provided in Section 7 to highlight some of the more significant linguistic and sociohistorical findings of the chapter, also suggesting limitations to the present study and areas of future research.

2. Amerindian populations of northwestern Colombia

Spanish conquistadors arrived along the Caribbean and Pacific lowland areas of present-day Colombia and began to make their way toward the Andean highlands in the early 16th century. For this early period, there are no clear estimates of how many languages may have been spoken in Colombia, but those languages with the most vitality today are found in the extreme west and east, the dense rainforests of the Pacific lowlands and in the Amazon, respectively, the latter being outside the scope of the present chapter. In terms of genetic affiliation, at the time of conquest the indigenous languages of western half of the country belonged primarily to the Chibchan (e.g., Kuna, Muisca) and Chocoan families (see highlighted areas in Maps 1 and 2, respectively), but also included Barbacoan languages and several isolates such as Nasa Yuwe (further discussed in Section 5). The Chibchan language-speaking communities in northwestern Colombia, particularly the Kuna, declined significantly in this region during the colonial period, having been displaced into the Darien region of Panama by Chocoan groups and Spanish conquistadors by the early 18th century (Vargas Sarmiento 1993; Werner Cantor 2000; Williams 2004).

The present analysis makes no argument that *contemporary* contact between speakers of Spanish and Amerindian languages contributed to the semantic change in Antioquia discussed here, given the degree to which the former group far outsizes the latter. Rather, sociohistorical evidence indicates that in northwestern Colombia, the demographic disproportion in the early colonial period was the inverse, with Amerindians vastly outnumbering Europeans even as Spanish language use expanded among the indigenous population.

Map 1. Geographic distribution of Chibchan languages[4]

Map 2. Geographic distribution of Chocoan languages[5]

As demonstrated in Map 2, the Chocoan family is in large part concentrated in the Pacific lowlands, but also reaches into the largely highland province of Antioquia in northwestern Colombia. The Chocoan languages Embera Chamí and Embera Catío are used as native languages today by sizeable communities near the municipalities of Jardín and Ituango, roughly 150 km south and north, respectively, of Antioquia's capital Medellín. The areas highlighted in red in Maps 3 and 4, reproduced from Breogan2008 (2022a, b) show the approximate distribution of speakers of these two Chocoan varieties at present.

A significant consideration, and some debate (Herrera Ángel 2017), surround the size and density of pre-Columbian peoples of northwestern Colombia. Parsons (1949: 29) argues that "[p]opulation estimates for aboriginal Colombia have generally been unrealistically low […]. Yet the overwhelming evidence of the early chronicles, the incredibly numerous Indian graves (*guacas*), and the extensive old fields all point to a very dense peopling of the Antioqueño country." This author estimates that in the northwestern corner of the region (Urabá) alone "there were at least 300,000 inhabitants at the time of the Conquest" (1949: 30).

---

4. Reproduced with Creative Commons (CC) CC0 1.0 Universal Public Domain Dedication. https://creativecommons.org/publicdomain/zero/1.0/deed.en.

5. Reproduced with Creative Commons (CC) CC0 1.0 Universal Public Domain Dedication.

Chapter 11. The contact origin(s) of 'hand' and 'foot' > 'limb' in Antioquian Spanish   269

Map 3. Contemporary distribution of Embera Chamí speakers[6]

Map 4. Contemporary distribution of Embera Catío speakers[7]

The limitations to our knowledge about Amerindian communities residing in the present-day department of Antioquia at first contact with Europeans are not unique to northwestern Colombia. These gaps in information are exacerbated, however, by a setting that was distinct from those that characterized early colonial Peru and New Spain (Mexico), where the existence of the massive pre-Columbian empires reinforced the notion of monolithic ethnolinguistic ecologies in those colonies. Broadly speaking, when the Spanish arrived in northwestern South America, they did not encounter large, sedentary, hierarchically structured indigenous societies there as they had in the Peru and Mexico. However, the coastlines, riverbeds, and cordilleras of the western half of Colombia were some

---

6. Reproduced with Creative Commons (CC) Attribution-ShareAlike 4.0 International license. https://creativecommons.org/licenses/by-sa/4.0/deed.en.

7. Reproduced with Creative Commons (CC) Attribution-ShareAlike 4.0 International license.

of the earliest areas explored and written about by Spanish chroniclers in South America. As such, there is a wealth of primary material in the diaries and letters of conquistadors, priests, and chroniclers from the first half of the 16th century to documenting and laying claim to the lands and lives of the peoples they came across in their early *entradas*. Some of these writings are set forth and summarized below to demonstrate the continuous presence of Chocoan speaking peoples in Antioquia from earliest European contacts.

Restrepo Tirado (1892: 3–25) used chroniclers' accounts to enumerate the names of indigenous groups and their leaders by contemporary department, noting ethnolinguistic overlap where present. In general, the impression Restrepo Tirado gives of the earliest Spanish colonists' experiences in Antioquia is one of "wonder and pleasant surprise" at the "innumerable populations" of indigenous peoples (15, my translation). Restrepo Tirado notes that "[O]n the banks of the Cauca River, the Spanish found [...] populations extending beyond view under the domain of the Cacique *Nutibara*, to whom all those residing in the valley up to the Abibe mountain ridge paid tribute" (9–10, italics in original, my translation).[8]

Approaching the region of what would become the colonial capital of Antioquia – in colonial documents referred to simply as 'Antioquia', now 'Santa Fe de Antioquia' – Restrepo Tirado (1892) describes the 'valle de Buriticá' as a particularly dense area of population, stating that between Antioquia and Buriticá there were many houses as well as a large town (16). Another ethnonym Restrepo Tirado points out that is easily traced to the department of Antioquia is Ituango, described as having a population of 100 houses (16). Ituango is the name of a small municipality in northern Antioquia, notably in close proximity to the Jaidukama *resguardo* 'reservation', where an Embera (Catío)-speaking indigenous community resides (Imbett et al. 2018).

In summary, Restrepo Tirado (1892: 18) provides a tripartite division of the ethnolinguistic affiliations of the groups living in Antioquia at the time of Spanish arrival, between: (i) Catíos, who were "situated on lands comprising the western edge of the Cauca [River] and the Serranía de Abibe"; (ii) Nutabes, between the Cauca River and the Porce River; and (iii) the Tahamíes, between the Porce River and the Magdalena River. Restrepo Tirado's Catío group is one of the two macro-dialects of the Embera language (see Loewen 1960); the region this author

---

8. Of particular note in this passage is the name Nutibara, which is the name borne now by a small mountain (Cerro Nutibara) that sits in the center of Medellín, capital of Antioquia. As for the other (non-italicized) name in the above quotation, Abibe, Restrepo continues: "[t]he Cacique of Abibe was independent and had his capital on the side of the mountain of the same name" (10). Here of geographic note is the Serranía de Abibe, part of the northwestern extreme of the western cordillera of the Andes in Colombia; today it aligns with the border between the departments of Antioquia and Córdoba, northwest of Medellín.

delimits for Catíos would have included two of the early mining centers of colonial New Granada, that is, Buriticá and Santa Fe de Antioquia, as well as the contemporary city of Ituango. On the other hand, the area described by Restrepo as being occupied by Nutabes comprises the region where the villa and eventual city of Medellín began to grow precipitously in the 18th century, when a new phase of highland gold mining propelled the economy of Antioquia (Twinam 1982). The Tahamí region circumscribed by Restrepo points towards eastern Antioquia, a region that would develop mining centers such as Rionegro and Marinilla, which saw the beginnings of larger-scale settlement in the 18th century (see Maps 6–8 in Section 6).

Restrepo Tirado's (1892) outline is similar to conclusions drawn by Hernández de Alba (1948) on the history of contemporary Amerindian populations in northwestern Colombia. Hernández de Alba outlines a tripartite division of dozens of cohesive communities, consistently named across archival sources:

> The ethnology of the peoples who occupied the territory which, at the time of the Conquest, was called 'between the three rivers' – the Magdalena, Cauca, and Atrato Rivers – will be treated in three divisions. The first includes the tribes of the right bank of the Cauca River, the *Quimbaya, Carrapa, Picara, Paucura, Pozo*, and *Arma*. The second division includes the several tribes from the *Ancerma* to the *Abibe*, between the left bank of the Cauca River and the Atrato River, which was formerly called the San Juan River and the Río Grande del Darién. The third comprises the *Aburrá (Avurrá), Nutabe, Urezo, Tahamí*, and *Yamicí* of the Province of Aburrá. (1948: 307, italics in original)

The second and third divisions are relevant to the present discussion, the first corresponding to languages spoken primarily in the contemporary departments of Cauca and Valle del Cauca. For geographic orientation with respect to the river names discussed above, refer to Map 5, below, adapted from Milenioscuro 2009.[9] Most importantly for our purposes, Hernández de Alba claims definitively that "Almost without exception these tribes speak dialects of the *Chocó* language" (1948: 308, *italics in original*).[10]

Loewen (1963: 243) also demonstrates that many ethnic groups across western Colombia in the contemporary departments of Antioquia and its surroundings

---

9. Reproduced with Creative Commons (CC) Attribution-ShareAlike Unported license. https://creativecommons.org/licenses/by-sa/3.0/deed.en

10. Rivet (1943–1946) posited based on rudimentary word lists that 'Nutabe' and what has been called 'Old Catío' (see, e.g., Adelaar & Muysken 2004: 49) would have been in fact Chibchan, not Chocoan languages. The cited source of Rivet's word lists for Nutabe and Old Catío is Vásquez de Espinosa (1942 [1628]: 33–34]), who collected the word lists in the "city of Cáceres," 230 km north of Medellín, and outside the sociocultural realm at issue in this study.

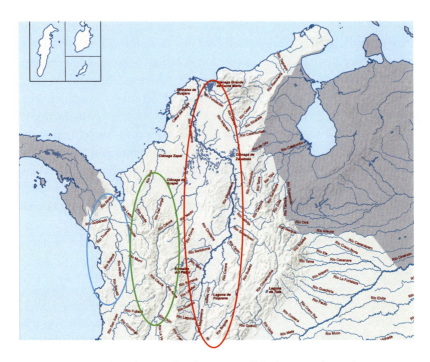

Map 5. Major rivers of northern Colombia: Atrato (blue), Cauca (green) and Magdalena (red)

would most likely have spoken Chocoan languages and that "names such as Urabá, Quimbaya, Paparo ... may represent extinct Chocó peoples". Loewen further hypothesizes that:

> Chocó speaking peoples now extinct ... may have extended beyond the present limits. ... In several older sources ..., the Nutave and Tahami are listed as inhabiting the Nechi River east of the Cauca River. Both appear to be Chocó words: tahami ~ tahamia, even today, would indicate *those people who live far out*; while Nutave, modern [i̯nt ͪape], would indicate (*those people*) *living higher up*.
>
> (1963: 239, emphasis in original)

Loewen's conclusions about the peoples of northwestern Colombia leading up to the time of Spanish conquest are supported by the archaeological record as well. Helms (1979) proposes that "Quimbaya and Dabeiba may have been part of the same exchange network in the early sixteenth century" (154), while, at the same time, "Dabeiba ... appears to have acted as a middleman between gold-collecting centers of the Cauca valley, particularly the Buriticá mines in the vicinity of Antioquia" (156). The significance of Dabeiba to the peoples of northwestern Colombia was recognized in Vasco Núñez de Balboa's first expedition into the interior of

Colombia in 1515, as evidenced in a letter he wrote to the king Charles V in June of that same year. In this letter, he states that he had traveled to the "province of Davaybe" and "received information about the mines that are inland [...]. And this this was true, there are large mines [...] and that all the *caciques* collect it" (Núñez de Balboa 1864 [1515]: 532–533, my translation).

From the above accounts, the emerging view of the linguistic ecology of northwestern Colombia at the time of Spanish conquest is a patchwork; some communities were large and served crucial sociopolitical and commercial roles, while others would have been small and rather peripheral to these central hubs of power. All were likely interconnected to one degree or another, however, by patterns of pre-Columbian commerce which would be built upon and repurposed by Spanish colonial authorities.[11] The totality of evidence presented above demonstrates that peoples speaking Chocoan languages were present in and around virtually all areas of economic and political interest to colonial authorities in Antioquia, in particular (Santa Fe de) Antioquia and Medellín. Chocoan peoples' knowledge of gold-mining practices suited specifically to the region were later relied upon by Spanish settlers, their *criollo* and *mestizo* children, as well as West Africans and their descendants for most of the colonial period (Colmenares 1978; Twinam 1982).

3. Language contact in early colonial Antioquia (16th century)

This chapter makes the case that the semantic change 'hand' > 'arm' and 'foot' > 'leg' in Antioquia arose through language contact, specifically the innovation of transfer-derived variants via language shift, wherein the number of shifting speakers (i.e., Spanish learners) far outnumbered the number of L1 Spanish speakers. The current section hones in on interactions among Europeans, Amerindians, and African(-descendants) that likely facilitated this change.

Some of the earliest insights into interethnic contacts in the geographic region that today comprises the department of Antioquia come from the Spanish chronicler Pedro Cieza de León's *Parte Primera de la Chrónica del Perú* (1864 [1553]: 39–92). Cieza de León travelled alongside Juan de Badillo inland from the Caribbean through the Urabá region, passing through early Spanish settlements in Buriticá and Antioquia, among others. Buriticá attracted the Spanish in particular due to its easily accessible gold deposits and proximity to the colonial capi-

---

11. Maps of pre-Columbian commercial hubs can be found in Helms (1979:152), Trimborn (1942:121), and West (1952:53). On the distribution of Amerindian peoples at the time of Spanish conquest, see Parsons (1949:32) and Vargas Sarmiento (1993:98).

tal of the region, Antioquia (contemporary 'Santa Fe de Antioquia'). By the time Cieza de León arrived, he referred to what must have been a well-known site, "the rich and famous hill of Buritica, whence such a vast quantity of gold has been taken in times past" (56).

Lode mining (i.e., excavating), which spurred the early gold rush to Buriticá, gave way to alluvial or placer mining (i.e., panning or sluicing from riverine sources), which was the norm across Antioquia (Colmenares 1978: 252–253). Cieza de León writes:

> This city of Antioquia is situated in a valley between the famous, notable, and rich rivers of Darien [Atrato] and Santa Martha [Cauca], for these valleys are between the two Cordilleras. The position of the city is very good, with wide plains, near a small river. [...] *All the rivers are full of very fine gold*, and their banks are shaded by many kinds of fruit-trees. *Antioquia is surrounded by extensive provinces, inhabited by Indians, very rich in gold, who use smalls scales to weigh it.*
>
> (1864 [1553]: 52, my emphasis)

Throughout the 16th century and beyond, the colonial economy of western Colombia, including Antioquia, was based primarily upon the forced labor of Amerindians and West Africans for the purposes of gold mining (Colmenares 1978, 1979). Twinam points out that "[a]s early as 1550, African slaves were mining Buriticá, and by 1583 two hundred Spaniards controlled a force of three hundred blacks and fifteen hundred Indians" (1982: 17). Cieza de Leon's chronicle mentions enslaved Africans working alongside the indigenous population in Antioquia, making note that "during the summer the Indians and Negroes get much wealth from the banks, and hereafter, when there are more Negroes, they will procure more gold" (1864 [1553]: 58). As direct labor for gold mining throughout western Colombia was shifted onto the shoulders of enslaved Africans, the indigenous population continued as a vital element of the colonial demographic makeup.

To varying degrees, Antioquia's Amerindian and West African(-descendant) communities either resisted and removed themselves from direct contact with the settlers and their offspring, especially through *cimarronaje* 'marronage', or they persisted in variably more-or-less close contact with Spanish-speaking settlers along with the growth of Spanish colonial power in New Granada (see Jiménez Meneses 2004; Williams 2004). Parsons comments on one form of the latter possibility:

> Within a very few years after the Conquest the aborigines of Antioquia had been so reduced in numbers [...] that those who remained formed an amorphous and disordered group which *lost its cultural identity with amazing rapidity. The subjugation of these remnants was a frequent activity of the captains of Antioquia for*

two centuries; expeditions against the Chocóes were recruited in the capital on at least a dozen occasions until the Indians began to weary of the game and yielded themselves up to the missionaries of the Cañasgordas and Urrao missions.

(1949: 30, my emphasis)

The emphasized segment of the above quote is crucial to the present analysis, as it points to a concrete constellation of social circumstances that led to the adoption of Spanish on a wide scale by the indigenous population in Antioquia in the early colonial period.

Colombian historian Álvaro Restrepo Euse posited the following: "One can easily deduce, that the Colony of Antioquia did not exceed, originally, six hundred Spaniards, who in their crossings with the Indians produced the white population that in the year 1600 served as the foundation for the colonization of the territory" (1903: 59). However, Robledo's (1864 [1539]) account also provides evidence that, as in many other cases of the Spanish Americas, enslaved Africans were present as the earliest settlements were being established in 16th-century Antioquia. In describing his and other Spanish colonists' ability to wrest control of the region surrounding Santa Fe de Antioquia from indigenous resistance and revolts, the author paints a scene where "it weren't for the Blacks [sic: *negros*] that were with them with axes and hoes, we wouldn't have saved a single horse" (Robledo 1864 [1539]: 408, my translation).

To summarize, archival evidence indicates that speakers of Chocoan languages were the most widespread geographically as well as demographically in Antioquia's early colonial period. Chocoan varieties (Embera Chamí, Embera Catío) would thus form the source language(s) from which Antioquian Spanish would be influenced via L1 transfer in language shift, some features of which were reinforced as West Africans were trafficked to the growing settlements in and around Santa Fe de Antioquia and Medellín. Early interactions between Amerindians, Europeans, and West Africans led to the community-wide adoption of contact-induced linguistic forms, including the uses of *mano* and *pie* for upper and lower limbs.

4. Origins of African(-descendant)s in Antioquia

In this section, various strands of evidence are weighed to determine from which regions of West Africa the African(-descendant) population in colonial Antioquia arrived, and, by proxy, the language backgrounds of those communities. The author is unaware of any contemporaneous documents tracing specific groups of enslaved Africans trafficked from coastal ports to work in the early gold mines of Antioquia. Data extracted from the online *Transatlantic Slave Trade Database* (Voyages Database 2009), however, indicate that among the enslaved Africans disembarking in Cartagena and Santa Marta – the closest ports of entry for enslaved Africans to the area under discussion – three main groups prevailed demographically in the 16th century, as shown in Table 1:

Table 1. Origins of enslaved Africans in Cartagena and Santa Marta, Colombia, 1514–1600

	Portuguese Guinea	Cape Verde	West Central Africa	Other[*]
Enslaved persons	20,684	20,482	18,756	12,211
Percent of total	28.67%	28.39%	26.00%	16.93%

[*] Important to note here as well is that included in the 'Other' category are two sizeable groups: 'Senegambia and offshore Atlantic' (10.43%) and São Tomé (4.43%), from which early varieties of Portuguese-lexified Creole languages may have arrived in Colombia as well. The remaining groups – 'Congo River', 'Princes Island and Elmina', Sierra Leone, and Luanda – consisted each of less than 500 individuals, though they do demonstrate a relatively wide range of origins for this early phase of Spanish trafficking of enslaved Africans into colonial Colombia. It should also be noted that a large chunk of the data set for this period (31,155 or 43.19%) pertains to those enslaved Africans for which no port of origin was specified. Lacking evidence, no assumptions were made as to the ethnolinguistic origins of those individuals.

Each of these groups must be considered not just in percentages relative to one another but also in terms of raw numbers given their early time of arrival in the colony, and the relatively small number of Spanish settlers inland.

For the purposes of brevity, we will not enumerate all possible candidate substrate languages that could have arrived from 'Portuguese Guinea', 'Cape Verde', or 'West Central Africa', as defined in the database. Rather, a few assumptions must be made to both simplify and clarify our analysis of the most plausible West African substrates at play in Antioquia in the early colonial period. Our first assumption is that 'West Central Africa' was an area where people who may have been enslaved and trafficked to Colombia predominantly spoke languages of the Bantu-H subgroup. This assumption is justified by Eltis and Richardson (2010: 136–137), who demonstrate the presence of the Kongo kingdom in a broad region of West Central Africa, which experienced the most intense impact of the slave trade during the 16th century. Even into the 17th century, Heywood and Thornton (2007: 56) indicate that "[a]lthough the region was divided into a multiplicity of kingdoms and smaller political entities, in the entire region only two languages, Kikongo and Kimbundu, were spoken."

The second assumption is that the only languages that were spoken widely enough in 'Portuguese Guinea' – roughly, contemporary Guinea Bissau – and

'Cape Verde', as listed in the database, would have been the Atlantic Portuguese-based Creole languages that emerged there through the course of early Portuguese exploration, later colonization, and finally the trans-Atlantic slave trade. A concomitant assumption here is that these Atlantic Portuguese-based Creole languages would have already emerged in the period under discussion. Sociohistorical and linguistic evidence supports this hypothesis. Jacobs (2010) posits that "UGPC [Upper Guinea Portuguese Creole, referred to by its speakers as Kriyol] emerged and nativized in the late 15th to early 16th century on Santiago [Cape Verde], from where it was taken to the mainland by native Cape Verdeans who settled in and around Cacheu [Guinea Bissau] in the late 16th century" (290). Thus, it is plausible that some or many among those who arrived from these regions disembarking in Cartagena – and from there, Antioquia – would have been familiar with a Portuguese-based Creole, as well as one or more other languages.

Thus, the substrate languages most likely to have been represented among early arrivals of West Africans in Antioquia were Kikongo (as a representative of the typologically similar Bantu-H subgroup), Cape Verdean Portuguese Creole (Caboverdianu) and Guinea Bissau Portuguese Creole (Kriyol).

It is important to take note of the demographic persistence of both Amerindian and West African(-descendant) populations well after the initial period of contact and foundation discussed here. Table 2 summarizes the demographic makeup of six representative settlements catalogued in a series of censuses across Colombia in the second half of the 18th century (note that, in the table, 'Antioquia' designates the city, not the department).

Table 2. Demographics of six settlements in Antioquia, 1776 (adapted from McFarlane 1993: 362–363; Tovar Pinzón et al. 1994: 102–123)

	'Whites'	'Slaves of all colors'	'Free people of all colors'	'Indians'
Antioquia	1,235	8,121	6,360	–
Medellín	2,653	2,501	9,100	–
Rionegro	551	686	2,953	–
Peñol	1	–	–	696
Buriticá	1	–	–	364
Sabanalarga	1	–	–	547

In the three most significant settlements in terms of population, an overwhelming majority of the population consisted of *libres de todos los colores* 'free people of all colors' and *esclavos de todos los colores* 'slaves of all colors'.[12] The data in Table 2 strongly suggest that the non-'White' population vastly outnumbered 'Whites' in Antioquia throughout the colonial period, even into the last quarter of the 18th century.

Language contact and shift scenarios plausibly would have played out frequently, perhaps in parallel, in cities like Medellín and (Santa Fe de) Antioquia, where populations of African origin predominated, as well as in small settlements where it is apparent from the census data that large indigenous communities were accompanied by a single European priest, as in the case of Peñol and Sabanalarga. The above is precisely the type of social setting where we would expect substratum transfer through language shift (see Section 1) to occur. Thomason and Kaufman have argued that

> [i]f an entire large population shifts to the language of a much smaller group of conquering invaders over one or two generations, the shifting speakers are unlikely to be fully bilingual in the TL [target language = here, Spanish] before they abandon their native language [here, Embera, Kikongo, Caboverdianu, and Kriyol], so we can expect to find extensive substratum interference in the TL.
>
> (Thomason & Kaufman 1988: 199)

Any transfer of limb partonomy in such a scenario of widespread L2 acquisition can be considered a likely case of *source language agentivity* in the sense articulated in van Coetsem (2000: 5, 54ff), with the 'source languages' in this case being those of Amerindian and West African origin that were most relevant to the sociohistorical context of Antioquia. It is precisely in this sort of social and linguistic context, depicted in the archival accounts and data throughout Sections 2, 3, and 4, that the innovation 'hand' / 'foot' > 'limb' is reconstructed here.

An analysis based on sociohistorical *and* synchronic data is critical insofar as the synchronic pattern in Examples (1) and (2), above, points typologically to a past context of intense language contact and shift. The nature of the innovative pattern, which involves the semantics of core vocabulary, and the process from which it originates (i.e., L1 semantic transfer) lend further support to the above account, as discussed below.

---

12. One modification that has been made from McFarlane's (1993: 362–363) table, besides summarizing the information held there, is the inclusion of the full terms, 'slaves *of all colors*' and 'free people *of all colors*' as they appear in the original documents, accessible online through the *Archivo General de la Nación de Colombia*. The abbreviation does not faithfully render the complexity of racial perception in the late colonial era when this census was prepared, which would have included, inevitably, the offspring of Amerindians and West Africans (as well as *mestizos* and African-descendants of a variety of backgrounds) within the two groups designated 'of all colors'.

5. Linguistic analysis: Substrates and processes

In this section, I outline the linguistic data and processes relevant to the analysis of limb partonomy patterns as a case of substrate transfer in Antioquian Spanish through adult second language acquisition in the early colonial period. Here it is worth returning to the apparent uniqueness of this variety in the use of *mano* and *pie* to refer to 'hand + arm' and 'foot + leg', as compared to other varieties of Spanish. According to the *World Atlas of Linguistic Structures* (WALS), the "identifying" of these two parts of the upper limb with one lexeme occurs in 228 out of 617 (37%) of the languages surveyed (Brown 2013).[13]

Crosslinguistically then, the Antioquian Spanish pattern is less common though not a rarity. It occurs within the Indo-European family, such as in Russian and Greek, as revealed in the Database of Cross-Linguistic Co-lexifications by searching for co-lexifications of the concepts 'arm' + 'hand' and 'foot' + 'leg' (Rzymski et al. 2020). However, while not coded by either of the above databases, to the author's knowledge the only Romance language exhibiting the 'identity' pattern for 'hand' + 'arm' and 'foot' + 'leg' is Romanian (McClure 1975: 79). In that case a contact origin is of course probable, inherited through the Balkan Sprachbund, which had a predominance of languages with congruent limb partonomies. Meanwhile, this pattern and process is analogous to several well-attested examples from the Atlantic Portuguese-based Creole languages of Guinea-Bissau, Cape Verde, and São Tomé e Príncipe (Ferraz 1976: 36; 1979: 100–101). In each of these languages, words derived from the same two Ibero-Romance etyma – *mão* and *pé* – were relexified by adults through naturalistic L2 acquisition based upon L1 patterns from West African languages of the Atlantic, Kwa, Mande, and Bantu subgroups, among others (Parkvall & Baker 2012: 237–239).

---

13. Two points of clarification should be made here. First, WALS has an entry for 'hand' and 'arm', but not 'foot' and 'leg', so no large-scale typological evidence can be offered on the latter. Second, both relevant Chocoan languages ('Catío' and 'Embera Northern') have been misidentified by the compilers of the atlas as having 'different' lexemes. The citation to which WALS makes reference for both languages is Huber & Reed's (1992) comparative dictionary, data from which is included in Table 3. In said dictionary, the confusion apparently lies in the Chocan language entries for 'hand' (19), which includes a post-posed *hã*; Huber & Reed gloss this entry more specifically as 'palm of the hand' in a footnote, though it might be more appropriate to use 'palm of the limb', *hã* being the 'palm'. This was verified by a Colombian researcher of Embera Catío (Llerena, p.c., 2017).

5.1 Limb partonomy in plausible substrate candidate languages

Table 3 shows patterns of limb partonomy in four Chocoan languages and three Chibchan[14] languages as compiled in the comparative dictionaries of Huber and Reed (1992: 19, 22, 25, 29) and Loewen (1957: 44a, 219a) and an early Kuna dictionary (Pinart 1890: 15, 37, 44). All four Chocoan varieties listed here are spoken contemporarily throughout the area comprising the western cordillera of the Andes in Colombia, the bridge between the department of Chocó in the west and Antioquia and Córdoba to the east – i.e., the area where Antioquian Spanish most plausibly developed. In all four languages it is readily apparent that one lexeme each can be used for 'hand, arm' and 'foot, leg', respectively. Each of the three Chibchan languages also show overlapping 'hand' / 'arm' and or 'foot' / 'leg' concepts, though Kuna presents the least similar pattern and would have been the most relevant to the colonial context discussed here (see footnote 14).

Table 3. Limb partonomy in Chocoan and Chibchan languages of northwestern Colombia

	'hand'	'arm'	'foot'	'leg'
Embera Catío (Chocoan)	huwá	huwá	hérṹ	hérṹ
Embera Chamí (Chocoan)	húa	húa	hírṹ	hírṹ
Embera Tadó (Chocoan)	húa	húa	hírá̃ / bɨ́ri	hīrá̃
Wounaan (Chocoan)	húa	húa	bɨ	bɨ
Kuna (Chibchan)	chúncal	chíncal guál	mali	tugúal yocór
Ika (Chibchan)	gúnni	gúnni	dʒúʔkwit	dʒúʔkwit
Dímina (Chibchan)	gúla	gura, gúla	kina	kina

It should be noted briefly as well that a similar pattern obtains in the Nasa Yuwe language, insofar as *cuse* is equivalent to *mano* 'hand', while *cuse pil* equals *antebrazo* 'forearm, lower part of arm', suggesting that *cuse* is equivalent to both

---

14. An anonymous reviewer of this chapter rightly recommended that the limb partonomy in Chibchan be included here as well. Kuna is the most plausible candidate, in geographical terms, given the sociohistorical discussion above, though a consultation of Huber & Reed's (1992) comparative dictionary demonstrates that Ika and Dímina have complete overlap between 'hand' and 'arm', 'foot' and 'leg'. Both are spoken in and around the Sierra Nevada de Santa Marta, over 800 kilometers to the northeast of Medellín, closest the city of Barranquilla. Four additional Chibchan languages, also spoken either in the area of Santa Marta or along the border with Venezuela show overlap between 'foot' and 'leg', but not 'hand' and 'arm'. Thus, while the linguistic evidence would appear to leave some room for ambiguity, the sociohistorical evidence, as a whole, points more heavily towards L1 transfer from (a) Chocoan as opposed to Chibchan language(s).

'hand' and 'limb'; more obviously, *chinda* is glossed as *pie, pierna* 'foot, leg' (Slocum & Gerdel 1983: 76, 375, 436, 453), showing a lower limb partonomy analogous to that of Antioquian Spanish. Nasa Yuwe (alternatively known as Páez), is considered a language isolate, but since colonial Antioquia lies well to the north of areas where Nasa Yuwe speakers reside currently, it is unlikely to have had an intense (or any) effect on the development of Spanish there. Even so, the presence of this semantic pattern in all these northwestern indigenous Colombian languages suggests the possibility of an areal feature shared by the languages of this region prior to colonization.

Critical to the evidence in support of a substrate transfer account is that the languages most spoken by enslaved Africans also exhibited a similar pattern. Table 4 draws together data from Laman (1964: 303, 304, 328) and Parkvall & Baker (2012: 237–238) demonstrating that each of these languages is analogous to Chocoan languages and Antioquian Spanish in as much as they present a congruent pattern of non-distinction between 'hand' vs. 'arm' and 'foot' vs. 'leg'.

Table 4. Limb partonomy in Kikongo, Caboverdianu (Cape Verde), and Kriyol (Guinea Bissau)

	'hand'	'arm'	'foot'	'leg'
Kikongo (Bantu)	kóoko	kóoko	kúulu	kúulu
Caboverdianu* (Portuguese-based Creole)	mo	mo	pe	pe
Kriyol (Portuguese-based Creole)	mõ	mõ	pe	pe

* The gloss in Parkvall & Baker (2012: 237) for the Santiago variety of Caboverdianu *mo* is in fact 'hand and **lower** arm'; a similar incomplete overlap is true for *pe*, which is glossed as 'foot and **lower** leg' (239). On the other hand, the *Atlas of Pidgin and Creole Structures Online* (abbrev. APiCS) reports that the Santiago variety of Caboverdianu has two distinct terms, *mo* for 'hand' and *brásu* for 'arm', differentiating the upper arm (Huber & APiCS Consortium 2013). However, the existence of a dictionary entry for both 'hand' and 'arm' does not mean that the former cannot be used in reference to the latter (Majid & van Staden 2015); indeed, this partial overlap is analogous to the pattern found in the Colombian Spanish varieties discussed here.

In summary, each of the substrate languages plausibly involved the emergence of a unique colonial variety of Spanish in Antioquia features the pattern under analysis here. This congruence of limb partonomy between four languages – one (four) Amerindian and three West African – is sociohistorically coincidental, but it was likely crucial for both the innovation and the preservation of this feature in the new variety, as Baptista (2020) has argued, for instance, in the case of several features in Creole languages. In the presence of features that align among speakers of various L1 backgrounds, transfer is more likely, especially in contexts of naturalistic L2 acquisition, as explored next.

5.2 Community change through adult learning: L1 transfer with substrate congruence

In this section, I briefly outline the linguistic processes that gave rise to the contemporary usage of *mano* for 'upper limb' in Antioquian Spanish as in (1), above. It should be noted that, for the reasons of space, the following discussion concerning 'hand' and 'arm' is completely analogous for the lower limb domain in Antioquia, that is, the area referred to as either *pie* 'foot' or *pierna* 'leg' in canonical Spanish. In Antioquia *pie* may be used for 'leg, lower limb', as seen in (2) above, and the lexical data in Section 5.1 show that an analogous process of L1 transfer is equally plausible for the lower limb domain, derived from the lexical semantics of Embera and reinforced by Kikongo, Caboverdianu, and Kriyol limb partonomies. The typological congruence of limb partonomy among the most predominant L1s spoken by the Amerindian and West African populations of Antioquia had a central role in emerging varieties of Antioquian Spanish as used, initially, by L2 Spanish speakers, and then adopted by L1 Spanish speakers with little or no knowledge of or direct contact with these substrate languages.

As illustrated in Figure 1, the canonical Spanish pattern for upper limb autonomy is one in which *mano* 'hand' is sharply distinguished from *brazo* 'arm'. For speakers of Spanish varieties with this pattern, including other regions of Colombia – where Chocoan languages were not spoken at the time of Spanish conquest and the early trafficking of enslaved West Africans was less demographically significant –, the extended use of *mano* to refer to anything above the wrist is not only unreported, but several informants have claimed it impossible.

In contrast to the strictly distinguishing pattern of 'hand' versus 'arm' reference, Figure 2 demonstrates an underspecification of the upper limb in each of the relevant substrate languages. The present study hypothesizes that adult language learners, who comprised the demographic majority in the context of early colonial Antioquia, identified *mano* with *húa, kóoko* or *mo/mõ* in their primary language. Accumulated reproductions of *mano* with L1 semantics associating it with the entire upper limb domain made it more likely for younger individual L2 Spanish learners as well as perhaps some adult L1 speakers in the community to replicate this option.

The literature on Creole languages has noted this non-differentiating pattern in English-based Creole languages as well, such as Nicaraguan, San Andrés, and Jamaican Creole Englishes (Bartens 2011: 220; Holm 1982 [1978]: 217; Parkvall & Baker 2012: 237–239). In these varieties, it is generally associated with substrate semantic transfer, with the specific substrate source language(s) of the pattern varying depending on the sociohistorical profile of the language or contact variety. Thus, despite its diverse origins, this pattern appears most frequently in analy-

Chapter 11. The contact origin(s) of 'hand' and 'foot' > 'limb' in Antioquian Spanish

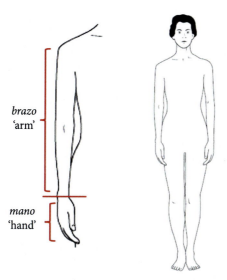

Figure 1. Upper limb partonomy in Spanish (Ibero-Romance), presumed superstrate[15]

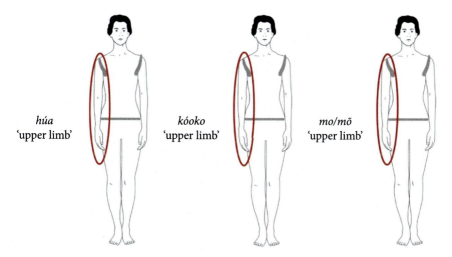

Figure 2. Plausible substrate pattern: Embera, Kikongo, and Atlantic Portuguese-based Creoles

ses as an instance of L1 transfer through adult acquisition. More recent evidence from at least some L2 learning settings suggests that, if this semantic mapping is present in the learner's L1, it may be copied onto the L2. Indeed, the identification

---

15. All body partonomy figures are adapted from the template in van Staden & Majid (2006), in accordance with the permissions for reproduction outlined therein.

of 'hand' with the entire limb is one of the first examples of L1 'interference' in language contact outlined in Weinreich (1953), who noted that it is a common feature of L2 English as used by L1 Russian speakers, in which *ruka* is often generalized for both 'hand' and 'arm' (1953: 7–8).

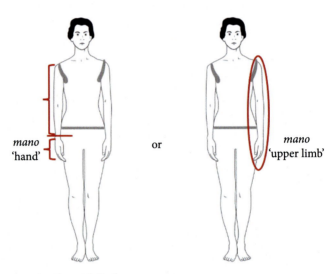

Figure 3. Antioquian Spanish limb partonomy

Figure 3 highlights an ambiguity of reference in the contemporary senses of *mano* in Antioquian Spanish. To the left-hand side, *mano* has a restrictive meaning, contrastive with the term *brazo* 'arm', as in the canonical pattern in Figure 1. Meanwhile, on the right we see that *mano* is not actually restricted, since the range of reference goes well beyond that which is usually delimited by *brazo*. This co-existence of *brazo* 'arm' and *mano* 'upper limb' is similar to 'overlapping' patterns used in contact languages such as Bahamian Creole, Sri Lankan Portuguese, as well as the São Vicente variety of Caboverdianu (Huber & the APiCS Consortium 2013).

6. Language acquisition and the historical sociolinguistics of Antioquian Spanish

Antioquian Spanish is not typically referred to as a contact variety, and today's Antioquians are largely monolingual in Spanish.[16] In spite of this, the preceding

---

16. Indeed, the present author, upon first noting the variants of *mano* and *pie* discussed here and verifying their usage and acceptability among monolingual Spanish speakers from Medel-

discussion makes frequent reference to (naturalistic) (second) language acquisition and learning, L1 transfer and other terms from the SLA literature, in conjunction with concepts and constructs most often associated with studies on language contact, such as substrate languages and language shift. A linkage between contemporary monolingual Antioquian Spanish and language acquisition must be made, however, because the synchronic pattern of use of 'hand' for 'arm' and 'foot' for 'leg' in (1) and (2), originated by way of a historical sociolinguistic process, substratum transfer through language shift, as the above historical and linguistic evidence shows.

Adopting a sociohistorical-acquisitional approach, the present study outlines the contours of a complex social fabric in 16th-century Antioquia and one linguistic outcome of the language contact that took place during that period. The predominant population, Amerindian communities speaking Chocoan languages, would have been the most balanced in terms of age demographics, given that there was an overrepresentation of adult males among Europeans and West Africans during that period. By the late 18th century, however, enslaved and free West African(-descendant)s were numerically predominant in central Antioquia, suggesting that many children as well as adults comprised this group. In Table 2 we also see evidence that Amerindians were still being congregated into *corregimientos*, where Spanish clergy (*corregidores*, lit. 'correctors') were charged with teaching Catholicism and the Spanish language to several hundreds of individuals. By this latter period, the region had been gradually populated by small mining-oriented settlements, as depicted in the chronological progression of maps in Figure 4, below, adapted from Milenioscuro (2012a, b, c).[17]

The centralization of colonial power in (Santa Fe de) Antioquia is reflected in its early appearance in the top left-hand side of Figure 4, depicting the year 1580. The colonial capital of Antioquia was a site where Chocoan-language speakers lived alongside one another, with *ladino* or Spanish-speaking individuals who served as interpreters for many court complaints brought there by Chocoan speakers from neighboring regions (Williams 2004: 195–196).

Subsequent settlements of Medellín, and later Rionegro and Marinilla indicate that the greatest mining activity shifted to the east, a change which is reflected in

---

lín and surrounding municipalities, did not immediately arrive upon a language contact-based analysis. Insight here is credited to J. Clancy Clements, who noted its similarity to the outcome of other (unrelated) situations of language contact with clear substrate influence, including Korlai Portuguese, which demonstrates the same pattern via transfer from the Marathi words *hat* 'hand and arm' and *pay* 'foot and leg' (Clements 1996: 11).

17. Reproduced with Creative Commons (CC) Attribution-ShareAlike license. https://creativecommons.org/licenses/by-sa/3.0/legalcode.

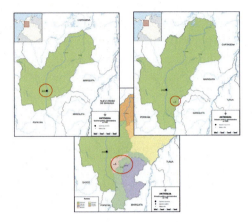

Figure 4. Antioquia in 1580 (top left, Antioquia circled), 1650 (top right, Medellín circled), and 1760 (bottom center, Medellín, Rionegro, and Marinilla circled)

the gradually increasing commercial and demographic significance of Medellín, which would eventually become the department's capital once Colombia became independent from Spain in 1826 (Twinam 1982). In these three settlements crucial to Antioquia's steady economic rise, one would have expected frequent interaction between Spanish-speakers and West African(-descendant)s, some being born in Antioquia, others arriving from other regions, and yet many still arriving directly from West Central Africa (Congo, Angola), and other increasingly diverse regions of West Africa such as Benin, Ghana, and Nigeria, among others. In this setting, what may be assumed as the prevailing method of Spanish-language learning (in spite of the *corregidores*' efforts) was naturalistic second language acquisition, which can lead to diachronic changes for the entire continuum of contact varieties, ranging from Creole languages and mixed languages to the colonial varieties of the Americas (for an overview, see Winford 2020).

The incorporation of L1 Embera-, Kikongo-, Caboverdianu-, and Kriyol-speaking individuals, among others, into early Antioquian settlements between the 16th and 18th centuries involved, at the most fundamental level, the learning of Spanish. This was achieved by both adults as well as children, with language shifts occurring in all but a few Embera-speaking communities, and among all West Africans. With these shifts, traces of speakers' first or heritage languages were transferred into the emerging variety of Spanish in Antioquia. That so few contact-induced features persist in Antioquian Spanish is due in part perhaps to the presence of children, language shifts taking place within one to two generations in most cases, and Spanish learners only demographically dominant in the early colonial period. The persistence of the feature discussed here is attributable to several local sociolinguistic triggers, including the typological congruence of this feature across sociohistorically-relevant Amerindian and West African substrate languages, and the numerical predominance of substrate language speakers.

From an acquisitional perspective, the role of transfer is paramount to the present discussion. According to Odlin (1989: 27): "Transfer is the influence resulting from similarities and differences between the target language and any other language that has been previously (and perhaps imperfectly) acquired". While this definition and much of the theoretical discussion of transfer as a process focuses on adult SLA in contemporary, non-naturalistic or classroom contexts (Schwartz & Sprouse 1996), transfer or 'substratum influence/interference' is also present in the language contact literature, especially in the genesis of pidgins and/or creole languages, albeit with much debate about its relative status alongside other 'universal' processes of second language acquisition (on this question, see Chapter 5 in this volume). One example from the literature on Creole languages that relies heavily on transfer is Lefebvre's *Relexification Hypothesis* (1998, 2001), which argues that the L1 is the starting point for all acquisition in naturalistic second language contexts, especially Creole genesis (see also Sprouse 2006). Lefebvre argues that the lexical semantics of *all* of a speaker's L1 'strings' (i.e., words, phrases) are relabeled by similar L2 (or L3, etc.) words, each carrying the full semantic and distributional constraints as in the L1, all the while superficially appearing to approximate an L2 word/phrase. Indeed, relexification as such would adequately describe the process outlined here in the specific case of limb partonomy semantics in Antioquian Spanish.

In the context of historical language contact and shift, Thomason and Kaufman argue that

> it is the sociolinguistic history of the speakers, and not the structure of their language, that is the primary determinant of the linguistic outcome of language contact. Purely linguistic considerations are relevant but strictly secondary overall. [...] Both the direction of the interference and the extent of interference are socially determined; so, to a considerable degree, are the kinds of features transferred from one language to another. (Thomason & Kaufman 1988: 35)

While those authors frequently use the term '(substratum) *interference* through shift' (39–53ff; see also Chapter 1, Section 4.4 in this volume), the present analysis substitutes the term 'transfer',[18] signaling that the relevant shift has already occurred, and that the discussion herein applies to monolingual varieties of

---

18. However, as a reviewer of this chapter highlighted, the origin of the pattern portrayed here was very much an active process, involving adaptive innovations by adults and children at varying levels of bilingualism, in which case, the term 'interference' is not inaccurate.

Antioquian Spanish. Thomason and Kaufman discuss this question, positing that "the greatest amount of interference through shift will occur in the absence of full (perfect) bilingualism, though of course the shifting group will normally be partially bilingual during the shifting period" (41). Finally, these authors argue that "in changes resulting from imperfect learning of a second language, *the TL [target language] is not so much accepting the changes as giving in to them*, since it is the shifting speakers, not the original TL speakers, who initiate the changes" (43, my emphasis). When communication is not impeded among the speech community, innovations are accepted from a variety of sources and in all components of language, including, as shown here, the semantics of body partonomy. Overall, the acquisitional action of source language speakers as the originators of innovations in situations of language contact is in full agreement with agency-based models of language change (see Chapter 4 in this volume).

Given the sociohistorical and linguistic evidence presented above, I submit that a speech community demographically dominated by L1 speakers of languages identifying with one lexeme 'extremity' and 'limb' shifted by necessity to the exclusive use of Spanish over the course of (less than) one to three generations and thus introduced the semantic extension *mano* 'hand' > 'upper limb' and *pierna* 'foot' > 'lower limb' in Antioquian Spanish.

7. Conclusion

The apparent synchronic ambiguity in the meanings of *mano* and *pie* in Antioquian Spanish is a window into a history of language contact in a region not often associated with Amerindian or African(-descendant) people. Here linguistic and historical evidence has been offered in support of the hypothesis that the semantic change 'hand' and 'foot' > 'limb' would have taken place through intense contact between Amerindian, West African, and European peoples in Antioquia during its foundation in the colonial period (mid- to late-16th century). As is common in historical sociolinguistic approaches to language change, no 'smoking gun' evidence from the relevant time period has been uncovered – for instance, a metalinguistic comment by a contemporary missionary educator regarding limb reference among indigenous or West African learners of Spanish – but neither is it the case that are there extant (or historically documented) varieties of Spanish wherein this change has occurred and an internal explanation is plausible.

Aside from continued research into original archival documents, from which one could expect additional insight, the present combination of historical sociolinguistic and acquisitional lenses to the apparently unique case of Antioquian Spanish limb partonomy is enlightening in itself. Here a plausible sociohistorical scenario has been outlined that explains puzzling synchronic data on the basis of the specific and local instances of language contact and shift in the distant past, as well as the extant information from the fragmentary historical record for this variety. One may presume that the more researchers consider less-commonly explored variants in language usage in the Spanish varieties of the Americas, such as the patterns of limb partonomy as explored here, the more likely it is that more cases of substrate influence will be found than have been previously discussed in the literature.

Abbreviations

REFL reflexive
DAT dative

References

Adelaar, William & Pieter Muysken. 2004. *The languages of the Andes* [Cambridge Language Surveys]. Cambridge: Cambridge University Press.

Baptista, Marlyse. 2020. Competition, selection, and the role of congruence in Creole genesis and development. *Language* 96(1). 160–199.

Bartens, Angela. 2011. Substrate features in Nicaraguan, Providence and San Andrés Creole Englishes. In Claire Lefebvre (ed.), *Creoles, their substrates, and language typology*, 201–224. Amsterdam: John Benjamins.

Breogan2008. 2022a. Mapa da lingua emberá catío. *Wikimedia Commons.* https://commons.wikimedia.org/wiki/File:Ember%C3%A1_cat%C3%ADo.png (15 December 2021).

Breogan2008. 2022b. Mapa da lingua emberá chamí. *Wikimedia Commons.* https://commons.wikimedia.org/wiki/File:Ember%C3%A1_cat%C3%ADo.png (15 December 2021).

Brown, Cecil. 2013. 'Hand' and 'arm'. In Matthew Dryer & Martin Haspelmath (eds.), *The world atlas of linguistic structures*. https://wals.info/chapter/129. (15 January 2022).

Cieza de León, Pedro de. 1864. *The travels of Pedro de Cieza de León, A.D. 1532–50, contained in the first part of his Chronicle of Peru*. Trans. by Clements R. Markham. London: Hakluyt Society.

Clements, J. Clancy. 1996. *The formation and development of Korlai Portuguese*. Amsterdam: John Benjamins.

Colmenares, Germán. 1978. *Historia económica y social de Colombia 1537–1719*. Bogotá, Colombia: Editorial La Carreta.

Colmenares, Germán. 1979. *Historia económica y social de Colombia, Tomo II. Popayán: Una sociedad esclavista 1680–1800*. Bogotá, Colombia: Editorial La Carreta.

Eltis, David & David Richardson. 2010. *Atlas of the transatlantic slave trade*. New Haven, CT: Yale University Press.

Ferraz, Luiz. 1976. The origin and development of four creoles in the Gulf of Guinea. *African Studies* 35(1). 33–38.
Ferraz, Luiz. 1979. *The creole of São Tomé*. Johannesburg: Witwatersrand University Press.
Helms, Mary. 1979. *Ancient Panama: Chiefs in search of power* [Texas Pan American Series]. Austin, TX: University of Texas Press.
Hernández de Alba, Gregorio. 1948. Sub-Andean tribes of the northwest Cauca valley. In Julian Steward, *Handbook of South American Indians (vol. 4): The Circum-Caribbean tribes*, 297–327. Washington, DC: Smithsonian Institution.
Herrera Ángel, Marta. 2017. La demografía colonial como proyecto político: Jaime Jaramillo y la ideología de la 'modernidad'. *Anuario Colombiano de Historia Social y de la Cultura* 44. 49–69.
Heywood, Linda & John Thornton. 2007. *Central Africans, Atlantic creoles, and the foundation of the Americas, 1585–1660*. Cambridge: Cambridge University Press.
Holm, John. 1982 [1978]. *The creole English of Nicaragua's Miskito Coast: Its sociolinguistic history and a comparative study of its lexicon and syntax*. Ann Arbor, MI: University Microfilms International.
Huber, Magnus & the APiCS Consortium. 2013. 'Hand' and 'arm'. In Susanne Maria Michaelis, Philippe Maurer, Martin Haspelmath & Magnus Huber (eds.), *The atlas of pidgin and creole language structures*. Oxford: Oxford University Press.
Huber, Randall & Robert Reed. (coord.). 1992. *Vocabulario comparativo: Palabras selectas de lenguas indígenas de Colombia*. Bogotá: Instituto Lingüístico de Verano.
Imbett Vargas, Erika Solange & Álvaro David Monterroza Ríos. 2018. Análisis de artefactos identitarios de la comunidad indígena Emberá Katío (Resguardo Jaidukama – Ituango, Colombia). *El Ágora USB* 18(1). 173–186.
Jacobs, Bart. 2010. Upper Guinea Creole: Evidence of a Santiago birth. *Journal of Pidgin and Creole Languages*. 25(2). 289–343.
Jiménez Meneses, Orián. 2004. *El Chocó: Un paraíso del demonio. Nóvita, Citará y el Baudó, siglo XVIII*. Medellín, Colombia: Editorial Universidad de Antioquia
Laman, Karl Edvard. 1964. *Dictionnaire Kikongo-Français*. Ridgewood, NJ: Gregg Press.
Lefebvre, Claire. 1998. *Creole genesis and the acquisition of grammar: The case of Haitian Creole*. Cambridge: Cambridge University Press.
Llerena, Ernesto. 2017. Personal correspondence. January 1, 2017.
Lefebvre, Claire. 2001. Relexification in creole genesis and its effects on the development of the creole. In Norval Smith & Tonjes Veenstra (eds.), *Creolization and contact*, 9–42. Amsterdam: John Benjamins.
Loewen, Jacob. 1957. *Comparative dictionary: Chocó dialects-Spanish-English*. Cali: Mennonite Brethren Board of Missions.
Loewen, Jacob. 1960. Dialectología de la familia lingüística Chocó. *Revista Colombiana de Antropología* 9. 9–22.
Loewen, Jacob. 1963. Chocó I: Introduction and bibliography. *International Journal of American Linguistics* 29(3). 239–263.
Majid, Asifa & Miriam van Staden. 2015. Can nomenclature for the body be explained by embodiment theories. *Topics in Cognitive Science* 7. 570–594.

Matras, Yaron & Jeanette Sakel. 2007. Investigating the mechanisms of pattern replication in language convergence. *Studies in Language* 31(4). 829–865.

McClure, Erica. 1975. Ethno-anatomy: The structure of the domain. *Anthropological Linguistics* 17(2). 78–88.

McFarlane, Anthony. 1993. *Colombia before independence: Economy, society, and politics under Bourbon rule.* Cambridge: Cambridge University Press.

Milenioscuro. 2009. Mapa de los ríos de Colombia. *Wikimedia Commons.* https://commons.wikimedia.org/wiki/File:Mapa_de_Colombia_(r%C3%ADos).svg. (15 January 2022).

Milenioscuro. 2012a. Territorio y división político-administrativa de Antioquia en 1580. *Wikimedia Commons.* https://commons.wikimedia.org/wiki/File:Antioquia_(1580).svg. (15 January 2022).

Milenioscuro. 2012b. Territorio y división político-administrativa de Antioquia en 1644. *Wikimedia Commons.* https://commons.wikimedia.org/wiki/File:Antioquia_(1650).svg. (15 January 2022).

Milenioscuro. 2012c. Territorio y división político-administrativa de Antioquia en 1760. *Wikimedia Commons.* https://commons.wikimedia.org/wiki/File:Antioquia_(1760).svg. (15 January 2022).

Núñez de Balboa, Vasco. 1864. Carta del adelantado Vasco Núñez de Balboa. In Joaquin F. Pacheco, Francisco de Cárdenas & Luis Torres de Mendoza (eds.), *Colección de documentos inéditos relativos al descubrimiento, conquista y colonización de las posesiones españolas de América y Oceania* (vol. 2), 526–538. Madrid: Imprenta de J. M. Pérez. Originally published in 1515.

Odlin, Terence. 1989. *Language transfer: Cross-linguistic influence in language learning.* Cambridge: Cambridge University Press.

Parkvall, Mikael & Philip Baker. 2012. Idiomatic (potential) calques and semantic borrowing. In Angela Bartens & Philip Baker (eds.), *Black through white: African words and calques which survived slavery in creoles and transplanted European languages*, 231–248. London: Battlebridge Publications.

Parsons, James. 1949. *Antioqueño colonization in western Colombia.* Berkeley: University of California Press.

Pinart, Alphonse Louis. 1890. *Vocabulario castellano-cuna.* Paris: Ernest Leroux.

PRESEEA. 2014. *Corpus del proyecto para el estudio sociolingüístico del español de España y de América.* Alcalá de Henares: Universidad de Alcalá. http://preseea.linguas.net. (15 January 2022).

Raynor, Eliot. 2017. Ambigüedad y metonimia en el uso de *mano* y *pie* en el español colombiano noroccidental. *Trabajos finales para las memorias del XVIII Congreso Internacional de ALFAL.* https://www.mundoalfal.org/es/content/actas. (15 January 2022).

Raynor, Eliot. 2021. Colonial-era language shifts and the sources of substrate body partonomy in the Spanish of northwestern Colombia. *University of Pennsylvania Working Papers in Linguistics*, 27(1). 189–193.

Restrepo Euse, Álvaro. 1903. *Historia de Antioquía (departamento de Colombia) desde la conquista hasta el año 1900.* Medellín: Imprenta Oficial.

Restrepo Tirado, Ernesto. 1892. *Estudios sobre los aborígenes de Colombia: Primera parte.* Bogotá: Imprenta de la Luz.

Rivet, Paul. 1943–1946. Nouvelle contribution à l'étude de l'ethnologie précolombienne de Colombie. *Journal de la Societé des Américanistes de Paris* 35. 25–39.

Robledo, Jorge. 1864. Relación del descubrimiento de las provincias de Antiochia. In Joaquin F. Pacheco, Francisco de Cárdenas & Luis Torres de Mendoza (eds.), *Colección de documentos inéditos relativos al descubrimiento, conquista y colonización de las posesiones españolas de América y Oceania* (vol. 2), 291–356. Madrid: Imprenta de J. M. Pérez.

Rzymski, Christoph, Tiago Tresoldi, Simon J. Greenhill, Mei-Shin Wu, Nathanel E. Schweikhard, Maria Koptjevskaja-Tamm, Volker Gast, Timotheus A. Bodt, Abbie Hantgan, Gereon A. Kaiping, Sophie Chang, Yunfan Lai, Natalia Morozova, Heini Arjava, Nataliia Hübler, Ezequiel Koile, Steve Pepper, Mariann Proos, Briana van Epps, Ingrid Blanco, Carolin Hundt, Sergei Monakhov, Kristina Pianykh, Sallona Ramesh, Russell D. Gray, Robert Forkel and Johann-Mattis List. 2020. The Database of Cross-Linguistic Colexifications, reproducible analysis of cross-linguistic polysemies. *Scientific Data* 7. 1–12. Article 13.

Schwartz, Bonnie & Rex Sprouse. 1996. L2 cognitive states and the Full Transfer/Full Access model. *Second Language Research* 12(1). 40–72.

Slocum, Marianna & Florence Gerdel. 1983. *Diccionario páez-español español-páez*. Lomalinda, Colombia: Townsend.

Sprouse, Rex. 2006. Full transfer and relexification: Second language acquisition and creole genesis. In Claire Lefebvre, Lydia White & Christine Jourdan (eds.), *L2 acquisition and creole genesis: Dialogues*, 169–181. Amsterdam: John Benjamins.

Thomason, Sarah & Terrence Kaufman. 1988. *Language contact, creolization, and genetic linguistics*. Berkeley, CA: University of California Press.

Tovar Pinzón, Hermes, Jorge Andrés Tovar Mora & Camilo Ernesto Tovar Mora (eds.). 1994. *Convocatoria al poder del número: Censos y estadísticas de la Nueva Granada (1750–1830)*. Bogotá: Archivo General de la Nación.

Trimborn, Hermann. 1942. Der Handel im Caucatal. *Zeitschrift für Ethnologie* 1(6). 112–126.

Twinam, Ann. 1982. *Miners, merchants, and farmers in colonial Colombia*. Austin: University of Texas Press.

van Coetsem, Frans. 2000. *A general and unified theory of the transmission process in language contact*. Heidelberg: Winter.

Van Staden, Miriam & Asifa Majid. 2006. Body colouring task. *Language Sciences* 28(2–3). 158–161.

Vargas Sarmiento, Patricia. 1993. *Los embera y los cuna: Impacto y reacción ante la ocupación española. Siglos XVI y XVII*. Bogotá: Instituto Colombiano de Antropología.

Vázquez de Espinosa, Antonio. 1942. *Compendium and description of the West Indies* (trans. by Charles Upton Clark). Washington, DC: Smithsonian. Originally published in 1628.

Voyages Database. 2009. *Slave voyages: The Transatlantic Slave Trade Database*. http://slavevoyages.org. (15 January 2022).

Weinreich, Uriel. 1953. *Languages in contact: Findings and problems*. The Hague, Netherlands: Mouton.

Werner Cantor, Erik. 2000. *Ni aniquilados, ni vencidos: Los emberá y la gente negra del Atrato bajo el dominio español. Siglo XVIII*. Bogotá, Colombia: Instituto Colombiano de Antropología e Historia.

West, Robert. 1952. *Colonial placer mining in Colombia*. Baton Rouge, LA: Louisiana State University Press.

Wilkins, David. 1996. Natural tendencies of semantic change and the search for cognates. In Mark Durie & Malcolm Ross (eds.), *The comparative method reviewed: Regularity and irregularity in language change*, 264–304. Oxford: Oxford University Press.

Williams, Caroline. 2004. *Between resistance and adaptation: Indigenous peoples and the colonisation of the Chocó 1510–1753*. Liverpool: Liverpool University Press.

Winford, Donald. 2020. The New Spanishes in the context of contact linguistics: Toward a unified approach. In Luis Ortiz López, Rosa Guzzardo Tamargo & Melvin González-Rivera (eds.), *Hispanic contact linguistics: Theoretical, methodological and empirical perspectives*, 12–41. Amsterdam: John Benjamins.

CHAPTER 12

Adult L2 acquisition of *for*-complementation in Chinese Pidgin English and Hong Kong English
A sociohistorical perspective

Michelle Li
Saint Francis University, Hong Kong

This paper examines the emergence of *for*-complementation in Chinese Pidgin English (CPE) and Hong Kong English (HKE) from a sociohistorical perspective. Although CPE and HKE arise under different contact situations and time periods, surprisingly speakers of these varieties show parallelism in the use of *for* to introduce purposive clauses. The origins of *for* as a complementizer in CPE will be argued to be contributed by convergence of meanings and functions in Cantonese and English – the major input languages in the feature pools of both varieties. It will be shown that L2 learning provided the mechanism for the emergence of *for* in purposive clauses in CPE and HKE. Variation in sentential complementation in these two varieties of English supports one of the tenets in variationist historical sociolinguistics, namely synchronic and diachronic variation can inform and complement each other.

Keywords: complementizers, substrate influence, Chinese Pidgin English, Hong Kong English, feature pool, historical sociolinguistics

1. Introduction

In recent decades, new research development in historical sociolinguistics has made significant contributions to language change and variation. This can be seen in the increasing number of monographs and handbooks discussing theories, methods, and new findings on sociohistorical accounts of language change (e.g., Hernández-Campoy & Conde-Silvestre 2012; Russi 2016; Rutten & van der Wal 2014). Since the 1960s, synchronic variation has become the mainstream in studies of language change (see Chapter 1, Section 4.3 in this volume). One of the major challenges faced by historical linguists is the incompleteness of historical data. However, the development in theories and methodologies in synchronic variationist sociolinguistics, as well as the growing body of literature on the acquisition of variation by speakers of different ages (see Chapters 2 and 3 in this volume), provide new insights to diachronic studies. Labov's (1972: 101) *Uniformitarian Principle*, which states that "the linguistic processes taking place around us are the same as those that have operated to produce the historical record," has become a popular core tenet for historical sociolinguistics.

Like variationist sociolinguistics, research in historical sociolinguistics also emphasizes the social meaning of linguistic variables. For example, Romaine (2005: 1696) states that "language is both a historical and social product, and must therefore be explained with reference to the historical and social forces which have shaped its use." Focusing on expressions of sentential complementation in Chinese Pidgin English (CPE) and Hong Kong English (HKE), two varieties of English developed under different sociohistorical circumstances and time periods but sharing several key sociohistorical triggers, this chapter examines the linguistic and social factors contributing to the innovative use of *for* as a complementizer in these varieties.

CPE, which emerged in the 18th century, was in use for more than two hundred years until its demise around the mid-20th century. HKE, on the other hand, is a local variety of English currently spoken in Hong Kong. Despite the significant temporal gap in their formation periods and differences in the sociohistorical settings, examples of *for* taking up the function of complementizer are attested in both CPE (1) as well as my sample of HKE (2) (for more information on this sample, see Section 5). The social and linguistic factors leading to the emergence of this shared feature will be discussed in Section 7.

(1) must make go chop chop **for** see dat doctor man (Tilden 1831–1832)
    must make go quickly COMP see ART doctor man
    '(You) must go to see the doctor quickly.'

(2) We will put more human resources **for** control the flow of people.

In English-lexified pidgin and creole studies, *for* as a complementizer is a commonly quoted feature, but this use in L2 varieties of English is an under-researched area. In *The Electronic World Atlas of Varieties of English* (eWAVE) (Kortmann et al. 2020), a database containing examples of 235 morphosyntactic features for 77 varieties of English, the pervasiveness of a *for*-based complementizer (Feature 201) is quantified. This distribution is shown in Table 1.

As can be seen in Table 1, the use of this feature is either absent or rare in most L1 and L2 varieties of English; on the contrary, it is commonly seen in English-lexified pidgins and creoles. Though CPE is not one of the languages included in

Table 1. Frequency of occurrence of a *for*-based complementizer in different varieties of English (Kortmann et al. 2020)

Value variety*	A	B	C	D	X	?
Traditional L1 varieties (10)	0	0	3	6	1	0
High-contact L1 varieties (23)	0	0	3	17	3	0
Indigenized L2 varieties (18)	0	0	1	12	2	3
English-based pidgins (7)	2	1	0	2	2	0
English-based creoles (19)	11	4	1	3	0	0
Total (77)	13	5	8	40	8	3

A feature is pervasive or obligatory
B feature is neither pervasive nor extremely rare
C feature exists, but is extremely rare
D attested absence of feature
X feature is not applicable (given the structural make-up of the variety/P[idgin]/C[reole])
? no information on feature is available
* The numbers in parentheses refer to the numbers of varieties. The database entry for this feature can be accessed here: https://ewave-atlas.org/parameters/201#2/7.0/7.6

the eWAVE database, examples such as (1) show that the feature is attested in CPE. According to the database, HKE receives value D (attested absence of feature). Although previous studies on HKE have not mentioned this feature, this paper shows that it exists in some speakers of HKE. Using Mufwene's (2008) *feature pool* framework, this paper examines the sociohistorical origins of *for*-complementation in both CPE and HKE through an acquisitional lens. It will be shown that similarities in the input available to learners, as well as influence from their L1, contributed to the emergence of this feature.[1]

The remainder of the paper is organized as follows. Sections 2 and 3 introduce the sociohistorical background of CPE and forms of sentential complementation in this pidgin. Section 4 presents different complementizers attested in CPE and Section 5 discusses their origins. Section 6 examines the use of *for*-complementation in HKE and compares it with CPE, emphasizing the role of L2 acquisition as the sociohistorical basis for the presence of this feature in both varieties. Section 7 puts this analysis in a larger context, by discussing the relationship between language acquisition and historical sociolinguistics, and how this relationship can be used productively to study the emergence of specific constructions in historical varieties such as the ones surveyed in this chapter. Section 8 provides some concluding remarks.

---

1. See Chapters 3, 4, 5 and 6 in this volume for an overview of the literature on the various forms in which the acquisitional action of adult L2 speakers may shape the diachronic evolution at the level of the community.

2. Chinese Pidgin English: Historical background

Although the Portuguese were the first Europeans to establish trade with China and settle in Macao in the 16th century, it was the British who dominated the trade between China and the West starting in the 18th century. As a result, the emergence of Chinese Pidgin English was a response to the need for a common language to facilitate interethnic business transactions. Alongside the lexifier (i.e., English), words of Chinese, Portuguese, Malay and Indian origins were also incorporated in CPE. The grammar of the pidgin showed significant influence from Cantonese, the substrate language, in elements such as *piecee* 'piece' as a classifier (Baker & Mühlhäusler 1990), the multipurpose preposition *long* 'along' (Li 2011), topicalization (Matthews & Li 2013), and serial verb constructions (Escure 2009).

Hall (1944) divides the history of CPE into four stages: (1) origin at Canton and Macao, ca. 1715–1748; (2) 'classical' period in Canton, 1748–1842; (3) period of expansion and greatest use, in Hong Kong, Treaty Ports, and Yangtze Valley, 1842-ca. 1890; and (4) decline, 1890–1940s. The 19th century not only marked the golden era of China trade but also the spread of CPE to other treaty ports.[2] Foreigners staying in Canton were subject to different types of restrictions; some of which were related to language. For instance, foreigners were not allowed to learn the Chinese language, while the Chinese despised the English and were reluctant to learn theirs. Under such circumstances, CPE might have acted as a more ethnically neutral language and kept the Chinese and foreigners at arm's length from each other linguistically and socially, given the two groups' hostility towards each other (Baker 1990). In the 19th century, a robust body of pedagogical texts in CPE for a Chinese audience attests to the importance of this code for interethnic communication (see this section below and Section 3). By contrast, English was unlikely to serve as the target language as people just needed enough English to get by. Entering the 20th century, while sociopolitical changes such as cessation of rights and privileges to foreigners in Mainland China diminished interactions between Chinese and foreigners and consequently the need for CPE, foreigners and merchant houses moved to Hong Kong and CPE continued to be spoken in the colony. However, the availability of English education resulted in negative attitudes towards use of the pidgin.

---

2. Besides Canton, the other four other treaty ports were Amoy (Xiamen), Foochow (Fuzhou), Ningbo and Shanghai. These ports were opened after the First Opium War (1839–1842). Hong Kong Island was ceded to the British Empire in 1842 after the signing of the Treaty of Nanking. British occupation expanded to the Kowloon Peninsula and New Territories after the Second Opium War.

By this time, use of CPE was limited to people of the lower class such as the *amahs* (female servants). The language eventually phased out around the 1960s/1970s.

Records of CPE were usually presented as reconstructed or remembered forms by foreigners. People who wanted to learn CPE typically learnt it orally from someone who already spoke the pidgin. In the 19th century, phrasebooks containing a few hundred words in pidgin became available for literate Chinese to teach or learn CPE (Bolton 2003; Shi 1993). Besides glossaries, dialogues in pidgin were found in *The Chinese and English Instructor* (published in 1862, transcribed in Li et al. 2005), a six-volume book compiled by the Cantonese merchant 唐廷樞 Tong Ting-kü [Tang Tingshu]. A characteristic feature of these Chinese sources is that Chinese characters are used to transcribe the pidgin. In its heyday (i.e., 19th century), CPE was learnt by adults such as foreign traders, Chinese merchants (*compradors*), *linguists* (interpreters), servants, etc. who entered the interethnic social networks where the use of the pidgin was common.

3. Verb complementation in CPE

Variability in sentential complementation has been a constant interest in pidgin and creole studies. Previous studies include the types and grammaticalization of complementizers in Sranan (Plag 1993), Gullah and Berbice Dutch (Holm 2000). There is a body of research on the use of complementizers in different creole languages, generally adapted from an element meaning 'for' in the respective lexifiers (Bickerton 1981; Byrne 1984; Mufwene 1989; Lefebvre & Loranger 2006; Plag 1993; Washabaugh 1975; Winford 1985). Some examples include Saramaccan *fu* (< English *for*) in (3) (Lefebvre & Loranger 2006), Mauritian Creole *pu* (< French *pour*) in (4) (Adone 1994: 30), and Papiamentu *pa* (< Portuguese *para*) in (5) (Lefebvre & Therrien 2015: 254).

(3) Mi duingi hen **fu** a bi go.
I force him FU he TNS go
'I forced him to go.'

(4) li ti al lafrañs **pu** marye me li pa fin kapav.
s/he TNS go France TO marry but s/he NEG ASP can
'She went to France to marry but she did not.'

(5) Mi ta deseá **pa** e bai.
1SG TA wish PA 3SG go
'I want him to go.'

In CPE, complement clauses can be expressed variably. This section will examine three types of complementation: juxtaposition, *for*-complementation and *to*-complementation.³ The data come from a corpus of CPE comprising a variety of sources in Chinese and English language sources (Baker 2003a, b).⁴

3.1 Juxtaposition

Juxtaposition, i.e., zero complementizer, of the matrix and complement clauses is the predominant sentential complementation pattern attested in both English and Chinese language sources of CPE. Take the high frequency verbs *think* and *want* as illustrated in (6) and (7) respectively as examples: zero complementizer (indicated as Ø in these examples) is used in both cases.

(6) Me think Ø you good man   (Ruschenberger 1838: 261)
1SG think Ø you good man
'I think (that) you are a good man.'

(7) my wantchee Ø build one houso   (Tong 1862: VI.57)
1SG want   Ø build ART house
'I want to build a house.'

A main source for zero complementizer is Cantonese, the substrate language, which does not require overt complementizers before complement clauses. This is shown in (7′), which is the translation of (7) in Cantonese.⁵ Juxtaposition is also reinforced by the fact that the complementizer *that* is optional in English.

(7′) ngo5 soeng2 Ø hei2 jat1 gaan1 uk1
1SG want Ø build one CL   house
'I want to build a house.'

---

3. Li (2017) discusses the use of *so* as a complementizer in CPE. Similar to the case of *for* and *to*, the complementizer *so* coexists with juxtaposition and is attested in English language sources only.

4. The English language sources were compiled by the late Philip Baker. The sources were taken from a wide range of genres ranging from travelogues, memoirs, magazine/newspaper articles, etc. dated from the 18th to 20th century. The Chinese sources are more homogenous in form; they are manuals for teaching and learning CPE in the 19th century.

5. Yeung (2006) argues that in Cantonese *waa6* 'say' functions as a complementizer; whereas Chappell (2008) proposes that *waa6* is a semi-complementizer. The status of *waa6* is still controversial.

3.2 *For*-complementation

The use of overt complementizer is attested in some sources. As in many pidgins and creoles, prepositions are a common source for complementizers in CPE. The number of prepositions in CPE is very small but they are multifunctional. For example, the word *long* is a preposition and a noun conjunction (Li 2011). The word *for* in CPE also has dual functions: the prepositional usage of *for* is shown in (8a–b), whereas in (9a–b) *for* functions as a complementizer. Note that the complementizer function is only attested in English language sources, not in Chinese language sources (for more on this, see Section 4). The example in (9) is from an early 19th-century source, quoted in Jenkins (1944).

(8) a. My can settle that pidgin **for** you   (Tong 1862: IV.32)
    1SG can settle DEM business PREP 2SG
    'I will get the matter arranged for you.'
  b. Can me trust that man go Nankin **for** pigeon buy silk
    Can 1SG trust DEM man go Nanking PREP business buy silk
                                          (Ruschenberger 1838: 263)
    'Can I trust that man to go to Nanking for business – to buy silk?'

(9) a. Now my flinde, Misser Tillen, you must go long my **for** catche
    Now 1POSS friend Mr. Tilden 2SG mus go PREP 1SG COMP catch
    chow chow tiffin and den can make see My No.1
    eat   tiffin and then can make see 1POSS first-class
    Book loom (library).   (Jenkins 1944: 13)
    library
    'Now my friend, Mr Tilden, you must go with me to get something to eat and then visit my first-class library.'
  b. my too much fear some war-ship-mans want **for** make bobbily long
    1SG too much fear some sailors   want COMP make trouble PREP
    china-mans.   (Tilden 1834–1836: 968)
    Chinese
    'I fear very much that some sailors want to make trouble for the Chinese.'

3.3 *To*-complementation

The example in (10) resembles the use of *to*-infinitive clauses in Standard English.

(10) he so sick he wanchy too much **to** see her.   (Loines 1953: 133)
    3SG so sick 3SG want very much COMP see 3SG
    'He was so sick that he wanted to see her very much.'

In addition to the complementizers *for* and *to*, there is a rare occurrence of complementation by means of *for to*, as shown in (11). Although this structure occurs only once in the corpus used in the present study, it should not be overlooked since it may have contributed to the diversity of input in the feature pool of CPE.

(11) Oh! that be **for to** take care and guard Josh, and see no man hurt him.
      Oh that COP COMP take care and guard god and see no man hurt 3SG
      (Fanning 1924: 191)
      'Oh, that is used for the purpose of taking care and guarding the god, and to make sure that nobody hurts him.'

This form is reminiscent of the Middle English *for to* construction, which is often used to introduce purposive infinitives (van Gelderen 1998). Though no longer used in Modern English, *for to* infinitives survive in dialectal varieties of English such as the Belfast English example in (12).

(12) I went to the shop **for to** get bread. (Henry 1995: 83)

In Modern English, *for* must be followed by an NP serving as the subject of the infinitive clause, thus creating the structure [*for* NP *to* VP]. This construction is attested once only in CPE corpus, as shown in (13).

(13) ebely man must make for   he   one piece paper **for**   dead flindes **to** gib
      every man must make PREP 3SG one piece paper PREP dead friends to give
      to   Quie.   (Tilden 1834–1836: 833)
      PREP Devil
      'Everyone must make a piece of paper for him; for the dead to give to the Devil'

To summarize, CPE had several options to express sentential complementation. Juxtaposition is the most common means. Other options are *for* and *to* as complementizers; both are used to indicate purpose clauses.

4. Variable use of complementizers in CPE

In this section, we will focus on the use of overt complementizers *for* and *to* in CPE as shown in (14) and (15).

(14) Now – one ting   more my like **for**   speak to   you my   flinde.
      now   one thing more 1SG like COMP speak PREP 2SG 1POSS friend
                                    (Tilden 1819; transcribed in Jenkins 1944: 16)
      'Now there's one more thing I would like to tell you, my friend.'

(15) you can go long my son **for** make see she my wifes and she my
 2SG can go PREP 1SG son COMP make see 3SG 3POSS wives and 3SG 3POSS
 young daughters so fashion can do suppose you like **to** see she.
 young daughters so fashion can do suppose 2SG like COMP see 3SG

(Tilden 1819; transcribed in Jenkins 1944: 19)

'You can go with my son to visit my wives and my young daughters; it can be done if you want to see them.'

Variable expressions of verb complementation suggest that, at least for some speakers of CPE, multiple options were available in their language ecology.[6] Alternation between *for* and *to* such as in (14) and (15) could be related to at least two factors: (a) both are prepositions and have partially overlapping meaning, particularly when denoting direction; and (b) both can be used to introduce the same type of clauses, specifically purpose clauses. Table 2 shows the distribution of these two complementizers in this same CPE corpus (see Section 3), according to the types of sources and the time periods in which they appear.

Table 2. Distribution of *for* and *to* functioning as complementizers in CPE

	English sources (1721–1842)	English sources (1843–1990)	Chinese sources (ca. mid-19th c.)	Total
for	27	1	0	28
to	13	6	1	20

A striking contrast shown in the table is the imbalance of occurrences of the complementizers in different sources. Near absence of complementizers in the Chinese sources is likely due to strong substrate influence, which could have favored juxtaposing clauses without overt conjunctions. Attestations of the complementizers *for* and *to* concentrate between the 18th to the mid-19th century, with the number of *for* doubles that of *to*. From the mid-19th century onwards, use of complementizers decreases sharply, especially *for*.

The cause of the decrease is unclear, but it is worth mentioning that many attestations of *for* and *to* are found in the American supercargo[7] Bryant Tilden's journals, written between 1819–1837. Despite the relatively high number of occurrences of *for* and *to* in this single source, Tilden's journals contain other characteristic features of CPE which are also attested in other English sources. These

---

6. See Chapter 3 in this volume for an overview of the literature on the acquisition of variation by L2 learners.

7. A supercargo represents the ship's owner on board a merchant ship and is in charge of the cargo and its sale.

coincidences suggest that these data are representative of at least some forms of CPE. The stabilization of CPE, perhaps aided by the availability of phrasebooks written in Chinese in the 19th century, seems to have reduced the options and eventually reinforced the use of juxtaposition as the most frequent complementizer. Even so, the availability of these complementizers in the historical record for CPE begs the question of which sources early speakers of CPE would have relied on to select them, a point to which we turn in the next section.

5. Origins of *for* as a complementizer in CPE

This section focuses on the sources that contribute to the use of *for* as a complementizer in CPE. Bickerton (1980) argues that the modal auxiliary function of *fi* in Caribbean English creoles is the source of complementizer *fi* introducing a sentential complement. Washabaugh (1975, 1980) assumes a prepositional origin for complementizer *fi* in Providence Island Creole. A third proposal is put forward by Winford (1985) who argues that, as *fi* in Caribbean English creoles exhibits both verbal and prepositional functions, these two functions might originate from a common semantic element which he labels 'directional' *fi*. Support for this proposal comes from the substrate languages of Caribbean English creoles, such as Twi, where *fi* functions both as a verb meaning 'to come or go from' and a preposition. In Hawai'i Creole English, *for* is multifunctional: as a preposition *for* is a directional or goal marker as in (16), and as a complementizer *for* is commonly used to express purpose such as (17) (Siegel 2008: 101).

(16) See, mama, what good policeman been give **for** me?
    'See, mama, what the nice policeman gave me?'

(17) He ask me **for** cheer you up.
    'He asked me to cheer you up.'

Siegel (2000, 2007) compares the semantics of *for* in Hawai'i Creole English and *para* in Portuguese and discovers their similarities. In Portuguese, *para* expresses a range of meanings including 'for', 'with a view to', 'for the purpose of', 'in order to', or 'intended for'. The complementizer use of *para* in Portuguese is shown in (18).

(18) Estão-se a preparar **para** sair.   (Siegel 2007: 75)
    'They're getting ready to go out.'

Due to their semantic and syntactic similarities, Siegel (2007) proposes that the functions of *for* in Hawai'i Creole are based on the functions of *para* in Portuguese, one of its substrate languages.

With this crosslinguistic evidence in mind, it will be argued that *for*-complementation in CPE emerged from the converging meanings and functions of the corresponding morphemes in the lexifier (English) as well as in the substrate language (Cantonese). In English, *for* is one of the most semantically versatile prepositions: some of its meanings are clearly directional, for example 'towards' in (19), 'intention' in (20), and 'purpose' in (21).

(19) They were heading **for** the airport.

(20) I've bought pizzas **for** the kids.

(21) The cats are not **for** sale.

In (22a–b), *for* is used to indicate cause or reason (note that the use of *for* as a complementizer, as in 22b, is now commonly perceived as archaic or literary).

(22) a. My brother was fined **for** speeding.
　　 b. He has moved to the countryside **for** he wanted to build a farm.

Though uncommon in CPE, the 'because' meaning of *for* is found in (23a), similar to the meaning of (22a), and bimorphemic *what for* is used as a question word like (23b).

(23) a. Here can make handsome face, for　too muchee handsome face have got
　　　　 here can make handsome face CONJ too much　 handsome face have got
　　　　　　　　　　　　　　　　　　　　　　　　　　　　　(Spencer 1925: I.227)
　　　　 'I can paint a beautiful portrait of you because you are handsome.'
　　 b. **what for** you wantchee money　　　　　　　　　　　　(Tong 1862: 54)
　　　　 what for 2SG want　　money
　　　　 'What do you want money for?'

Besides prepositional or conjunctive uses of *for* in English, elements of Cantonese may have offered additional support for complementizer *for* in CPE. Directional and motion verbs such as 'go' and 'come' often develop grammatical functions, for example *be going to* in English (Hopper & Traugott 2003: 80–86). In many languages, motion verbs such as 'go' and 'come' serve as sources of grammatical functions such as markers of purposive clauses (Heine & Kuteva 2004). Two Cantonese motion verbs – *heoi3* 'go to' and *lai4* 'come to' – show development from verbs to purpose markers as in the sentences in (24) below.

(24) a. ngo5 heoi3 gin3 gong1
　　　　 1SG　go to　see　job
　　　　 'I went to have an interview.'

b. ngo5 lai4   gin3 gong1
    1SG come to see job
    'I came for an interview.'
c. ngo3 m4 soeng5 heoi3 nam2 ni1 go3 man6tai4
    1SG NEG want   go   think DEM CL   problem
    'I don't want to think about this problem.'
d. ngo5 maai5 ni1 bou6 gei1   lai4 zing2 min6 baau1
    1SG buy DEM CL equipment come make bread
    'I bought this equipment for making bread.'

As verbs, *heoi3* and *lai4* are used as motion verbs as in (24a–b). Yiu (2005: 124–125) examines primary and extended meanings of *heoi3* and *lai4* and she shows that one of their meanings is to introduce purpose clauses, which can be regarded as metaphorical goals. The primary lexical meaning of these verbs is weakened in (24c–d), where they encode 'purpose' instead of 'spatial movement'. Such semantic change is accompanied by the verbs acting more like a preposition marking purposive clause. However, since *for* does not have a verbal function, we may wonder whether these two Cantonese verbs provided reinforcement for the development of *for* as complementizer – if so, what were the similarities and how did they work?

Washabaugh (1980) and Winford (1985) argue that the semantic properties of 'locational' and 'directional' are central to the uses of *for* as a preposition and a complementizer. This claim is supported by the functions and origins of *for* in CPE. Given the parallelism in meaning and function between Cantonese *heoi3/lai4* and CPE *for*, it is legitimate to hypothesize that the local substrate provided input for the various uses of *for*. With respect to meaning, both *heoi3/lai4* and *for* embed directionality. Moreover, an irrealis meaning is present when *heoi3/lai4* and *for* are used to introduce purposive clauses.

The close mapping in the prepositional and complementizer functions of *for* in English and Cantonese *heoi3/lai4* allowed early speakers of CPE to draw from these various sources in their repertoires to create prepositional and complementizer uses of *for*. In this sense, although CPE *for* does not have a verbal function, the emergence of *for* as a complementizer in CPE mirrors the developments seen in other English-based pidgin and creole varieties., its use as a complementizer (often with a purpose reading) mirrors the similar semantic change in Cantonese *heoi3/lai4*. Therefore, in addition to English, its seems that speakers of CPE also transferred some of the meanings and functions of other sources to CPE *for*, such as these two motion verbs in Cantonese,[8] among other possible sources (see Section 7), all of which were part of their linguistic repertoires (see Chapter 4 in this volume).

Up to this point, the argument has been necessarily historical. To fill in the gaps in the historical record, we now turn to additional evidence from a present-day ecology, namely Hong Kong English, which exhibits several key sociohistorical and acquisitional parallelisms with CPE.

6. Verb complementation in Hong Kong English

In this section we focus on a contemporary variety spoken in Hong Kong, namely Hong Kong English. Since CPE is no longer being acquired, present-day contact between Cantonese and English in Hong Kong provides a partial sociohistorical analogue to the acquisitional choices of CPE speakers. First, a brief sociolinguistic overview of the use of English in Hong Kong will be given, followed by discussions on the use of *for* to introduce purpose clause in in HKE.

Britain occupied Hong Kong Island in 1841 and declared the island a colony in 1842. In subsequent years, Kowloon Peninsular and New Territories became British possessions in 1860 and 1899 respectively. The colonial period of Hong Kong ended in 1997 when China took over its sovereignty. English has been present in Hong Kong since its foundation as a colony as an administrative and official language.[9] Pidgin English, though lacking official recognition, was a more commonly used variety during the early colonial period. Demographically, Hong Kong is today a predominantly Cantonese-speaking society with nearly 90% of the population using Cantonese as their usual language. Though important in areas such as administration, law, business and education, English is mainly used as a second language (Census and Statistics Department 2016). Children in Hong Kong typically begin to receive formal instruction in English from kindergarten. In primary and secondary education, English is a mandatory language subject taught mainly by local teachers and some schools adopt English as the medium of instruction. Most post-secondary education institutions adopt the English language policy for teaching and learning. While schools emphasize the acquisition of Standard English, in recent decades there has been an increasing awareness of HKE as a local variety (Bolton 2002; Gisborne 2009; Setter et al. 2010; Wong

---

8. An earlier draft of this chapter commented exclusively on *heoi4* in this section. I thank an anonymous reviewer for pointing out the similarities between *heoi4* and *lai4* to introduce purpose clauses.

9. Chinese was declared a co-official language in 1974.

2017). In Schneider's (2007:133) *Dynamic Model* for the evolutionary cycle of new Englishes, HKE is categorized as Phase 3 (*nativization*), a stage characterized by widespread bilingualism and the development of markedly local patterns in phonology, morphology and syntax rooted in L2 acquisition (see Section 7 for more on the language ecology of HKE).

Though CPE and HKE arose in distinctly different sociohistorical circumstances and show considerable grammatical differences, both varieties use complementizer *for* to introduce purposive clauses. An interesting question, therefore, is whether similar acquisitional strategies have led to such semantic and structural parallelism in both contact varieties.

The available data to answer these questions are limited given that acquisition of verb complementation by L1 Chinese learners of English is insufficiently researched. Some studies include Romasanta (2019), who examines the choice between finite *that*/zero-complement clauses and gerunds of the verb *regret* in American English, British English, Hong Kong English, and Nigerian English. Hsin (2012) investigates the acquisition of five complementizers – *that, whether, if, for, whether-to* – by Chinese EFL learners and finds that all complementizers except *for* are acquired satisfactorily by the learners. Interestingly, while many Hong Kong students are able to produce the target *to*-infinitive complement clauses, examples of use of purpose complementizer *for* in (25a–d), which are very similar to the recorded CPE examples (see Section 5), are found in some students' compositions.[10] The examples of HKE in this study were taken from a collection of compositions written by students attending English courses in a post-secondary institution in Hong Kong.

(25) a. We will put more human resources **for** control the flow of people.
 b. We will set up more guideline **for** discipline the flow in next exhibition.
 c. The post operative medication, Aspirin, is needed to give him **for** control blood pressure through oral with 100mg.
 d. He says "Unity within diversity" event is an opportunity **for** raise public awareness and building understanding to public citizen.

A caveat is that due to the limited data, it is not possible at this stage to offer generalizations on the verbs that select *for*. However, at the semantic level, this type of clause introduced by *for* is clearly purposive in both CPE and HKE, as shown by the examples included in this study. Syntactically, an apparent difference is that in CPE, the verbs include complement-taking verbs such as *want*, whereas in the

---

10. An anonymous reviewer raised the question of the conventionality of using *for* as in the examples in (25). The feature is not a widely recognized in the literature of HKE. However, the lack of attention to this use of *for* could also be related to the type of corpus under scrutiny.

HKE examples the clauses introduced by *for* in (25) are all adjuncts expressing purpose. In other words, complementizer *for* in CPE seemed to have a broader syntactic range than in HKE.[11]

Though the data come from a small and specific group of Hong Kong students, the acquisition of the values of *for* deserves explanation since the use of *for* in (25a–d) conspicuously departs from the standard variety of English that these students are exposed to in the classroom. A possible explanation could be related to the partially overlap in meaning of *for* and *to*. In the discussion of CPE, it has been shown that *for* and *to* are used as prepositions and complementizers; the directional meaning in both words is a likely source for introducing purposive complement clauses. In addition, the shared linguistic background of the speakers of CPE and HKE, both involving contact between Cantonese and English, may also explain the co-existence of *for* and *to* for similar functions.

The presence of these complementizers in the historical record of CPE and HKE alike suggests that speakers of both varieties shared at least some of the same sociolinguistic and acquisitional motivations to select these options. The next section examines the characteristics of the speakers and the linguistic ecologies of CPE and HKE within the *feature pool* framework (Mufwene 2008).

7. Language acquisition and the historical sociolinguistics of *for*-complementation

Many researchers have invoked language acquisition theory and processes to explain the mechanisms of pidginization and creolization. For example, Bickerton's (1981) *Language Bioprogram Hypothesis* aimed to investigate the role of first language acquisition on creolization. While some of his arguments have been largely refuted since, more recent evidence does indicate that, in some contexts, L1 acquisition may result in language change. For instance, O'Shannessy (2020) shows that a distinct sociolinguistic context has resulted in the emergence of a new auxiliary system in the mixed language Light Warlpiri, with young children as the main agents of this innovation (see also Chapter 8 in this volume). By contrast, some authors (most notably Plag 2008a, b and Chaudenson 2001) regard creolization as the result of incomplete acquisition of the target language by adults. In a similar vein, Siegel (2008) examines the influence of language transfer, particularly substrate influence, on pidginization and creolization.

In this section, Mufwene's (2008) proposal of a *feature pool* will be used to explain the ecologies and variations in verb complementation in CPE and HKE.

---

11. I would like to thank an anonymous reviewer for pointing out this difference.

Based on Charles Darwin's theory of the biological evolution of species, the *feature pool* represents an evolutionary approach to language analogous to the evolution of biological species. Two key tenets of the model are *competition* and *selection*. The feature pool of a particular ecology is contributed by variants from all the languages and varieties participating in that ecology. Variants, be they lexical, phonological, syntactic, semantic or pragmatic, compete with each other at all levels of grammar. The grammar of an emerging contact variety is made up of different *idiolects* which are shaped by the inputs available to the individuals. During the processes of competition and selection, speakers select different subsets of variants and create their own idiolects. According to Mufwene (2008: 117), an idiolect is characterized as follows:

> Variation among individual speakers' personalities and histories of social interactions produces inter-idiolectal variation of the kind where no speaker replicates anybody else's idiolect, although those of speakers who evolve in the same communication networks are more similar to each other. That is, although all speakers/learners select their features (albeit with some modification) from the same pool, they do not select exactly the same variants.

The idiolect is an important component in language creation because it is at this level that individual variation is evident; that is, individual speakers recombine features in ways that are unique and idiosyncratic according to their environments and experiences of contact and learning. Individuals contribute to the feature pool through interactions with each other; such interactions in turn will affect the trajectory of language evolution (see Chapter 4 for a similar proposal). At the communal level, selection and competition of variants of the same feature pool show characteristics of *blending inheritance* (Mufwene 2001, 2008). This means that individual speakers can modify or adjust their idiolects during their interactions with other speakers throughout their lifespan. As a result, such mutual dependence between individual speakers constitutes a dynamic part in the evolution of any language.

Since the variants in the feature pool are fundamental to determining combinations of features and reorganization of the linguistic system, an examination of the feature pools of CPE and HKE is needed in order to explain their linguistic characteristics. Though developing at different times, the two most important input languages of CPE and HKE are identical in both settings, namely Cantonese and English. However, in the case of CPE, we can assume, in addition to the standard varieties, that the English traders and ship crews spoke a variety of dialects. Variation in the lexifier is shown in the different types of sentential complementation in CPE, for example the standard *to*-infinitive complementation, the *for to* construction, *for*-complementation, and juxtaposition (see Section 3). Besides

Cantonese and English, Macau Pidgin Portuguese (MPP) (Li & Matthews 2016), which was used before CPE, could have been a source of input too. In their examination of a phrasebook on MPP, Li and Matthews (2016) show that MPP and CPE share several lexical and grammatical features. In MPP, one way to introduce complement clauses is by the morpheme *polo*, which like *for* is both a preposition and a complementizer.[12] MPP *polo* could have provided yet another model for the use of *for* in CPE. Moreover, the use of *for* may also be affected by the semantically similar verbs *heoi3* and *lai4* in the substrate language, Cantonese, as explained above (Section 5). The available evidence strongly suggests that the feature pool of CPE was contributed by multiple languages.

The language ecology of HKE partly overlaps with that of CPE; however, it also differs from CPE in significant ways. As in CPE, Cantonese (the community language) and English are important contributors in the feature pool of HKE. Speakers of other Chinese varieties such as Hakka, Chaozhou and Mandarin are also part of the local ecology but in much smaller numbers than Cantonese. Compared with CPE, the variety of English in the feature pool of HKE is more consistent, normally the standard variety as most people learn English as a second language in school setting. As observed above (Section 5), the syntactic range of complementizer *for* in HKE appears to be more restricted than in CPE, allowing only for adjunct phrases expressing purpose (*for* + infinitive) and not for other types of constructions (e.g., complement-taking verb *want*). The less variable input for HKE learners may be at the root of these differences.[13]

Besides *for*-complementation, there are other phonological and grammatical aspects where HKE also resembles CPE, for example the use of *have* in expressions of existence and possession (Chan 2004). Despite such similarities, evidence of a direct historical connection between the two varieties of English is lacking.[14] In fact, they differ significantly in other aspects of their respective sociohistorical contexts, including the process of acquisition, transmission, and domains of use. From a sociohistorical perspective, CPE emerged in condition where a makeshift language was needed to resolve communication barrier among people speaking

---

12. The form *polo* in Macau Pidgin Portuguese may be a fusion of the forms and functions of Portuguese *por* and *para* (Li & Matthews 2016: 175).

13. See also Chapter 3 in this volume for the role of variation in the input on adult L2 acquisition.

14. Use of Chinese Pidgin English faded out in the 1960s/1970s. By that time, the concept of Hong Kong English was not recognized, at least academically. Interest in Hong Kong English as a distinct variety is likely a result of Kachru (1992) and others' (McArthur 1998) research on World Englishes. Systematic corpus-based studies on Hong Kong English began in the 2000s. The significant gap between the demise of CPE in Hong Kong and the current concept of Hong Kong English seems to support the historical discontinuity between the two varieties.

different native languages. People just learnt enough English to get by and the output need not be a complete replication of the lexifier (Mufwene 2001). Its use was restricted to business-related activities. With respect to methods of transmission, CPE was transmitted primarily through an oral manner and was learnt with minimal supervision. It was not until the 19th century that written material on CPE was available and speakers could learn the language more consistently. In contrast, the use of English in Hong Kong was initially a colonial policy, and it is still supported by the school system and other institutions. Most children receive formal instruction in English as early as ages 2–3 years. As a result, the mode of learning, the quantity and quality of input differ markedly from those of CPE.

Having explained the language ecologies of CPE and HKE, we will examine how they affect the linguistic outputs of the two varieties. The influence of Cantonese and the lack of need or intention to replicate L1 English completely could explain the strong preference for zero complementizer in CPE but its rarity in HKE. The use of complementizer *for* in place of *to* in CPE and HKE in purposive clauses may seem puzzling, but its selection can be attributed to the partial similarity between the sociohistorical embedding of language acquisition in both cases. Multiple factors seemed to have conspired to produce this structure. These factors include the multiple semantic value of *for* as a preposition and the historical availability of purpose constructions with *for* in English (Section 4), as well as the use of motion verbs *heoi3* and *lai4* as markers of purpose in Cantonese. Today, the overlapping functions and meanings of *for* and *to* may continue to create difficulties for some students in HKE, especially those who are more Cantonese-dominant bilingual speakers.[15] Notwithstanding these differences, several of the same linguistic processes are at work for a historical variety and a contemporary variety of English. These linguistic parallelisms can be explained by a model of linguistic evolution where learners have access to several similar sources and rely on elements from their L1s and their L2s to configure the grammar of their respective idiolects.

From a lifespan language acquisition perspective, although we may regard the use of complementizer *for* as simply L2 learner errors, the sociolinguistic context of CPE and HKE clearly offered speakers sufficient motivation to select this option, at least as one possible variant for the syntactic expression of purpose. Schneider (2007: 86) argues that structural innovations such as those associated with verb complementation may occur at Phase 3 *nativization*, a stage where HKE is said to belong. As advanced in Chapter 6, in a social context where L2 learners

---

15. See Chapter 5 in this volume for a closer look at the importance of transparency in bilingual acquisition, and Chapter 11 for another case study of the role of L1 semantics in language contact settings.

are socially and/or demographically prominent, these innovations may become part of the resulting variety. Although at this stage it cannot be said that such use of *for* among Hong Kong students is systematic or conventionalized, it may represent a domain of innovation in HKE.

8. Conclusion

The work by Weinreich et al. (1968) changed the focus of language variation from language as an autonomous system to a variationist approach which emphasizes the integration of linguistic and social processes to explain language variation and change. One of the central principles of variationist sociolinguistics is that linguistic variables have social meaning, and they are distributed systematically (Tagliamonte 2012). Another milestone of variationist sociolinguistics is the relationship between synchronic language variation and diachronic processes. Labov's (1972) *Uniformitarian Principle*, which states that synchronic linguistic variation can be used to reconstruct at least some of the sociolinguistic processes occurring in the past, has been widely used as a guiding principle in the study of historical variation (see Section 1). The growing body of research on language acquisition across the lifespan and language change, surveyed and applied throughout this volume, has also added to our knowledge of the dynamics of change at the individual and community level. The present study on variable expressions of verb-complementation in CPE and HKE has uncovered an area, namely *for* to introduce purposive clauses, where synchronic variation parallels diachronic variation. The application of Mufwene's feature pool concept is compatible with variationist (historical) sociolinguistics: as Romaine (2016: 21) states, "[v]ariation arises from competition between grammars or elements within them. Socially speaking, these grammars are instantiated in communities and individuals."

This paper compares variation in complementation strategies, in particular marking of purposive clause, in two varieties of English: Chinese Pidgin English, a historical variety, and Hong Kong English, a present-day variety. Several options are available: zero complementizer (via juxtaposition) and use of prepositional complementizers *to* and *for*. In CPE, the origins of *for* can be attributed to partial convergence in meanings and functions of *for* in English and the motion verbs *heoi3* 'go to' and *lai4* 'come to' in Cantonese. Though far apart in time, the use of *for* in introducing purpose is also found in HKE. This chapter has shown that the selection of *for* in CPE and HKE can be attributed to the fact that the variants in the feature pools of CPE and HKE partly overlap, and that learners had similar motivations to select this syntactic variant for their emerging idiolects. This study contributes to variationist sociolinguistics research as it shows that despite separation in time when the feature pools show some similarities, a linguistic structure in a historical variety may resurface in a contemporary variety with a very similar (albeit not identical) syntactic profile. This is shown in the case of the functions of *for* in CPE and HKE. It supports the view that contemporary data and acquisition-based contact and language change theory can be deployed to understand language creation and language variation in the past.

Funding

The work described in this paper was fully supported by a grant from the Research Grants Council of the Hong Kong Special Administrative Region, China (UGC/FDS11/H01/18).

Acknowledgements

I would like to thank the reviewers for their helpful comments.

Abbreviations

ART	article	NEG	negation
ASP	aspect	POSS	possessive
CL	classifier	PREP	preposition
COMP	complementizer	SG	singular
COP	copula	TNS	tense
DEM	demonstrative		

References

Adone, Dany. 1994. *The acquisition of Mauritius Creole*. Amsterdam: John Benjamins.
Baker, Philip. 1990. Off target? *Journal of Pidgin and Creole Languages* 5. 107–119.
Baker, Philip & Peter Mühlhäusler. 1990. From business to pidgin. *Journal of Asian-Pacific Communication* 1(1). 87–115.
Baker, Philip. 2003a. CPE1: Corpus of Chinese Pidgin English as attested in English language sources (1721–1842).
Baker, Philip. 2003b. CPE2: Corpus of Chinese Pidgin English as attested in English language sources (1843–1990).
Bickerton, Derek. 1980. Decreolization and the creole continuum. In Albert Valdman & Arnold Highfield (eds.), *Theoretical orientations in creole studies*, 109–128. New York: Academic Press.

Bickerton, Derek. 1981. *Roots of language.* Ann Arbor, MI: Karoma Press.

Bolton, Kingsley. 2002. *Hong Kong English: Autonomy and creativity.* Hong Kong: Hong Kong University Press.

Bolton, Kingsley. 2003. *Chinese Englishes: A sociolinguistic history.* Cambridge: Cambridge University Press.

Byrne, Francis. 1984. Fi and fu: Origins and functions in some Caribbean English-based Creoles. *Lingua* 62(1–2). 97–120.

Census and Statistics Department. 2016. *Population by-census – main results.* Hong Kong: Hong Kong Special Administrative Region.

Chan, Alice Y. W. 2004. Syntactic Transfer: Evidence from the Interlanguage of Hong Kong Chinese ESL Learners. *The Modern Language Journal* 88, 56–74.

Chappell, Hilary. 2008. Variation in the grammaticalization of complementizers from Verba Dicendi in Sinitic languages". *Linguistic Typology* 12. 45–98.

Chaudenson, Robert. 2001. *Creolization of language and culture.* London: Routledge.

Escure, Geneviève. 2009. Is serialization simple? Evidence from Chinese Pidgin English. In Nicholas Faraclas & Thomas Klein (eds.), *Simplicity and complexity in creoles and pidgins,* 109–123. London: Battlebridge.

Fanning, Edmund. 1924. *Voyages and discoveries in the South Seas, 1792–1832.* Salem (Mass): Marine Research Society.

Gisborne, Nikolas. 2009. Aspects of the morphosyntactic typology of Hong Kong English. *English World-Wide* 30(2). 149–169.

Hall, Jr. Robert A. 1944. Chinese Pidgin English grammar and texts. *Journal of the American Oriental Society* 64(3). 95–113.

Heine, Bernd & Tania Kuteva. 2004. *World lexicon of grammaticalization.* Cambridge: Cambridge University Press.

Henry, Alison. 1995. *Belfast English and Standard English.* Oxford: Oxford University Press.

Hernández-Campoy, Juan Manuel & Juan Camilo Conde-Silvestre (eds.) 2012. *The handbook of historical sociolinguistics.* London: Blackwell-Wiley.

Holm, John. 2000. *An introduction to pidgins and creoles.* Cambridge: Cambridge University Press.

Hopper, Paul & Elizabeth Traugott. 2003. *Grammaticalization* (2nd edition). Cambridge: Cambridge University Press.

Hsin, Ai-li. 2012. The acquisition of English complementizers in canonical vs. noncanonical structures. *Taiwan Journal of TESOL* 9. 95–141.

Jenkins, Lawrence Waters (ed.). 1944. *Bryant Parrott Tilden of Salem, at a Chinese dinner party, Canton, 1819.* Princeton: Princeton University Press.

Kachru, Braj. 1992. *The other tongue: English across cultures.* 2nd edition. Urbana, IL: University of Illinois Press.

Kortmann, Bernd, Kerstin Lunkenheimer & Katharina Ehret (eds.). 2020. *The Electronic World Atlas of Varieties of English.* Zenodo. https://ewave-atlas.org/ (15 December 2021).

Labov, William. 1972. Some principles of linguistic methodology. *Language in Society* 1(1). 97–120.

Lefebvre, Claire & Virginie Loranger. 2006. On the properties of Saramaccan *FU*: Synchronic and diachronic perspectives. *Journal of Pidgin and Creole Languages* 21. 275–335.

Lefebvre, Claire & Isabelle Therrien. 2015. On the properties of Papiamentu *pa*. In Claire Lefebvre. *Functional Categories in Three Atlantic Creoles. Saramaccan, Haitian and Papiamentu*, 245–282. Amsterdam: John Benjamins.

Li, Michelle. 2011. Origins of a preposition: Chinese Pidgin English *long* and its implications for pidgin grammar. *Journal of Language Contact* 4(2). 269–294.

Li, Michelle. 2017. The emergence of *so* as a complementizer in Chinese Pidgin English. *English World-Wide* 38(1). 5–28.

Li, Michelle & Stephen Matthews. 2016. An outline of Macau Pidgin Portuguese. *Journal of Pidgin and Creole Languages* 31(1). 141–183.

Li, Michelle, Stephen Matthews & Geoff Smith. 2005. Pidgin English texts from *The Chinese and English Instructor*. Special issue of the *Hong Kong Journal of Applied Linguistics* 10. 79–167.

Loines, Elma (ed). 1953. *The China trade post-bag of the Seth Low family of Salem and New York*. Manchester (Maine): Falmoth Publishing House.

Matthews, Stephen & Michelle Li. 2013. Chinese Pidgin English. In Susanne Michaelis, Philippe Maurer, Martin Haspelmath & Magnus Huber (eds.), *Survey of pidgin and creole languages. Volume I: English-based and Dutch-based languages*, 206–213. Oxford: Oxford University Press.

McArthur, Tom. 1998. *The English languages*. Cambridge: Cambridge University Press.

Mufwene, Salikoko. 1989. Equivocal structures in some Gullah complex sentences. *American Speech* 64(3). 304–326.

Mufwene, Salikoko. 2001. *The ecology of language evolution*. Cambridge: Cambridge University Press.

Mufwene, Salikoko. 2008. *Language evolution: Contact, competition, and change*. London: Continuum.

O'Shannessy, Carmel. 2020. How ordinary child language acquisition processes can lead to the unusual outcome of a mixed language. *International Journal of Bilingualism* 25. 458–480.

Plag, Ingo. 1993. *Sentential complementation in Sranan*. Tübingen: Max Niemeyer.

Plag, Ingo. 2008a. Creoles as interlanguages: Syntactic structures. *Journal of Pidgin and Creole Languages* 23(2). 307–328.

Plag, Ingo. 2008b. Creoles as interlanguages: Inflectional morphology. *Journal of Pidgin and Creole Languages* 23(1). 109–130.

Romaine, Suzanne. 2005. Historical sociolinguistics/Historische Soziolinguistik. In Ulrich Ammon, Norbert Dittmar, Klaus Mattheier & Peter Trudgill (eds.), *Sociolinguistics/Soziolinguistik: An international handbook of the science of language and society/Ein internationales Handbuch zur Wissenschaft von Sprache und Gesellschaft*, volume 2, 1696–1703. Berlin: De Gruyter Mouton.

Romaine, Suzanne. 2016. The variationist approach. In Merja Kytö & Päivi Pahta (eds.), *The Cambridge handbook of English historical linguistics*, 19–35. Cambridge: Cambridge University Press.

Romasanta, Raquel P. 2019. Variability in verb complementation: Determinants of grammatical variation in indigenized L2 varieties of English. *Studies in Variation, Contacts and Change in English* vol. 20. https://varieng.helsinki.fi/series/volumes/20/romasanta/ (20 January 2022)

Ruschenberger, William Samuel. 1838. *Narrative of a voyage around the world, during the years 1835, 36, and 37; (...).* 2 vols. London: Richard Bentley.

Russi, Cinzia. 2016. *Current trends in historical sociolinguistics.* Berlin: De Gruyter Mouton.

Rutten, Gijsbert & Marijke van der Wal. 2014. *Letters as loot. A sociolinguistic approach to seventeenth and eighteenth-century Dutch.* Amsterdam: John Benjamins.

Schneider, Edgar. 2007. *Postcolonial English: Varieties around the world.* Cambridge: Cambridge University Press.

Setter, Jane, Cathy Wong & Brian Chan. 2010. *Dialect of English: Hong Kong English.* Edinburgh: Edinburgh University Press.

Shi, Dingxu. 1993. Learning Pidgin English through Chinese characters. In Francis Byrne & John Holm (eds.), *Atlantic meets the Pacific*, 459–465. Amsterdam: John Benjamins.

Siegel, Jeff. 2000. Substrate influence in Hawai'i Creole English. *Language in Society* 29(2). 197–236.

Siegel, Jeff. 2007. Recent evidence against the Language Bioprogram Hypothesis: The pivotal case of Hawai'i Creole. *Studies in Language* 31(1). 51–88.

Siegel, Jeff. 2008. *The emergence of pidgin and creole languages.* Oxford: Oxford University Press.

Spencer, Alfred. (ed.) 1925. *Memoirs of William Hickey.* 4 vols. London: Hurst & Blackett.

Tagliamonte, Sali A. 2012. *Variationist sociolinguistics: Change, observation, interpretation.* Malden, MA: Wiley-Blackwell.

Tilden, Bryant. 1831–1832. *Journal of fourth voyage to China, in ship Crusoe of Salem via Batavia, Singapore and Manila.* Unpublished manuscript.

Tilden, Bryant P. 1834–1836. *Journal. Sixth voyage to China, in Ship Surat 1834–1836.* Unpublished manuscript.

Tong, Ting-kü [Tang, Tingshu]. 1862. *The Chinese and English Instructor.* Canton: Wei Jin Tang.

van Gelderen, Elly. 1998. *For to* in the history of English. *American Journal of Germanic Language and Literature* 10(1). 45–72.

Washabaugh, William. 1975. On the development of complementizers in creolization. *Working papers on language universals* 17. 109–140.

Washabaugh, William. 1980. From preposition to complementizer in Caribbean English Creole. In Richard R. Day (ed.), *Issues in English Creoles: Papers from the 1975 Hawaii conference*, 97–109. Amsterdam: John Benjamins.

Weinreich, Uriel, William Labov & Marvin Herzog. 1968. Empirical foundations for a theory of language change. In Winfred Lehmann & Yakov Malkiel (eds.), *Directions for historical linguistics*, 95–188. Austin: University of Texas Press.

Winford, Donald. 1985. The syntax of *fi* complements in Caribbean English Creole. *Language* 61(3). 588–624.

Wong, May. 2017. *Hong Kong English: Exploring lexicogrammar and discourse from a corpus-linguistic perspective.* Basingstoke: Palgrave Macmillan.

Yeung, Ka-Wai. 2006. On the status of the complementizer waa6 in Cantonese. *Taiwan Journal of Linguistics* 4. 1–48.

Yiu, Yuk Man Carine. 2005. Spatial extension: Directional verbs in Cantonese. PhD thesis. Hong Kong University of Science and Technology.

PART IV

Future directions

CHAPTER 13

Towards an acquisitionally informed historical sociolinguistics

Israel Sanz-Sánchez
West Chester University

This conclusion chapter offers an overview of some of the main themes developed throughout the volume and highlights several important theoretical and methodological implications for the development of new acquisitionally informed research agendas in historical sociolinguistics. The use of acquisition theory and corpora as sources of information to interpret the sociohistorical and sociolinguistic archive is complicated by several methodological and analytical hurdles – nevertheless, it is argued here that acquisitional analogues between past and present and a knowledge of how various groups of learners process different forms of variation can do much to propel the study of language variation and change in historical situations. In addition, new technological developments and sources of data can furnish researchers additional information about how individual acquisitional trajectories may have contributed to the linguistic patterns attested in the archival record. Lastly, an acquisitionally informed perspective can also be a step to address structural inequalities in linguistic description and in the construction of knowledge in our field.

Keywords: language acquisition, language variation, language change, historical sociolinguistics

1. What lies ahead? Language acquisition across the lifespan and future research agendas in historical sociolinguistics

The chapters in this volume have showcased many potential applications of acquisition theory and data to a sociohistorical understanding of language variation and change. Specifically, they demonstrate several of the ways in which an acquisitionally-based perspective that treats language learning as a lifelong endeavor and as the starting point for the spread of innovations across the community can be instrumental in interpreting the extant archive that historical sociolinguists work with.

Following the general introduction to the possibilities of an acquisitionally informed historical sociolinguistics articulated in the introductory chapter in Part I, the contributions in Part II have highlighted various recent strands of research on language acquisition that focus on how individuals of various ages process different kinds of variable input in a broad range of social settings. In doing so, they have shared clues on how specific acquisitional strategies by particular groups of learners may yield specific linguistic changes. In Part III, these findings have been put to work. The goal in these chapters has been to interpret the historical linguistic evidence as attested across a variety of historical corpus types (epistolary corpora, audio recordings, naturalistic observation data, sociolinguistic interviews, demographic tallies, etc.) to better understand the attested local patterns of variation and change in several sociohistorical environments.

Beyond their specific area of focus, the chapters in this volume collectively demonstrate the viability of research agendas in historical sociolinguistics where the psycholinguistic element and its interaction with linguistic and social factors becomes more integrated in the explanation of language variation and change than has traditionally been the case. This approach supplements the contributions from other more common approaches in our field, such as the quantification of variable patterns in the historical record, the reconstruction of the social and demographic environments of specific historical ecologies, or the examination of the ideological and cultural scaffolding of language variation. Therefore, the incorporation of the acquisitional dimension does not replace nor invalidate research strands within our field that target specific aspects of the sociohistorical dynamics of language change. To the contrary, our argument is that all these research avenues are necessary because they complement each other, and that the acquisition-based lens can be enlisted to not only enrich those additional perspectives, but also to integrate them. Incorporating acquisition allows us to better understand how all these aspects may have interacted, which brings us closer to the ideal explanation of language change envisioned in Weinreich et al. (1968) (see Chapter 1 in this volume).

From a methodological perspective, the applications of acquisition theory and data to the available historical evidence proposed by the chapters in the present volume are as diverse and as multidimensional as the very historical sociolinguistic settings that the authors are seeking to investigate. Far from advocating for a single approach, the chapters offer a non-exhaustive array of suggestions for how to advance towards the interdisciplinary integration of language acquisition and historical sociolinguistics: some methodological or analytical protocols may be more appropriate for specific time periods, social contexts, and types of available sociolinguistic or linguistic data. In this sense, this volume is meant as a conversation starter rather than as a prescriptive treatise on how to use acquisition theory or data in our field. In addition, the strategies proposed in this volume necessarily stem from the theory, data, and tools that historical sociolinguists currently have at their disposal. In this respect, the conversation will surely be helped by the emergence and development of new data collection and analytical technologies, some of which have only recently begun to be explored (e.g., 'big data', artificial intelligence) (McShane & Nirenburg 2021). As more tools and data become available, the possibilities to study the historical sociolinguistic record through the lens of acquisition theory will certainly continue to expand. The prospects are exciting and given the fast development of new technologies and data sources, we cannot predict them all – a few tentative lines of inquiry are sketched in the following paragraphs.

Historical sociolinguists are used to thinking about language change as the collective result of multiple socially embedded individual acts of language learning and language use. From this perspective, connecting the progression of a given innovation to the linguistic behavior of the speakers in the community is ultimately the goal of every explanation of language change. In this sense, treating the socially situated nature of language acquisition as a key dimension of any change can help us identify its motivation at different levels better than if we were to only rely on sociolinguistic motivations. An awareness of how individuals at various points of their lifespan process different types of variation can shed light on who the likely originators of the specific innovation were, and how it may have caught on in a particular social and linguistic embedding. An acquisitionally informed approach can supplement observations of language change obtained from other angles.

For instance, in a recent contribution to the study of the rate of language change, the chapters in Nevalainen et al. (2020a) build on the theory of *punctuated equilibrium*, originally proposed for the spread of biological changes and adapted by Dixon (1997) to the study of language history. According to this theory, languages exist in a state of equilibrium that is unsettled ('punctuated') by specific events, bringing about an acceleration of change. In one of the papers in this collection (Nevalainen et al. 2020b), this theory is applied to a meta-analysis of a range of attested changes in Middle English documentation from the period 1150–1500. The authors calculate the rate of spread of these changes during specific time intervals within this period. They then connect the intervals when change rates accelerated to specific sociohistorical events that may have played a punctuating role, including the Norman Conquest and the sociolinguistic changes that followed it, and the Black Death. Their analysis confirms that the Middle English period was a time of accelerated change in the written evidence, with the period of maximum cumulative acceleration around the mid-14th-century. Some of these effects may be the consequence of changes in scribal practices, but as the authors acknowledge, the observed rates must ultimately also be a function of communal language change linked to demographic shifts and their sociolinguistic consequences – the data "do not manifest a direct impact of a single disruptive force, but can rather be associated [with] an accumulation in time and space of social and cultural changes, which were mediated in writing and unfolded over a longer period of time" (32). From an acquisitional perspective, as acknowledged elsewhere in the same collection, the question becomes how the alternation of periods of rapid language change and stasis can be understood as the byproduct of changes in the conditions of acquisition in the community (Nevalainen et al. 2020a: 12). As seen in the case studies in this volume, these changes may include shifts in the proportion of native vs. non-native speakers, the emergence of social networks where speakers of certain ages are able to negotiate new norms, or cultural pressures about age-appropriate sociolinguistic behavior.

A lifespan perspective on language acquisition also allows to us to understand how seemingly different sociolinguistic process may ultimately be rooted in shared human cognitive mechanisms operating in different ways at different points of our life. While specific sociolinguistic contexts have been connected to different processes of contact and change (e.g., pidginization and creolization has been attributed to L2 acquisition and nativization by children; koinéization has been linked to interdialectal accommodation among adults and dialectal focusing via L1 acquisition; and the incrementation of dialectal norms has been attributed to vernacular reorganization by older children and adolescents, to name but a few – see Chapter 1, Section 4), the application of these processes is ultimately regulated by the sociolinguistic conditions that allow for the acquisitional behavior of specific groups of speakers to shape the emergence of new varieties. This is certainly not a new argument in historical sociolinguistics. For instance, Table 1 shows some tentative correlations between community structure, forms of acquisition and linguistic outcomes, following Operstein (2015). Note that here, *transmission* is not used as in Labov (2007) to refer specifically to the acquisition of the full conditioning of a linguistic norm via L1 acquisition, but instead designates any form of linguistic perpetuation in the community. *Exoteric* and *esoteric* refer, respectively, to the predominant makeup of the local social networks (loose-knit vs. tight-knit communities):

Some of the correlations noted in Table 1 have also been noted in other work connecting sociolinguistic and linguistic typologies (Trudgill 2011; Winford 2017). In very general terms, this classification appears to predict linguistic outcomes based on specific conditions of acquisition in the community.

Several of the chapters in this collection fit more or less comfortably within these prototypical scenarios. For instance, the emergence of a new allophonic system of /æ/ studied by Christopher Strelluf in Chapter 9 exhibits many of the

Table 1. Community structure and associated forms of acquisition and linguistic outcomes (adapted from Operstein 2015: 12)

Type of community	Main form of acquisition driving transmission	Outcome
Exoteric, high contact	L2 acquisition	New languages
Esoteric, high contact	Bilingual L1 acquisition	Nativization of contact features
Esoteric, low contact	L1 acquisition	Gradual change

hallmarks of the gradual incrementation of a sociolinguistic norm by older children and adolescents in low-contact environments. The diachronic persistence of voice onset timing variation and final obstruent neutralization in the German heritage communities in Wisconsin researched by Samantha Litty in Chapter 10 can be understood as the sociohistorical remnant of what was originally a synchronically motivated feature generated by adult bilinguals. Similarly, the pattern of semantic imposition for body partonomy in Antioquia Spanish and the demographic and crosslinguistic evidence assessed by Eliot Raynor in Chapter 11 appear to be a good match for an L1-nativization scenario where younger learners conventionalized what was originally an adult L2 feature.

Other times, however, the interaction among acquisitional, sociolinguistic and linguistic factors appears to have followed paths that are not a good match for any of the typologies in Table 1. For instance, the young speakers of Río de la Plata Spanish studied by María Irene Moyna and Pablo Requena in Chapter 7 conventionalized the split between deontic and epistemic values in the early 1900s in a high-contact environment that included many sources, both native and non-native. The resulting norm was not based on the conventionalization of an L2 feature, but on the reinterpretation of the variable, more unsystematic input received from older speakers of diverse ethnolinguistic background (including L1 speakers) into a more predictable norm. Similarly, the creation of Light Warlpiri analyzed by Carmel O'Shannessy in Chapter 8 has taken place in an environment where the children have not just nativized bilingual adult input into new contact features in any of the languages, as observed in other high-contact ecologies. Instead, they have used the code-switching practices between English/Kriol and Warlpiri in adult speech as the steppingstone to a new mixed language, including elements of the source codes and new levels of grammatical complexity unattested among adults. In this process, the community's sociocultural acceptance towards linguistic innovation practices among children appears to have been key to the emergence of the new code. Even the case of *for* + infinitive purpose constructions in Chinese Pidgin English researched by Li in Chapter 12, which does not appear to have given rise to an L1-acquired norm, is sociolinguistically complex in that it demonstrates the speakers' ability to rely on various sources (Chinese, standard English, English dialects) to generate a new construction. In this process, access to various forms of input and social contexts of use seems to have motivated speakers to incorporate the new construction to their repertoires.

While some of these changes challenge the descriptive typologies outlined in Table 1, the speakers in these ecologies were ultimately not unlike those in other historical settings in that they used their age-specific cognitive affordances to navigate sociolinguistically and culturally complex landscapes and to produce combinations that were learnable by other speakers. By addressing the psycholinguistic aspect of attested language changes through a socially situated lens, historical sociolinguists can take one more step towards the more integrated, less compartmentalized model of language change envisioned by Winford (2017; also see Chapter 1, Section 6).

2. What's needed? Challenges and opportunities

As the preceding paragraphs (and chapters) have demonstrated, the future is rife with opportunities to apply acquisition theory and data to the historical sociolinguistic study of language variation and change. But we are not naïve. Despite the undeniable advances that have already taken place, the study of historical sociolinguistic variation and change from an acquisitionally informed perspective continues to pose theoretical and methodological challenges. As noted in Chapter 1 (Section 6), the almost complete lack of acquisitional data for most historical periods poses a significant hurdle. In the preceding chapters in this volume, the authors have offered various methodological suggestions to alleviate this lack of data (e.g., comparison between historical data and acquisition corpora collected through naturalistic observation and experimental studies, use of present-day L2 learner corpora, combination of written and audio sources, etc.). These studies leave no room to doubt that the potential for these methodologies to inform future sociohistorical approaches to language change should not be underestimated. Still, other challenges remain.

For instance, as the distribution of chapters in this volume and the literature review in Chapter 1 show, high-contact ecologies where the contributions from different kinds of learners are relatively easy to identify are still the primary areas of application of this acquisitional perspective. By contrast, an acquisitionally informed approach may appear to be less applicable to other sociolinguistic environments where variation patterns are harder to attribute to specific cohorts of learners. However, more difficult does not mean impossible. For instance, Christopher Strelluf's study (Chapter 9) of vowel change in a low-contact ecology offers a methodologically refined approach to the sociophonetic evidence furnished by two kinds of sources, i.e., audio recordings and sociolinguistic interviews. Since the year of birth is available for the individuals recorded in these sources, the combination of both corpora allows the author to compare the vowel systems of speakers across 150 years and consecutive generations, often among members of the same family. This apparent time approach also allows us to identify older children and adolescents as the propellers of change in this non-high-contact ecology. But even when audio records are not available, possibilities abound. Examples can be seen in Petré & Van de Velde (2018) or Anthonissen & Petré (2019), where the linguistic behavior of generations of writers is related to language changes and the input that each generational cohort may have received is reconstructed. These studies can also benefit from the mathematical modelling of language change, where various acquisitional assumptions are built into the learning agents and the best model to explain the changes that one sees in natural languages can be identified (Baxter & Croft 2016; Blythe & Croft 2021).

We also need to make progress in the study of many sociolinguistic contexts that have traditionally been neglected in historical sociolinguistic literature. Such contexts include most linguistic minorities and non-Western language communities, far too commonly excluded from canonical forms of thinking about 'typical' or otherwise assumedly 'normal' sociocultural conditions of language socialization, transmission, and learning. From an acquisitional perspective, this desideratum requires that acquisition data also be collected from such communities, since Western European languages and their colonial/diasporic manifestations are clearly overrepresented among the available acquisition corpora (e.g., many of the child language acquisition corpora featured on the CHILDES database and the vast majority of the L2 corpora listed by the Centre for English Corpus Linguistics at the Université Catholique de Louvain represent a handful of European languages like English, German, French, Italian or Spanish, with only a few Asian languages and virtually no African, Australasian or indigenous American languages). The acquisition-based perspective in historical sociolinguistic research that we have advocated for in this volume can only go as far as the acquisition data that are available to us and the theories that are built on these data allow us to. In this sense, acquisition scholars and historical sociolinguists alike have an opportunity to start addressing some of the structural inequalities and scales of Eurocentric bias that have permeated our fields (Canagarajah 2013), but only if we are aware of these biases to begin with. Otherwise, under the pretext of adopting a universally minded uniformitarian approach to language acquisition and change, we run the risk of perpetuating existing hierarchies and sociocultural biases that continue to favor certain linguistic and historical experiences over others.

Finally, we also need more interdisciplinary collaboration. Collective volumes such as this one are a great start, but this collaboration needs to happen on the ground, with acquisition researchers and historical sociolinguists working and thinking together. To this day, acquisition venues (conferences, journals, academic programs) and historical sociolinguistics fora are by and large still independent from each other. Only if this everyday interdisciplinary practice becomes part of how historical sociolinguists work will we be able to advance towards a more theoretically comprehensive, more methodologically productive and more socioculturally encompassing integration of language acquisition theory and historical sociolinguistics.

References

Anthonissen, Lynn & Peter Petré. 2019. Grammaticalization and the linguistic individual: New avenues in lifespan research. *Linguistics Vanguard* 5(2). 20180037.

Baxter, Gareth & William Croft. 2016. Modeling language change across the lifespan: Individual trajectories in community change. *Language Variation and Change* 28. 129–173.

Blythe, Richard & William Croft. 2021. How individuals change language. *PLoS ONE* 16(6). e0252582.

Canagarajah, Suresh. 2013. *Translingual practice: Global Englishes and cosmopolitan relations*. London: Routledge.

Centre for English Corpus Linguistics. 2022. Learner corpora around the world. https://uclouvain.be/en/research-institutes/ilc/cecl/learner-corpora-around-the-world.html (15 January 2022)

CHILDES. 2022. Child language data exchange system. https://childes.talkbank.org/ (15 January 2022)

Dixon, Robert. 1997. *The rise and fall of languages*. Cambridge: Cambridge University Press.

Labov, William. 2007. Transmission and diffusion. *Language* 83(2). 344–387.

McShane, Marjorie & Sergei Nirenburg. 2021. *Linguistics for the age of AI*. Cambridge, MA: The MIT Press.

Nevalainen, Terttu, Tanja Säily & Turo Vartiainen (eds). 2020a. *Comparative sociolinguistic perspectives on the rate of linguistic change*. Special issue of the *Journal of Historical Sociolinguistics*, 6(2).

Nevalainen, Terttu, Tanja Säily, Turo Vartiainen, Aatu Liimatta & Jefrey Lijffijt. 2020b. History of English as punctuated equilibria? A meta-analysis of the rate of linguistic change in Middle English. *Journal of Historical Sociolinguistics* 6(2). 20190008.

Operstein, Natalie. 2015. Contact-genetic linguistics: Toward a contact-based theory of language change. *Language Sciences* 48. 1–15.

Petré, Peter & Freek Van de Velde. 2018. The real-time dynamics of the individual and the community in grammaticalization. *Language* 94(4). 867–901.

Trudgill, Peter. 2011. *Sociolinguistic typology: Social determinants of linguistic complexity.* Oxford: Oxford University Press.

Weinreich, Uriel, William Labov & Marvin Herzog. 1968. Empirical foundations for a theory of language change. In Winfred Lehmann & Yakov Malkiel (eds.), *Directions for historical linguistics*, 95–195. Austin: University of Texas Press.

Winford, Donald. 2017. The ecology of language and the New Englishes: Toward an integrative framework. In Markku Filppula, Juhani Klemola, Anna Mauranen & Svetlana Vetchinnikova (eds.), *Changing English: Global and local perspectives*, 25–55. Berlin: De Gruyter Mouton.

Language index

A
Ambon Malay 112–113, 116–118
  see also Malay
Amerindian languages 266–267
Anglo-Norman French 140
Atlantic Creole languages 20
  see also English-based
    Creole languages;
    Portuguese-based Creole
    languages; Spanish-based
    Creole languages
Australasian languages 324

B
Bahamian Creole 284
  see also English-based
    Creole languages
Basque 52, 152

C
Caboverdianu 277–278, 281–282,
  284, 286
  see also Cape Verdean
    Portuguese Creole;
    Portuguese-based Creole
    languages
Canadian French 68
Cantonese 119, 297–299,
  304–306, 308–312
  see also Chinese
Cape Verdean Portuguese
  Creole 277
  see also Caboverdianu;
    Portuguese-based Creole
    languages
Caribbean English Creole 303
  see also English-based
    Creole languages
Chaozhou Chinese 310
  see also Chinese
Chibchan languages 267–268,
  271, 280
Chinese 21, 30, 66, 68, 109, 119,
  121–122, 138, 294–313, 323
Chocoan languages 267–268,
  270–273, 275, 279–282, 285

Chûgoku Japanese 94
  see also Japanese
Classic Warlpiri 192–193
  see also Warlpiri
Classical Latin 154
Cocoliche 155
Creoles 16–19, 20, 22, 27, 70–71,
  130, 132, 281–282, 286–287, 295,
  298, 300, 305, 308, 321
  see also English-based
    Creole languages;
    Portuguese-based Creole
    languages; Spanish-based
    Creole languages
Czech 235

D
Danish 86
Dutch 20, 85, 91, 93, 95–98, 110,
  112–121, 298
  Berbice Dutch 298
  Early Modern Dutch 20,
    85, 95
  Iowa Dutch 115
  Middle Dutch 96
  Surinamese Dutch 115
  Virgin Island Dutch 115

E
Egyptian Arabic 68
Emberá 266, 270, 278–280,
  282–283, 286
  Emberá Catío 268–270,
    275, 279–280
  Emberá Chamí 268–269,
    275, 280
  Emberá Tadó 280
English:
  Australian English 182, 185
  Belfast English 301
  Black South African
    English 138
  British English 20, 132–133,
    135–136, 139–140, 205, 307
  Canadian English 10, 50,
    89

Chinese Pidgin English
  (CPE) 30, 295, 297, 310,
  312, 322
Hong Kong English
  (HKE) 130, 132, 135, 303
Indian English 22, 136, 139,
  140
Latinx English 78
Middle English 49–50, 301,
  320
Missouri English 23, 30,
  212, 225
Multicultural London
  English (MLE) 132–133
New Englishes 138, 140, 307
New Zealand Englishes 23,
  204
Nigerian English 307
North American Englishes
  50, 204–206, 228
Philadelphia English 46,
  66, 206–207
Scottish English 47
Singapore English 22, 119,
  138, 140
Tristan da Cunha English
  21
Wisconsin English 239,
  241, 244–247, 259
  see also English-based
    Creole languages
English-based Creole languages
  282, 296, 303, 305
  see also Bahamian Creole;
    Caribbean English
    Creole; Gullah; Hawai'i
    Creole English; Jamaican
    Creole English; Kriol;
    Nicaraguan Creole
    English; Providence
    Island Creole; San Andrés
    Creole English

F
Frisian 98

G

German 30, 91, 96–98, 114, 121, 234–260, 322, 324
  see also Pennsylvania German; Wisconsin German
Germanic languages 95–96
Gothic 12
Guaraní 52, 152
Guinea Bissau Portuguese Creole 276–277, 279, 281
  see also Portuguese-based Creole languages
Gullah 298
  see also English-based Creole languages
Gurindji Kriol 183, 188, 195
  see also Kriol

H

Hakka Chinese 310
  see also Chinese
Hawai'i Creole English 130, 132, 135, 303
  see also English-based Creole languages
Hindi 139
Hispano Romance 154

I

Ibero-Romance 279, 283
Indo-Aryan languages 139
Israeli Sign Language 23
Italian 70, 140, 155, 257, 324

J

Jamaican Creole English 282
  see also English-based Creole languages
Japanese 94
  see also Chûgoku Japanese

K

Kikongo 266, 276–278, 281–283, 286
Korlai Portuguese 285
  see also Portuguese-based Creole languages
Kriol 51, 182–197, 322
  see also English-based Creole languages

L

Light Warlpiri 23, 30, 179–198

M

Macau Pidgin Portuguese (MPP) 310
  see also Portuguese
Malay 117
  see also Ambon Malay
Mandarin Chinese 310
  see also Chinese
Marathi 285
Montreal French 86

N

Nicaraguan Creole English 282
  see also English-based Creole languages
Nicaraguan Sign Language 23, 130, 181
Norwegian 49, 133–134, 235

P

Páez 281
Papiamento/Papiamentu 20, 93, 298
Pennsylvania German 205, 248
  see also German
Persian 133
Pidgins 16–19, 27, 70–71, 130, 183, 281, 287, 295–296, 300, 308, 321
Portuguese 20–21, 110, 121, 152, 297–298, 303, 310
  Barranquenho Portuguese 21
  Brazilian Portuguese 177
  Mozambique Portuguese 68
  see also Caboverdianu; Cape Verdean Portuguese Creole; Guinea Bissau Portuguese Creole; Korlai Portuguese; Macau Pidgin Portuguese (MPP); Portuguese-based Creole languages; Sri Lankan Portuguese; Upper Guinea Portuguese Creole
Portuguese-based Creole languages 20, 277, 279, 281, 283, 276
  see also Caboverdianu; Cape Verdean Portuguese Creole; Guinea Bissau Portuguese Creole; Korlai Portuguese; Sri Lankan Portuguese; Upper Guinea Portuguese Creole
Proto-Austronesian 265
Proto-Germanic 50
Providence Island Creole 305
  see also English-based Creole languages; San Andrés Creole English

Q

Quechua 21, 52, 114

R

Romanian 54, 279
Russian 53, 91, 94, 258, 279, 284

S

San Andrés Creole English 282
  see also English-based Creole languages; Providence Island Creole
Spanish:
  Amazonian Spanish 78
  Antioquian Spanish 266–267, 275, 279–288
  Argentinian Spanish 150–174
  Chilean Spanish 46
  Colombian Spanish 30, 281
  Latin American Spanish 20, 23, 166
  Peninsular Spanish 68, 152, 154–155
  Peruvian Spanish 75
  Puerto Rican Spanish 66, 72
  Rioplatense (RPS) 24, 30, 150–175, 322
  see also Spanish-based Creole languages
Spanish-based Creole languages 21
Sri Lankan Portuguese 284
  see also Portuguese-based Creole languages

T
Turkish   107, 117–119

U
Ukrainian   91, 258
Upper Guinea Portuguese Creole   277
   see also Portuguese-based Creole languages

W
Warlpiri   179–198
West African languages   266–267, 276, 279, 281, 287
West Germanic languages   95–96
Western European languages   324

Wisconsin German   236–237, 246–247, 257–259
   see also German

Y
Yagua   75

Subject index

A
/ae/:
　/æ/　30, 49, 86, 203–229, 321
　/ae/ raising　49, 50, 205, 207, 214–215, 225–228
　/æ/ systems　205–208, 221, 225, 228
　tense vs lax /æ/　46, 205
Aboriginal　30, 182, 185
abrupt creolization　130
　see also creole languages
acquisition:
　acquisition corpora　23, 323–324
　acquisition of (socio)linguistic variation　25, 44, 47, 65, 68, 77, 79
　acquisition of variable patterns　45–46, 48, 65
　bilingual acquisition　3, 18, 29, 44, 105, 121–122, 137, 235, 239, 244, 256–257, 319
　early acquisition of sociolinguistic variation　46–47
　monolingual acquisition　3, 7, 29, 46, 52–55, 73, 99, 109–110, 115, 120, 122, 158, 189, 239, 251–259
　second dialect acquisition (SDA)　10, 16, 87–88, 90
　second language acquisition (SLA)　90, 64–79, 88, 133, 137, 139, 143, 266, 279, 285–287
　timing of acquisition　46–48, 57, 164
　see also adolescents; adults; bilingualism; children; classroom acquisition settings; critical period; development in language acquisition; errors in acquisition; naturalistic acquisition; optimal periods; Western vs. non-Western acquisition contexts
actuation　12, 14, 18, 27, 30, 57, 174, 229
address forms in Spanish　24, 153–159
adolescents:
　adolescence　4–6, 10–11, 14–16, 18, 21–23, 48, 87–88, 109–110, 118–119, 128–134, 203–205, 207–213, 215, 218, 227, 229, 250, 321–322, 324
　adolescent peak　14, 109
　adolescent role in language innovation　18, 208, 211
　post-adolescent changes　15–16
　see also incrementation; vernacular reorganization
adults:
　adult acquisition of sociolinguistic variation　68
　adulthood　4–5, 11, 45, 51, 55–57, 64–79, 97, 128, 133–134, 180, 215
　adult input　7, 57, 180, 182, 186, 322
　adult learners　6, 17, 50, 52, 65–66, 70, 74, 108–109, 114–115, 282
　adult role in language innovation　30
　adult vernacular lability　85
　adults as agents of language change　266
　late acquisition by adults　89
　see also errors in acquisition; heritage speakers

African-descendant population　267, 274–275, 277, 285–286, 288
　see also slaves (African); West Africa
age:
　age of onset　104, 108, 111, 116, 119, 122, 255
　age-graded variation　14–15
　aging (as a process)　4–5, 11
　as a biological vs. cultural construct　4–5
/ai/ raising　50
allomorph　191–194
Amazon region　75, 78
Amerindian population　266–271, 273–288
Amsterdam　95–98
Antilles　154
Antioquia region　264–289
Antwerp　95–98
Appalachia　206
apparent time (change)　6, 14–15, 69, 85, 185, 208, 215, 218–219, 221, 225–226, 324
archival recordings　30, 203–204, 212
Argentina　150, 152–153, 155, 164
artificial language　48–50, 108
Aruba　93
Aspect Hypothesis　74
Asunción　152
audio data　236, 238, 240, 245, 250, 259
　audio recordings　30, 174, 235, 238, 242, 250, 258, 319, 324
Auslautverhärtung　234, 244
Autonomous Development Hypothesis　113, 120

B
bad data problem (in historical sociolinguistics)　98, 141, 204
Basic Variety　70
Bergen　88, 133

bilingualism:
  bilingual children 29, 45, 51–57, 92, 196
  bilingual effects 51–52, 54–55
  bilingual innovations 51, 55
  bilingual language development 45–46
  bilingual mode 116
  bilingual optimization strategies 105–107, 119–120
  bilingual settings 110
  bilinguals as agents of language change 17
  long-term communal bilingualism 114, 116
  see also code-switching; heritage speakers; rely on more languages strategy; rely on one language strategy
Bioprogram Hypothesis 19, 308
blending inheritance 309
body partonomy 283, 288, 322
borrowing transfer 91
  see also recipient language (RL)
Bottleneck Hypothesis 141
brain 4, 8–9, 12, 88–89, 110, 142
  brain maturation 4
  brain plasticity 4, 88–90, 108
  see also neurocognitive maturation
Brazil 116–117
Britain 10, 133, 152, 306
Buenos Aires 151–153, 155, 158, 160, 170, 172

C
California 206
Cambodia 66
Canada 121, 206, 208
Cape Verde 276–277, 279, 281
caregivers 5–6, 14, 44, 46–48, 54, 131, 167, 208, 210–211, 215, 222, 224–225, 229
cascade principle 115, 151, 186
case marking 118, 191–194, 197
  dative case 50, 93, 119, 184, 191–194
  ergative-absolutive pattern 50, 191

ergative case 50, 184, 187, 191–194
Cauca department 271, 273
census data 251, 266, 277–278
  see also US Census
cessatives 159–162, 164–165
changes in progress 49, 72, 85–86, 195–196, 207, 216–217
Chicago 54, 205
children:
  child heritage speakers 10, 45, 51–56
  child acquisition of sociolinguistic variation 44, 47
  child language acquisition 5, 10, 12, 29, 49, 51, 56–57, 129, 131, 173, 181, 185, 190, 195, 324
  child-initiated language change 46, 49, 51, 56, 180–181
  childhood 4–7, 10, 14–15, 20, 53–55, 85, 88–89, 110, 128–129, 131–132, 134, 210–213, 251, 256–258
  children as agents of language change 56, 118, 181, 197, 308
  children's innovations 45, 48–51, 56–57, 114, 173, 180–182, 186–188, 190, 195–197, 211, 287, 208, 322
  early childhood 5–6, 14, 54, 89
  late acquisition of grammatical variation by children 48, 151
  late childhood 6
  see also bilingualism; errors in acquisition; heritage speakers
Cincinnati 205
classroom acquisition settings 70, 76, 137–138, 142, 151, 287, 308
  see also teachers
clitics:
  in Spanish 53–55
  in Portuguese 67–68
code-switching 9, 30, 182–183, 185–187, 189–190, 196, 322
Colombia 30, 264–289

colonialism:
  colonial plantation settings 19
  colonization 20–21, 27, 71, 78, 143, 152, 154–155, 171, 182–183, 204, 236, 266–271, 273–282, 285–288, 306–311
  colonizers 19, 140
  see also post-colonial settings
competition 114, 150, 160, 170–171, 207, 309, 312
complementation (and complementizer) 30, 295–313
complexity in grammar 16, 22, 45, 48, 53, 138, 156, 158–159, 171, 186, 311
congruence 107, 266, 279, 281–282
Constructive Nonconformity Principle 76
contact-induced changes:
  contact-induced grammaticalization 118–119
  contact-induced interference 107
  contact-induced language change 51–52, 55, 74, 94, 104, 109, 112, 116, 118, 121–122, 179–180, 185, 275, 286
  see also dialect; language contact
Controller First Principle 70
convergence 72–73, 114, 312
copula (and copular verbs) 71, 72
Córdoba (city in Argentina) 164, 175
Córdoba (region of Colombia) 270, 280
creole languages 16, 19–22, 27, 70–71, 130, 132, 135, 183, 276–277, 279, 281–284, 286–287, 295–296, 298, 300, 303, 305
critical period 5–6, 10, 14, 88, 129, 131
  Critical Period Hypothesis 88
  see also optimal periods

cross-linguistic influence   45,
    51–52, 55, 93, 98, 114, 116, 118,
    120
    cross-linguistic transfer   90,
        92–94, 181
    see also borrowing transfer;
        imposition; interference;
        language contact;
        substratum; transfer (L1)

D
Darien region   267, 271
demographic change   16, 95–96,
    152
development in language
    acquisition:
    developmental factors   5,
        7–8, 13, 51, 68, 69, 104, 115,
        119, 138, 140, 165, 180, 204
    developmental errors   180
    developmental view of
        language acquisition   7
diachronic change   26, 45, 69, 75,
    141, 174, 286
dialect:
    dialect contact   16, 29, 45,
        84–85, 87–91, 93–95,
        97–99, 107, 137, 237
    difficulty hierarchy (in
        dialect acquisition)   88,
        94
    see also acquisition;
        koineization; new dialect
        formation
differential object marking   54
diffusion   15, 129, 131, 133–134,
    140, 205
direct object clitic   53–54
dominance in bi/
    multilingualism   17–18, 30,
    53–54, 56, 90, 92–96, 98–99,
    119, 128, 141–142, 235–236, 239,
    241, 250–259

E
ecology of language   22, 24, 73,
    133, 137, 140, 143, 273, 302,
    306–307, 309–310, 323–324
    see also feature pool
ego-documents   121, 170, 237
England   87, 109
entrenchment   108, 119–120
environmental determinants   4

errors in acquisition:
    child acquisition   13
    non-native adult
        acquisition   5–6, 138, 140,
        311
esoteric vs. exoteric
    communities   321–322
Eurocentric bias in acquisition
    research   324
exemplar theory   209
experimental studies of
    acquisition   6, 9, 23–24, 30, 49,
    92–93, 113, 120, 142, 152, 165,
    167, 323

F
F1/F2   209, 213–215, 217
Failed Features Hypothesis   141
feature pool   18, 114, 132–133, 172,
    296, 301, 308–310, 312–313
    see also ecology of language
Feature Reassembly Hypothesis
    141
feature variation   235
final obstruent neutralization
    (FOT)   235, 244–250, 260
First Noun Strategy   70
Flanders   95–96
form-meaning mapping   8, 74,
    113
fossilization   137
frequency   6, 8–10, 13, 21, 48–50,
    53, 57, 64, 67–70, 86, 98, 108,
    112–113, 156, 160–162, 170, 188,
    214, 243, 296, 299
Full Transfer/Full Access
    Hypothesis   141

G
gender mismatches   53, 55
generation   6, 13–15, 19, 21, 45,
    49–72, 77–78, 109, 115, 121–122,
    127–128, 130–131, 133–138, 142,
    159, 180–181, 186–187, 190–191,
    196, 204, 206–207, 210–211,
    214–215, 218–219, 221, 225, 227,
    236–237, 249, 251, 256, 258–259,
    278, 287–288, 324
    generational change   15, 128,
        130
    see also age
generativism   7, 12–13, 105, 112
Groningen   95

Guinea Bissau   276–277, 279, 281
Guizhou province   89

H
heritage speakers   45, 51–57,
    112–113, 244, 259
    see also adults; children
historical sociophonetics
    203–204, 208
Hong Kong   30, 128, 140, 295,
    297, 306–308, 310–313

I
Iberian Peninsula   153
Illinois   248
immigration (and immigrant)
    16, 18, 21, 29, 66, 71, 76, 128,
    135–136, 153, 155, 170, 172, 204,
    234–237, 249, 257–259
    see also migration
imposition   17–18, 30, 91, 120,
    143, 248, 250, 322
    imposition transfer   91
    see also language contact;
        sourcelanguage (SL);
        transfer (L1)
improvised language strategies
    106–107, 113
incrementation   10–11, 14, 22–23,
    30, 46, 49, 86, 109, 131,
    203–229, 321
    incrementation model   46
    see also vernacular
        reorganization
(ing) in L1 English   46
(ing) in L2 English   66, 68
indexicality   137, 142
India   128, 135–136, 138–140, 297
Indigenous communities   270,
    278
innovation   5, 11, 13, 16–18, 27–28,
    30, 45, 48–51, 54–57, 109–110,
    114, 116, 121–122, 134–136, 138,
    173, 180–182, 186–188, 190,
    195–197, 208, 211, 223, 273, 278,
    281, 287–288, 309, 311–312,
    319–320, 322
input demand   22
interdisciplinarity in historical
    sociolinguistics   2, 25, 71, 319,
    325
interface effects   22, 140
Interface Hypothesis   75, 139–140

interference 17, 107, 114, 235, 278, 284, 287–288
  see also cross-linguistic influence; imposition; language contact; transfer (L1)
interlanguage 5, 17, 19, 22, 67, 69–70, 78, 153, 155
intermediate forms 92, 94, 239
Interpretability Hypothesis 141
invariant structures 55
irregular 10, 22–23, 57, 115, 166, 180
Italy 153
item-per-item learning 108

K
Kansas 121, 207
Kansas City 205, 207, 208–209, 212–213, 215, 219, 221, 227–229
koinéization 94, 98, 132–133, 154, 196, 321
  see also dialect; new dialect formation

L
Lajamanu 182–183, 198
language acquisition across the lifespan 2–3, 6–7, 12–24, 27, 89, 98–99, 107, 204, 312
Language Acquisition Device 5
language contact 16–19, 22–24, 27, 29, 65, 70–71, 73, 75–76, 79, 85–86, 90–91, 94, 98, 104–105, 107–110, 112, 115, 117–118, 120, 137, 142, 204, 235, 243, 265–266, 273, 278, 284–285, 287–289, 311
  see also bilingualism; contact-induced changes; cross-linguistic influence; imposition; substratum; transfer (L1)
language shift 17, 99, 236, 253, 258, 266, 273, 275, 278, 285–286
Leiden 97
lexical conditioning 55
life stage 4–5, 84–85, 87, 90, 107–109, 128–129, 132, 134, 142
lingua franca 183
logical problem in language change 12
London 18, 128, 132–133, 135

M
Madison 237–238
Massachusetts 69
Medellín 264, 268, 270–271, 273, 275, 277–278, 280, 285–286
Mexico 52, 54, 68, 154, 269
Michigan 121, 206
Midwest region 206, 235
migration (*and* migrant) 16, 66, 71, 87–89, 94–95, 97, 128, 133–136, 143, 153, 155, 170, 172, 206, 208
  see also immigration
Milton Keynes 132–135
Milwaukee 248
Mirror-Image Hypothesis 71–72, 79
Missouri 204–229
mixed input 45–51, 56, 182, 189
mixed language 30, 51, 183–197, 286, 308, 322
mobility in speakers and communities 76–77, 85–87, 89, 226
modality 151, 156–158, 160, 164–165
  deontic modality 157–158, 164–165
  epistemic modality 49, 151, 157–158, 160–165, 167–172, 322
  modal verb *must* 49
momentum-based model 46
monolingual mode 111
Montevideo 150–153, 155, 160–161, 170, 172
multiethnolects 18, 136, 143

N
native-like forms 67
  see also errors in acquisition 67, 88, 131–132
naturalistic acquisition:
  data 9, 30, 162, 170, 319, 323
  L2 naturalistic acquisition 69, 75, 78, 142, 266, 279, 281, 285–287
  see also acquisition
ne-deletion in French 72
negation 69, 72, 138, 157
Netherlands 93, 95–96, 112–113, 116–119, 121

neurocognitive maturation 3
  see also brain
new dialect formation 10, 17, 21, 45, 128–129, 132, 136–138
  see also koineization; dialect
New Granada 266, 271, 274
New Orleans 205–206
New Spain 269
New York 89, 205–206
New Zealand 23, 135–136, 204
Nonconformity Hypothesis (*and* Nonconformity Principle) 76
normative pressures 23, 72, 154, 172–173, 190
Northern Territory 182
null objects 52–53, 55

O
old age (*and* elderly) 5, 11
optimal periods 10
  see also critical period
oral history 212
orthography (*and* orthographic variation) 96–98, 242–243, 247–249, 253, 255–257

P
Pacific Northwest region 206
panel studies 9, 20, 73, 85–86, 204, 210
peers (influence in acquisition) 6, 10, 14, 18, 23, 46, 57, 67, 88, 109, 121, 131–133, 135, 172–173, 184, 186, 190, 210, 225, 229
Pennsylvania 205, 248
Peru 154, 269, 273
Philadelphia 46, 66, 205–207
phonology (*and* phonological variation) 4, 10–11, 13, 30, 88–89, 91, 94, 110, 118–119, 131, 134–135, 171, 181, 194, 206, 213, 227–229, 235, 237–239, 242, 248–250, 252, 254, 256, 258, 307, 309–310
  phonological mergers 23–24
pidgins (*and* pidginization) 16, 19, 27, 70–71, 130, 183, 281, 287, 295–298, 300, 305–306, 308, 310, 312, 321
post-colonial settings 20, 22, 27, 29, 129, 132–133, 137–138, 140

pre-Columbian 268–269, 273
predictable variation 9
preposition 55, 71, 118, 297, 300, 302–305, 308, 310–312
present progressive 73, 75
preventives 159, 160–162, 165
probabilistic processing in language acquisition 208, 210–211, 218–219, 225
probability-matching 10, 108, 121
Prototype Hypothesis 74
psycholinguistic factors 4, 10, 16–18, 22, 27, 91, 319, 323
Puerto Rico 66, 72
punctuated equilibrium 320
purposive clause 301, 304–305, 307–308, 311–312

Q
quantitative boosts 49

R
reanalysis 12–13, 50–51, 129–130, 135, 186–187
recipient language (RL) 17, 91
    recipient language agentivity 91
    see also language contact
regularization 10, 69, 129, 134, 180, 182, 187, 191, 196–197
relexification 19, 287
Relexification Hypothesis 298
'rely on more languages' strategy 107, 116–120, 122
    see also bilingualism; language contact
'rely on one language' strategy 107, 108, 111–115
    see also bilingualism; language contact
repertoire 7, 14–15, 18, 22, 24, 29, 67, 85–86, 90–91, 93, 95–97, 99, 106, 141, 182, 305–306, 323
restricted input 45, 51–52
retrograde change 15
reverse-U model of incrementation 211
Río de la Plata region 24, 30, 151–175, 322
rule-based learning 108
-s deletion 46

S
salience:
    acoustic salience 113
    perceptual salience 21
San Francisco 122
Santa Fe de Antioquia 270–271, 273–275, 278, 285
São Tomé e Príncipe 279
Scotland 47
selection of language features 24–25, 30, 74, 155–156, 159, 165, 171–172, 309, 311–312
semantic extension 94, 117, 288
sentence completion task 165–166
simple present 73–75
slaves (African) 71, 266, 274–278, 281–282, 285
social embedding of a change 11, 14, 24, 26, 109, 127, 136, 311, 320
social network 4, 28, 89, 132, 170, 190, 298, 321
socioeconomic index (SEI) 213, 228
sociolinguistic interviews 30, 66, 204, 207, 212–213, 319, 324
sociophonetics 22, 30, 86, 142, 203–205, 208, 211–213, 227–229, 257–259, 324
source language (SL) 17, 120, 182, 184–186, 196, 275, 284, 288
    source language agentivity 91, 278
    see also language contact
South Midland region 206
Spain 68, 154, 269, 286
St. Louis 205, 207, 212–213
stability 6, 15, 75, 107, 112–113, 116, 159
stasis 321
Stockholm 128, 136
structural inequalities 324
structural priming 92–93
structured vs. unstructured variation 21, 54–55, 110
stylistic reinterpretation 130
subject pronoun expression 48, 55, 66–67, 73, 92
Subset Principle 138
substratum 266, 285, 287
    substrate influence 22, 266, 285–289, 302, 308
    see also cross-linguistic influence; imposition; language contact; transfer (L1)
syllable-final 171, 235, 244, 256, 259–260
syllable-initial 235, 243, 250, 256

T
-t/-d deletion 48
target forms 167
teachers 155, 175, 306
    see also classroom acquisition settings
Tehran 133
tense-mood-aspect (TMA) 19, 70–71, 186–187, 189
transfer (L1) 22, 52, 78, 90–94, 96–97, 153, 181, 265–266, 273, 275, 278–287, 305, 308
    see also borrowing transfer; cross-linguistic influence; imposition; interference; language contact; substratum
transmission 14–15, 26, 49, 110, 115, 121–122, 129–133, 137–138, 186, 203–205, 208, 211–212, 214–229, 310–311, 321–322, 324
    vertical vs. horizontal 121–122, 186, 229
transparency 22, 112, 113, 311
trend studies 9, 14, 85
Turkey 117, 119
tuteo 151–152, 154–174
    see also voseo
twins 221–222
typology 17, 70, 73, 75, 185

U
/u/ fronting 49
uniformitarianism (and Uniformitarian Principle) 4, 26, 151, 181, 257, 295, 312, 324
Universal Grammar 5, 130
Uruguay 150, 152–153, 155
US Census 213
US South region 77–78, 206
usage-based approaches 9, 13–14, 105, 112
Utrecht 97

V

variable input   13, 56, 173,
    180–181, 310, 319
vernacular reorganization   14,
    321
    see also adolescents;
        incrementation
vernacular universal   18
Vietnam   66

voice onset time (VOT)   235,
    238–243
voseo   151–152, 154–174
    see also tuteo

W

weak biases   49
West Africa   266–267, 273–279,
    281–282, 285–288

Western vs. non-Western
    acquisition contexts   5, 9, 16,
    29, 128–129, 132, 136–141, 324
Wisconsin   234–260, 322
word order   19, 49, 113, 181,
    193–194
written sources   235, 237,
    242–243, 247, 250